Reading Woman

Reading Woman

ESSAYS IN FEMINIST CRITICISM

Mary Jacobus

METHUEN

First published in Great Britain in 1986 by
Methuen & Co. Ltd
11 New Fetter Lane, London EC4P 4EE
First published as a University Paperback in 1987

© 1986 Columbia University Press

Printed in Great Britain by
J.W. Arrowsmith Ltd, Bristol

British Library Cataloguing in Publication Data

Jacobus, Mary
    Reading woman : essays in feminist
    criticism.—(University paperbacks).
    1. Feminist literary criticism—History
    I. Title.
    809   PN98.W64

ISBN 0-416-92460-3

For Reeve and Frances and in memory of my father

Contents

Illustrations

Preface

Reading Woman **began** as a collection of feminist literary criticism focusing on texts by women writers. As it evolved, it became not just a book of feminist readings, but a book about both "reading" and "woman"—whether as reader, as writer, or as read; and especially as represented in and by Freudian and Lacanian psychoanalysis. In their different ways, all the essays included address both the question of feminist reading and the related (for me, inseparable) question of reading "woman" as a figure for sexual difference. They are also linked by a preoccupation with the relation between women and theory, especially (but not only) psychoanalytic theory. What is the status and function of "woman" in the Freudian text? And what is the status and function of theory within feminist criticism? Feminist readings of writing by and about women—concerned with the representation of women, and with the relation between reading, writing, and sexual difference—intersect here with readings of feminist theory itself.

    To position myself as a feminist critic, both geographically and intellectually, it seems worth saying that in 1980 I moved from England to the United States. One effect of that move, paradoxically, was to take me closer to France. Recent Anglo-American feminist criticism has been invigorated, often transformed, by its encounter with French feminism, particularly psychoanalytic feminism. The essays included in this book are no exception. For me at least, existing literary and feminist concerns have often been radically reformulated in the light of writings by (and about) Hélène Cixous, Sarah Kofman, Julia Kristeva and Luce Irigaray—to name only the best known—as well as by the interpretative writings in England of Lacanian feminists such as Juliet Mitchell and Jacqueline Rose;

or, in the United States, Jane Gallop and Shoshana Felman. It is scarcely possible to write feminist literary criticism in the 1980s without acknowledging the influence of critics, theorists, and mediators such as these, whether French or Franco-feminist. Their work, it seems to me, has significantly changed the scope, method, and assumptions of Anglo-American criticism since its first new wave over a decade ago.

My own feminist literary criticism began in the early 1970s in the wake of writing by Mary Ellmann and Kate Millett, at a time when feminist literary criticism, however energetic, was relatively untheoretical in its critique of literature and of the assumptions governing conventional criticism. Such criticism attempted to shift the ground, to place the accent elsewhere, to expose the interestedness of phallocriticism, and to privilege the writing, perspective, and experience of women. Elaine Showalter later called this attempt "gynocritics." In the course of rereading my own previously published essays for inclusion in this book, it became clear to me that the significant break for many feminist critics, and certainly for myself, occurred as a result of the intellectual and political influence of French feminist thinking from the mid-1970s on. For that reason, I have chosen not to include anything written before 1978. As in criticism generally, French theory (structuralist, post-structuralist, deconstructive, and psychoanalytic) has infiltrated and often polarized feminist literary criticism. The theoretical transformation which has taken place in feminist criticism during the past five years or so is particularly associated with two connected, ongoing feminist "projects": that of bringing the insights of psychoanalysis to bear in a feminist context, and that of bringing a feminist critique to bear on psychoanalysis. My own writing has been, and continues to be, shaped by this double project, as well as by the impact of literary theory on feminist criticism (and vice versa).

A second major impetus in contemporary feminist literary criticism has come from teaching. Here too, my own writing has been stimulated and transformed by the opportunity to teach in a flourishing women's studies program and by the energy and insights of the feminist criticism to which women's studies have given rise. In America at least, the institutional acceptance and funding of women's studies programs and courses (however precarious or embattled) have allowed a generation of teachers and students to teach and study in ways that reflect the feminist critique of traditional concepts of literary curricula and the literary canon. One consequence has been the growing impact of feminist theory and criticism on the institution of literary criticism itself. These gains are now increasingly under threat in the United States from a government intent on imposing its ideology not only on women, the family, and on sexual and racial issues, but also on the reproduction of teaching, learning, and culture both within and outside universities. Feminist criticism in a multiplicity of disciplines (and interdisciplines) represents a sustained and vocal alternative to this ideology and is by now surely—I hope—too well established, if only in an academic context, to go away quietly if conservative views of the role of the humanities prevail. The attempt to belittle or deny the intellectual significance and achievement of both women's studies and black studies is an alarming aspect of reactions to the transforming effect within universities of courses and programs set up during the past decade. Such courses have done more than provide the context for feminist criticism; they have been crucial for the political, sexual, and racial awareness of an entire generation of students.

In the wake of this political and educational backlash, feminist anxiety about the masculine appropriation of feminist studies within the academy, and especially within literary criticism, seems—however well founded—relatively unimportant. Nonetheless, it is an irony that the very impact of feminist criticism on the institution of literary criticism and theory risks turning feminism into yet another ingredient in the existing mix or plurality, rather than constituting a critique of that pluralized, universalizing melange itself. Literary study has been, and continues to be, fundamentally challenged by and increasingly responsive to the concerns of the women's movement and the impact of women's studies, as well as the critique produced by feminist literary criticism. Appropriation of that critique, rather than recognition of its implications for critical practice, risks not simply diluting it, but silencing it. This is not to say that one has to be female in order to write feminist criticism; but no one, I think, can afford to become involved in the debate and practice of feminist criticism without confronting the implications for their own critical position of that debate, that practice. Whether feminist or not, critics can't avoid situating themselves (and being situated) in relation to the feminist literary criticism and theory they speak for or about. Though it says much for the state of feminist literary criticism that accounts of contemporary critical theory can no longer ignore a feminist critique, these accounts themselves—by standing outside feminist critical debate—risk seeming immune to it. One function of feminist criticism is to put that immunity in question.

My own criticism has been enabled by the existence of a community of Anglo- and Franco-American feminist critics, by now too large and disparate to be represented by selected names. This book is intended as a contribution to a dialogue within feminist literary criticism itself. The position I've chosen to take, though often responding to the pioneering writing in the 1970s of feminist literary critics, "herstorians," and interpreters such as Elaine Showalter, Sandra Gilbert, and Susan Gubar, seems (to me at least) to be an argument with and against the finally untheorized, experiential, and literary-herstorical tendency of much feminist criticism in the United States. For some, it may seem that my own writing is insufficiently rooted in history, whether from a traditional or from a Marxist point of view. The alert feminist reader will also see that the criticism in this collection, as well as reflecting only certain aspects of feminist literary study, focuses in detail on a select group of writers. Mary Wollstonecraft, Mary Shelley, Charlotte Brontë, George Eliot, Charlotte Perkins Gilman, and Virginia Woolf are hardly forgotten or neglected woman writers; nor can Freud, whose texts would continue to engage me for their literary interest alone, be considered an underexposed author today. But while choosing to write about the major formative influences on a particular feminist literary context—my own—or on a major formative influence on "theory" as that term is currently understood, I have tried to raise theoretical questions that are relevant to other feminist concerns, other feminisms. These writers and these questions are the ones that preoccupy me, even (as it must seem to some) at the cost of excluding less well-known writing by women, whether from the same or from other contexts; or at the cost of refusing other questions of major feminist concern, such as the remaking of the literary canon and the recovery of "lost" women writers; or, still more damagingly, at the cost of seeming to deny the distorting effects on feminist criticism and theory of ignoring the writing and criticism of black, Afro-American, or third world women. Like literary study in general, feminist criticism can be called to account for neglecting these different strands in the feminist enterprise. With the inscription of women's cultural, historical, and social oppression, the recognition of ethnic and racial as well as sexual difference—whether in literature, in culture, or in society generally—remains a major task for feminist criticism to undertake.

But for better or worse, my own feminist writing occupies the position I've tried to outline. In admitting to this position, with its limitations as well as its polemicizing tendency, I should say that for me there is a role for a feminist criticism which attempts to read literary and psychoanalytic texts with particular theoretical ends in view—that the pursuit, practice, and investigation of "theory" by way of "reading" (my practice in this book) is a worthwhile and defensible contribution to feminist literary criticism; and that the hostility to both theory and psychoanalysis, whether on the part of traditional literary scholars or from within a divided and multi-faceted feminist movement itself, seems to me misplaced. Feminist literary criticism must speak to, and with, other modes of feminist and literary study, other feminist and critical aims and perspectives, without seeking to elide, deny, or universalize differences which make the contemporary feminist enterprise so necessary, so challenging, and so difficult. This book engages some of the issues confronting feminist critics, whether like or unlike myself, from a particular, declared perspective, that of a psychoanalytically and theoretically informed feminism. Its limitations, as they will surely seem to some, may be the limitations of that perspective; but they are also my own. Its possibilities, I would argue, are those of a feminist literary criticism committed to the view that issues of theory—theories of reading, textuality, and language; theories of the (gendered) subject—have implications beyond their immediate context; that although the dialogues betwen sexual and racial difference, or between feminism and Marxism, are not specifically engaged here, the dialogue of theoretical differences necessarily abuts on and provokes them.

Acknowledgments

Besides the debts to contemporary feminist critics and theorists acknowledged in my text and notes, I am indebted to the following people for their generous comments, discussion, disagreement, or information during the writing of the essays included in this book: Lauren Berlant, Penny Boumelha, Cynthia Chase, Jonathan Culler, Ian Donaldson, Zillah Eisenstein, Maud Ellmann, Shoshana Felman, Mary Lowenthal Felstiner, Sander Gilman, Sneja Gunew, Neil Hertz, Sarah Kofman, Laurie Langbauer, Dorothy Mermin, Mary Nyquist, Reeve Parker, Eve Sedgwick, and Elaine Showalter; to the members of the Marxist-Feminist Literature Collective (London, 1977–78); members of the Psychoanalysis and Feminism Reading Group (Cornell, 1980–81); and to the graduate students in a seminar on Psychoanalysis and Feminist Criticism (Cornell, 1984). My thanks to Ann Cvetkovich for her help in preparing and checking the manuscript and to Phillis Mollock (Ithaca) and Richard Larson (Canberra) for word-processing it. On the domestic front, Cassandra Britton, Kusum Dave, and Allison Dugdale have all provided indispensible support as well as timely feminist interjections. I am especially grateful to the Humanities Research Centre, Australian National University, Canberra, for a Visiting Fellowship in 1985 which gave me the time to complete this book and the benefit of an unfamiliar but congenial setting in which to do so, that of Australian feminism.

"The Difference of View" and "The Buried Letter: *Villette*" first appeared in this form in Mary Jacobus, ed., *Women Writing and Writing about Women* (London: Croom Helm, 1979); "Men of Maxims and *The Mill on the Floss*" first appeared in *Critical Inquiry* (Winter 1981), 8(2), reprinted in Elizabeth Abel, ed., *Writing and Sexual Difference* (Chicago: University of Chicago Press, 1982); "Is There a Woman in This Text?" first appeared in *New Literary History* (Autumn 1982), 14(1). I am grateful for permission to reprint them here.

Note: Throughout the text, references to the works of Freud are to *The Standard Edition of the Complete Psychological Works of Sigmund Freud*, 24 vols., James Strachey, ed. (London: Hogarth Press, 1953–74), cited *SE*, with volume and page number(s).

Reading Woman

I. READING WOMAN (READING)

Reading Woman (Reading)

"**It was a change** in Orlando herself that dictated her choice of a woman's dress and of a woman's sex. And perhaps in this she was only expressing rather more openly than usual . . . something that happens to most people without being thus plainly expressed. For here again, we come to a dilemma. Different though the sexes are, they intermix. In every human being a vacillation from one sex to the other takes place, and often it is only the clothes that keep the male or female likeness, while underneath the sex is the very opposite of what it is above. Of the complications and confusions which thus result every one has had experience" (Virginia Woolf, *Orlando*).[1]

Or, "it is clothes that wear us and not we them"; Woolf's *Orlando* (1928) again. Can we say the same of language—that words speak us and not we them—and hence of reading too? What would "reading woman" mean if the object of our reading (woman as text) and the reading subject (reader as already read) were gendered only as the result of the reading process? What if, to put it another way, there were no gender identity except as constituted by clothes, or by language—just as there is no "literal" meaning to oppose to metaphor, but only metaphors of literalness. As Shoshana Felman puts it,

> if it is clothes alone, i.e., a cultural sign, an institution, which determine our reading of the sexes, which determine masculine and feminine and insure sexual opposition as an orderly, hierarchical polarity; if indeed clothes make the *man*— or the woman—are not sex roles as such, inherently, but travesties?[2]

In Woolf's novel, Orlando's transvestism is not simply a travesty which mimics or exaggerates the signs by which gender identity is culturally instituted and maintained; rather, Orlando might be said to dress up at (cross-)dressing, exposing the dilemma ("here again, we come to a dilemma") or impossible choice of gender; as the *OED* has it, "A choice between two . . . alternatives, which are or appear equally unfavorable; a position of doubt or perplexity, a 'fix.'" In Felman's words, transvestite roles become "travesties of a travesty," since there is no unequivocal gender identity to render ambiguous in the first place, but only the masquerade of masculine and feminine.

If there is no literal referent to start with, no identity or essence, the production of sexual difference can be viewed as textual, like the production of meaning. Once we cease to see the origin of gender identity as biological or anatomical—as given—but rather as instituted by and in language, "reading woman" can be posed as a process of differentiation for which psychoanalysis provides a model. In Freudian terms, the subject acquires both gender and subjectivity by its passage through the Oedipus and castration complexes; in Lacanian terms, the subject's entry into the symbolic order, and hence the subject's gender, are determined by relation to the phallus and (it amounts to the same thing) by taking up a predetermined position within language.[3] In order to read as women, we have to be positioned as already-read (and hence gendered); by the same token, what reads us is a signifying system that simultaneously produces difference (meaning) and sexual difference (gender). We might go further and say that in constituting woman as our object when we read, we not only read in gender, but constitute ourselves as readers. The stabilizing, specular image of woman in the text makes reading possible by assuring us that we have women's faces too—or men's, for that matter, since "woman" serves also as a figure for or reflection of "man."[4] Reading woman becomes a form of autobiography or self-constitution that is finally indistinguishable from writing (woman). Putting a face on the text and putting a gender in it "keeps the male or female likeness" (in Woolf's words) while concealing that "vacillation from one sex to another" which both women and men must keep, or keep at bay, in order to recognize themselves as subjects at all. The monster in the text is not woman, or the woman writer; rather, it is this repressed vacillation of gender or the instability of identity—the ambiguity of subjectivity itself which returns to wreak havoc on consciousness, on hierarchy, and on unitary schemes designed to repress the otherness of femininity.

Feminist critics have traditionally concerned themselves with the woman writer, and especially with what Woolf calls "the difference of view, the difference of standard."[5] Women's writing occupies an unchallenged place in the politics of feminist criticism and in the classroom; yet the category itself remains problematic (defined by authorship? by style or by language? by refusal of the very categories "masculine" or "feminine"?). More recently, feminist criticism has concerned itself with the woman reader—with woman as the producer of her own system of meanings; meanings that may challenge or subvert patriarchal readings and undo the traditional hierarchy of gender.[6] So much so that Jonathan Culler can make the question of "Reading as a Woman" an exemplary instance for his discussion of readers and reading in *On Deconstruction* (1982). "For a woman to read as a woman," he concludes, paraphrasing Peggy Kamuf's "Writing Like a Woman," "is not to repeat an identity or an experience that is given but to play a role she constructs with reference to her identity as a woman, which is also a construct, so that the series can continue: a woman reading as a woman reading as a woman."[7] The appeal to "experience," whether reader's or writer's, short-circuits this process and creates an illusory wholeness or identity, denying the internal division which simultaneously produces the gendered subject and the reading subject. Since "reading woman" necessarily entails both a theory of reading and a theory of woman—a theory of subjectivity and a theory of gender—I want to look at the double question of reading woman (reading) or woman reading (woman) from the perspective of three feminist essays which raise these theoretical issues by way of the metaphor of transvestism ("the clothes that wear us"). The first is Sandra Gilbert's "Costumes of the Mind: Transvestism as Metaphor in Modern Literature"; the second is a review article by Elaine Showalter, "Critical Cross-Dressing: Male Feminists

and the Woman of the Year"; and the third is Shoshana Felman's "Rereading Femininity."[8] Each of these three feminist
critics has been highly influential in defining what "reading
woman" might mean, whether for Anglo-American readers or,
in the case of Felman, in a Franco-American context; yet they
reveal strikingly different assumptions about both gender and
textuality—so much so that the first two essays deploy the metaphor of transvestism in the context of a theory of gender identity which the third essay, Felman's, sets out to deconstruct.
Perhaps this difference can be attributed to the fact that while
Gilbert and Showalter have attempted to construct a feminist
literary and critical "herstory," Felman situates herself at the
intersection of literature and psychoanalysis. Significantly, for
my purposes at least, Felman's essay takes as its point of departure a rereading of Freud's 1932 lecture, "On Femininity." The
intervention of psychoanalysis in the context of feminist criticism and theory, I shall argue, makes all the (sexual) difference. Read as a history of the way in which "the difference of
view" is produced, rather than an attempt to describe what it
consists of, psychoanalysis frees women's writing from the determinism of origin or essence while providing feminist criticism with a way to refuse the institutionalization of sexual and
textual difference as gender identity and hence as questions
that cannot be posed at all.

Sandra Gilbert's "Costumes of the Mind" is an
"argumentative history" (Gilbert's own phrase) designed to rewrite literary history in feminist terms. A speculative account of
twentieth-century modernism based on differing uses of the
transvestism metaphor by men and women, her essay cham-
pions the (female) opponents of sexual hierarchy. Whereas
Joyce in the Nighttown episode of *Ulysses*, Lawrence in "The
Fox," and Eliot in *The Wasteland* all portray gender disorder or
the blurring of sexual distinctions either as a means of endorsing conservative views of male dominance, or as nightmare
(Gilbert argues), feminist transvestism becomes a means to
subvert and repudiate the hierarchical views of the male modernists. Woolf's *Orlando*, for instance, portrays gender identity
as fluid, multiple, and interchangeable; in Gilbert's phrase,

"insouciant shiftings" (Woolf's "vacillation from one sex to the other") replace the fixity of gender identity. Gilbert clearly privileges this vision of the happily multiform self or genderless identity beyond sexual divisions which she sees in the "utopian" androgyny of writing by Djuna Barnes and H.D. The culminating metaphor of her essay, fittingly, is the gesture by which the heroines in writing by Atwood, Chopin, and Plath all discard their clothes in order to "shatter the established paradigms of dominance and submission associated with the hierarchy of gender and restore the primordial chaos of transvestism or genderlessness."[9] Although Gilbert does not ask whether this fantasy of utopian androgyny or primordial genderlessness could ever be realized, she does ask what might account for the differing gender ideologies of male and female modernists. In the last resort, however, her inquiry is limited by a theory of gender in which the relation between body and subject remains unmediated by either the unconscious or language. The answers she provides—psychobiography on one hand, literary history on the other—reveal the unquestioned argument that underpins her "argumentative history." For all her sympathy with Woolf's tranvestite metaphor, her assumptions about both identity and history are ones that finally reproduce the very fixities which *Orlando* is supposed to unsettle.

To take identity first. In order to account for the specifically male anxieties which Gilbert sees as energizing the "nightmare fantasies" of the male modernists, she invokes Joyce's ambivalent relation to mother, church, and country; Lawrence's mother-dominated childhood; and Eliot's clouded first marriage. But if psychobiography fixes gender identity thus, what price the "insouciant shiftings" of *Orlando*? And what factors in the formative years and relationships of female modernists might account for their differing view of gender arrangements? Are men constituted by their object relations, while women remain somehow immune to such identity fixes and fixations? What the answer to these questions might be we never learn, since for Gilbert the modernist writer is already unambiguously gendered, either male (hierarchical, conservative) or female (insouciantly shifting, feminist). Significantly, Gilbert quotes extensively from Robert Stoller's *Sex and Gender*

(1975) on the subject of male transvestism; in Stoller's terms, gender identity is either male or female, a "core identity" that is only rendered equivocal by unsatisfactory object relations and that may in fact uncannily correspond to biological and genetic factors even where it appears anomalous, as in the case of the boy raised as a girl who effortlessly adapts to his "new" gender ("Although he would seem to fit into the category of those rare people who have no difficulty in shifting their gender identity. . . . He never did shift his identity. He always felt . . . that he was a male").[10] Like Nancy Chodorow in *The Reproduction of Mothering* (1978), which also draws on Stoller's work, Gilbert ultimately assumes (by implication at least) the possibility of what Chodorow calls "the establishment of an unambiguous and unquestioned gender identity."[11] For Stoller, in fact, there is really no shifting at all, but only mistaken identity.

Gilbert, however, is primarily a revisionary literary herstorian and interpreter rather than a theorist (or even a psychoanalytic reader); and so it is no surprise that her account of twentieth-century modernism turns on what is often seen as its crucially determining (his)torical event—the differing implications for men and women of World War I. While the war years left men figuratively and literally shattered, Gilbert argues, they offered women the chance to redress their previously disinherited state. Every white feather given to a young man thereby dispatched to the trenches might mean another job for a woman; every angel in the house—every Red Cross nurse—became an avenging angel of death. The figure of the female angel of destruction, familiar from Gilbert and Gubar's *The Madwoman in the Attic* (1979), gives Gilbert's account of literary modernism a mythic dimension which itself derives from the myths of male modernists such as Yeats (Herodias' castrating daughters in "Nineteen Hundred and Nineteen," for instance). Why should the turn to history give birth to this vision of avenging female monstrosity? Is it possible that where the text of history is concerned, women can only be monsters or aberrations, since history itself (as Gilbert duly notes) is a conspiracy to marginalize or repress them? Hence the view of history offered in Woolf's *Between the Acts* (1941) by Miss La Trobe, who seems, in Gilbert's words, "to want to fragment history in order to ruin it" rather than "shoring up fragments of history against her ruin."[12] On the face of it, Gilbert endorses Woolf's modernist and feminist theory of history both here and in *Orlando*, where "shifts in literary style, shifts in historical styles, changing modalities of all kinds . . . remind us that . . . all is in flux." Yet in the last resort her own position turns out to be closer to that of the male modernist who, in her own words, "insists that the ultimate reality underlying history . . . is and must be the Truth of Gender"[13] than to the view that the ultimate reality underlying gender is history. Perhaps it is not so much the monster, woman, to which history gives birth, as the monster flux. Like identity, the very notion of (literary) history attempts to repress ambiguity and division; and what is repressed necessarily returns, in the language of the unconscious, as an avenging monster.

If Gilbert can be seen as falling back on the disorders of history to fix the still more threatening disorders of gender identity, what of Elaine Showalter's unsettling juxtaposition of recent forays into feminist criticism by male critics, on one hand, and Dustin Hoffman's 1982 film, *Tootsie*, on the other? "Critical Cross-Dressing" asks, shrewdly and wittily, whether the conversion to feminist criticism by male theorists such as Jonathan Culler in *On Deconstruction* and Terry Eagleton in *The Rape of Clarissa* (1982) is merely a form of transvestism akin to female impersonation—an appropriation which, like cross-dressing in *Tootsie*, can be viewed as a way of promoting masculine power while ostensibly masking it. Showalter's initial question ("Is male feminism a form of critical cross-dressing, a fashion risk of the 1980s that is both radical chic and power play?")[14] leads to others that are especially germane to feminist criticism; questions such as: is reading learned, and can men learn to read as feminists? Is "reading as a woman" fundamentally differentiated from "reading as a man," and if so, by what (political, sociological, or ideological) differences? Showalter persuasively unmasks *Tootsie* as not so much a feminist film but rather a film that reveals Hoffman's sense of the actor's career as feminine—passive, vulnerable, and physically exposed. Accordingly she diagnoses its transvestism, as Gilbert diagnoses that of the male modernists, in terms once more derived from Robert Stoller's *Sex and Gender*. For Stoller, the transvestite man sets out to prove that he is better than a biological woman because he is a woman with a penis.[15] *Tootsie*, Showalter argues, has it both ways. Michael Dorsey becomes a female star while still being able to lift heavy suitcases and grab taxis. But, while this is acute and apt, what has it to do with reading? Has Showalter allowed two different questions, that of female impersonation and that of reading as a woman, to become elided? Are they really the same (or at least analogous) questions, as she implies, or are they questions whose very conflation reveals an underlying contradiction in her theory of gender?

Contrasting Eagleton and Culler, Showalter represents the first as the Dustin Hoffman of literary theory—the Marxist critic who fears (like Lovelace himself in Richardson's novel) that he is effeminized by writing, and whose appropriation of feminist criticism attempts to recuperate its "phallic" power, just as Lovelace in Eagleton's own analysis attempts to recover Clarissa's imaginary phallic power by raping her. This "phallic criticism" is for Showalter simply "another raid on the resources of the feminine in order to modernize male dominance."[16] The effect, she observes, is to silence or marginalize feminist criticism by speaking for it, while simultaneously silencing the "something equivocal and personal in [Eagleton's] own polemic" which she sees as motivating his criticism. What is this "something equivocal"? Showalter's phrase occurs in the context of what is arguably her central thesis about reading and writing as a woman:

> Like other kinds of criticism . . . feminist criticism is both reading and writing, both the interpretation of a text and the independent production of meaning. It is through the autonomous act of writing, and the confrontation with the anxiety that it generates, that feminist criticism is both reading and writing, both the interpretation of a text and the independent production of meaning. It is through the autonomous act of writing, and the confrontation with the anxiety that it generates, that feminist critics have developed theories of women's writing, *theories proved on our own pulses*. (p. 147; my italics)

Just as *Tootsie* reveals Hoffman's sense of the actor's career as feminine, and just as *Clarissa* reveals Richardson's anxiety about the feminizing effects of writing, so for the Marxist critic (Showalter suggests) there may be something effeminate about literary criticism as opposed to revolutionary action. But if one sees writing itself as feminine—and here Showalter's view is unclear—then there can be no specifically feminist theory of women's writing as opposed to men's, and no way in which such theories can be proved experientially on the pulses of women. Showalter comes close to glimpsing that textuality at once produces gender and simultaneously produces equivocation, only to repress that insight with the language of the body ("proved on our own pulses"). By invoking the experience of being biologically female, she closes the very question which she opens in her discussion of Eagleton.

Culler's argument, as Showalter accurately recapitulates it, is precisely to "demonstrate some difficulties in the feminist appeal to the woman reader's experience, an experience and an identity which is always constructed rather than given." For Culler, " 'reading as a woman' is always a paradoxical act, in that the identity as 'Woman' must always be deferred" (pp. 139, 141). With apparent approval, Showalter summarizes Culler's analysis of feminist theories of reading, including his insistence that the appeal to female experience as a source of authority is always a double or divided request since the condition of being a woman is simultaneously seen as given and as created. She then proceeds to her own question, apropos of Culler's work: namely, "can a *man* read as a woman?" Noting that while Culler never presents himself as a feminist critic, he does offer a feminist reading of Freud's *Moses and Monotheism* (1939), she asks further "whether a male feminist is in fact a man reading as a woman reading as a woman?" Showalter is ready to concede that Culler has avoided the pitfall of female impersonation by reading "not as a *woman*, but as a man and a feminist"(p. 142). But one might well ask why it matters. If reading as a woman is a paradoxical act, reading as a man must involve a similarly double or divided demand. Showalter comes close to implying that while reading as a woman may (if she accepts Culler's view of the matter) involve constructing a gender identity, reading as a man does not. In other words, her theory of gender identity remains ultimately untouched by

Culler's argument. Though ostensibly careful to distinguish between the essentialist "woman" reader and the "feminist"
reader (a reader who may be male or female), Showalter
chooses to emphasize what she calls feminist reading because
"it has the important aspect of offering male readers a way to
produce feminist criticism that avoids female impersonation"
(p. 143). But again, if criticism—like reading and writing— can
be viewed as all a matter of cross-dressing anyway, Culler's
avoidance of female impersonation is neither here nor there.
Ironically, Culler's "feminist" reading of *Moses and Monotheism*
is designed to show why "the promotion of the paternal"
should produce patriarchal criticism's characteristic concern
with legitimacy of meaning and with the prevention of illegiti-
mate interpretations. This very preoccupation with legitimacy
and illegitimacy, this very preference for unambiguous meanings and stable origins, is precisely what underlies Showalter's
unease about the shiftiness of critical cross-dressing in the
academy.

Showalter' energetic polemic is fueled by understandable professional anxiety about preserving an area in criticism that is specific to women. This anxiety is played out most
clearly in her final paragraph, which culminates in a comic
apocalyptic fantasy. "Without closing the door on male feminists," she writes, "I think that Franco-American theory has
gone much too far in discounting the importance of signature
and gender in authorship."[17] Though she warns against essentialist simplicities ("Culler's deconstructive priorities lead him
to overstate the essentialist dilemma of defining the *woman*
reader"), it is surely essentialism—whether theoretical or professional—that we glimpse here, for without essentialism identity itself comes into question, and with it "the importance of
signature and gender in authorship" (what one might call the
Moses and Monotheism principle, or the insistence on legitimate
origin). "Going much too far" for Showalter means the cover of
the *Diacritics* special issue of summer 1982, enigmatically entitled *"Cherchez la femme: feminist critique/feminine text."* Here is
her description:

> On a white background is a figure in a black tuxedo and high
> heels, resting one knee on a bentwood chair à la Marlene

Dietrich. The figure has no hands or head. On the back cover, a dress, hat, gloves, and shoes arrange themselves in a graceful bodiless tableau in space. No "vulgar" feminist, the chic Diacritical covergirl hints at the ephemera of gender identities, of gender signatures.[18]

To invoke *Orlando* once more, the cover says: "it is clothes that wear us and not we them." For Showalter this graphic display of the metaphoricity of clothes risks dispersing gender identity altogether, leaving only the headless (i.e., silent) woman, the *corps morcelé* of nightmare.

　　　Hence the form taken by Showalter's dream of the feminist literary conference of the future: the demonic woman rises to speak, but mutates into a column of fire; the Diacritical woman rises to speak, but she is headless; and finally the third panelist, a transvestite male, takes the podium: "He is forceful, he is articulate; he is talking about Heidegger or Derrida or Lévi-Strauss or Brecht. He is wearing a dress." The phallic critic, or rather, the deconstructive or Marxist critic, has successfully usurped the feminist. Showalter is surely right to be canny about the appropriative moves of the masculine critical establishment vis-à-vis feminist criticism. But the very uncanniness of this final vision should alert the reader to what has been elided by her argument—namely, woman and text, body and subject. Showalter comes dangerously close to endorsing a position she has earlier derided, that of Lewis Lapham opposing the admission of women to the Century Club ("The clarity of gender makes possible the human dialectic"); in her own text, the reemergence of gender hierarchy necessarily brings with it the accompanying specter of gender disorder. But in the last resort, her fantasy reveals what is troubling about the fashion for female impersonation—the uneasy recognition that when the text takes off its clothes, it is indeed disembodied, uncanny, and silent. In other words, the very discontinuity of (female) body and (feminine) text is the scandal that experientially based theories of the woman reader displace onto the scandal of critical cross-dressing in the 1980s.

　　　Showalter views critical cross-dressers with all the suspicion that Joyce, Lawrence, and Eliot bring to transvestism. What theoretical argument might provide a less residually conservative theory of gender, a more revisionary reading of woman? Shoshana Felman's "Rereading Femininity" approaches the question of the woman reader (woman as other) "otherwise"; that is, in the light of psychoanalytic theory.[19] Freud's question, "What is femininity?" asks, Felman points out, "what is femininity—*for men?*" As she elaborates it, the question is rather, "what does the question—'what is femininity—*for men?*' mean *for women?*" A short answer to this longer question might be: the silencing or elimination of woman. Felman's reading of a story by Balzac, "The Girl with the Golden Eyes," in the light of Freud's lecture "On Femininity" poses, in her own words, "the double question of the reading of sexual difference and of the intervention of sexual difference in the very act of reading." Read as the story of a triangular relationship (the interference of an affair between a man and a woman in an existing affair between two women), Balzac's text, Felman argues, "at once explores and puts in question the very structure of opposition betwen the sexes, as well as the respective definitions of masculinity and femininity."[24] Her analysis of the way in which class struggle and gender struggle both spring from a *division* which is institutionalized as an authoritative *order* by *hierarchy* (her terms) neatly deconstructs the conservative ideology of Gilbert's male modernists. Like Eagleton's Lovelace or Showalter's Eagleton, the rake in Balzac's story can be viewed as a man in search of his own phallus—a man for whom the girl with the golden eyes is only a narcissistic reflection of his desire. In this conventional polarity of masculine and feminine, woman serves only as a metaphor for man; he alone has a proper identity, since woman is always a figurative substitute for man. Hence her final reduction to the *corps morcelé*—in Balzac's story, literally a bloody and mutilated corpse—of Showalter's nightmare. In this scheme of things, woman's only function is to mediate desire or to serve as a medium of exchange. Deprived of her function, she is expendable.

Felman's reading of "The Girl with the Golden Eyes" is also designed as a lesson in how not to read—"how to *stop reading* through the exclusive blind reference to a masculine signified"(p. 27). But just as the rake, Henri, reads Paquita (the girl with the golden eyes) in terms of a masculine signified, so Paquita herself can only read "in the feminine." Bound erotically to a Marquise whom we later learn is Henri's half-sister, Paquita loves Henri for his ambiguous resemblance to a woman. In the famous transvestite scene from Balzac's story, she dresses Henri in the Marquise's clothes so that he may better resemble her beloved. For Felman, in fact,

> Balzac's text could be viewed . . . as a rhetorical dramatization and a philosophical reflection on the constitutive relationship between transvestism and sexuality, i.e., on the constitutive relationship between sex roles and clothing. If it is clothes, the text seems to suggest, if it is clothes alone, i.e., a cultural sign, an institution, which determine masculine and feminine and insure sexual opposition as an orderly, hierarchical polarity; if indeed clothes make the *man*—or the woman—are not sex roles as such, inherently, but travesties? Are not sex roles but travesties of the ambiguous complexity of real sexuality, of real sexual difference?(p. 28)

Henri and Paquita, Felman concludes, "are thus but transvestisms of the other sex's deceptively unequivocal identity; that is, they are travesties of a travesty." Like words, gender identity can be travestied or exchanged; there is no "proper" referent, male or female, only the masquerade of masculinity and femininity. At the climax of her ecstatic sexual intercourse with Henri, Paquita cries out: "Oh! Mariquita"—as Felman points out, a name which links that of Henri (de Marsay), Paquita herself, and the Marquise, thereby subverting the conventional opposition of masculine and feminine and staging "the ambiguous complexity of real sexuality." In addition, the name "Mariquita" means in Spanish, according to Felman, "an effeminate man"; we are told that Paquita's ecstatic cry pierces Henri's heart. The challenge here is not just to sexual hierarchy (Henri finds a woman installed in his place) but, Felman argues, to the smooth functioning of representation. Where Henri had previously found his ideal self—an imaginary, unequivocal sexual identity—reflected in Paquita's golden eyes, he now finds only division and the evidence of ironic misrecognition. The betrayer that must be cast out is the principle of difference, here redefined as femininity itself. Although the jealous Marquise forestalls Henri's revenge on Paquita, brother and sister come face to face over her dead body with the principle of ambiguity which each embodies for the other. Henri's discovery, that his rival is not other, but the same, installs his double as feminine. In Felman's words, "Since Henri himself has a woman's face, the feminine, Henri discovers, is not *outside* the masculine, its reassuring canny *opposite*, it is *inside* the masculine, its uncanny *difference from itself*" (p. 41). Inside every transvestite man, a woman is struggling to get out (a view of transvestism radically opposed to that of Stoller).

Femininity, in Felman's terms, "*inhabits* masculinity" as otherness or disruption; it is the uncanny of repression itself. Another name for it, though Felman does not invoke it, might be "bisexuality"—a bisexuality that necessarily returns as monstrosity. Henri first describes the girl with the golden eyes as "the woman of [his] dreams":

> She is the original of that ravishing picture called *La Femme Caressant sa Chimère*, the warmest, the most infernal inspiration of the genius of antiquity; a holy poem prostituted by those who have copied it for frescoes and mosaics; for a heap of bourgeois who see in this gem nothing more than a gewgaw and hang it on their watch-chains—whereas, it is the whole woman, an abyss of pleasure into which one plunges and finds no end. . . . And here I am today waiting for this girl whose chimera I am, asking nothing better than to pose as the monster in the fresco.[21]

What can we make of this strange allusion to "La Femme Caressant sa Chimère," seemingly an antique Pompeian fresco? Balzac apparently has in mind a passage from Henri Latouche's Neapolitan novel, *Fragoletta* (1829) where, during a visit to the Palazzo Studii, Latouche's characters discuss this and other paintings:

> "Et cette femme caressant une Chimère . . . c'est donc là une idée de tous les temps? Ce monstre aux ailes de colombe at aux nageoires de poisson est un bien bizarre objet d'affection; mais que de grâces dans l'attitude et particulièrement dans les bras de cette femme!" "Et que d'amour dans son regard . . . . On sent que rien de réel n'obtiendra jamais un tel culte de sa part."[22]

Balzac himself described the central character of Latouche's novel as "cet être inexprimable, qui n'a pas de sexe complet, et dans le coeur duquel luttent la timidité d'une femme et l'énergie d'un homme, qui aime la soeur, est aimé du frère, et ne peut rien rendre à l'un ni à l'autre. . . ."; "comme *l'Hermaphrodite*," he concludes, "*Fragoletta* restera monument".[23] The reference here is to Polyclitus's hermaphroditic statue, a discussion of which follows closely after that of the fresco and provides the centerpiece for Latouche's representation of the bisexual as an emblem of love. Elsewhere in Balzac's writing, "ce monstre" is, of course, the bisexual;[24] and the monster whom Henri views in his imagination as the object of Paquita's desire is himself—monstrous not by contrast with her ideality, but because, as we duly discover, his own gender identity is ambiguous. When Henri vows vengeance on Paquita for daring to love a woman in the guise of a man, he attempts to destroy the monster of bisexuality that always lurks within. Ironically, her death confronts him more surely with what she screens, the woman who is his monstrous or ambiguous double—with the femininity which he must deny if he is to maintain the illusion of unequivocal gender identity on which his masculinity depends.

Balzac's rake and his half-sister are alike in seeing Paquita as an object of exchange to be possessed or discarded at will (like her mother, "She comes from a country where women are not beings, but things—chattels, with which one does as one wills, which one buys, sells, and slays").[25] Whether viewed as an object of exchange or as the mediator of desire, Paquita transgresses the system in which she is inscribed by daring to be a desiring subject in her own right, and one whose desire disrupts the hierarchical opposition of masculine and feminine. As she intervenes in Balzac's story to reveal the scandalous interchangeability of man and woman—each standing for the other—so Felman herself, she points out, intervenes in Freud's lecture "On Femininity." Felman disrupts Freud's text as Paquita ruins representation in Balzac's story by daring to be at once a desiring and a speaking subject. Freud had posed the problem of femininity as a problem for men; the question *of* women is opened in a manner which closes it *for* them. As Felman writes,

In assuming here my place as a speaking subject, I have then *interfered*, through female utterance and reading, in Freud's male writing. I have *enacted* sexual difference in the very act of reading Freud's interrogation of it; enacted it as precisely difference, with the purpose not of rejecting Freud's interrogation, but of displacing it, of carrying it beyond its *stated* question, by disrupting the transparency and misleadingly self-evident universality of its male enunciation.[26]

But—one might ask—is Freud's text so misleadingly, so self-evidently and universalizing "male" after all? Doesn't textuality itself (like Eagleton's writing) always contain "something equivocal"?

Freud's fictive "lecture" actually starts a paragraph earlier than Felman's opening quotation implies ("Today's lecture . . . may serve to give you an example of a detailed piece of analytic work"). It begins conventionally enough, at first sight, with the time-honored words, "Ladies and Gentlemen"—only to announce a problem: "All the while I am preparing to talk to you I am struggling with an internal difficulty" (*SE*, 22:112). What is this "internal difficulty"? Surely nothing else but the recognition by Freud of his own ambiguous relation to discourse (Felman's "enunciation"), and hence to gender as well. He is, he confesses, "uncertain . . . of the extent of [his] license"; how far can he go? (Like Franco-American theory in Showalter's polemic, could he go "much too far"?) Should an introduction to psychoanalysis such as these *New Introductory Lectures* have been left "without alteration or supplement" (*SE* 22:112), he asks? One might ask, in turn, why a lecture "On Femininity" should take the appearance of "alteration or supplement." *Alteration* (an everyday euphemism for the neutering of domestic pets) and *supplement* (après Derrida, an academic euphemism for writing-as-masturbation) are terms that suggest unmanning effects, as if both theory and writing reenact the internal division by means of which sexual identity is constituted (or should I say, "fixed"?).

Freud proposes, he tells his imaginary audience, to bring forward "nothing but observed facts." But it is precisely the evidence of observation—the empiricism of scientific inquiry—that his lecture dismantles at the outset:

When you meet a human being, the first distinction you make is "male or female?" and you are accustomed to make the distinction with unhesitating certainty. Anatomical science shares your certainty at one point and not much further. The male sexual product, the spermatozoon, and its vehicle are male; the ovum and the organism that harbours it are female. . . . [But] Science next tells you something that runs counter to your expectations and is probably calculated to confuse your feelings. It draws your attention to the fact that portions of the male sexual apparatus also appear in women's bodies, though in an atrophied state, and vice versa in the alternative case. It regards their occurrence as indications of *bisexuality,* as though an individual is not a man or a woman but always both. (*SE* 22:113-14)

If anatomical science can provide only an ambiguous answer to the riddle of gender, then, Freud writes "you are bound to . . . conclude that what constitutes masculinity or femininity is an unknown characteristic which anatomy cannot lay hold of" (*SE* 22:114). Could "psychology" provide an answer, perhaps? No, since it merely reinscribes in the realm of mental life either anatomy or conventional attributions of gender to qualities such as activity or passivity. If "psychology too is unable to solve the riddle of femininity" (*SE* 22:116), what of psychoanalysis? For Freud, psychoanalytic inquiry would take the form of an aporia, refusing the idea of a secret or "essence" altogether. Instead of demanding an answer to the riddle against which so many heads have knocked—"Heads in hieroglyphic bonnets,/Heads in turbans and black birettas . . ." (*SE* 22:113n.)[27]—psychoanalysis asks how differentiation itself comes about: "In conformity with its peculiar nature, psychoanalysis does not try to describe what a woman is—that would be a task it could scarcely perform—but sets about enquiring how she comes into being" (*SE* 22:116). The "peculiar nature" of psychoanalysis, Freud suggests, is not to describe what is, knocking its head against the opaque reality of observation or representation, but rather to uncover the process by which that reality or set of representations is constructed.

The outlines of what Freud calls "the prehistory of women"—a process of sexual differentiation founded on the

differing operations on boy and girl of the Oedipus and castration complexes—forms (in Gilbert's phrase) an "argumentative
history" with which feminists in turn have argued; arguing, that
is, both with Freud and among themselves.[28] Rather than rehearsing here that (pre)history or the debate which surrounds
"On Femininity," I want simply to invoke the crucial but problematic thesis of bisexuality put forward in Freud's lecture.
Though he at first thought of bisexuality in terms of an undifferentiated sexual nature prior to the institution of sexual
difference, Freud came to see bisexuality, in the words of Juliet
Mitchell and Jacqueline Rose—whose *Feminine Sexuality* (1983)
contains the most sustained account of a revised, Lacanian
Freud—as standing for "the very uncertainty of sexual division
itself" and as inseparable from "the divison and precariousness
of human subjectivity."[29] This Lacanian reading of sexual difference would emphasize in particular what Rose calls "the
availability to all subjects of both positions in relation to that
difference itself." Lacan and language simultaneously install
the subject in sexual difference, and sexual difference in the
subject: "For Lacan, men and women are only ever in language. . . . All speaking beings must line themselves up on one
side or the other of this division, but anyone can cross over and
inscribe themselves on the opposite side from that to which
they are anatomically destined."[30] But as Stephen Heath points
out in *The Sexual Fix* (1984), bisexuality works both ways in
theoretical arguments, functioning "as the beginning of an alternative representation, as an insistence against the one position, the fixed sexual order, man and woman;" but also
returning "as a confirmation of that fixity, a strategy in which
differences . . . are neutralized into the given system of identity."[31] On one hand, bisexuality as crossing over or shifting: on
the other, bisexuality as the old fix. Though he seems to start by
dissolving the opposition beween masculine and feminine,
Freud ends by reaffirming the old order; masculinity provides
the measure for the feminine. For Sarah Kofman in *The Enigma
of Woman* (1985), Freud first masters sexual difference by posit-
ing an original masculinity in women, making the girl's bisexuality more pronounced than the boy's, and then establishes a
norm of bisexuality which predisposes women to hysteria; the

sign of feminine sexual difference becomes the sign of feminine neurosis.[32] The binary opposition returns to obliterate sexual difference while restoring sexual hierarchy.

Yet a resourceful reading of Freud's "On Femininity" (such as Kofman provides) might reveal that the very bisexuality posited for women makes them, not a derivative of man, but rather, in their complexity, a model for sexuality in general. As Culler puts it, "the moves by which psychoanalysis establishes a hierarchical opposition between man and woman rely on premises that reverse this hierarchy."[33] Reversal becomes the first and necessary step, the point of leverage for dismantling a theoretical structure in which the feminine is produced only as a negative term; as lack. If, from a Lacanian point of view, "masquerade" (cross-dressing?) "is the very definition of 'femininity' precisely because it is constructed with reference to a male sign,"[34] that definition, in turn, is itself clearly a form of masquerade, an imposture. Freud's account of the "peculiar nature" of psychoanalysis ("psycho-analysis does not try to describe what a woman is . . . but sets about enquiring how she comes into being," *SE* 22:116) could well be rephrased as Rose's Lacanian account of the "peculiar nature" of femininity: "Psychoanalysis does not produce that definition. It gives an account of how that definition is produced."[35] Hence the importance of psychoanalysis for any account of women's relation to, and constitution by, discourse. But there is another side to it. Reread, not as given, but as produced, "femininity"—woman—also demands a rereading of the text of psychoanalysis. Hence the importance of feminist criticism for any account of the constitution of psychoanalytic discourse. The theoretical reversal reveals the role played by woman in sustaining Freud's theory of gender. But it also reveals how that theory can be reread to produce a theoretical formulation in which the emphasis shifts from "woman" to "reading."

Orlando too might be called an "argumentative history"—the history of a woman writer. Orlando's gender shift from masculine to feminine occurs during the reign of Charles I at approximately the moment when (according to Woolf's literary-historical scheme) it was possible for the first time to become a woman writer and not the suicidal Judith Shakespeare of *A Room of One's Own* (1929). Though at once lover and beloved, Orlando is also a poet whose writing provides a history of literary possibilities from 1500 to Woolf's own age. Indeed, like *A Room of One's Own*, *Orlando* can be read as the history of its own writing. Though she lightheartedly takes issue with essentialist notions of gender—such as "(1) that Orlando had always been a woman, (2) that Orlando is at this moment a man"[36]—Woolf's underlying concern is with questions of writing. The convergence of Orlando and authorial concerns, or gender and writing, is most clearly marked when Orlando, having married and so met the requirements of the spirit of her age (at this point, the Victorian age) "could write, and write she did. She wrote. She wrote. She wrote." With this, Orlando's biographer, and the text, break off for a long digression on the mind of the writer at work. The life of a writer refuses to be written. Woolf as biographer can only invoke processes that are at once Orlando's and her own: "this mere woolgathering; this thinking; this sitting in a chair day in, day out, with a cigarette and a sheet of paper and a pen and an ink pot."[37] Writing and thinking, Orlando neither thinks of a gamekeeper (like Lady Chatterley) nor pens him a note (the only forms of thinking and writing nobody objects to in a woman); she is, Woolf observes, "one of those monsters of iniquity who do not love." This monster who will neither love nor (like Henri de Marsay) kill, is "no better than a corpse," a mere body: "if . . . the subject of one's biography will neither love nor kill, but will only think and imagine, we may conclude that he or she is no better than a corpse and so leave her."[38] Looking out of the window, the only resource left, the biographer searches for other signs of life; returning from her year's imaginative absorption, Orlando-as-writer similarly pushes aside her pen, comes to the window with her completed manuscript, and exclaims: "Done!" Life is most fully present when the life of the writer and the writing of the life merge, breaking down the distinction between subject and object; between woman as writer or woman as written, woman as reader or woman as read. Orlando and her biographer, in other words, create each other by mutual substitution; the masquerade—Orlando's transvestite progress through the literary ages—is that of writing, where fictive and multiple selves are the only self, the only truth, the writer knows.

What Gilbert calls "a revisionary biography"[39] can be seen as autobiography; specifically, as female autobiography. Woolf wrote to Vita Sackville-West apropos of *Orlando*, "it sprung upon me how I could revolutionise biography in a night."[40] In a review of Harold Nicolson's biography, *Some People* (1927), written while she was at work on *Orlando*, Woolf described "the new biography" as one in which we realize that the figure which has been most completely and most subtly displayed is that of the author"; one in which we realize that "Truth of fact and truth of fiction are incompatible" and "the life which is increasingly real to us is the fictive life."[41] *Orlando* culminates—or rather, fails to culminate—with a mock peroration in which the (auto)biographical subject meditates inconclusively on herself as woman writer; on the "true self" that is "a woman. Yes, but a million other things as well." In the face of such irrepressible diversity, such multiplicity of shifting selves, the biographer throws in her hand:

> But (here another self came skipping over the top of her mind like the beam from a lighthouse). Fame! (She laughed.) Fame! Seven editions. A prize. Photographs in the evening papers (. . . we must here snatch time to remark how discomposing it is for her biographer that this culmination and peroration should be dashed from us on a laugh casually like this; but the truth is that when we write of a woman, everything is out of place—culminations and perorations; the accent never falls where it does with a man).[42]

"When we write of a woman, everything is out of place." Or, as Barbara Johnson has written apropos of women and autobiography, "the monstrousness of selfhood is intimately embedded within the question of female autobiography. Yet how could it be otherwise, since the very notion of a self, the very shape of human life stories, has always, from St. Augustine to Freud, been modeled on the man."[43]

Orlando "discomposes" or undoes her (auto)biographer because the displaced accent also displaces the writing subject. "When we write of a woman everything is out of place;" displacement, not hierarchy, becomes the order of the day. These multiple displacements—from one self to another, from masculine to feminine, from biography to autobiography, from reader to writer—constitute the "insouciant shiftings" of writerly non-identity or otherness which simultaneously preclude both closure (culminations and perorations) and certainty (truth). "If you want to know more about femininity," Freud inconclusively concludes his lecture, "enquire from your own experience of life, or turn to the poets" (*SE* 22:135). When literature turns from experience to psychoanalysis for an answer to the riddle of femininity, psychoanalysis turns the question back to literature, since it is in language—in reading and in writing woman—that femininity at once discloses and discomposes itself, endlessly displacing the fixity of gender identity by the play of difference and division which simultaneously creates and uncreates gender, identity, and meaning. "The difference (of view)" which we look for in reading woman (reading) is surely nothing other than this disclosure, this discomposition, which puts the institution of difference in question without erasing the question of difference itself.

II. FEMINIST READINGS

1. The Difference of View

For George Eliot, as for her heroines (wrote Virginia Woolf),

> The burden and the complexity of womanhood were not enough; she must reach beyond the sanctuary and pluck for herself the strange bright fruits of art and knowledge. Clasping them as few women have ever clasped them, she would not renounce her own inheritance—*the difference of view, the difference of standard.*[1]

The terms here are worth lingering on; they bring to light a hidden problem as well as articulating an obvious one. The problem explicitly located is, in one way or another, central to feminist literary criticism: that is, the nature of women's access to culture and their entry into literary discourse. The demand for education ("the strange bright fruits of art and knowledge") provides the emancipatory thrust of much nineteenth- and twentieth-century feminism, and goes back to Mary Wollstonecraft's attempt to appropriate the language of Enlightenment Reason for her own sex in *A Vindication of the Rights of Woman* (1792). But this access to a male-dominated culture may equally be felt to bring with it alienation, repression, division—a silencing of the "feminine," a loss of women's inheritance. The problem, then, is not George Eliot's alone; it is that of women's writing (and of feminist literary criticism) itself. To propose a difference of view, a difference of standard—to begin to ask what the difference might be—is to call into question the very terms that constitute the difference.

The terms used by Virginia Woolf, therefore, also uncover something of the rift experienced by women writers in a patriarchal society, where language itself may reinscribe the structures by which they are oppressed. Reaching beyond the sanctuary, transgressing the boundaries of womanhood (*womanhood:* the sacred hearth, at once home, womb and tomb; something is being stilled into silence, for the burden of womanhood is also the burden of the mystery)—the movement becomes an exit from the sacred into the profane. In this scheme, woman as silent bearer of ideology (virgin, wife, mother) is the necessary sacrifice to male secularity, worldliness, and tampering with forbidden knowledge. She is the term by which patriarchy creates a reserve of purity and silence in the materiality of its traffic with the world and its noisy discourse. Feminized, the Faustian hero becomes a militant adventuress, Eve, plucking "the strange bright fruits" that bring both knowledge and unhappiness. The archetypal gesture installs George Eliot in a specifically Judeo-Christian drama, that of sin and death; the fall is from innocence (mindlessness?) into mortality. It's not surprising, therefore, that Virginia Woolf should end her essay with what amounts to a funeral oration. For her, George Eliot was literally worn into the grave by the battle with "sex and health and convention" which attended her quest for "more knowledge and more freedom."

In this traditional drama, a lively sense of sin is matched with a weighty sense of ancient female suffering and hopeless desire; but George Eliot's heroines, Virginia Woolf tells us, no longer suffer in silence:

> The ancient consciousness of woman, charged with suffering and sensibility, and for so many ages dumb, seems in them to have brimmed and overflowed and uttered a demand for something—they scarcely know what—for something that is perhaps incompatible with the facts of human existence.[2]

(That notion of dumbness and utterance, of demand for an impossible desire, forms a recurrent motif in both women's writing and feminist literary criticism.) What is striking here is the association of ancient suffering and modern desire with women's inheritance, as if they were almost synonymous. This is elegy, not affirmation. Elegy which, in Virginia Woolf's case, one might justifiably link with the death of a mother or mothering step-sister. Our mothers were killed by the burden and the complexity of womanhood; or, like George Eliot, died in giving birth to their writing (as Dorothea rests in an unvisited tomb in order that "George Eliot" may write her epitaph). Such, at any rate, seems to be the melancholy inference. It's surely significant that for at least one woman looking back at another, the price of combining womanhood and writing seemed so high—that the transgression of writing seemed to bring with it mortal consequences; the sacrifice not only of happiness, but of life itself.

Contemporary feminist criticism is more likely to stress pleasure than suffering—the freeing of repressed feminine desire; jouissance and *"la mère qui jouit"* (no longer barred from sexual pleasure) as against the burden of womanhood. Recent French writing about women and literature, marked as it is by the conjunction of neo-Freudian psychoanalysis and structuralism, has particularly tended to diagnose the repression of women's desire by representation itself, and by the order of language as instated by the Law of the Father: the Symbolic order, predicated on lack and castration. In this theoretical scheme, femininity—heterogeneity, otherness—becomes the repressed term by which discourse is made possible. The feminine takes its place with the absence, silence, or incoherence that discourse represses; in what Julia Kristeva would call the *semiotic,* the pre-oedipal phase of rhythmic, onomatopoeic babble which precedes the Symbolic but remains inscribed in those pleasurable and rupturing aspects of language identified particularly with avant-garde literary practice.[3] But here again, there's a problem for feminist criticism. Women's access to discourse involves submission to phallocentricity, to the masculine and the symbolic: refusal, on the other hand, risks reinscribing the feminine as a yet more marginal madness or nonsense. When we speak (as feminist writers and theorists often do) of the need for a special language for women, what then do we mean?

Not, surely, a refusal of language itself; nor a return to a specifically feminine linguistic domain which in fact marks the place of women's oppression and confinement. Rather, a process that is played out within language, across boundaries. The dream of a language freed from the Freudian notion of castration, by which female difference is defined as lack rather than otherness, is at first sight essentially theoretical, millennial and Utopian. Its usefulness lies in allying feminism and the avant-garde in a common political challenge to the very discourse which makes them possible; the terms of language itself, as well as the terms of psychoanalysis and of literary criticism, are called into question—subverted from within. Woman and artist, the feminine and the avant-garde, are elided in the privileged zone of contemporary intellectual and esthetic concern: writing. Such a move has the advantage of freeing off the "feminine" from the religion-bound, ultimately conservative and doom-ridden concept of difference-as-opposition which underlies Virginia Woolf's reading of the "case" of George Eliot. *Difference* is redefined, not as male *versus* female—not as biologically constituted—but as a multiplicity, ambiguity and heterogeneity which is that of textuality itself. Writing, the production of meaning, becomes the site both of challenge and otherness; rather than (as in more traditional approaches) simply yielding the themes and representation of female oppression. *Difference*, in fact, becomes a traversal of the boundaries inscribed in Virginia Woolf's terms, but a traversal that exposes these very boundaries for what they are—the product of phallocentric discourse and of women's relation to patriarchal culture. Though necessarily working within "male" discourse, women's writing (in this scheme) would work ceaselessly to deconstruct it: to write what cannot be written.

So much for one formulation of the question: what is the nature (the difference) of women's writing? Another way to pose the question is to explore the extent to which patriarchal representation, by contrast, "silences" women—the extent to which *woman* or *womanhood*, considered not as an image but as a sign, becomes the site of both contradiction and repression. For D. H. Lawrence, woman is "the unutterable which man must forever continue to try to utter"; she achieves womanhood at the point where she is silenced (like Sue Bridehead) and installed within the sanctuary.[4] If writing is a transgression punishable by death, being written about, by however loving a father, can also prove fatal. Take the disquieting way in which Hardy, in a famous scene from *Tess of the D'Urbervilles* (1891), reveals the sign *woman* to be a rich source of mythic confusion, ideological contradiction, and erotic fascination:

> She was yawning, and he saw the red interior of her mouth as if it had been a snake's. She had stretched one arm so high above her coiled-up cable of hair that he could see its satin delicacy above the sunburn; her face was flushed with sleep, and her eyelids hung heavy over their pupils. The brim-fulness of her nature breathed from her. It was a moment when a woman's soul is more incarnate than at any other time; when the most spiritual beauty bespeaks itself flesh; and sex takes the outside place in the presentation.[5]

Sex having taken the outside place in the presentation, it's not surprising that within a short space Tess should become first feline, and then Eve. The language of incarnation (body and soul, presence and absence) signals an underlying structure which comes near to collapse before the threat of female sexuality. Though Hardy seems to be salvaging Tess's body for spirituality (the vessel is brim-full), the yawning mouth opens up a split in the very terms he uses. The incarnate state of Tess's soul appears to be as close to sleep—to unconsciousness—as is compatible with going about her work. At the same time, the snake-mouth marks the point of (desired) entry to an interior which is offered to us as simply yet more body (she is all red inside, *not* all soul). Fascination with this unknown, unrepresentable, interiorized sexuality is surely at the center of male fantasies of seduction and engulfment. No wonder that Hardy goes on to make Tess, not the object of male gaze, but the mirror in which the male is reflected ("*she* regarded *him* as Eve at her second waking might have regarded Adam"; my italics): Otherness is domesticated, made safe, through narcissism—the female mouth can't utter, only receive and confirm the male.

Tess's silence, like her purity, makes female desire dumb; places her on the side of unconsciousness and, finally, death. "Shut up already" might be the hidden message which a feminist critique uncovers. But to stop at such readings (or at exposing the reproduction of sexist ideology by male critics) is to take only the first step toward uttering an alternative. Utterance, though, brings the problem home for women writers (as for feminist critics). The options polarize along familiar lines: appropriation or separatism. Can women adapt traditionally male dominated modes of writing and analysis to the articulation of female oppression and desire? Or should we rather reject tools that may simply reinscribe our marginality and deny the specificity of our experience, instead forging others of our own?—reverting, perhaps, to the traditionally feminine in order to revalidate its forms (formlessness?) and preoccupations; rediscovering subjectivity, the language of feeling, ourselves. The risks on either side are illuminatingly played out in the writing of feminism's founding mother herself: Mary Wollstonecraft. *The Rights of Woman*, in claiming sense for women rather than sensibility, pays a price that is reflected in its own prose. Putting herself outside the confines of a despised femininity, aligning herself with "sense," Mary Wollstonecraft also eschews "pretty feminine phrases" as a male conspiracy designed to soften female slavery. Linguistic pleasure (literary language) is placed on the side of the feminine, then banned, like female desire:

> I shall disdain to cull my phrases or polish my style. I aim at being useful, and sincerity will render me unaffected; for, wishing rather to persuade by the force of my arguments than dazzle by the elegance of my language, I shall not waste my time in rounding periods, or in fabricating the turgid bombast of artificial feelings, which, coming from the head, never reach the heart. I shall be employed about things, not words! and, anxious to render my sex more respectable members of society, I shall try to avoid that flowery diction which has slided from essays into novels, and from novels into familiar letters and conversations.[6]

A swagger of busy self-presentation makes this as much the creation of an alienated persona as it is a feminist preface to *Lyrical Ballads*. A plainspoken utilitarian speaks not so much *for* women, or *as* a woman, but *against* them—over their silent bodies, and over (having attempted to cast it out) the body of the text too: "I shall be employed about things, not words!"

Speaking both for and as a woman (rather than "like" a woman): this is the problem of women's writing. For the feminist critic, the problem may resolve itself as one of style. For Mary Wollstonecraft, the solution lay in fiction that gave her access not only (paradoxically) to her own situation as a woman, but to literariness. *The Wrongs of Woman: or, Maria* (1798) negates both the title and the assumptions of her earlier essay in order to show how, if "sense" excludes women, "sensibility" confines them—yet offers a radical challenge to patriarchy; a challenge which it must repress. (When the heroine pleads her own case in a court of law, the judge alludes to "the fallacy of letting women plead their feelings. . . .What virtuous woman thought of her feelings?", thereby exposing the double bind.) The prison of sensibility is created by patriarchy to contain women; thus they experience desire without Law, wielding language without power. Marginalized, the language of feeling can only ally itself with insanity—an insanity which, displaced into writing, produces a moment of imaginative and linguistic excess over-brimming the container of fiction, and swamping the distinction between author and character:

> What is the view of the fallen column, the mouldering arch, of the most exquisite workmanship, when compared with this living memento of the fragility, the instability, of reason, and the wild luxuriancy of noxious passions? Enthusiasm turned adrift, like some rich stream overflowing its banks, rushes forward with destructive velocity, inspiring a sublime concentration of thought. *Thus thought Maria*—These are the ravages over which humanity must ever mournfully ponder. . . .It is not over the decaying productions of the mind, embodied with the happiest art, we grieve most bitterly. The view of what has been done by man, produces a melancholy, yet aggrandizing, sense of what remains to be achieved by human intellect; but a mental convulsion, which, like the devastation of an earthquake, throws all the elements of thought and imagination into confusion, makes contemplation giddy, and we fearfully ask on what ground we ourselves stand.[7]

This is what it means for women to be on the side of madness as well as silence. Like the rich stream overflowing its banks, a wash of desire throws all the elements of thought and imagination into confusion. By contrast with the ruins of (male) cultural imperialism, the earthquake is feminized; it demands "on

what ground we ourselves stand," opening onto a feminist sublime where all foundations are called into question.

Mary Wollstonecraft's concern in this passage for
"words," not "things," makes it a crucial moment for both
women's writing and feminist literary criticism. A mental con-
vulsion breaches the impasse between undifferentiated disap-
pearance into a "male" text and the prison of sensibility.
Rejecting the essentialism that keeps women subjected as well
as subjective, it also rejects mastery and dominance. Madness
imagined as revolution, or the articulation of Utopian desire
("a demand for something—they scarcely know what"), represent gestures past the impasse played out in Mary Wollstonecraft's prose. In writing, such gestures may release possibilities
repressed by a dominant ideology or its discourse. The transgression of literary boundaries—moments when structures are
shaken, when language refuses to lie down meekly, or the marginal is brought into sudden focus, or intelligibility itself refused—reveal not only the conditions of possibility within
which women's writing exists, but what it would be like to
revolutionize them. In the same way, the moment of desire (the
moment when the writer most clearly installs herself in her
writing) becomes a refusal of mastery, an opting for rupture
and possibility, which can in itself make women's writing a
challenge to the literary structures it necessarily inhabits.

"Thus thought Maria"—the container overflowing
with authorial Enthusiasm—has its analogue in a famous
"awkward break" noticed by Virginia Woolf in *A Room of One's
Own* (1929). Her example is Charlotte Brontë's intrusion into
Jane Eyre (1847) with what Woolf rightly identifies as a protest
against the confinement of the nineteenth-century woman
writer:

> It is in vain to say human beings ought to be satisfied with
> tranquillity: they must have action; and they will make it if
> they cannot find it. . . .Women are supposed to be very calm
> generally: but women feel just as men feel; they need exercise
> for their faculties, and a field for their efforts as much as their
> brothers do; they suffer from too rigid a restraint, too abso-
> lute a stagnation, precisely as men would suffer. . . .It is
> thoughtless to condemn them, or laugh at them, if they seek

to do more or learn more than custom has pronounced necessary for their sex.

> *When thus alone, I not unfrequently heard Grace Poole's laugh.*[8]

("That is an awkward break, I thought," comments Virginia Woolf.) The author herself has burst the bounds of "too rigid a restraint"—making action if she cannot find it. By a breach of fictional decorum, writing enacts protest as well as articulating it.

The point is not simply that excess of energy disrupts the text; it is that the disruption reveals what the novel cannot say within its legitimate confines, and hence reveals its fictionality. The unacceptable text gets the blue pencil from Virginia Woolf ("the woman who wrote those pages . . . will write in a rage where she should write calmly. . . .She will write of herself where she should write of her characters. She is at war with her lot"); but it also opens up a rift in her own seamless web. What she herself cannot say without loss of calmness (rage has been banned in the interests of literature) is uttered instead by another woman writer. The overflow in *Jane Eyre* washes into *A Room of One's Own*. This oblique recuperation of feminist energy has implications for feminist criticism as well as for fiction; might, in fact, be said to characterize the practice of the feminist critic, for whom the relation between author and text (her own text) is equally charged. Editing into her writing the outburst edited out of Charlotte Brontë's, Virginia Woolf creates a point of instability which unsettles her own urbane and polished decorum. The rift exposes the fiction of authorial control and objectivity, revealing other possible fictions, other kinds of writing; exposes, for a moment, its own terms.

The slippage here is both seductive and threatening. Seductive, because passion is involved; threatening, because the structures on which both fiction and criticism depend are seen to be built on words alone. And perhaps the correction of authorial transgression—the domestication of authorial desire—may be necessary in the interests of writing itself. Take a significant moment of self-censorship like that which closes the "Finale" of *Middlemarch* (1871–72). George Eliot's compas-

sionately magisterial verdict on the "determining acts" of Dorothea's life ("the mixed result of young and noble impulse
struggling amidst the conditions of an imperfect social state, in
which great feelings will often take the aspect of error, and
great faith the aspect of illusion") cancels what had originally
been "an awkward break" in the final pages of the first edition:

> They were the mixed results of young and noble impulse
> struggling under prosaic conditions. Among the many re-
> marks passed on her mistakes, it was never said in the neigh-
> bourhood of Middlemarch that such mistakes could not have
> happened if the society into which she was born had not
> smiled on . . . modes of education which make a woman's
> knowledge another name for motley ignorance—on rules of
> conduct which are in flat contradiction with its own loudly-
> asserted beliefs. While this is the social air in which mortals
> begin to breathe, there will be collisions such as those in
> Dorothea's life, where great feelings will take the aspect of
> error, and great faith the aspect of illusion.[9]

Here authorial indignation risks turning the neighborhood
of Middlemarch into "social air," and uncovering fiction as
polemic.

Whether the cancellation springs from loss of nerve
or aesthetic judgment, it makes George Eliot (so to speak) the
heir of Virginia Woolf as well as Charlotte Brontë. In doing so,
it opens up the possibility of the author's dissolution into her
own text; the closing sentences of the novel point beyond the
"Finale" to their own writing—to the full nature that has its
strength broken by being diverted into channels whose effect is
incalculably diffusive:

> Her finely-touched spirit had still its fine issues, though they
> were not widely visible. Her full nature, like that river of
> which Cyrus broke the strength, spent itself in channels
> which had no great name on the earth. But the effect of her
> being on those around her was incalculably diffusive: for the
> growing good of the world is partly dependent on unhistoric
> acts; and that things are not so ill with you and me as they
> might have been, is half owing to the number who lived
> faithfully a hidden life, and rest in unvisited tombs.[10]

Earlier, George Eliot has referred to Casaubon's turgid schol-
arship as "minor monumental productions"; monuments to
dead languages. By contrast with this sterile imperialism (Casaubon *versus* the world), we have the unhistoric acts that make
for growing good. Though a new Saint Theresa will find no
conventual life to reform, a new Antigone no Creon to oppose
with self-immolation ("the medium in which their ardent
deeds took shape is forever gone"), still, the writer may find
another "medium" of her own for ardent deeds. Dorothea's
hidden life and entombment make her a silent reformer, an
unremembered protester; but her silence and anonymity are
the sacrifice which allows George Eliot speech and name.

    If the gain seems marginal, this may be because
writing is itself marginal, unhistoric; if diffusive, incalculably
so. But the possibility glimpsed at the end of *Middlemarch*—that
of Enthusiasm overflowing into ink—points to the silent sub-
versiveness of writing, its power to destabilize the ground on
which we stand. In *A Room of One's Own*, Virginia Woolf dissolves "truth" (the withheld "nugget of truth") into "the lies
that flow from my pen"; the subject of women and writing
becomes a fiction: "I propose, making use of all the liberties
and licences of a novelist, to tell you the story."[11] As hard fact
dissolves into fluid fiction, so the authorial "I" becomes "only a
convenient term for somebody who has no real being"; many
"I"s, many Marys ("Mary Beton, Mary Seton, Mary Carmi-
chael" and I)—a plurality contrasted to the unified "I" which
falls as a dominating phallic shadow across the male page, like
Casaubon's monumental egotism. And as the subject "I" is dis-
solved into writing, so boundaries themselves are called into
question; rendered, not terra firma, but fiction too. Once returned to its proper medium (the Cam), the thought-fish which
swims through *A Room of One's Own* "as it darted and sank, and
flashed hither and thither, set up such a wash and tumult of
ideas that it was impossible to sit still." The story becomes
the narrative of its own inception, then of the arrest of verbal
energy—this darting, flashing, linguistic play—by the figure of
a man, representative of the Law, of the phallic "I" that bars
and bounds:

It was thus that I found myself walking with extreme rapidity across a grass plot. Instantly a man's figure rose to intercept me. Nor did I at first understand that the gesticulations of a curious-looking object, in a cut-away coat and evening shirt, were aimed at me. His face expressed horror and indignation. Instinct rather than reason came to my help; he was a Beadle; I was a woman. This was the turf; there was the path. Only the Fellows and Scholars are allowed here; the gravel is the place for me. Such thoughts were the work of a moment. As I regained the path the arms of the Beadle sank, his face assumed its usual repose. (pp.5–6)

The protest against male exclusiveness is obvious enough; so is the comical reduction of an educational institution to a grass plot and a clockwork beadle. Acquiescing in the terms of her trespass, Virginia Woolf yet shows, with pleasurable oblique-ness (via her short cut), that these terms are arbitrary—a matter of cut-away coats and gravel paths.

Woolf's satire, in delineating the confines within which women must walk ("This was the turf; there was the path") traverses and exposes them. The story she tells is in fact that of her own oblique relation, as a woman writer, to the dominant culture and to patriarchal institutions (she labels them Oxbridge, the educational system which inscribes her marginality). At once within this culture and outside it, the woman writer experiences not only exclusion, but an inter-nalized split. Elsewhere in *A Room of One's Own* she puts it like this:

if one is a woman one is often surprised by a sudden splitting off of consciousness, say in walking down Whitehall, when from being the natural inheritor of that civilisation, she be-comes, on the contrary, outside of it, alien and critical. (p. 101)

"Alien and critical"—the stance glimpsed behind the urbane and playful style of *A Room of One's Own*. Though Virginia Woolf never fails to remind us that the matter of inheritance is abso-lutely a matter of access to power, property and education, an experienced division forms part of that inheritance too. To recognize both the split and the means by which it is constituted, to challenge its terms while necessarily working within them— that is the hidden narrative of the trespass on the grass. But what about that elusive thought-fish? For Virginia Woolf, rage drove it into hiding; the rage that for her distorts Charlotte Brontë's fiction ("She will write in a rage where she should write calmly"). It is in this light, perhaps, that we should reread her famous remarks about androgyny—not as a naive attempt to transcend the determinants of gender and culture (though it is that too), but rather as a harmonizing gesture, a simul-taneous enactment of desire and repression by which the split is closed with an essentially Utopian vision of undivided con-sciousness. The repressive male/female opposition which "interferes with the unity of the mind" gives way to a mind paradoxically conceived of not as one, but as heterogeneous, open to the play of difference: "resonant and porous . . . it transmits emotion without impediment . . . it is naturally cre-ative, incandescent, and undivided" (p. 102). That's as good a description as one could wish, not of the mind, but of Virginia Woolf's own prose—and of the play of difference perpetually enacted within writing.

The gesture toward androgyny is millennial, like all dreams of another language or mode of being; but its effect is to remove the area of debate (and the trespass) from biological determination to the field of signs; from gender to representa-tion ("words" not "things"). And in holding open other pos-sibilities—otherness itself—such writing posits "the difference of view" as a matter of rewriting. "A woman writing thinks back through her mothers"; thinking back through the mother becomes a gesture at once of recuperation and of revision. The rediscovery of a female literary tradition need not mean a re-turn to specifically "female" (that is, potentially confining) do-mains, any more than the feminist colonizing of Marxist, psychoanalytic, or post-structuralist modes of thought neces-sarily means a loss of that alien and critical relation which is one aspect of women's inheritance. Rather, they involve a rec-ognition that all attempts to inscribe female differences within writing are a matter of inscribing women within fictions of one kind or another (whether literary, critical, or psychoanalytic); and hence, that what is at stake for both women writing and writing about women is the rewriting of these fictions—the work of revision which makes "the difference of view" a question rather than an answer, and a question to be asked not simply of women, but of writing too.

2. The Buried Letter: *Villette*

"Is this enough? Is it to live? . . . Does virtue lie in abnegation of self? I do not believe it. . . . Each human being has his share of rights. I suspect it would conduce to the happiness and welfare of all, if each knew his allotment, and held to it as tenaciously as the martyr to his creed. Queer thoughts these, that surge in my mind: are they right thoughts? I am not certain."

Caroline Helstone's assertion of the inalienable rights of self, in Brontë's *Shirley* (1849),[1] I take to be the seed of her *Villette* (1853)—in which repression returns vengefully on the heroine in the form of a ghostly nun. But *Villette* is not simply about the perils of repression. It is a text formally fissured by its own repressions, concealing a buried letter. Lucy Snowe writes two letters to Graham Bretton, one "under the dry, stinting check of Reason," the other "according to the full, liberal impulse of Feeling"—one for his benefit, censored and punishingly rational, the other for hers, an outpouring of her innermost self.[2] The same doubleness informs the novel as a whole, making it secretive, unstable and subversive. The narrative and representational conventions of Victorian realism are constantly threatened by an incompletely repressed Romanticism. Supernatural haunting and satanic revolt, delusion and dream, disrupt a text which can give no formal recognition to either Romantic or Gothic modes. The buried letter of Romanticism becomes the discourse of the Other, as the novel's unconscious—not just Lucy's—struggles for articulation within the confines of mid-nineteenth-century realism. The resulting distortions and mutilations in themselves constitute an aspect of the novel's meaning, like the distortions of a dream text. But there is more to be found in *Villette* than the incompatibility of realist and Romantic modes. It is haunted by the unacknowledged phantom of feminism, and by the strangeness of fiction itself. Its displacements and substitutions, like its silences and dislocations, are a reminder that fiction is the peculiar reserve both of repression and of the *Unheimliche*—the uncanny which, in Freud's words, "is in reality nothing new or alien, but something which is familiar and old-established in the mind and which has become alienated from it only through the process of repression."[3] Lucy's haunted self-estrangement encodes the novel's alienation from its ghostly subtext.

"Why is *Villette* disagreeable?" asked Matthew Arnold—"Because the writer's mind contains nothing but hunger, rebellion and rage, and therefore that is all she can, in fact put into her book."[4] The same qualities inspired Kate Millett's polemicizing of *Villette* as a radical feminist text ("one long meditation on a prison break").[5] Arnold and Millett are alike in proposing an unmediated relationship between author and work. It is easy to dismiss this collapsing of Charlotte Brontë and her fictional creation, Lucy Snowe; in her letters the novelist writes punitively of her heroine, "I can hardly express what subtlety of thought made me decide upon giving her a cold name" and "I am not leniently disposed towards Miss *Frost* . . . . I never meant to appoint her lines in pleasant places."[6] Yet the assumption that autobiographical release fuels the novel is natural enough, and not only because the letters evince the same straining after dissociation as the novel itself. For *Villette*, belonging as it appears to do to the tradition of the *roman personnel* (the lived fiction), invites its readers to make just such a covert identification between Charlotte Brontë and her creation—and then frustrates it. The novel's real oddity lies in perversely withholding its true subject, Lucy Snowe, by an act of repression which mimics hers. Her invisibility is more than evasive; it is devious, duplicitous. Lucy lies to us. Her deliberate ruses, omissions and falsifications break the unwritten contract of first-person narrative (the confidence between reader and "I") and unsettle our faith in the reliability of the text. "I, Lucy Snowe, plead guiltless of that curse, an overheated and discursive imagination" (p. 69), she tells us; but the same sentence goes on to speak of the infant Paulina's incommensurately powerful grief "haunting" the room—as Lucy herself will later be haunted by the "discursive" imagination she denies. "I, Lucy Snowe, was calm," she insists again, after a heartrending account of Paulina's parting from her father (disclosing the lie): "she dropped on her knees at a chair with a cry—'Papa!' It was low and long; a sort of 'Why has thou forsaken me?'" (p. 79). Riven with such contradictions, Lucy's narrative calls itself into question by forcing us to misread it. "I seemed to hold two lives—the life of thought, and that of reality" (p. 140), she tells us later; the hidden life of thought strives ceaselessly to evade her censorship in the very language she uses: that of supernatural haunting and the Christian Passion—the product of an inverted martyrdom in which Lucy renounces her share of rights instead of cleaving to them.

At the start of the novel, Lucy observes and narrates another's drama, the diminutive Paulina's. Of her own painful circumstances we learn only that she has been shipwrecked in the metaphoric tempest which recurs at moments of crisis through the novel: "To this hour, when I have the nightmare, it repeats the rush and saltiness of briny waves in my throat, and their icy pressure on my lungs" (p. 94). Paulina's grief—that of the abandoned child cast among strangers—has in any case already acted out Lucy's. Asking no pity for herself, Lucy earlier had invoked it for her surrogate: "How will she get through this world, or battle with this life? How will she bear the shocks and repulses, the humiliations and desolations . . . ?" (p. 93). So, too, Paulina's premature love for the adolescent Graham Bretton is at once a displacement and a prefiguration of Lucy's future relationship with him; just as later, Miss Marchmont's state of erotic arrest and confinement are annexed to Lucy herself: "Two hot, close rooms thus became my world. . . . All within me became narrowed to my lot" (p. 97). As the novel quarries deeper into Lucy's subconscious, the displacement becomes more bizarre. Confined alone at the Rue Fossette during the long vacation, she finds herself looking after a cretin—a creature conjured from nowhere to be her "strange, deformed companion," an image of deranged self who "would sit for hours together moping and mowing and distorting her features with indescribable grimaces" (p. 229). That the heartsick Miss Marchmont and the untamed cretin, warped in mind and body, are aspects of Lucy's repression (as Paulina had been an aspect of her loss) hardly needs emphasizing. Her regression from child to invalid to cretin parodies and reverses the Romantic quest for self which is the real "plot" (the conspiracy of silence) of *Villette*. "Who *are* you, Miss Snowe?" asks Ginevra Fanshawe inquisitively— "But *are* you anybody? . . . Do—*do* tell me who you are!" (pp. 392, 394). And, "If you really are the nobody I once thought you, you must be a cool hand" (p. 393). A cool hand indeed; for Lucy's invisibility is a calculated deception—a blank screen on which others project their view of her. To Graham Bretton she is "a being inoffensive as a shadow"; to M. Paul, denouncing her in a melodramatic hiss, she is dangerously, sexually, insurgent—"vous avez l'air bien triste, soumise, rêveuse, mais vous ne l'êtes pas. . . . Sauvage! la flamme à l'âme, l'éclair aux yeux!" (p. 404).

Lucy withholds her true identity from us as well as from the characters whose presence as actors in the novel defines her absence. The most disconcerting of her reticences, and the least functional, concerns her recognition of the medical attendant at the Rue Fossette (Dr. John) as Graham Bretton. The "idea, new, sudden, and startling" (p. 163) which strikes Lucy as she observes him one day at the Pensionnat Beck is not disclosed to the reader until her return to the scene of her and Paulina's childhood love, the reconstituted Bretton household: "I first recognized him on that occasion, noted several chapters back. . . . To *say* anything on the subject, to *hint* at my discovery, had not suited my habit of thought" (p. 248). Instead of declaring herself, Lucy prefers to retain her social invisibility— at this stage she is still employed as a nursery-governess. Her strategic silence conceals the private life which Mme. Beck's system of surveillance is at pains to detect, while she herself sets about detecting the clandestine flirtation between Dr. John ("Isadore," in this role) and Ginevra, much as she had earlier observed the love game between Graham and the infant Paulina. The novel is full of such voyeurisms (Mme. Beck herself is scarcely more on the watch than Lucy)—exhibitions in which Lucy casts herself as an onlooker, passive yet all powerful. Even when she takes the stage herself, during the school play of Chapter 14, she contrives to combine the two roles—at once spectator and participant in the sexual drama which she enacts between "Isadore," Ginevra, and her gallant, de Hamal (between the "Ours" or sincere lover, the coquette, and the fop whose part Lucy plays). Here the divide between stage and audience, watcher and watched, is piquantly removed in the interests of a more complex and ambiguous drama; Lucy also crosses the sexual divide—impersonating a man while clad as a woman from the waist down. In the same way, the frisson lies in Lucy's nonsubservience to her spectator role, as the game of master/slave in *Jane Eyre* is spiced by Jane's insubordination to her master. Jane discovers a taste for sexual mastery in preference to the more conventional role of mistress: Lucy discovers in herself "a keen relish for dramatic expression" and, carried away by she knows not what, transforms her part into an unorthodox piece of intersexual rivalry—"I acted to please myself" (p. 211).

"But it would not do for a mere looker-on at life" (p. 211). Lucy's invisibility is an aspect of her oppression: the actress, Vashti, is an aspect of her hidden revolt. As a middle-class woman, Lucy can only be employed within the home or its educational colony, the school; but that "home," since she is employee and not "mistress," must remain alien. Though increasingly professionalized, the role of teacher retains many of the anomalies of the governess figure in her differing guises (mother substitute, educator, companion). The governess is peculiarly the victim of middle-class sexual ideology, for the only role open to her is that of bringing up children while marriage and motherhood themselves are paradoxically taboo for her within the family that employs her. Economically nonnegotiable (nonexchangeable), she is denied both social and sexual recognition: "No one knows exactly how to treat her."[7] Significantly, Lucy prefers the relative independence of remaining a teacher in Mme. Beck's pensionnat to Mr. Home's offer of employment as Paulina's companion; while Mme. Beck sees in Lucy's bid to marry M. Paul a threat to the economic and family interests on which her establishment is founded (Lucy will ultimately set up a rival school). Charlotte Brontë's letters have much to say both about the "condition of woman" question and about being a governess; but this, finally, of the woman whose destiny it is to be unmarried:

> when patience had done its utmost and industry its best, whether in the case of women or operatives, and when both are baffled, and pain and want triumph, the sufferer is free, is entitled, at last to send up to Heaven any piercing cry for relief, if by that he can hope to obtain succour.[8]

In *Villette*, that piercing cry is uttered by an actress whose release of "hunger, rebellion and rage" sets the theater literally alight with its revolutionary force.

Vashti is a female version of the central Romantic protagonist, the satanic rebel and fallen angel whose damnation is a function of divine tyranny (Blake's Urizen, Byron's Jehovah of sacrifices, Shelley's Jupiter):

> Pain, for her, has no result in good; tears water no harvest of wisdom: on sickness, on death itself, she looks with the eye of a rebel. Wicked, perhaps, she is, but also she is strong; and her strength has conquered Beauty, has overcome Grace, and bound both at her side, captives peerlessly fair, and docile as fair. Even in the uttermost frenzy of energy is each maenad movement royally, imperially, incedingly upborne. Her hair, flying loose in revel or war, is still an angel's hair, and glorious under a halo. Fallen, insurgent, banished, she remembers the heaven where she rebelled. Heaven's light, following her exile, pierces its confines, and discloses their forlorn remoteness. (p. 340)

Villette can only be silent about the true nature and origin of Lucy's oppression; like Charlotte Brontë's letters, it neither questions the enshrining of marriage within Victorian sexual ideology, nor pursues its economic and social consequences for women. But what the novel cannot say is eloquently inscribed in its subtext—in the "discursive" activity of Lucy's (over-) heated imagination, and in the agitated notation and heightened language which signal it. Here her mingled identification, revulsion and admiration are tellingly juxtaposed with Graham Bretton's indifference to the spectacle. We witness not only his lack of affinity "for what belonged to storm, what was wild and intense, dangerous, sudden, and flaming"—for the Romantic mode which defines Lucy's own insurgent inner life; we witness also his sexual judgment on "a woman, not an artist: it was a branding judgement" (pp. 341, 342). "Branded" as a fallen woman, a rebel against conventional morality, Vashti is at once déclassé and thereby permitted to retain her potency—a demonic symbol of sexual energy created by a woman (actress/author) in contrast to the static, male-fabricated images of woman exhibited for Lucy's inspection in an earlier chapter: Cleopatra on one hand, the *Jeune Fille/Mariée/Jeune Mère/Veuve* on the other (woman as sexual object or as bearer of ideology). "Where was the artist of the Cleopatra? Let *him* come and sit down and study this different vision" (p. 339; my italics), demands Lucy—in whose scandalous pink dress M. Paul detects a latent scarlet woman.

"*Heimlich* is a word the meaning of which develops in the direction of ambivalence, until it finally coincides with its opposite, *unheimlich.*" Thus Freud, for whom the uncanny in fiction provided "a much more fertile province than the uncanny in real life, for it contains the whole of the latter and something more besides" (*SE* 17:226, 249). Lucy's dreamlike propulsion from one world to another—from her childhood at Bretton, to Miss Marchmont's sickroom, to the Pensionnat Beck, and back again to Bretton—makes resourceful use of this fertile province, suspending the laws of probability for those of the mind. Narrative dislocation in *Villette* insists on the irreducible otherness, the strangeness and arbitrariness, of inner experience. Lucy's return to the past (or the return of her past?) is ushered in by a nightmare of estrangement—"Methought the well-loved dead . . . met me elsewhere, alienated" (p. 231)—and she recovers consciousness after her desperate visit to the confessional amidst the decor of the *Unheimliche:* "all my eye rested on struck it as spectral," "These articles of furniture could not be real, solid arm-chairs, looking-glasses, and washstands—they must be the ghosts of such articles" (pp. 237, 241). The real becomes spectral, the past alien, the familiar strange; the lost home (*heimlich*) and the uncanny (*unheimlich*) coincide. Like Vashti, Lucy is an exile from the paradisal world of Bretton; even when restored miraculously to it, she cannot remain there. Its true inmate is not the satanic rebel and fallen angel, but the angelic, spiritualized Paulina—whose surname, appropriately, is Home. By marrying her (it is she whom he rescues from the threatened conflagration in the theater) Graham Bretton ensures the continuation of the status quo. But their conventional love story—child bride taken in charge by medical father substitute—is upstaged by Lucy's more innovatory and disturbing inner drama. In this internalized theater, the part that doubles Lucy's is taken by a (supposed) ghost. Freud's essay on the uncanny offers a classic formulation of Gothic strategy: "the writer creates a kind of uncertainty in us . . . by not letting us know, no doubt purposely, whether he is taking us into the real world or into a purely fantastic one of his own creation." The effect of this uncertainty in Charlotte Brontë's novel is to challenge the monopolistic claims of realism on "reality"—to render its representations no less fictive and arbitrary than the Gothic and Romantic modes usually viewed as parasitic. Moreover, as Freud suggests, a peculiarly powerful effect is achieved when the writer pretends to move in the world of common reality and then oversteps it, "betraying us to the superstitiousness which we have ostensibly surmounted" (*SE* 17:250). The grudge which we feel against the attempted deceit is just that retained by readers and critics of *Villette* toward the nun of the Rue Fossette—in whom repression, the uncanny, and the unacknowledged phantom of feminism combine to subvert the novel's facade of realism.

A realist reading of *Villette* must relegate the nun to the level of Gothic machinery; indicatively both Kate Millett (for whom the novel is a manifesto of sexual politics) and Terry Eagleton (for whom it is a Marxist myth of power) ignore her ambiguous presence.[9] But just because the device is so cumbrous and unnecessary in realist terms—Ginevra's gallant dressed up for their clandestine assignations—it must have another function. In effect, it symbolizes not only Lucy's repression, but the novelist's freedom to evoke or inhibit the *Unheimliche;* to lift or impose censorship. The nun thus becomes the phantom or psychic reality which representation represses, evading the censorship of realism as de Hamal himself evades the forbidden ground of the Pensionnat Beck under Mme. Beck's censoring eyes. In his medical capacity, Graham Bretton diagnoses "a case of spectral illusion . . . resulting from long-continued mental conflict" (p. 330). But as it turns out, the rationalist explanation is debunked by the fictive reality of the novel itself: "doctors are so self-opinionated, so immovable in their dry, materialist views" (p. 338), Lucy comments with apparent perversity; yet the text vindicates her. The legend of the nun, buried alive in a vault under the Methuselah pear tree "for some sin against her vow" (p. 172), is introduced early on but lies dormant until passion threatens to reassert itself. The first apparition—summoned up, it seems, by Lucy's love for Graham Bretton—occurs when she plunges into the vaultlike depths of "the deep, black, cold garret" (p. 324) to enjoy his precious letter:

> Are there wicked things, not human, which envy human bliss? Are there evil influences haunting the air, and poisoning it for man? What was near me? . . .
>
> Something in that vast solitary garret sounded strangely. Most surely and certainly I heard, as it seemed, a stealthy foot on that floor: a sort of gliding out from the direction of the black recess haunted by the malefactor cloaks. I turned: my light was dim; the room was long—but, as I live! I saw in the middle of that ghostly chamber a figure all black or white; the skirts straight, narrow, black; the head bandaged, veiled, white.
>
> Say what you will, reader—tell me I was nervous, or mad; affirm that I was unsettled by the excitement of that letter; declare that I dreamed: this I vow—I saw there—in that room—on that night—an image like—a NUN. (p. 325)

The sheerest melodrama? or a bold refutation of "common reality"? Lucy's challenge—"Say what you will, reader"—defies us to find the narrative incredible or the author unreliable.

For the reader, there is no knowing how to take the nun; is Lucy deceiving us again? A brief admonitory sighting marks her visit to the theater (an unexplained light in the *grenier*); but the next full apparition occurs at a similar moment of high emotional significance—on the still, dim, electric evening when she buries her letters from Graham, and her love for him, in a hole under the Methuselah pear tree:

> the moon, so dim hitherto, seemed to shine out somewhat brighter: a ray gleamed even white before me, and a shadow became distinct and marked. I looked more narrowly, to make out the cause of this well-defined contrast appearing a little suddenly in the obscure alley: whiter and blacker it grew on my eye: it took shape with instantaneous transformation. I stood about three yards from a tall, sable-robed, snowy-veiled woman.
>
> Five minutes passed. I neither fled nor shrieked. She was there still. I spoke.
>
> "Who are you? and why do you come to me?"
>
> (p. 381)

Lucy here both hides a treasure and entombs a grief; does the nun confront her to assert their kinship? The third apparition—aroused to vengeful anger—is provoked by M. Paul's declaration of affinity between himself and Lucy ("we are alike—there is affinity. Do you see it, mademoiselle, when you look in the glass?"). The birth of love and the turbulent reactivation of repression occur simultaneously:

> Yes; there scarce stirred a breeze, and that heavy tree was convulsed, whilst the feathery shrubs stood still. For some minutes amongst the wood and leafage a rending and heaving went on. Dark as it was, it seemed to me that something more solid than either night-shadow, or branch-shadow, blackened out of the boles. At last the struggle ceased. What birth succeeded this travail? What Dryad was born of these throes? We watched fixedly. A sudden bell rang in the house—the prayer-bell. Instantly into our alley there came . . . an apparition, all black and white. With a sort of angry rush—close, close past our faces—swept swiftly the very NUN herself! Never had I seen her so clearly. She looked tall of stature, and fierce of gesture. As she went, the wind rose sobbing; the rain poured wild and cold; the whole night seemed to feel her. (p. 458)

Natural and supernatural are brought ambiguously into play; the nun is at once "solid," material, and capable of bringing about changes in the weather—"betraying us to the superstitiousness we have ostensibly surmounted."

Lucy's question ("Who are you?") remains un-answered, but the nun's ambiguous status—at once real and spectral, both a deceit practiced on Lucy and her psychic dou-ble—has important implications for the system of representa-tion employed in the novel. The configuration of characters around Lucy is equally expressive of her quest for identity and of her self-estrangement. Mrs. Bretton, Mme. Beck, Ginevra, the detestable Zélie de St. Pierre and the adorable Paulina are the images of women (the good and bad mothers, the rivals and sisters) through whom Lucy both defines and fails to recognize herself, placed as she is at the center of a distorting hall of mirrors in which each projection is obedient to her feelings of gratitude, rivalry, attraction, hatred or envy. No other woman in the novel has any identity except as Lucy herself bestows it. The absent center exerts a centripetal force on the other charac-ters, making them all facets of the consciousness whose pas-sions animate them. And yet such is the level which a realist reading of *Villette* would claim as stable, objective, autono-mous, in contrast to the phantasmal subjective world repre-sented by the nun and the Gothic hinterland to which she belongs. At this point one must acknowledge the powerful presence of fantasy in Charlotte Brontë's fiction. M. Paul, no less than Lucy's rivals (the images to whom she must submit or over whom she may triumph), is animated by a wish fulfillment which it is surely justifiable to see as Charlotte Brontë's own. But far from detracting from the fiction, the release of fantasy both energizes *Villette* and satisfies that part of the reader which also desires constantly to reject reality for the sake of an obe-dient, controllable, narcissistically pleasurable image of self and its relation to the world. From the scene in which Ginevra triumphantly contrasts herself and Lucy in the mirror, to Lucy's unexpected glimpse of herself in public with Graham Bretton and his mother ("a third person in a pink dress and black lace mantle . . . it might have been worse," p. 286), to M. Paul's declaration of affinity ("Do you see it . . . when you look in the glass? Do you observe that your forehead is shaped like mine—that your eyes are cut like mine?", p. 457), we trace, not so much the rehabilitation of the plain heroine, as the persistence of the Lacanian mirror phase.[10] Or, to put it in terms of text rather than plot, we too are confronted by an image in which signifier and signified have imaginary correspondence—by a seductive representational illusion which denies the lack or absence central to all signification. The nun stands opposed to this imaginary plenitude of sign or image. Too easily identified as the specter of repression, or as the double of Lucy's repressed self, she is nonetheless recalcitrantly other; "Who are you?" asks Lucy, not recognizing her. She is the joker in the pack, the alien, ex-centric self which no image can mirror—only the structure of language. Like the purloined letter in Lacan's reading of the Poe story, where the meaning of the letter (the autonomous signifier) lies in its function in the plot rather than its actual contents, the nun derives her significance from her place in the signifying chain.[11] She has one function in relation to Lucy, another in relation to M. Paul, and another again in relation to Ginevra. The different meanings intersect but do not merge; the threads cross and intertwine without becoming one. Her uncanniness lies in unsettling the "mirroring" conventions of representation present elsewhere in *Villette,* and in validating Gothic and Romantic modes, not as "discursive" and parasitic, but—because shifting, unstable, arbitrary and dominated by desire—as the system of signification which can more properly articulate the self.

What are we to make of Lucy's extraordinary narrative? Which level of the text finally claims priority? Pursuit of the nun to the novel's climax—the phantasmagoric scenes of Lucy's drugged nocturnal expedition to the illuminated park—provides an answer of sorts. The nun has by this time manifested herself in another guise, as the external obstacle to marriage between Lucy and M. Paul; that is, his supposed devotion to the dead, sainted Justine Marie (and, with her, to Roman Catholicism) whose nun-like portrait is pointedly exhibited to Lucy by Père Silas, as well as his guardianship of a bouncing, all too alive ward of the same name. Her presence at the climax of the novel perfectly illustrates Charlotte Brontë's deviousness, the strategy by which her heroine's consciousness at once distorts, and, in doing so, creates a truth that is essentially a fiction. In this coda-like sequence, all the characters of the novel are paraded before the apparently invisible Lucy in their happy family parties—the Brettons and Homes; the Becks, Père Silas and Mme. Walravens; and lastly, after an elaborate buildup of expectation and delay, M. Paul and his ward. Thus Lucy is ostensibly returned to her original role of excluded spectator. But there is a difference. This time it is she who is *metteur en scène* in a drama of her own making. First comes "the crisis and the revelation," the long-awaited arrival of the nun or her double, Justine Marie—heightened by Lucy's anticipatory memories of her earlier hauntings:

> It is over. The moment and the nun are come. The crisis and the revelation are passed by.
>
> The flambeau glares still within a yard, held up in a park-keeper's hand; its long eager tongue of flame almost licks the figure of the Expected—there—where she stands full in my sight! What is she like? What does she wear? How does she look? Who is she?
>
> There are many masks in the Park to-night, and as the hour wears late, so strange a feeling of revelry and mystery begins to spread abroad that scarce would you discredit me, reader, were I to say that she is like the nun of the attic, that she wears black skirts and white head-clothes, that she looks the resurrection of the flesh, and that she is a risen ghost.
>
> All falsities—all figments! We will not deal in this gear. Let us be honest, and cut, as heretofore, from the homely web of truth.
>
> *Homely,* though, is an ill-chosen word. What I see is not precisely homely. A girl of Villette stands there. . . .
> (pp. 562–63)

"*Heimlich* is a word the meaning of which develops in the direction of ambivalence." Once again it is the living and not the dead, the familiar and not the strange, that becomes uncanny; not least because the bathos fails to proceed as expected.

The transformation of spectral nun into bourgeois belle is followed by yet another audacious reversal—a denial of reality whereby Lucy invents an engagement between M. Paul and his ward, a fiction whose basis ("his nun was indeed buried") is the truth of her own autonomous imagination:

> Thus it must be. The revelation was indeed come.
> Presentiment had not been mistaken in her impulse; there is

a kind of presentiment which never *is* mistaken; it was I who had for a moment miscalculated; not seeing the true bearing of the oracle, I had thought she muttered of vision when, in truth, her prediction touched reality.

I might have paused longer upon what I saw; I might have deliberated ere I drew inferences. Some perhaps would have held the premises doubtful, the proofs insufficient; some slow sceptics would have incredulously examined, ere they conclusively accepted the project of a marriage between a poor and unselfish man of forty, and his wealthy ward of eighteen; but far from me such shifts and palliatives, far from me such temporary evasion of the actual, such coward fleeing from the dread, the swift-footed, the all-overtaking Fact, such feeble suspense of submission to her the sole sovereign, such paltering and faltering resistance to the Power whose errand is to march conquering and to conquer, such traitor defection from the TRUTH. (pp. 565–56)

Is this Lucy's final and most outrageous lie? or, as the text insists in the face of its heavily alliterative irony, the novel's central "truth"?—that the imagination usurps on the real to create its own fictions; that Lucy is essentially and inevitably single.

The self-torturing narrative and masochistic imagery ("I invoked Conviction to nail upon me the certainty, abhorred while embraced") speed Lucy back to her solitary dormitory in the Rue Fossette, to the effigy of the nun on her bed, and the empty garments which signal "the resurrection of the flesh":

Tempered by late incidents, my nerves disdained hysteria. Warm from illuminations, and music, and thronging thousands, thoroughly lashed up by a new scourge, I defied spectra. In a moment, without exclamation, I had rushed on the haunted couch; nothing leaped out, or sprung, or stirred; all the movement was mine, so was all the life, the reality, the substance, the force; as my instinct felt. I tore her up—the incubus! I held her on high—the goblin! I shook her loose— the mystery! And down she fell—down all round me—down in shreds and fragments—and I trode upon her. (p. 569)

The phrasing is odd and significant: "all the movement was

mine, so was all the life, the reality, the substance, the force." The wardrobe mockingly bequeathed to Lucy by the eloped Ginevra and de Hamal labels her as the nun of the Rue Fossette—at once accusing her of animating the specter from within herself, and forcing her to recognize its true identity.

But of course the narrative doesn't leave things here, although the ambiguous ending cunningly attempts to do so—at once uniting Lucy and M. Paul in their educational idyll, and severing them for ever. The final evasion ("Trouble no quiet, kind heart; leave sunny imaginations hope," p. 596) was clearly designed to satisfy the conventional novel reader as well as Charlotte Brontë's father. But there is more to it. Of the two letters she writes to Graham Bretton, Lucy tells us: "To speak truth, I compromised matters; I served two masters: I bowed down in the house of Rimmon, and lifted the heart at another shrine" (p. 334). The entire novel, not just its ending, bears the marks of this compromise—between Victorian romance and the Romantic imagination, between the realist novel and Gothicism. The relationship between the two texts is as arbitrary as that between the two letters; as the signified slides under the signifier, so the buried letter bears an ex-centric relation to the public version. This is not to say that the real meaning of *Villette,* "the TRUTH," lies in its ghostly subtext. Rather, it lies in the relationship between the two, which points to what the novel cannot say about itself—to the real conditions of its literary possibility. Instead of correcting the novel into a false coherence, we should see in its ruptured and ambiguous discourse the source of its uncanny power. The double ending, in reversing the truth/fiction hierarchy, not only reinstates fantasy as a dominant rather than parasitic version of reality, but at the same time suggests that there can be no firm ground; only a perpetual de-centering.

Fittingly, the sleight of hand is carried out with the aid of metaphors drawn from the Romantic paradox of creation-in-destruction. The tempest by which Lucy's earliest loss is signified becomes an apocalyptic upheaval prophesying rebirth as well as death when the time comes for her to leave Miss Marchmont ("disturbed volcanic action . . . rivers suddenly rushing above their banks ... strange high tides flowing furiously in on low sea-coasts," p. 98). In the same way, Lucy's loss of consciousness before her rebirth into the Bretton household, later in the novel, is heralded by renewed images of Shelleyan storm—"I only wished that I had wings and could ascend the gale, spread and repose my pinions on its strength, career in its course, sweep where it swept" (p. 230). There is thus a profound ambiguity in the Romantic cataclysm which shipwrecks Lucy's happiness at the end of the novel:

> The skies hang full and dark—a rack sails from the west; the clouds cast themselves into strange forms—arches and broad radiations; there rise resplendent mornings—glorious, royal, purple as monarch in his state; the heavens are one flame; so wild are they, they rival battle at its thickest—so bloody, they shame Victory in her pride. I know some signs of the sky; I have noted them ever since childhood. God, watch that sail! Oh! guard it!

>   .   .   .   .   .

> That storm roared frenzied for seven days. It did not cease till the Atlantic was strewn with wrecks: it did not lull till the deeps had gorged their full of sustenance. Not till the destroying angel of tempest had achieved his perfect work, would he fold the wings whose waft was thunder—the tremor of whose plumes was storm. (pp. 595–96)

John Martin and the Angel of Death transform Lucy's premonition of loss into an apocalyptic victory of the imagination. By admitting to the incompatibility of the world of thought and the world of reality, Lucy becomes a truly reliable narrator—single and double at the same time. And by tacitly affirming the centrality of shipwreck, loss and deprivation to the workings of her imagination, Charlotte Brontë also reveals the deepest sources of her own creativity.

A Bloomian reading would presumably see the nun as an emblem of repression in a belated text whose sexual anguish, like that of Tennyson's "Mariana," masks influence anxiety (note the analogous presence of the Methuselah pear tree and "Mariana"'s poplar).[12] A plausible case could be made for misreading *Villette* in the same way. Charlotte Brontë's imagina-

tion was nurtured on Romanticism ("that burning clime where
we have sojourned too long—its skies flame—the glow of sun-
set is always upon it"),[13] but the world of Angria had to be
repressed in the interests of Victorian realism: "When I first
began to write . . . I restrained imagination, eschewed romance, repressed excitement."[14] It was no more possible to
write a Romantic novel in the mid-nineteenth century than to
read one, as the bewildered and imperceptive reviews of
Wuthering Heights (1847) reveal. Unlike her sister, Emily Brontë
refused to bow down in the house of Rimmon, and in an
important sense, hers is the repressed presence in *Villette*.
Lucy's unwilling return to consciousness in the Bretton household ("Where my soul went during that swoon I cannot
tell. . . . She may have gone upward, and come in sight of her
eternal home. . . . I know she reentered her prison with pain,
with reluctance," p. 237) resembles nothing so much as Emily
Brontë's "Prisoner" after visionary flight: "Oh, dreadful is the
check—intense the agony/When the ear begins to hear and the
eye begins to see."[15] Her invocation "To Imagination" underlies
Villette's paean to the Imagination in the face of Reason's tyranny ("'But if I feel, may I *never* express?' 'Never!' declared
Reason," p. 307). Emily Brontë had written, "So hopeless is the
world without,/The world within I doubly prize," and welcomed a "benignant power,/Sure solacer of human cares"—

> Reason indeed may oft complain
> For Nature's sad reality,
> And tell the suffering heart how vain
> Its cherished dreams must always be;
> And truth may rudely trample down
> The flowers of Fancy newly blown.
>
> But thou art ever there to bring
> The hovering visions back and breathe
> New glories o'er the blighted spring
> And call a lovelier life from death,
> And whisper with a voice divine
> Of real worlds as bright as thine.[16]

Charlotte Brontë, in turn, creates one of the most
remarkable invocations to Imagination in Victorian literature—

a passage that criticism of *Villette* has proved consistently unable to assimilate, or even acknowledge:

> Often has Reason turned me out by night, in mid-winter, on
> cold snow. . . . Then, looking up, have I seen in the sky a
> head amidst circling stars, of which the midmost and the
> brightest lent a ray sympathetic and attent. A spirit, softer and
> better than Human Reason, has descended with quiet flight
> to the waste—bringing all round her a sphere of air borrowed
> of eternal summer; bringing perfume of flowers which cannot
> fade—fragrance of trees whose fruit is life; bringing breezes
> pure from a world whose day needs no sun to lighten it. My
> hunger has this good angel appeased with food, sweet and
> strange, gathered amongst gleaming angels. . . . Divine, com-
> passionate, succourable influence! When I bend the knee to
> other than God, it shall be at thy white and winged feet,
> beautiful on mountain or on plain. Temples have been reared
> to the Sun—altars dedicated to the Moon. Oh, greater glory!
> To thee neither hands build, nor lips consecrate; but hearts,
> through ages, are faithful to thy worship. A dwelling thou
> hast, too wide for walls, too high for dome—a temple whose
> floors are space—rites whose mysteries transpire in presence,
> to the kindling, the harmony of worlds! (p. 308)

The dizzying and visionary prose strains, like Shelley's poetry,
away from the actual toward enkindled abstractions that image
the human mind. But the deity that the temple of the heart
enshrines is female; like the embodiment of rebellion and rage
(Vashti), the spirit that succours the mind's hunger has been
triumphantly feminized.

"Nothing but hunger, rebellion and rage. . . . No
fine writing can hide this thoroughly, and it will be fatal to her
in the long run"—Arnold's prognosis was wrong (Charlotte
Brontë died of pregnancy), but revealingly poses a split between rebellion and "fine writing." The divorce of the Romantic imagination from its revolutionary impulse poses special
problems for Victorian Romantics. Where vision had once
meant a prophetic denunciation of the status quo and the imagining of radical alternatives, it comes to threaten madness or
mob violence. Losing its socially transforming role, it can only
turn inward to self-destructive solipsism. Charlotte Brontë's

own mistrust erupts in *Villette* with the fire that flames out during Vashti's performance or in the vacation nightmare which drives Lucy to the confessional; while the spectral nun (the Alastor of the Rue Fossette?) has to be laid in order to free Lucy from the burden of the autonomous imagination and allow her to become an economically independent headmistress. There are added complications for a woman writer. The drive to female emancipation, while fueled by revolutionary energy, had an ultimately conservative aim—successful integration into existing social structures; "I am a rising character: once an old lady's companion, then a nursery-governess, now a school-teacher," Lucy boasts ironically to Ginevra (p. 394). Moreover, while the novel's pervasive feminization of the Romantic Imagination is a triumph, it runs the attendant risk of creating a female ghetto. The annexing of special powers of feeling and intuition to women and its consequences (their relegation to incompetent dependency) has an equally strong Romantic tradition; women, idiots and children, like the debased version of the Romantic poet, become at once privileged and (legally) irresponsible. The problem is illuminated by situating Charlotte Brontë's novels within a specifically feminist tradition. *Villette*'s crushing opposition between Reason and Imagination is also present in Mary Wollstonecraft's writing. *The Rights of Woman*—directed against the infantilizing Rousseauistic ideal of feminine "sensibility"—not only advocates the advantages for women of a rational (rather than sentimental) education, but attempts to insert the author herself into the predominantly male discourse of Enlightenment Reason, or "sense." Yet, paradoxically, it is within this shaping Rousseauistic sensibility that Mary Wollstonecraft operates as both woman and writer—creating in her two highly autobiographical novels, *Mary* (1788) and, ten years later, *The Wrongs of Woman*, fictions which, even as they anatomize the constitution of femininity within the confines of "sensibility," cannot escape its informing preoccupations and literary influence.[17] Though their concepts of Reason differ, the same split is felt by Charlotte Brontë. In *Villette*, Reason is the wicked and "envenomed" stepmother as opposed to the succoring, nourishing, consoling "daughter of heaven," Imagination (pp. 308, 309). It is within this primal yet divisive relationship that the novelist herself is constituted as woman and writer—nurtured on Romanticism, fostered by uncongenial Reason. The duality haunts her novel, dividing it as Lucy is divided against herself.

It is surely no longer the case, as Kate Millett asserted in 1970, that literary criticism of the Brontës is "a long game of masculine prejudice wherein the player either proves they can't write and are hopeless primitives . . . or converts them into case histories from the wilds."[18] But feminist criticism still has a special task in relation to Charlotte Brontë's novels. That task is not to explain away, but to explain—to theorize—the incoherencies and compromises, inconsistencies and dislocations, which provoked the "can't write" jibe in the first place; to suggest, in other words, the source of Matthew Arnold's disquiet. It is enough to point to the part played by realism and Reason respectively in Charlotte Brontë's double quest for literary form and for female emancipation. To do so relocates her writing, not in a neurotic northern hinterland ("case histories from the wilds"), but in the mainstream of Victorian literary production—its legacy of Romanticism complicated in her case by the conflict between a revolutionary impulse toward feminism and its tendency to confine women within irrationality. And what of the feminist critic? Isn't she in the same position as Charlotte Brontë, the writer, and her character, Lucy Snowe?—bound, if she's to gain both a living and a hearing, to install herself within the prevailing conventions of academic literary criticism. To this extent, hers must also be an ex-centric text, a displacement into criticism of the hunger, rebellion, and rage which make Lucy an estranged image of self. Constituted within conditions essentially unchanged since those of Mary Wollstonecraft and Charlotte Brontë (i.e. patriarchy) and experiencing similar contradictions within herself and society, the feminist critic faces the same disjunction— removed, however, to the disjunction between literary response and critical discourse. The novel itself becomes the discourse of the Other, making its presence felt in the distortions and mutilations of critical selectivity. What strategy remains, beyond unsettling the illusory objectivity of criticism? Surely also to unfold a novel whose very repressions become an eloquent testimony to imaginative freedom, whose ruptures provide access to a double text, and whose doubles animate, as well as haunt, the fiction they trouble. In the last resort, the buried letter of Romanticism and the phantom of feminism both owe their uncanny power to their subterranean and unacknowledged presence—to repression itself, the subject of Charlotte Brontë's most haunting novel, and fiction's special reserve.

3. Men of Maxims and
The Mill on the Floss

"The first question to ask is therefore the following: how can women analyze their own exploitation, inscribe their own demands, within an order prescribed by the masculine? *Is a women's politics possible within that order?*" (Luce Irigaray)[1]

To rephrase the question: Can there be (a politics of) women's writing? What does it mean to say that women can analyze their exploitation only "within an order prescribed by the masculine"? And what theory of sexual difference can we turn to when we speak, as feminist critics are wont to do, of a specifically "feminine" practice in writing? Questions like these mark a current impasse in contemporary feminist criticism. Utopian attempts to define the specificity of women's writing—desired or hypothetical, but rarely empirically observed—either founder on the rock of essentialism (the text as body), gesture toward an avant-garde practice which turns out not to be specific to women, or, like Hélène Cixous in "The Laugh of the Medusa," do both.[2] If anatomy is not destiny, still less can it be language.

A politics of women's writing, then, if it is not to fall back on a biologically based theory of sexual difference, must address itself, as Luce Irigaray has done in "The Power of Discourse and the Subordination of the Feminine," to the position of mastery held not only by scientific discourse (Freudian theory, for instance), not only by philosophy, "the discourse of discourses," but by the logic of discourse itself. Rather than attempting to identify a specific practice, in other words, such a feminist politics would attempt to relocate sexual difference at the level of the text by undoing the repression of the "feminine" in all the systems of representation for which the Other (woman) must be reduced to the economy of the Same (man). In Irigaray's terms, "masculine" systems of representation are those whose self-reflexiveness and specularity disappropriate women of their relation to themselves and to other women; as in Freud's theory of sexual difference (woman equals man-minus), difference is swiftly converted into hierarchy. Femininity comes to signify a role, an image, a value imposed on women by the narcissistic and fundamentally misogynistic logic of such masculine systems. The question then becomes for Irigaray not "What is woman?" (still less Freud's desperate "What does a woman want?") but "How is the feminine determined by discourse itself?"—determined, that is, as lack or error or as an inverted reproduction of the masculine subject.[3]

Invisible or repressed, the hidden place of the feminine in language is the hypothesis which sustains the model of the textual universe, like ether. We know it must be there because we know ourselves struggling for self-definition in other terms, elsewhere, elsehow. We need it, so we invent it. When such an article of faith doesn't manifest itself as a mere rehearsal of sexual stereotypes, it haunts contemporary feminist criticism in its quest for specificity—whether of language, or literary tradition, or women's culture. After all, why study women's writing at all unless it is "women's writing" in the first place? The answer, I believe, must be a political one, and one whose impulse also fuels that gesture toward an elusive *"écriture féminine"* or specificity. To postulate, as Irigaray does, a "work of language" which undoes the repression of the feminine constitutes in itself an attack on the dominant ideology, the very means by which we know what we know and think what we think. So too the emphasis on women's writing politicizes in a flagrant and polemical fashion the "difference" which has traditionally been elided by criticism and by the canon formations of literary history. To label a text as that of a woman, and to write about it for that reason, makes vividly legible what the critical institution has either ignored or acknowledged only under the sign of inferiority. We need the term "women's writing" if only to remind us of the social conditions under which women wrote and still write—to remind us that the conditions of their (re)production are the economic and educational disadvantages, the sexual and material organizations of society, which, rather than biology, form the crucial determinants of women's writing.

Feminist criticism, it seems to me, ultimately has to invoke as its starting point this underlying political assumption. To base its theory on a specificity of language or literary tradition or culture is already to have moved one step on in the argument, if not already to have begged the question, since by then one is confronted by what Nancy Miller, in a recent essay on women's fiction, has called "the irreducibly complicated relationship women have historically had to the language of the dominant culture."[4] Perhaps that is why, baffled in their attempts to specify the feminine, feminist critics have so often turned to an analysis of this relationship as it is manifested and thematized in writing by and about women. The project is, and can't escape being, an ideological one; concerned, that is, with the functioning and reproduction of sexual ideology in particular—whether in the overtly theoretical terms of Luce Irigaray or in the fictional terms of, for instance, George Eliot. To quote Miller again, the aim would be to show that "the maxims that pass for the truth of human experience, and the encoding of that experience in literature, are organizations, when they are not fantasies, of the dominant culture."[5]

But Irigaray's "women's politics," her feminist argument, goes beyond ideology critique in its effort to recover "the place of the feminine" in discourse. The "work of language" which she envisages would undo representation altogether, even to the extent of refusing the linearity of reading. "*Après-coup*," the retroactive effect of a word ending, opens up the structure of language to reveal the repression on which meaning depends; and repression is the place of the feminine. By contrast, the "style" of women—*écriture féminine*—would privilege not the look but the tactile, the simultaneous, the fluid. Yet at the same time, we discover, such a style can't be sustained as a thesis or made the object of a position; if not exactly "nothing," it is nonetheless a kind of discursive practice that can't be thought, still less written. Like her style, woman herself is alleged by Irigaray to be an unimaginable concept within the existing order. Elaborating a theory of which woman is either the subject or the object merely reinstalls the feminine within a logic that represses, censors, or misrecognizes it. Within that logic, woman can only signify an excess or a deranging power. Woman for Irigaray is always the "something else" that points to the possibility of another language, asserts that the masculine is not all, does not have a monopoly on value, or, still less, "the abusive privilege of appropriation." She tries to strike through the theoretical machinery itself, suspending its pretension to the production of a single truth, a univocal meaning. Woman would thus find herself on the side of everything in language that is multiple, duplicitous, unreliable, and resistant to the binary oppositions on which theories of sexual difference such as Freud's depend.[6]

Irigaray's argument is seductive precisely because it puts all systems in question, leaving process and fluidity instead of fixity and form. At the same time, it necessarily concedes that women have access to language only by recourse to systems of representation that are masculine. Given the coherence of the systems at work in discourse, whether Freudian or critical, how is the work of language of which she speaks to be undertaken at all? Her answer is "mimetism," the role historically assigned to women—that of reproduction, but deliberately assumed; an acting out or role playing within the text which allows the woman writer to know better and hence to expose what it is she mimics. Irigaray, in fact, seems to be saying that there is no "outside" of discourse, no alternative practice available to the woman writer apart from the process of undoing itself:

> To play with mimesis is thus, for a woman, to try to recover the place of her exploitation by discourse, without allowing herself to be simply reduced to it. It means to resubmit herself—inasmuch as she is on the side of the "perceptible," of "matter"—to "ideas," in particular to ideas about herself, that are elaborated in/by a masculine logic, but so as to make "visible," by an effect of playful repetition, what was supposed to remain invisible: the cover-up of a possible operation of the feminine in language. It also means "to unveil"

the fact that, if women are such good mimics, it is because they are not simply resorbed in this function. *They also remain elsewhere.*[7]

Within the systems of discourse and representation which repress the feminine, woman can only resubmit herself to them; but by refusing to be reduced by them, she points to the place and manner of her exploitation. "A possible operation of the feminine in language" becomes, then, the revelation of its repression, through an effect of playful rehearsal, rather than a demonstrably feminine linguistic practice.

Irigaray's main usefulness to the feminist critic lies in this half-glimpsed possibility of undoing the ideas about women elaborated in and by masculine logic, a project at once analytic and ideological. Her attack on centrism in general, and phallocentrism in particular, allows the feminist critic to ally herself "otherwise," with the "elsewhere" to which Irigaray gestures, in a stance of dissociation and resistance which typically characterizes that of feminist criticism in its relation to the dominant culture or "order prescribed by the masculine." But like Irigaray herself in "The Power of Discourse," feminist criticism remains imbricated within the forms of intelligibility—reading and writing, the logic of discourse—against which it pushes. What makes the "difference," then? Surely, the direction from which that criticism comes—the elsewhere that it invokes, the putting in question of our social organization of gender; its wishfulness, even, in imagining alternatives. It follows that what pleases the feminist critic most (this one, at any rate) is to light on a text that seems to do her arguing, or some of it, for her—especially a text whose story is the same as hers; hence, perhaps, the drift toward narrative in recent works of feminist criticism such as Sandra Gilbert and Susan Gubar's influential *The Madwoman in the Attic.*[8] What's usually going on in such criticism—perhaps in all feminist criticism—is a specificity of relationship that amounts to a distinctive practice. Criticism takes literature as its object, yes; but here literature in a different sense is likely to become the subject, the feminist critic, the woman writer, woman herself.

This charged and doubled relationship, an almost inescapable aspect of feminist criticism, is at once transgressive and liberating, since what it brings to light is the hidden or unspoken ideological premise of criticism itself. *Engagée* perforce, feminist criticism calls neutrality into question, like other avowedly political analyses of literature. I want now to undertake a "symptomatic" reading of a thematically relevant chapter from Eliot's *The Mill on the Floss* (1860) in the hope that this quintessentially critical activity will bring to light if not "a possible operation of the feminine in language" at least one mode of its recovery—language itself. I will return later to the final chapter of Irigaray's *This Sex Which Is Not One* in which an escape from masculine systems of representation is glimpsed through the metaphors of female desire itself.

Nancy Miller's "maxims that pass for the truth of human experience" allude to Eliot's remark near the end of *The Mill on the Floss* that "the man of maxims is the popular representative of the minds that are guided in their moral judgment solely by general rules."[9] Miller's concern is the accusation of implausibility leveled at the plots of women's novels: Eliot's concern is the "special case" of Maggie Tulliver—"to lace ourselves up in formulas" is to ignore "the special circumstances that mark the individual lot." An argument for the individual makes itself felt as an argument against generalities. For Eliot herself, as for Dr. Kenn (the repository of her knowlege at this point in the novel), "the mysterious complexity of our life is not to be embraced by maxims" (p. 628). Though the context is the making of moral, not critical, judgments, I think that Eliot, as so often at such moments, is concerned also with both the making and the reading of fiction; with the making of another kind of special case. Though Maggie may be an "exceptional" woman, the ugly duckling of St. Ogg's, her story contravenes the norm, and in that respect it could be said to be all women's story. We recall an earlier moment, that of Tom Tulliver's harsh judgment of his sister ("You have not resolution to resist a thing that you know to be wrong"), and Maggie's rebellious murmuring that her life is "a planless riddle to him" only because he's incapable of feeling the mental needs which impel her, in his eyes, to wrongdoing or absurdity (pp. 504, 505). To Tom, the novel's chief upholder of general rules and patriarchal law (he makes his sister swear obedience to his prohibitions on the family Bible), the planless riddle of Maggie's life is only made sense of by a "Final Rescue" which involves her death: "In their death they were not divided" (p. 657). But the reunion of brother and sister in the floodwaters of the Ripple enacts both reconciliation and revenge, consummation and cataclysm; powerful authorial desires are at work.[10] To simplify this irreducible swirl of contradictory desire in the deluge that "rescues" Maggie as well as her brother would be to salvage a maxim as "jejune" as *"Mors omnibus est communis"* (one of the tags Maggie finds when she dips into her brother's Latin grammar) stripped of its saving Latin.[11] We might go further and say that to substitute a generality for the riddle of Maggie's life and death, or to translate Latin maxims into English commonplaces, would constitute a misreading of the novel as inept as Tom's misconstruction of his sister, or his Latin. Maggie's incomprehensible foreignness, her drift into error or impropriety on the river with Stephen Guest, is a "lapse" understood by the latitudinarian Dr. Kenn. For us, it also involves an understanding that planlessness, riddles, and impropriety—the enigmas, accidents, and incorrectness of language itself—are at odds with the closures of plot (here, the plot of incestuous reunion) and with interpretation itself, as well as with the finality of the maxims denounced by Eliot.

For all its healing of division, *The Mill on the Floss* uncovers the divide between the language or maxims of the dominant culture and the language itself which undoes them. In life, at any rate, they remain divided—indeed, death may be the price of unity—and feminist criticism might be said to install itself in the gap. A frequent move on the part of feminist criticism is to challenge the norms and aesthetic criteria of the dominant culture (as Miller does in defending Eliot), claiming, in effect, that "incorrectness" makes visible what is specific to women's writing. The culturally imposed or assumed "lapses" of women's writing are turned against the system that brings them into being—a system women writers necessarily inhabit. What surfaces in this gesture is the all-important question of women's access to knowledge and culture and to the power that goes with them. In writing by women, the question is often explicitly thematized in terms of education. Eliot's account of Tom's schooling in "School-Time," the opening chapter of Book 2, provides just such a thematic treatment—a lesson in antifeminist pedagogy which goes beyond its immediate implications for women's education to raise more far-reaching questions about the functioning of both sexual ideology and language. Take Maggie's puzzlement at one of the many maxims found in the Eton Grammar, a required text for the unfortunate Tom. As often, rules and examples prove hard to tell apart:

> The astronomer who hated women generally caused [Maggie] so much puzzling speculation that she one day asked Mr. Stelling if all astronomers hated women, or whether it was only this particular astronomer. But, forestalling his answer, she said,
>
> "I suppose it's all astronomers: because you know, they live up in high towers, and if the women came there, they might talk and hinder them from looking at the stars."
>
> Mr. Stelling liked her prattle immensely. (p. 220)

What we see here is a textbook example of the way in which individual misogyny becomes generalized—"maximized," as it were—in the form of a patriarchal put-down. Maggie may have trouble construing *"ad unam mulieres,"* or "all to a woman," but in essence she has got it right.[12] Just to prove her point, Mr. Stelling (who himself prefers the talk of women to star gazing) likes her "prattle," a term used only of the talk of women and children. Reduced to his idea of her, Maggie can only mimic man's talk.

Inappropriate as he is in other respects for Tom's future career, Mr. Stelling thus proves an excellent schoolmaster to his latent misogyny. His classroom is also an important scene of instruction for Maggie, who learns not only that all astronomers to a man hate women in general but that girls can't learn Latin; that they are quick and shallow, mere imitators ("this small apparatus of shallow quickness," Eliot playfully repeats); and that everybody hates clever women, even if they are amused by the prattle of clever little girls (pp. 214, 221, 216). It's hard not to read with one eye on her creator. Maggie, it emerges, rather fancies herself as a linguist, and Eliot too seems wishfully to imply that she has what one might call a "gift" for languages—a gift, perhaps, for ambiguity too. Women, we learn, don't just talk, they double-talk, like language itself; that's just the trouble for boys like Tom:

> "I know what Latin is very well," said Maggie, confidently. "Latin's a language. There are Latin words in the Dictionary. There's bonus, a gift."
>
> "Now, you're just wrong there, Miss Maggie!" said Tom, secretly astonished. "You think you're very wise! But 'bonus' means 'good,' as it happens—bonus, bona, bonum."
>
> "Well, that's no reason why it shouldn't mean 'gift,' " said Maggie stoutly. "It may mean several things. Almost every word does." (p. 214)

And if words may mean several things, general rules or maxims may prove less universal than they claim to be and lose their authority. Perhaps only "this particular astronomer" was a woman-hater or hated only one woman in particular. Special cases or particular contexts—"the special circumstances that mark the individual lot" (p. 628)—determine or render indeterminate not only judgment but meaning too. The rules of language itself make Tom's rote learning troublesome to him. How can he hope to construe his sister when her relation to language proves so treacherous—her difference so shifting a play of possibility, like the difference within language itself, destabilizing terms such as "wrong" and "good"?

Maggie, a little parody of her author's procedures in *The Mill on the Floss*, decides "to skip the rule in the syntax—the examples became so absorbing":

> These mysterious sentences snatched from an unknown context,—like strange horns of beasts and leaves of unknown plants, brought from some far-off region, gave boundless scope to her imagination, and were all the more fascinating because they were in a peculiar tongue of their own, which she could learn to interpret. It was really very interesting—the Latin Grammar that Tom had said no girls could learn: and she was proud because she found it interesting. The most fragmentary examples were her favourites. *Mors omnibus est communis* would have been jejune, only she liked to know the

Latin; but the fortunate gentleman whom every one congrat-
ulated because he had a son "endowed with *such* a disposition" afforded her a great deal of pleasant conjecture, and she
was quite lost in the "thick grove penetrable by no star,"
when Tom called out,

"Now, then, Magsie, give us the Grammar!" (pp. 217–18)

Whereas maxims lace her up in formulas, "these mysterious
sentences" give boundless scope to Maggie's imagination; for
her, as for her author (who makes them foretell her story), they
are whole fictional worlds, alternative realities, transformations of the familiar into the exotic and strange. In their foreignness she finds herself, until roused by Tom's peremptory
call, as she is later to be recalled by his voice from the Red
Deeps. Here, however, it is Maggie who teaches Tom his most
important lesson, that the "dead" languages had once been
living: "that there had once been people upon the earth who
were so fortunate as to know Latin without learning it through
the medium of the Eton Grammar" (p. 221). The idea—or,
rather, fantasy—of a language that is innate rather than acquired, native rather than incomprehensibly foreign, is a consoling one for the unbookish miller's son; but it holds out hope
for Maggie too, and presumably also for her creator. Though
Latin stands in for cultural imperialism and for the outlines of a
peculiarly masculine and elitist classical education from which
women have traditionally been excluded, Maggie can learn to
interpret it. The "peculiar tongue" had once been spoken by
women, after all—and they had not needed to learn it from Mr.
Stelling or the institutions he perpetuates. Who knows, she
might even become an astronomer herself, or, like Eliot, a
writer who by her pen name had refused the institutionalization of sexual difference as cultural exclusion. Tom and Mr.
Stelling tell Maggie that "Girls never learn such things";
"They've a great deal of superficial cleverness but they couldn't
go far into anything" (pp. 214, 221). But going far into things—
and going far—is the author's prerogative in *The Mill on the
Floss*. Though Maggie's quest for knowlege ends in death, as
Virginia Woolf thought Eliot's own had ended,[13] killing off this
small apparatus of shallow quickness may have been the necessary sacrifice in order for Eliot herself to become an interpreter

of the exotic possibilities contained in mysterious sentences. Maggie—unassimilable, incomprehensible, "fallen"—is her text, a "dead" language which thereby gives all the greater scope to authorial imaginings, making it possible for the writer to come into being.

We recognize in "School-Time" Eliot's investment—humorous, affectionate, and rather innocently self-lovingly—in Maggie's gifts and haphazard acquisition of knowledge. In particular, we recognize a defense of the "irregular" education which until recently had been the lot of most women, if educated at all. Earlier in the same chapter, in the context of Mr. Stelling's teaching methods (that is, his unquestioning reliance on Euclid and the Eton Grammar), Eliot refers whimsically to "Mr. Broderip's amiable beaver" which "busied himself as earnestly in constructing a dam, in a room up three pairs of stairs in London, as if he had been laying his foundation in a stream or lake in Upper Canada. It was 'Binny's' function to build" (p. 206). Binny the beaver, a pet from the pages of W. J. Broderip's *Leaves from the Note Book of a Naturalist* (1852), constructed his dam with sweeping brushes and warming pans, "handbrushes, rush-baskets, books, boots, sticks, clothes, dried turf or anything portable."[14] A domesticated *bricoleur*, Binny makes do with what he can find. A few lines later, we hear of Mr. Stelling's "educated" condescension toward "the display of various or special knowledge made by irregularly educated people" (p. 207). Mr. Broderip's beaver, it turns out, does double duty as an illustration of Mr. Stelling's "regular" (not to say "rote") mode of instruction—he can do no otherwise, conditioned as he is—and as a defense of Eliot's own display of irregularly acquired "various or special knowledge." Like Maggie's, this is knowledge drawn directly from books, without the aid of a patriarchal pedagogue. Mr. Stelling and the institutions he subscribes to (Aristotle, deaneries, prebends, Great Britain, and Protestantism—the Establishment, in fact) are lined up against the author-as-eager-beaver. Eliot's mischievous impugning of authority and authorities—specifically, cultural authority—becomes increasingly explicit until, a page or so later, culture itelf comes under attack. Finding Tom's brain "peculiarly impervious to etymology and demonstration," Mr. Stelling concludes that it "was peculiarly in need of being ploughed and harrowed by these patent implements: it was his favourite metaphor, that the classics and geometry constituted that culture of the mind which prepared it for the reception of any subsequent crop." As Eliot rather wittily observes, the regimen proves "as uncomfortable for Tom Tulliver as if he had been plied with cheese in order to remedy a gastric weakness which prevented him from digesting it" (p. 208). Nor is Eliot only, or simply, being funny. The bonus or gift of language is at work here, translating dead metaphor into organic tract.

Like Maggie herself, the metaphor here is improper, disrespectful of authorities, and, as Tom later complains of his sister, not to be relied on. Developing the implications of changing her metaphor from agriculture to digestion, Eliot drastically undermines the realist illusion of her fictional world, revealing it to be no more than a blank page inscribed with a succession of arbitrary metaphoric substitutions:

> It is astonishing what a different result one gets by changing the metaphor! Once call the brain an intellectual stomach, and one's ingenious conception of the classics and geometry as ploughs and harrows seems to settle nothing. But then, it is open to some one else to follow great authorities and call the mind a sheet of white paper or a mirror, in which case one's knowledge of the digestive process becomes quite irrelevant. It was doubtless an ingenious idea to call the camel the ship of the desert, but it would hardly lead one far in training that useful beast. O Aristotle! if you had had the advantage of being "the freshest modern" instead of the greatest ancient, would you not have mingled your praise of metaphorical speech as a sign of high intelligence, with a lamentation that intelligence so rarely shows itself in speech without metaphor,—that we can so seldom declare what a thing is, except by saying it is something else? (pp. 208–9)

In the *Poetics* Aristotle says: "It is a great thing to make use of . . . double words and rare words . . . but by far the greatest thing is the use of metaphor. That alone cannot be learned; it is the token of genius. *For the right use of metaphor means an eye for resemblances.*"[15] Of course there's authorial self-congratulation lurking in this passage, as there is in Eliot's affectionate parade of Maggie's gifts. But an eye for resemblances (between Binny and Mr. Stelling, for instance, or brain and stomach) is also here a satiric eye. Culture as (in)digestion makes Euclid and the Eton Grammer hard to swallow; Aristotle loses his authority to the author herself. On one level, this is science calling culture into question, making empiricism the order of the day. But there's something unsettling to the mind, or, rather, stomach, in this dizzy progression from culture, digestive tract, and tabula rasa to ship of the desert (which sounds like a textbook example of metaphor). The blank page may take what imprint the author chooses to give it. But the price one pays for such freedom is the recognition that language, thus viewed, is endlessly duplicitous rather than single-minded (as Tom would have it be); that metaphor is a kind of impropriety or oxymoronic otherness; and that "we can so seldom declare what a thing is, except by saying it is something else."

Error, then, must creep in where there's a story to tell, especially a woman's story. Maggie's "wrong-doing and absurdity," as the fall of women often does, not only puts her on the side of error in Tom's scheme of things but gives her a history; "the happiest women," Eliot reminds us, "like the happiest nations, have no history" (p. 494). Impropriety and metaphor belong together on the same side as a fall from absolute truth or unitary schemes of knowledge (maxims). Knowledge in *The Mill on the Floss* is guarded by a traditional patriarchal prohibition which, by a curious slippage, makes the fruit itself as indigestible as the ban and its thick rind. The adolescent Maggie, "with her soul's hunger and her illusions of self-flattery," begins "to nibble at this thick-rinded fruit of the tree of knowledge, filling her vacant hours with Latin, geometry, and the forms of the syllogism" (p. 380). But the Latin, Euclid, and Logic, which Maggie imagines "would surely be a considerable step in masculine wisdom," leave her dissatisfied, like a thirsty traveler in a trackless desert. What does Eliot substitute for this mental diet? After Maggie's chance discovery of Thomas à Kempis, we're told that "the old books, Virgil, Euclid, and Aldrich—that wrinkled fruit of the tree of knowledge—had been all laid by" for a doctrine that announces: "And if he should attain to all knowledge, he is yet far off" (pp. 387, 383). Though the fruits of patriarchal knowledge no longer seem worth the eating, can we view Thomas à Kempis as anything more than an opiate for the hunger pains of oppression? Surely not. The morality of submission and renunciation is only a sublimated version of Tom's plainspoken patriarchal prohibition, as the satanic mocker, Philip Wakem, doesn't fail to point out. Yet in the last resort, Eliot makes her heroine live and die by this inherited morality of female suffering—as if, in the economy of the text, it was necessary for Maggie to die renouncing in order for her author to release the flood of desire that is language itself.[16] Why?

The Mill on the Floss gestures toward a largely un-acted error, the elopement with Stephen Guest which would have placed Maggie finally outside the laws of St. Ogg's. Instead of this unrealized fall, we are offered a moment of attempted transcendence in the timeless death embrace which abolishes the history of division between brother and sister—"living through again in one supreme moment, the days when they had clasped their little hands in love" (p. 655). What is striking about the novel's ending is its banishing not simply of division but of sexual difference as the origin of that division. The fantasy is of a world where brother and sister might roam together, "indifferently," as it were, without either conflict or hierarchy. We know that their childhood was not like that at all, and we can scarcely avoid concluding that death is a high price to pay for such imaginary union. In another sense, too, the abolition of difference marks the death of desire for Maggie; "The Last Conflict" (the title of the book's closing chapter) is resolved by her final renunciation of Guest, resolved, moreover, with the help of "the little old book that she had long ago learned by heart" (p. 648). Through Thomas à Kempis, Eliot achieves a simultaneous management of both knowledge and desire, evoking an "invisible" or "supreme teacher" within the soul, whose voice promises "entrance into that satisfaction which [Maggie] had so long been craving in vain" (p. 384). Repressing the problematic issue of book learning, this "invisible teacher" is an aspect of the self which one might call the voice of conscience or, alternatively, sublimated maxims. In "the little old book," Maggie finds the authorized version of her own and Eliot's story, "written down by a hand that waited for the heart's prompting . . . the chronicle of a solitary, hidden anguish . . . a lasting record of human needs and human consolations, the voice of a brother who, ages ago, felt and suffered and renounced" (pp. 384–85).

Where might we look for an alternative version or, for that matter, for another model of difference, one that did not merely substitute unity for division and did not pay the price of death or transcendence? Back to the schoolroom, where we find Tom painfully committing to memory the Eton Grammar's "Rules for the Genders of Nouns," the names of trees being feminine, while some birds, animals, and fish "*dicta epicoena* . . . are said to be epicene."[17] In epicene language, as distinct from language imagined as either neutral or androgynous, gender is variable at will, a mere metaphor. The rules for the genders of nouns, like prescriptions about "masculine" or "feminine" species of knowledge, are seen to be entirely arbitrary. Thus the lament of David for Saul and Jonathan can be appropriated as the epitaph of brother and sister ("In their death they were not divided"), and "the voice of a brother who, ages ago, felt and suffered and renounced" can double as the voice of a sister-author, the passionately epicene George Eliot. One answer, then, to my earlier question (why does Eliot sacrifice her heroine to the morality of renunciation?) is that Eliot saw in Thomas à Kempis a language of desire, but desire managed as knowledge is also managed—sublimated, that is, not as renunciation but as writing. In such epicene writing, the woman writer finds herself, or finds herself in metaphor.

For Irigaray, the price paid by the woman writer for attempting to inscribe the claims of women "within an order prescribed by the masculine" may ultimately be death; the problem as she sees it is this: "[How can we] disengage ourselves, *alive*, from their concepts?"[18] The final, lyrical chapter of *This Sex Which Is Not One*, "When Our Lips Speak Together," is, or tries to be, the alternative she proposes. It begins boldly: "If we keep on speaking the same language together, we're going to reproduce the same history" (p. 205). This would be a history of disappropriation, the record of the woman writer's self loss as, attempting to swallow or incorporate an alien language, she is swallowed up by it in turn:

> Outside, you try to conform to an alien order. Exiled from yourself, you fuse with everything you meet. You imitate whatever comes close. You become whatever touches you. In your eagerness to find yourself again, you move indefinitely far from yourself. From me. Taking one model after another, passing from master to master, changing face, form, and language with each new power that dominates you. You/we are sundered; as you allow yourself to be abused, you become an impassive travesty. (p. 210)

This, perhaps, is what Miller means by "a posture of imposture," "the uncomfortable posture of all woman writers in our culture, within and without the text."[19] Miming has become absorption into an alien order. One thinks of Maggie, a consumer who is in turn consumed by what she reads, an imitative "apparatus" who, like the alienated women imagined by Irigaray, can only speak their desire as "spoken machines, speaking machines." Speaking the same language, spoken in the language of the Same ("If we keep on speaking sameness, if we speak to each other as men have been doing for centuries, as we have been taught to speak, we'll miss each other, fail ourselves"), she can only be reproduced as the history of a fall or a failure (p. 205). Eliot herself, of course, never so much as gestures toward Irigaray's jubilant utopian love language between two women—a language of desire whose object ("my indifferent one") is that internal (in)difference which, in another context, Barbara Johnson calls "not a difference between . . . but a difference within. Far from constituting the text's unique identity, it is that which subverts the very idea of identity." What is destroyed, conceptually, is the "unequivocal domination of one mode of signifying over another."[20] Irigaray's experiment in "When Our Lips Speak Together" is of this kind, an attempt to release the subtext of female desire, thereby undoing repression and depriving metalanguage of its claim to truth. "The exhausting labor of copying, miming" is no longer enough (p. 207).

But for all Irigaray's experimentalism, the "difference" is not to be located at the level of the sentence, as Miller reminds us.[21] Rather, what we find in "When Our Lips Speak Together" is writing designed to indicate the cultural determinants that bound the woman writer and, for Irigaray, deprive her of her most fundamental relationship: her relationship to herself. In fact, what seems most specifically "feminine" about Irigaray's practice is not its experimentalism as such but its dialogue of one/two, its fantasy of the two-in-one: "In *life* they are not divided," to rephrase David's lament. The lips that speak together (the lips of female lovers) are here imagined as initiating a dialogue not of conflict or reunion, like Maggie and Tom's, but of mutuality, lack of boundaries, continuity. If both Irigaray and Eliot kill off the woman engulfed by masculine logic and language, both end also—and need to end—by releasing a swirl of (im)possibility:

> These rivers flow into no single, definitive sea. These streams are without fixed banks, this body without fixed boundaries. This unceasing mobility. This life—which will perhaps be called our restlessness, whims, pretenses, or lies. All this remains very strange to anyone claiming to stand on solid ground. (p. 215)

Is that, finally, why Maggie must be drowned, sacrificed as a mimetic "apparatus" (much as the solidity of St. Ogg's is swept away) to the flood whose murmuring waters swell the "low murmur" of Maggie's lips as they repeat the words of Thomas à Kempis? When the praying Maggie feels the flow of water at her knees, the literal seems to have merged with a figural flow; as Eliot writes, "the whole thing had been so rapid—so dreamlike—that the threads of ordinary association were broken" (p. 651). It is surely at this moment in the novel that we move most clearly into the unbounded realm of desire, if not of wish fulfillment. It is at this moment of inundation, in fact, that the thematics of female desire surface most clearly.[22]

We will look in vain for a specifically feminine linguistic practice in *The Mill on the Floss*; "a possible operation of the feminine in language" is always elsewhere, not yet, not here, unless it simply reinscribes the exclusions, confines, and irregularities of Maggie's education. But what we may find in both Eliot and Irigaray is a critique which gestures beyond cultural boundaries, indicating the perimeters within which their writing is produced. For the astronomer who hates women in general, the feminist critic may wish to substitute an author who vindicates one woman in particular or, like Irigaray, inscribes the claims of all women. In part a critic of ideology, she will also want to uncover the ways in which maxims or *idées reçues* function in the service of institutionalizing and "maximizing" misogyny, or simply deny difference. But in the last resort, her practice and her theory come together in Eliot's lament about metaphor—"that we can so seldom declare what a thing is, except by saying it is something else." The necessary utopianism of feminist criticism may be the attempt to declare what is by saying something else—that "something else" which presses both Irigaray and Eliot to conclude their very different works with an imaginative reaching beyond analytic and realistic modes to the metaphors of unbounded female desire in which each finds herself as a woman writing.

III. WOMEN AND THEORY

1. Is There a Woman in This Text?

Let me start with an anecdote. Readers of Stanley Fish's *Is There a Text in This Class? The Authority of Interpretive Communities* (1980) will recognize in my title an allusion to the anecdote which gives him his. It's also, appropriately enough, an interpreter's joke (though at whose expense is not immediately clear); and, since it involves the triangulation of two men and a woman, a joke that falls structurally into a category defined by Freud as at once seductive and aggressive. Seductive, because you'll recall that for Freud this is always the aim of the sexual joke directed at a woman; aggressive, because the presence of another man turns desire to hostility, enlisting the originally interfering third party as an ally. The function of this kind of joke is both to humiliate and to eliminate the woman, becoming a joke at the precise point when it is directed no longer at her but at the onlooker-turned-listener.[1] Here, then, is Fish's anec-joke, which involves two male professors of differing critical persuasions and a female student whose theoretical innocence has already been violated by one of them:

> On the first day of the new semester a colleague at Johns Hopkins University was approached by a student who, as it turned out, had just taken a course from me. She put to him what I think you would agree is a perfectly straightforward question: "Is there a text in this class?" Responding with a confidence so perfect that he was unaware of it (although in telling the story, he refers to this moment as "walking into the trap"), my colleague said, "Yes; it's the *Norton Anthology of Literature*," whereupon the trap (set not by the student but by the infinite capacity of language for being appropriated) was sprung: "No, no," she said, "I mean in this class do we believe in poems and things, or is it just us?"[2]

Despite the ritual allusion to language's infinite capacity for appropriation, it's not hard to see that the student here, rather than language, is being appropriated as two professors vie for possession of the untutored female mind. But the woman student—described by the unnamed professor as "one of Fish's victims"—is not simply the victim of Fishy doctrine (parodically rendered as the instability of the text and the unavailability of determinate meanings); she's also the fall doll who sets Fish's theoretical discourse in motion—the idiot questioner disguised as dumb blonde. For one professor after another's ego, she voices a satisfyingly reductive version of Fish's critical position; but for Fish himself, she provides the opportunity to complicate it and finally cast it out in favor of a more finely tuned position (limited indeterminacy and a situational definition of meaning). By the end of the book the trap contains, not Fish's unwary colleague, still less the agile Fish, but the dumb blonde's misinterpretation.

If an anecdote tells us something the teller knows, a joke may reveal something he doesn't. Fish's anecdote tells us that he doesn't hold the absurd view ascribed to him by his opponents, that poems and things are "just us." But his joke tells us something else. Of the many constitutive meanings in this first-day-of-term encounter that Fish goes on to ponder, there is one he does not mention: the interpretive wrinkle introduced by the sexual triangle. Of course it could be argued that in most American universities, and especially at Johns Hopkins, such gender arrangements are the norm—and so they are. But the overwhelming likelihood that in the interpretive community which concerns Fish—the English department of a major university—two professors at odds about critical theory will be male, and the student female, doesn't quite account for the effect. One has only to substitute a male "victim" for laughter to turn to pedagogic exasperation (can't students get *anything* right?). Lurking behind Fish's bonhomous opening gambit is a tinge of gender harassment—not institutional but structural. There's no reason to think Fish himself anything but well disposed toward women students, or indeed feminist criticism, though one might justifiably take him to task for ignoring gender as a constitutive element in the interpretive community, especially in the light of current feminist concern with the woman reader. Rather, we glimpse here a paradigm commonly found when professors anxiously rebut their critics or covertly compete with one another. One might speculate that the function of the female "victim" in scenarios of this kind is to provide the mute sacrifice on which theory itself may be founded; the woman is silenced so that the theorist can make the truth come out of her mouth. Freud himself, in similar circumstances, rebuts doubts thrown on his professional competence and on the rightness of his theories with his "Dream of Irma's Injection," obliging a recalcitrant young patient to swallow the interpreter's "solution" which she has resisted in real life. If (as the dream enabled him triumphantly to prove) *when the work of interpretation has been completed, we perceive that a dream is the fulfilment of a wish,*" then Freud not only exonerates himself as physician and as analyst, but enacts a satisfying revenge on resistant patient and skeptical colleagues alike.[3] The sickly Irma has violence done to her body—in particular, to her remarkable oral cavity—in order that Freud's solution to the secret of dreams may be swallowed by his readers. One might say that the wish fulfilled by this dream is that dreams should be the fulfillment of wishes.

Like Fish's anec-joke, Freud's dream can be misread as an example of the role frequently played by women in a theoretical context. It's no part of my purpose to indict "theory" as such—on the contrary; still less to imply, as some feminist critics have tended to do, that theory is of itself "male," a dangerous abstraction which denies the specificity of female experience and serves chiefly to promote men in the academy. Instead, I want to offer some thoughts about the relation between women and theory—about the deflection of gender harassment (aggression against the class of women) or sexual harassment (aggression against the bodies of women) onto the "body" of the text. The result might be called textual harassment, the specular appropriation of woman, or even her elimination altogether. It's not just that women figure conveniently as mirrors for acts of narcissistic self-completion on the part of some male theorists, or that the shutting up of a female "victim" can open theoretical discourse. It's also a matter of the adversarial relation between rival theorists which often seems to underlie a triangle such as the one in Fish's anecdote. This triangle characteristically invokes its third (female) term only in the interests of the original rivalry and works finally to get rid of the woman, leaving theorist and theorist face to face. My first extended example of the textual relation between a woman and a theory will be *Delusions and Dreams in Jensen's Gradiva* (1907), Freud's reading of a fin-de-siècle novella. Painstaking yet wishful, Freud's practice is a reminder that the word *theory* comes from the Greek verb to look on, view, or contemplate, and that self-regard can never be far away in such a context. My second example will center on Mary Shelley's *Frankenstein* (1818), and especially on Frankenstein's uncreation of his female monster, while drawing on a theoretical debate which similarly has as its focus the elimination of the woman. Finally, I'll return briefly to another way of asking the question "Is there a woman in this text?" in order to relocate it within current feminist critical theory—putting the question back where it belongs for feminist critics themselves.

Gradiva Rediviva

> Then thou our fancy of itself bereaving,
> Dost make us Marble with too much conceaving . . .
> —Milton, "On Shakespear"

Recognizing the violence done by Freud to the literary text in the interests of analytical "truth," Sarah Kofman writes in *Quatre romans analytiques* (1973) of the impossibility of analytic interpretation without countertransference; "the unconscious of the analysis, like that of everyone, can never be eliminated."[4] What form does this countertransference take in the case of Freud's analysis of Jensen's "Pompeian phantasy," *Gradiva* (1903)? Freud himself was bound to read it in the light of his own theories, but did he also read his theories into it?[5] As it happens, he was himself alert to the possibility of having found in Jensen's "phantasy" only what he wanted to find: "Is it not rather we who have slipped into this charming poetic story a secret meaning very far from its author's intentions?" (*SE* 9:43). If so, then he is implicated in the same delusional structure as Jensen's archeologist hero—guilty of "introducing into an innocent work of art purposes of which its creator had no notion," and demonstrating "once more how easy it is to find what one is looking for" (*SE* 9:91).[6] Constructing an elaborate theory on the basis of his delusion, the young archeologist not only finds what he's looking for, but—and this is his chief value for Freud—reveals the artist-neurotic within the scientific scholar. In this sense (like Gradiva's own therapeutic dealings with the deluded hero), Freud's treatment of the novella might be said to take up the same "ground" as the delusion itself. For Kofman, in fact, the hero's "cure" at the hands of Gradiva parallels Freud's cure of the text—a cure whereby literature is ultimately consigned to the status of delusion, becoming a mere device "for catching the carp truth: that of the literary text which must confirm that of psychoanalysis."[7] Against his own better practice, Kofman argues, Freud is forced to align himself with the metaphysics of logocentricity—with "truth" as opposed to "fiction." But perhaps there is another way of looking at the analytical countertransference at work in *Delusions and Dreams*. Freud's reading of Jensen's "phantasy" proceeds by means of a series of important but unstated parallels between the role of Gradiva herself and that of the literary text; between the relation of a marble image to a living woman or of "fiction" to real life. Above all, the doubling of Gradiva and the text bears on another unstated parallel, between "woman" and "theory."

One might start by asking what are the resemblances between Norbert Hanold, the young archeologist, and Freud himself. Jensen's hero is at once a "scientist" and a fantasist; his archeological obsession provides the basis for a delusion at odds with rational judgment and empirical realities, so that the original instrument of repression (archeology, or "science" itself) becomes the vehicle for the return of the repressed. Defending himself against Eros, or life, Hanold becomes preoccupied with an ancient bas-relief of a young girl whom he identifies as being of Hellenic origin and names "Gradiva" or "the girl who steps along" (after the war god *Mars Gradivus*, "striding into battle"), an allusion to her distinctive lift of the foot (figure 1).[8] Norbert Hanold, we're told, "took no interest in living women; the science of which he was the servant had taken that interest away from him and displaced it on to women of marble or bronze" (*SE* 9:45–46). His fixation on a buried past and his unconscious mourning for the lost erotic possibilities of the present are vividly symbolized by a dream of Gradiva's transformation from a living woman, stepping along with her characteristic gait, into a recumbent marble form buried by the ashes of Vesuvius. Freud's own relation to his "science" has something in common with Hanold's. "The author of *The Interpretation of Dreams,*" he writes, "has ventured, in the face of the reproaches of strict science, to become a partisan of antiquity and superstition" (*SE* 9:7). Whereas "strict science" explains dreaming as a purely physiological process, the imaginative writer sides with the ancients, with the superstitious public, and with Freud himself to recognize "a whole host of things between heaven and earth of which our philosophy has not yet let us dream" (*SE* 9:8). The ghost of Hamlet's murdered father becomes evidence for the uncanny power of the repressed—the unconscious itself, with its challenge to a materialist outlook. For Freud too "science" becomes at once the instrument of repression and the means by which it is overcome. What returns is "life," or "Zoë"—the Greek name given by Jensen to his flesh-and-blood Gradiva; for the sculpted girl has a living double. Like the young archeologist, who "had surrendered his interest in life in exchange for an interest in the remains of classical antiquity and who was now brought back to real life by a roundabout path which was strange but perfectly logical" (*SE* 9:10), a physiologically based science is revivified by what might be called the buried life of the mind.

Hence Freud's identification with his hero's growing impatience at a science unable to carry him back into the buried past of Pompeii: "What (science) taught was a lifeless, archeological way of looking at things, and what came from its mouth was a dead, philological language" (*SE* 9:16). Like the real life Zoë's father, Hanold has been something of an "archaeopteryx"—a "compromise idea," Freud suggests, by which Zoë wittily satirizes both her father and her oblivious lover, identifying them with "the bird-like monstrosity which be-

Figure 1. Frontispiece to Sigmund Freud, *Jensen's "Gradiva"*
and Other Works (*SE* 9).

longs to the archeology of zoology" (*SE* 9:33). Zoë's father, whom we see in hot pursuit of the lizard *faraglionensis* among the ruins of Pompeii, has preferred the taxonomy of zoology to life itself; both he and Hanold, until now, have been "absorbed by science and held apart by it from life and from Zoë" (*SE* 9:33). In a comically deluded moment, Hanold addresses the unlooked-for noontide apparition of Gradiva in Greek and Latin, forgetting, as he has done all along, that she is "a German girl of flesh and blood" (*SE* 9:18); what comes from the mouth of science is a dead philological language. Ostensibly, the incident shows that "his science was now completely in the service of his imagination" (*SE* 9:18). But it also raises a problem which Freud too must address in appropriate words. No less than Zoë's father, he runs the risk of becoming a taxonomist of life or, like Norbert Hanold, a strict scientist locked into a deadening technical vocabulary. As he embarks on the second, analytic phase of his reading of Jensen's novella in the light of his theories of dreams, neurosis, and therapy, we find Freud anxious to "repeat" or "reproduce" it "in correct psychological technical terms," "with the technical terminology of our science" (*SE* 9:47, 44). Yet he is dissatisfied with the taxonomy of mental illness available to him—"erotomania," "fetishism," "*dégeneré,*" and the like—because "all such systems of nomenclature and classification of the different kinds of delusion . . . have something precarious and barren about them" (*SE* 9:45). The "strict psychiatrist" who would investigate Hanold's delusion in terms of heredity and degeneracy must give way to the student of the imagination, allied to artist and neurotic, and ultimately to Zoë herself, since her wooing of the young archeologist from his delusion is the model for Freud's own wooing of science.

If the story of Norbert Hanold's awakening to life and love provides Freud with an analogy for the awakening of "strict psychiatry" to the existence of the unconscious, *Delusions and Dreams* also reveals a submerged concern with what might be called questions of mimesis; that is, with the relation between art object and observed life, the fidelity of literature to psychic laws and processes, and the status of the imagination itself in relation to Freudian theory. The central *donnée* of Jensen's "Pompeian phantasy" is "the far-reaching resemblance between the sculpture and the live girl" (*SE* 9:42), the improbable "premiss that Zoë was in every detail a duplicate of the relief" (*SE* 9:70), the coincidence of there existing in antiquity a bas-relief which perfectly represents the appearance, and especially the characteristic walk, of a young girl of fin de siècle Germany. Another *donnée*, equally unlikely, is that Zoë's family name, "Bertgang," might readily suggest translation as "Gradiva"; fantastically, Freud allows himself to speculate that Zoë's family may be of ancient descent, having earned their name from their womenfolk's distinctive way of walking (*SE* 9:42). The peculiarity here doesn't lie in the fact of Hanold's repressed erotic feelings for his forgotten childhood playmate (for that is what she turns out to be) having settled unknowingly on her marble likeness. Rather, it lies in the uncanny priority of the representation over what it represents. This peculiarity exactly parallels the priority of Freudian theory over the literary text. As Gradiva is to Zoë, so theory is to Jensen's novella. At first sight, Freud had seemed to be arguing for the priority of literary insight over that of "science"; as he poses it initially, the question is not whether "this imaginative representation of the genesis of a delusion can hold its own before the judgment of science," since instead "it is science that cannot hold its own before the achievement of the author" (*SE* 9:53). But by an unexpected sleight of hand, Freud ceases to emphasize the secondary status of science, instead asserting that his own prior views support all that Jensen has written: "Does our author stand alone, then, in the face of united science? No, that is not the case (if, that is, I may count my own works as part of science), since for a number of years . . . I myself have supported all the views that I have here extracted from Jensen's *Gradiva* and stated in technical terms" (*SE* 9:53). This is the payoff for Freud's cautious but stealthily appropriative reading of Jensen's novella. Just as the marble bas-relief can figure in Jensen's "phantasy" without seeming fantastic— indeed, seeming rather to authenticate it, since such a bas-relief actually existed—so Freudian theory, granted independent existence, authenticates Jensen's literary insight, becoming the model for both art and life.

The resemblance of a marble bas-relief to a living girl is the single unexplained and inexplicable "premiss" on which Jensen's novella and Freud's interpretation both depend. The double (Gradiva/Zoë) is also crucial to the way in which *Delusions and Dreams* poses the relation between theory and literary text, and in particular the relation between desire and the uncanny. Like Hanold, who sees in the sculpted figure "something 'of today' . . . as though the artist had had a glimpse in the street and captured it 'from the life' " (*SE* 9:11), Freud goes through the motions of testing Jensen's "phantasy" against empirical observation. Hanold takes to studying the feet of women in the street as a "scientific task," trying to discover whether Gradiva's gait has been rendered by the artist "in a life-like manner"; desire masks itself as "an ostensibly scientific problem which called for a solution" (*SE* 9:11–12). The increasingly bodily nature of his curiosity surfaces later, when he encounters the supposed ghost of Gradiva (actually Zoë) among the ruins of Pompeii. He longs to know "would one feel anything if one touched her hand?" (*SE* 9:23) and seizes an opportunity to slap it (a piece of erotic aggression not lost on Freud). The question asked by the young archeologist at this point doubles exactly with the reader's, who as yet has no means of knowing from Jensen's narrative that a flesh-and-blood Zoë exists. In the second part of his analysis Freud takes a similar tack. Is Jensen's story indeed only a "phantasy" (like Hanold's delusion) which renounces the portrayal of reality? Can his account of the construction of a delusion be verified from other sources? Does it lie within the bounds of possibility, like the sculptor's depiction of Gradiva's foot? (*SE* 9:41, 80). Ostensibly, Freud's answer is to assert its mimetic accuracy—Jensen's novella is "so faithfully copied from reality that we should not object if *Gradiva* were described not as a phantasy but as a psychiatric study" (*SE* 9:41). Yet it is important to remember the earlier moment in Freud's account when the apparition of Gradiva amidst the ruins of Pompeii produces an experience of confusion and uncertainty, not only for Hanold but for the reader, forcing the conclusion that she is either "a hallucination or a midday ghost" (*SE* 9:17). The unexpected discovery that—whether *rediviva* or not—she is corporeally present introduces the element of the uncanny, literally marking the return of the repressed. In his retelling of the story, Freud halts us here. The pause is significant, for both Gradiva and the text are alike in being uncanny, not because they are dead but because they are alive—living embodiments of desire. In Jensen's and Freud's texts, then, the uncanny moment occurs when what is supposed dead (Gradiva or science) comes to life again as "Zoë" or "theory."

While seeming to test Jensen's "phantasy" against reality, Freud ends by suggesting that what is uncanny about his science of the mind (as about the unconscious) is that it is something we have always known but have forgotten, just as Hanold has forgotten his childhood playmate. Ostensibly, theory turns out to be life itself. But in the context of Gradiva's apparition in the streets of Pompeii, Freud has earlier asked whether the author intends to leave us in a world "governed by the laws of science" or to transport us into an imaginary one (*SE* 9:17). Though he asserts that Jensen's story obeys the laws of science, these laws have a curious provenance. Like the resemblance of Gradiva and Zoë, the coincidence of Hanold's meeting with Gradiva in Pompeii, the very place to which he has fled in his unconscious avoidance of Eros, is represented as an illustration of "the fatal truth that has laid it down that flight is precisely an instrument that delivers one over to what one is fleeing from" (*SE* 9:42). As for the transporting of Zoë herself from Germany to Pompeii, this is merely an instance of the author guiding his characters "towards a happy destiny, in spite of all the laws of necessity" (*SE* 9:69); part, as it were, of the dream—and we know that Freud has throughout derived his "rules . . . for the solution of dreams" from his own *Interpretation of Dreams* (*SE* 9:57). Not only is there no such thing as chance, but "the laws of science" or mental life turn out to be uniquely authorized. Freud's complicity in the authorial manipulations of Jensen's text bears on an otherwise unrelated moment when he intrudes his own experience into the narrative. Recalling the uncanny resemblance between a dead woman and her sister, whose unexpected appearance in his consulting room momentarily convinced him "that the dead can come back to life" (*SE* 9:71), Freud not only implicates himself in the

delusional structure; he reveals his own residual belief in the
omnipotence of thought. Having considered himself responsible for the woman's death, he sees in her apparent restoration
to life a restoration of his infallibility as a doctor. The *revenant*
doubles as his own lost ideal. Commenting on Freud's account
of the narcissistic "essence of woman" who must fully correspond to male desire, Sarah Kofman writes that "men's fascination with this eternal feminine is nothing but fascination with
their own double, and the feeling of uncanniness,
Unheimlichkeit, that men experience is the same as what one
feels in the face of any double, any ghost, in the face of the
abrupt reappearance of what one thought had been overcome
or lost forever."[9] If Freud's experience of the uncanny in his
consulting room was nothing less than a pang of gratified narcissism, then the sighting of Gradiva by the deluded Hanold, by
the confused reader, and by Freud himself becomes the magical
moment when the fantasists of archeology, literature, and psychoanalysis confront themselves restored to wholeness.

    It is surely in this moment that we can identify the
countertransferential aspect of *Delusions and Dreams*. Like the
doll Olympia in Hoffmann's "The Sandman," who replies only
"Ach, Ach" to all that Nathanael proposes, the sculptured Gradiva had been a love object posing none of the risks of forbidden or potentially castrating sexuality.[10] But is the live Zoë
finally very different? For all his emphasis on the accuracy of
the copy—whether Gradiva's of Zoë or Jensen's of life—Freud
implies that mimetic representation inevitably involves distortion or lack. Substituting Zoë for Gradiva, Hanold replaces his
delusion "by the thing of which it could only have been a
distorted and inadequate copy" (*SE* 9:37). Similarly, "dream-
images have to be regarded as something distorted," a mere
copy of the dream thoughts they (mis)"represent" (*SE* 9:59).
The work of interpretation, then, seems to involve correcting
the distortion and restoring dream thoughts to an imaginary
wholeness. Despite his reductive statement that interpreting a
dream (or, by analogy, a literary text) involves translating
"manifest content" into "latent dream-thoughts" (*SE* 9:59),
Freud seems actually to be proposing something more like the
effect of the *revenant's* apparition in his consulting room. Both

delusion and theory become a desired supplement to the empirically observed world of the "strict psychiatrist." That Zoë herself, no less than Gradiva, is made in the image of Hanold's, Jensen's, and Freud's own desire emerges most clearly from the charming concluding scene of the "Pompeian phantasy." In a moment which Freud takes evident pleasure in rehearsing, Norbert Hanold asks Zoë Bertgang to step back once more into his dream of Gradiva and reenact for him the distinctive lift of the foot on which his delusion has centered:

> The delusion had now been conquered by a beautiful reality; but before the two lovers left Pompeii it was still to be honoured once again. When they reached the Herculenean Gate, where, at the entrance to the Via Consolare, the street is crossed by some ancient stepping-stones, Norbert Hanold paused and asked the girl to go ahead of him. She understood him "and, pulling up her dress a little with her left hand, Zoë Bertgang, Gradiva *rediviva*, walked past, held in his eyes, which seemed to gaze as though in a dream; so, with her quietly tripping gait, she stepped through the sunlight over the stepping-stones to the other side of the street." (*SE* 9:39-40)

"With the triumph of love," Freud concludes, "what was beautiful and precious in the delusion found recognition as well" (*SE* 9:40). This, unmistakably, is the Pygmalion story, in which the coming to life of the ideal beloved, modeled on the lover's desire, figures the artist's narcissistic relation to his Galatea-like creation. Nathanael's Olympia is simply the demonic version of the same myth. In the passage Freud quotes so affectingly, we witness not only the triumph of love but the triumph of specular appropriation ("held in his eyes, which seemed to gaze as though in a dream"). Freud's proof that theory is only the life we have forgotten turns on a moment when the living Zoë gets reappropriated as an uncanny representation: Gradiva *rediviva*.

The Bride of Frankenstein

Many and long were the conversations between Lord Byron and Shelley, to which I was a devout but nearly silent listener. During one

> of these, various philosophical doctrines were discussed, and among
> others the nature of the principle of life, and whether there was any
> probability of its ever being discovered and communicated.
>
> —Mary Shelley, "Introduction" to *Frankenstein*

Lacan ventriloquizes the meaning of Freud's "Dream of Irma's Injection" as a plea for forgiveness for having transgressed a limit previously uncrossed, that of curing the sick whom before no one had wished or dared to cure; "for to transgress a limit hitherto imposed on human activity is always culpable."[11] The magical word of Freud's dream solution ("Trimethylamin"), linked by Freud himself to the chemistry of sexual processes, suggests that Freud's morbid fascination with Irma's deep throat figures the broken taboo—that of looking too closely at "the immensely powerful factor of sexuality" which he believed to be the origin of the nervous disorders he aimed to cure (*SE* 4:116–17). In his *Autobiographical Study* (1925), recalling that as a boy he was moved "by a sort of curiosity" about human concerns, Freud speaks of the influence on him both of an older boy and of the theories of Darwin, which "held out hopes of an extraordinary advance in our understanding of the world" (*SE* 20:8). The two impulses behind his decision to become a medical student were male bonding and curiosity about the origins of life; later, his work in physiology was to focus on the central nervous system. His remark apropos of Norbert Hanold's researches into women's feet, that "the scientific motivation might be said to serve as a pretext for the unconscious erotic one" (*SE* 9:52), could stand as the epigraph not only to his own researches but to all scientific quests for the origins of life, whether organic or mental. Before moving on to *Frankenstein Or the Modern Prometheus*, whose own origins—according to Mary Shelley herself—lie in conversations between Byron and Shelley about "the nature of the principle of life,"[12] I want to look briefly at another scientific autobiography, James Watson's *The Double Helix: A Personal Account of the Discovery of the Structure of DNA* (1968). Watson's and Crick's pursuit of "the Rosetta Stone for unraveling the true secret of life,"[13] the very basis of genetic reproduction, unexpectedly repeats the paradigm of the scientific triangle which Mary Shelley had anticipated in her gothic novel, bringing together motifs of curiosity, ambition, and scientific inquiry in the context of an undercurrent of male bonding which has as its necessary victim a woman.

One might speculate that the unconscious motive of Watson's pursuit of the structures of DNA was twofold: that of engaging in intense oedipal rivalry with a distinguished older scientist, Linus Pauling, while attaching himself closely to another (younger) man, Francis Crick; or perhaps, as one scientific observer has suggested, Pauling and Crick were really interchangeable—"The love and the competition are one and the same."[14] In any event, both kinds of oedipal relation—rivalry or love—are profoundly misogynistic, demanding as they do the sacrifice of a living woman. As is well known, the "race" for the secret of DNA involved not only Watson and Crick in Cambridge versus Pauling at California Institute of Technology, but a London-based team consisting of Maurice Wilkins, who later received the Nobel prize along with the Cambridge pair, and a young woman named Rosalind Franklin. The competition derived some of its excitement from contrasting temperaments and styles, but above all from the radically different approaches involved. While Watson and Crick adopted the inspirational, hit-or-miss methods of theoretical model building, the London-based team used as its principal research tool the findings of X-ray diffraction—painstakingly empirical techniques of measuring molecular cell structures. This is the context in which a misogynistic element enters, and for a while dominates, Watson's "personal account." Wilkins' co-researcher, whom Watson refers to throughout as "Rosy," as if she were a kind of scientific charlady, had been brought in because of her expertise in X-ray diffraction technique; presumably Wilkins hoped that she would speed up his research. But "Rosy" refused to regard herself as Wilkins' assistant (which she was not) and—worse still—persisted in thinking that DNA was as much her problem as his. In Watson's eyes, this made her a furious feminist who ultimately posed a threat not simply to men but to science itself: "Clearly," he writes, "Rosy had to go or be put in her place. The former was obviously preferable because, given her belligerent moods, it would be very difficult for Maurice [Wilkins] to maintain a dominant position that would allow him to think unhindered about DNA" (p. 20). And go she finally did, but not before she had unknowingly provided the empirical data on which Watson and Crick based their final model of the double helix.

For Norbert Hanold, science becomes a discarded, unlovely mistress, or "an old, dried up, tedious aunt, the dullest and most unwanted creature in the world" (*SE* 9:65). Something similar happens to "Rosy" in *The Double Helix;* at once virago and dowd, she is represented as the sour spinster science by which theory knows itself young and virile. Not content with stressing her lack of feminine desirability—the absence of lipstick or attractive clothes—Watson speculates that she is "the product of an unsatisfied mother who unduly stressed the desirability of professional careers that could save bright girls from marriages to dull men" (p. 20); how unlike Zoë. Later, giving an important talk on DNA (whose implications Watson was at that point in no position to understand), she is represented as the product of "careful, unemotional crystallographic training," and hence as hostile to the idea of using "tinker-toy-like structures" for solving theoretical problems in biology. As she calls for more refined crystallographic analysis, Watson labels her the schoolmarm "labwork": "Certainly," he recalls, "a bad way to go out into the foulness of a heavy, foggy November night was to be told by a woman to refrain from venturing an opinion about a subject for which you were not trained. It was a sure way of bringing back unpleasant memories of lower school" (p. 52). In her sympathetic biography of Rosalind Franklin, Anne Sayre was struck by one detail in Watson's recollection of this talk, his reference to "Rosy's" glasses ("momentarily I wondered how she would look if she took off her glasses"). Ms. Franklin did not wear glasses.[15] For her biographer, this was the giveaway that Watson had substituted fiction for fact—just as he failed to give "Rosy" credit for providing him with crucial data. For us, perhaps, it throws light on other, seemingly unrelated aspects of Watson's account: his allusions to what he calls "popsies"; the preoccupation with the sexual life of Cambridge au pair girls which (according to Watson) constituted Crick's main topic of conversation apart from DNA; and his habit of referring to plausible theoretical solutions as "pretty." In his recent book, *Life Itself* (1981), Crick playfully calls RNA and DNA "the dumb blondes of the bio-molecular world."[16] Like Gradiva, the model of the double helix is narcissistically invested with desire; unlike "Rosy"— Nathanael's Klara to the Olympian DNA—the double helix re-plies only "Ach, Ach" when spoken to.

Brash and unconsciously misogynistic as it is, *The Double Helix* offers a clear-cut view of the Girardian triangle at work. The "pretty" object of desire (whether the solution to DNA or a Nobel prize) is pursued less for itself than for being desired by another scientist. The function of the object of desire is thus to mediate relations between men; female desire is im-possible except as a mimetic reflection of male desire.[17] The same paradigm shapes Mary Shelley's *Frankenstein*—at once a drama of Promethean scientific enquiry and of oedipal rivalry, a myth of creation that encompasses both a quest for the origins of life and the bond of love and hate between creator and crea-tion; "Did I request thee, Maker, from my clay/To mould Me man?" (*Paradise Lost*, X:743–44) demands the novel's Miltonic epigraph, in Adam's words to God. Significantly, what Mary Shelley recalls at the inception of her novel are conversations between Byron and Shelley in which she took almost no part. Perhaps we should see *Frankenstein* not simply as a reworking of Milton's creation myth in the light of Romantic ideology but as an implicit critique of that ideology for its exclusive emphasis on oedipal politics.[18] *Frankenstein* would thus become the novel that most accurately represents the condition of both men and women under the predominantly oedipal forms of Byronic and Shelleyan Romanticism. Read in this light, the monster's tragedy is his confinement to the destructive inten-sities of a one-to-one relationship with his maker, and his ex-clusion from other relations—whether familial or with a female counterpart. The most striking absence in *Frankenstein*, after all, is Eve's. Refusing to create a female monster, Frankenstein pays the price of losing his own bride. When the primary bond of paternity unites scientist and his creation so exclusively, women who get in the way must fall victim to the struggle. Indeed, if we look in this text for a female author, we find only a dismembered corpse whose successful animation would threaten the entire structure of the myth. It was more appropriate than he knew for James Whale to cast the same actress, Elsa Lanchester, as both the angelic Mary Shelley and the demonic female monster in his 1935 film sequel to the novel, *The Bride of Frankenstein* (figure 2).[19]

In Mary Shelley's own version, Frankenstein's creation of the monster is immediately followed by the vivid nightmare and yet more appalling awakening which had been her own waking dream and the starting point of her novel. Frankenstein's postpartum nightmare strikingly conflates the body of his long neglected fiancée and childhood sweetheart, Elizabeth, with that of his dead mother:

> I thought I saw Elizabeth, in the bloom of health, walking in the streets of Ingolstadt. Delighted and surprised, I embraced her; but as I imprinted the first kiss on her lips, they became

Figure 2. Elsa Lanchester as the monsteress in the Universal film
The Bride of Frankenstein (1935).

> livid with the hue of death; her features appeared to change, and I thought that I held the corpse of my dead mother in my arms; a shroud enveloped her form, and I saw the grave-worms crawling in the folds of the flannel. I started from my sleep with horror; a cold dew covered my forehead, my teeth chattered, and every limb became convulsed; when, by the dim and yellow light of the moon, as it forced its way through the window shutters, I beheld the wretch—the miserable monster whom I had created. (p. 58)

The composite image, mingling eroticism and the horror of corruption, transforms Frankenstein's latently incestuous brother-sister relationship with Elizabeth into the forbidden relationship with the mother.

The grave as well as the source of life, bringing birth, sex, and death together in one appalling place, the incestuously embraced mother figures Frankenstein's unnatural pursuit of nature's secrets in his charnel house labors. Like Irma's throat, the mother's shrouded form is unwrapped to reveal decay and deformity in the flesh itself.[20] It's not just that the exclusion of woman from creation symbolically "kills" the mother, but that Frankenstein's forbidden researches give to the "facts of life" the aspect of mortality. Elizabeth in turn comes to represent not the object of desire but its death. In a bizarre pun, the monster—"the demonical corpse to which I had so miserably given life"—is compared to "a mummy again endued with animation" (p. 58). Exchanging a woman for a monster, Frankenstein has perhaps preferred monstrosity to this vision of corrupt female flesh. From this moment on, the narrative must move inexorably toward the elimination of both female monster and Elizabeth herself on her wedding night. Only when the two females who double one another in the novel—the hideous travesty of a woman and her anodyne ideal—have canceled each other out is the way clear for the scene of passionate mourning in which the monster hangs, loverlike, over Frankenstein's deathbed at the conclusion of Walton's narrative.

In Mary Shelley's novel, intense identification with an oedipal conflict exists at the expense of identification with women. At best, women are the bearers of a traditional ideology of love, nurturance, and domesticity; at worst, they are

passive victims. And yet, for the monster himself, women become a major problem (one that Frankenstein largely avoids by
immersing himself in his scientific studies). A curious thread in
the plot focuses not on the image of the hostile father (Franken-
stein/God) but on that of the dead mother who comes to symbolize to the monster his loveless state. Literally unmothered,
he fantasizes acceptance by a series of women but founders in
imagined rebuffs and ends in violence. Though it is a little boy
(Frankenstein's younger brother) who provokes the monster's
first murder by his rejection, the child bears the fatal image of
the mother—the same whose shroud had crawled with grave-
worms in Frankenstein's nightmare:

> As I fixed my eyes on the child, I saw something glittering on
> his breast: I took it; it was a portrait of a most lovely woman.
> In spite of my malignity, it softened and attracted me. For a
> few moments I gazed with delight on her dark eyes, fringed
> by deep lashes, and her lovely lips; but presently my rage
> returned: I remembered that I was for ever deprived of the
> delights that such beautiful creatures could bestow; and that
> she whose resemblance I contemplated would, in regarding
> me, have changed that air of divine benignity to one ex-
> pressive of disgust and affright.
>
> Can you wonder that such thoughts transported
> me with rage? (p. 143)

Immediately after the monster has his vision of this lovely but
inaccessible woman, shifting in imagination from looks of be-
nignity to disgust, he finds the Frankenstein's servant girl Justine asleep in a nearby barn: "She was young: not indeed so
beautiful as her whose portrait I held; but of an agreeable aspect, and blooming in the loveliness of youth and health. Here,
I thought, is one of those whose joy-imparting smiles are bestowed on all but me. And then I bent over her, and whispered,
'Awake, fairest, thy lover is near—he who would give his life
but to obtain one look of affection from thine eyes: my beloved,
awake!' " (p. 143). But in this travesty of the lover's *aubade,* the
beloved's awakening will shatter the dream, so she must sleep
forever. On Justine's person the monster wreaks his revenge on
all women, planting among her clothes the incriminating evidence of the mother's portrait as the supposed motive for her
murder of the little boy. She is duly tried and executed, even

confessing to the crime—for in the monstrous logic of the text, she is as guilty as the monster claims: "The crime had its source in her: be hers the punishment!" (p. 144).

In this bizarre parody of the Fall, Eve is to blame for having been desired. By the same monstrous logic, if woman is the cause of the monster's crimes, then the only cure is a mate, "one as horrible and deformed as myself" (p. 144). The monster's demand for a mate provides the basis for James Whale's sequel. In *The Bride of Frankenstein*, Frankenstein and his crazed collaborator Dr. Praetorius undertake what neither Mary Shelley nor her hero could quite bring themselves to do—embody woman as fully monstrous. Shelley's Frankenstein gives several different reasons for dismembering the female corpse which he is on the point of animating: that she might prove even more malignant than her mate; that between them they might breed a race of monsters to prey on mankind; and that "they might even hate each other"—he loathing her for a deformity worse than his because it "came before his eyes in the female form," while "she also might turn in disgust from him to the superior beauty of man" (p. 165). This last fear, taken up by James Whale's horror movie, is a demonic parody of the moment in Milton's creation myth when Eve prefers her own image to that of Adam—"less fair,/Less winning soft, less amiably mild,/Than that smooth watery image" (*Paradise Lost*, IV:478–80). As in Renaissance representations of the Fall, where the serpent's face is hers, Eve appears in the guise of the narcissistic woman—that self-sufficient (the more desirable because self-sufficient) adorer of her own image (figure 3).[21] God tells her firmly that Adam is "he/Whose image thou art" (*Paradise Lost*, IV:471–2), but she knows better. If it is the function of *Paradise Lost* to cast out female self-love, it is the function of *The Bride of Frankenstein* to destroy its own monstrous version of Eve's rejection of Adam. Behind this fantasy lies yet another, that of the female monster who might desire men instead of monsters. The threat to male sexuality lies not only in her hideous deformity, refusing to accommodate the image of his desire, but in the dangerous autonomy of her refusal to mate in the image in which she was made. It is as if Irma's throat had suddenly found its voice.

At this juncture it seems appropriate to return to the

Figure 3. Raphael, *The Fall* (c. 1508–1511): Rome,
Vatican, Stanza della Segnature.

Girardian triangle and to Sarah Kofman's reading of Freud—in particular, to the Girard-Kofman argument over the narcissistic woman. Since the narcissistic woman has enjoyed some vogue as the point of resistance both to specular appropriation by male desire and to the phallocentric system whereby the term *woman* is reduced to *man-minus*, denying sexual difference, the argument is worth recapitulating.[22] Perhaps, too, the stakes are not quite what they seem. The theory of narcissism itself—an almost tautologous concept, given the reflexivity of looking at oneself as a love object—finds an apt emblem in this self-involved figure, who comes to represent for Girard the illusion at the center of Freud's theory, and for Freud himself, the barely repressed possibility that all love might turn out, at bottom, to be narcissistic. In "On Narcissism: An Introduction" (1914), Freud allows himself to speculate about a female type which he calls "the purest and truest one" (*SE* 14:88), a type who achieves the "self-sufficiency" of loving only herself. According to Freud, such women exercise a special attraction because—like children, cats, large beasts of prey, criminals, and "humorists"—they seem to have kept intact an original, primary narcissism which the adult male has lost. Her fascination is that of representing a lost paradise of narcissistic completeness, while leaving the lover forever unsatisfied. For once, Freud defines *woman* not in terms of lack but in terms of something she has; primary narcissism replaces the missing phallus. In Kofman's reading, the narcissistic woman is important because she refutes Freud's tendency elsewhere to reduce the "enigma" of woman to categories of penis envy, castration, and veiling. But, she writes, what is frightening about such a woman is "woman's indifference to man's desire, her self-sufficiency . . . it is what makes woman enigmatic, inaccessible, impenetrable."[23] And so Freud must finally redeem her, by way of pregnancy and motherhood, for the ethical superiority of object love. For Girard, however, the narcissistic woman had never been anything but a phantasmatic projection on Freud's part. Her self-sufficiency is an illusion, the strategy of a coquette aware that desire attracts desire, merely "the metaphysical transformation of the rival-model."[24] Failing to recognize the mimetic essence of desire, Freud has allowed himself to be entrapped by a woman.

In Kofman's eyes, Girard is responding to the intolerable idea of female self-sufficiency (as Freud himself does elsewhere) by denigrating it. But there is more at stake. Girard contends not simply that Freud is entrapped by a fantasy but that his entire theory of narcissism is a chimera. Freud's status as the theorist of desire is undermined in order to reduce narcissism to a merely mythical disguise for Girardian strife between doubles; eliminating the narcissistic woman, Girard also eliminates sexual difference, since in his scheme there is only male desire which the woman mimics. If the narcissistic woman stands, Eve-like, at the center of Freud's theory of desire, Girard's is the James Whale-like scenario of her destruction. What is left without her is the collaboration of Frankenstein and Dr. Praetorius—or, if you like, a struggle for primacy between Freud and Girard in which Girard employs Proust as his front man, using the metaphors of *À la recherche du temps perdu* to prove that Proust not only understood desire better than Freud but that he demystifies the concepts which buttress the theory of narcissism. The artist knows better than the scientist, for all his technical terms. There is a familiar ring to this. Freud's own arguments—about Jensen's *Gradiva*, for instance—are marshaled by Girard to prove the superiority of literary over scientific insight; Proust, moreover, doesn't really stand alone, since in this Freud himself supports him. But if all Girard wants to do is assert the primacy of the literary text as a source of theory, why his onslaught on the narcissistic woman? To start with, she is easier to unveil than Freudian theory; her coquettish self-sufficiency can stand in for its formidable appearance of wholeness. In addition, her elimination allows the literary text (Proust's) or the critical text (Girard's) to enjoy unmediated dialogue with the psychoanalytic text. Girard's final contention is not that Freud needs the narcissistic woman but that Freud and Proust (or rather, Girard) need one another: "a dialogue between the two, a dialogue of equals that has never occurred so far." But just as the monster comes finally to dominate Frankenstein, Girard has in mind something other than equality: "After countless Freudian readings of Proust, we can propose, for a change, a Proustian reading of Freud."[25] Next we will have the spectacle of the monster lamenting the destruction of his maker; for to destroy the loved and hated rival is to destroy what is, for Girard himself, the very essence of desire.

In Freud's reading of *Gradiva*, theory steals a march on the literary text which it invokes as proof of its rightness. In Girard's reading of Freud, the literary text usurps on theory—to reveal theory once more. The play of desire proves to be a power play; but either way, the name of the game is theoretical priority. Freud's tendency to suggest, despite himself, not that theory is life but rather that life is always theory, has some bearing on the narcissism debate. The threat posed by the narcissistic woman is that she may reveal the primacy of narcissism, undercutting object love and mimetic desire alike. Perhaps the ultimate function of both "life" (Zoë) and the narcissistic woman is to defend against formlessness; indeed, one might speculate that this is the chief function of woman as such in theoretical discourse.

Just as the threat of castration may localize an anxiety less unmanageable than that glimpsed in the abyss of Irma's throat—the formless depths of female sexuality—so representing theory as a woman may defend against the indeterminacy and impenetrability of theory itself. It is better to be threatened by even a female monster than to be possessed by a theory whose combined insubstantiality and self-sufficiency are those of delusion. The so-called theorist's dilemma may be one source of the difficulty: if a theory serves its purpose, it should establish relationships among observable phenomena, yet if these relationships are so established, theory can be dispensed with. The dispensability of a good theory has as its obverse Hegel's contention that the innovation of theory is to transform an ungraspable reality into something representable.[26] On one hand, the unprovability of theory is what constitutes its theoretical status; on the other hand, theory makes it possible to represent what would otherwise elude understanding. If we turn from Freud and Girard to feminist critical theory, it may be possible to see that feminists are caught in the dilemma of theory itself, particularly in their current concern not simply with sexual difference but with the issue of "the woman in the text," or gendered writing. If "theory" involves recourse either to the order of empirical observation (things as they are) or to delusion (things as they are not) or, on the contrary, a return to the field of representation (like patriarchal discourse, the traditional arena of women's oppression), would we do better to renounce it altogether?

And yet the question "Is there a woman in the text?" remains a central one—perhaps *the* central one—for feminist critics, and it is impossible to answer it without theory of some kind. The respective answers given by Anglo-American and French criticism are defined, in part at least, by the inherent paradox of "theory." In America the flight toward empiricism takes the form of an insistence on "woman's experience" as the ground of difference in writing. "Women's writing," "the woman reader," "female culture" occupy an almost unchallenged position of authority in feminist critical discourse of this kind. The assumption is of an unbroken continuity between "life" and "text"—a mimetic relation whereby women's writing, reading, or culture, instead of being produced, reflect a knowable reality.[27] Just as one can identify a woman biologically (the unstated argument would run), so one can with a little extra labor identify a woman's text, a woman reader, the essence of female culture. Of course the category of "women's writing" remains as strategically and politically important in classroom, curriculum, or interpretive community as the specificity of women's oppression is to the women's movement. And yet to leave the question there, with an easy recourse to the female signature or to female being, is either to beg it or to biologize it. To insist, for instance, that *Frankenstein* reflects Mary Shelley's experience of the trauma of parturition and postpartum depression may tell us about women's lives, but it reduces the text itself to a monstrous symptom. Equally, to see it as the product of "bibliogenesis"—a feminist rereading of *Paradise Lost* that, in exposing its misogynist politics, makes the monster's fall an image of woman's fall into the hell of sexuality—rewrites the novel in the image not of books but of female experience.[28] Feminist interpretations such as these have no option but to posit the woman author as origin and her life as the primary locus of meaning.

By contrast, the French insistence on *écriture féminine*—on woman as a writing-effect instead of an origin—asserts not the sexuality of the text but the textuality of sex. Gender difference, produced, not innate, becomes a matter of the structuring of a genderless libido in and through patriarchal discourse. Language itself would at once repress multiplicity and heterogeneity—true difference—by the tyranny of hierarchical oppositions (man/woman) and simultaneously work to overthrow that tyranny by interrogating the limits of meaning. The "feminine," in this scheme, is to be located in the gaps, the absences, the unsayable or unrepresentable of discourse and representation.[29] The feminine text becomes the elusive, phantasmal inhabitant of phallocentric discourse, as Gradiva *rediviva* haunts Freud's *Delusions and Dreams,* or, for the skeptical Girard, the narcissistic woman exercises her illusory power over the theory of narcissism. And yet, in its claim that women must write the body, that only the eruption of female jouissance can revolutionize discourse and challenge the Law of the Father, *écriture féminine* seems—however metaphorically—to be reaching not so much for essentialism (as it is often accused of doing) as for the conditions of representability. The theoretical abstraction of a "marked" writing that can't be observed at the level of the sentence but only glimpsed as an alternative libidinal economy almost invariably gives rise to gender-specific images of voice, touch, anatomy; to biologistic images of milk or jouissance. How else, after all, could the not-yet-written forms of *écriture féminine* represent themselves to our understanding? Not essentialism but representationalism is the French equivalent of Anglo-American empiricism—an alternative response to the indeterminacy and impenetrability of theory. If the woman in the text is "there," she is also "not there"—certainly not its object, not necessarily even its author. That may be why the heroine of feminist critical theory is not the silenced Irma, victim of Freudian theory, but the hysterical Dora whose body is her text and whose refusal to be the object of Freudian discourse makes her the subject of her own. Perhaps the question that feminist critics should ask themselves is not "Is there a woman in this text?" but rather: *"Is there a text in this woman?"*

2. Judith, Holofernes, and the Phallic Woman

I want to start with a footnote—not to my main text, which will be Freud's "Taboo of Virginity" (1917) but to his later essay on "Female Sexuality" (1931). Discussing the differing implications of the Oedipus and castration complexes for men and women, with their residue of masculine disparagement of women on one hand and feminine self-disparagement on the other, Freud slyly invokes the relations of psychoanalysis and feminism:

> It is to be anticipated that men analysts with feminist views, as well as our women analysts, will disagree with what I have said here. They will hardly fail to object that such notions spring from the "masculinity complex" of the male and are designed to justify on theoretical grounds his innate inclination to disparage and suppress women. But this sort of psycho-analytic argumentation reminds us here, as it so often does, of Dostoevsky's famous "knife that cuts both ways." The opponents of those who argue in this way will on their side think it quite natural that the female sex should refuse to accept a view which appears to contradict their eagerly coveted equality with men. The use of analysis as a weapon of controversy can clearly lead to no decision. (*SE* 21:230*n*.)

Freud refuses to take sides with a parade of judicious—one might almost say, antijudicial—impartiality. By withholding judgment, he seems to align himself with neither the prosecution nor the defense. That he himself had a judicial analogy in mind we know from tracing the Dostoevsky metaphor to its recent context elsewhere in Freud's writings, the 1928 essay on "Dostoevsky and Parricide," where he alludes to "the famous mockery of psychology" as a "knife that cuts both ways" in the speech for the defense at Mitya's trial in *The Brothers Karamazov*.[1] "A splendid piece of disguise," Freud observes, for we have only to reverse it to discover what Dostoevsky really meant: "It is not psychology that deserves the mockery, but the procedure of judicial enquiry. It is a matter of indifference who actually committed the crime; psychology is only concerned to know who desired it emotionally and who welcomed it when it was done" (*SE* 21:189). Analysts with feminist views might be tempted to reply that psychology itself has emotional desires; or at least that the "knife that cuts both ways" may slice unevenly for men and for women. Significantly, Freud's borrowed metaphor equates psychoanalysis itself with what had by this time become its centrally informing concept, the castration complex.[2] En route, the metaphor has also lost its original impartiality. Dostoevsky's phrase is actually rendered by the literal German of Freud's text as a "stick with two ends" (*"Stock mit zwei Enden"*). In the course of translation, we find that psychoanalysis develops a cutting edge, so that in the last sentence too it becomes an offensive "weapon" where in the original it had merely been put to "agonistic use" (*"Die agonale Verwendung der Analyse"*).[3] Freud's note says that there can be no winners in this battle of the sexes; the point must remain undecided. Yet in the Strachey translation, castration replaces the two-ended stick to make the cut, rather than undecidability, the mark of sexual difference.

The slippage here from the impartial to the partisan may reveal only the zeal of the translator. Determined to render justice to the text, Strachey overdetermines it. But perhaps translation, like psychology in Mitya's trial, is indifferent to Freudian intention, and "only concerned to know who desired [the crime] emotionally and who welcomed it when it was done." To say that misogynist desire speaks through Freud would be the crudest of feminist polemics—precisely the polemic Freud's footnote is designed to ward off. Yet the slippage, or slip, as Freud observes elsewhere, might be thought to occur "under the influence of disturbing affects" (*SE* 6:53*n*.). Again by Freud's own account, what could be more disturbing than the discovery of sexual difference? For the boy, you'll recall, "the discovery of the possibility of castration [is] . . . proved by the sight of the female genitals," while "the little girl discovers her own deficiency, from seeing a male genital" (*SE* 21:229, 233); the result is that boys disparage women, whom they regard as castrated, while girls are left with penis envy. This is the infantile form of the argument between analysts with feminist views and those who oppose them—an argument which Freud replays in *tu quoque* form ("you're afraid of castration," "no, you're castrated"). The increasing centrality of the castration complex to Freud's theory of sexual difference had found him embroiled in just such an argument. Karen Horney especially had noted the way in which only a hair's breadth separates the boy's view of the girl from psychoanalytic theory about feminine sexuality.[4] Although in retrospect (and in the light of a Lacanian rereading) Freud can be claimed to be arguing for sexual difference as the product of a division imposed by the castration complex—arguing, that is, from the symbolic rather than the anatomical—he nonetheless poses the discovery of sexual difference as a specular one ("the *sight* of the female genitals," "from *seeing* a male genital"). The sight here might be suspected of serving as a screen for a "site" of a different kind; that is, the site of a sexual difference which is unrepresentable because undecidable. In other words, the point on which Freud professes to be undecided has been settled by recourse to representation.

In his 1925 essay, "Some Psychical Consequences of the Anatomical Distinction between the Sexes," Freud offers an earlier and clearer statement of the process of perception which leads to the child's "theory" of castration. Here for the first time he explicitly addresses the notion that the Oedipus and castration complexes are not merely symmetrical for boys and girls; where for a boy the castration complex resolves the Oedipus complex (under the threat of castration, he ceases to desire his mother), for the girl it initiates the Oedipus complex by paving the way for the transferral of her affections from mother to father (seeing the mother's inferiority and blaming her for her own lack, she achieves a heterosexual love object). According to the story Freud tells, the boy, on first catching sight of a girl's genitals, "begins by showing irresolution and lack of interest; *he sees nothing or disavows what he has seen*, he softens it down or looks about for expedients for bringing it into line with his expectations" (*SE* 19:252; my italics). As Laplanche suggests, there is a telling ambiguity here; the boy at once sees nothing (can't see) and sees that there is nothing there (*"ne rien voir et voir rien, voir qu'il n'y a rien"*).[5] Since it is impossible not to see, not seeing leads to the conclusion that there's nothing to be seen. Only retrospectively, under the influence of castration anxiety, does the boy's irresolution become a decisive seeing, "arous[ing] a terrible storm of emotion in him" (*SE* 19:252) as he perceives the apparent reality of the threat of castration for himself. From this follow the dual or separate reactions, "horror of the mutilated creature or triumphant contempt for her," which later determines his relations to women. But when it comes to the girl, Freud's account differs in one important respect. Whereas for the boy it takes *"Nachträglichkeit"* or deferred action to give absence its traumatic meaning, in her case the sight of the boy's penis, "strikingly visible and of large proportions," at once forces her to recognize its superiority to her own clitoris and makes her fall prey to penis envy. Seeing something instead of nothing, she moves immediately from sight to decision, from representation to a theory about her own sexual inferiority: "She makes her judgement and her decision in a flash. She has seen it and knows that she is without it and wants to have it" (*SE* 19:252).[6] One might say that whereas seeing leads the girl to castration anxiety, castration anxiety leads the boy to see; that the ability to see sexual difference as a threatening sight is his defense against an original undecidability. To see something is better than seeing nothing, especially when it mirrors (even in a mutilated form) himself.

Apropos of the genesis of this infantile sexual theory, Laplanche alludes to a moment in the formulation of any theory which is characterized by its exceeding of the merely empirical and by its retrospectiveness—"the moment when theory is embodied [*prend corps*], when hesitations are suppressed and past steps are illuminated: the moment of 'so that was it!'" (*"c'était donc ça"*).[7] Or, the moment when indecision gives way to theory coincides with its embodiment. Though for the boy it is the girl who embodies his theory, he sees himself completed in her. It is also a narcissistic moment, then. The girl's lack is his gain, replacing a principle of difference with an economy of the same, thereby conserving the very thing he fears to lose. The form taken by his theory of castration obviously works to his advantage, since it reassures him that his own penis is still intact. But to whose advantage, theoretically speaking, does the castration complex work, and particularly (since it is most troubling of all to feminists) to whose advantage does the notion of penis envy work? An *ad hominem* feminist argument would at once reply: to Freud's advantage, of course; less reductively, one might say that it works to the advantage of what Sarah Kofman calls "the Freudian fiction."[8] The boy's original inability to decide exactly parallels Freud's initial claim that the use of psychoanalysis can lead to no decision between feminist analysts and their opponents, while the boy's later mutilation theory parallels Freud's own lapse into the decided view that women's assymmetrical passage through the Oedipus and castration complexes leaves them not only psychically scarred ("she develops, like a scar, a sense of inferiority") but actually inferior with regard to socialization and the formation of the superego ("We must not allow ourselves to be deflected from such conclusions by the denials of the feminists, who are anxious to force us to regard the two sexes as completely equal in position and worth" (*SE* 19:253, 258).[9] Penis envy can be seen as the defensive fiction which not only manages castration anxiety, but also sustains Freudian theory. An *"idée fixe"* designed to stabilize an original undecidability, the story of penis envy—by projecting the boy's threatened loss or "cut" onto the girl's scarred psyche—plays the same role as the Medusa's head which at once represents castration and provides a reassurance against it.[10] As penis envy insures the boy against lack (he has what she wants), it allows Freudian theory to become complete by projecting its own incompleteness on woman, thus solving "the enigma of woman" (*SE* 22:131) at her expense. It's surely no accident, therefore, that Freud's summarizing lecture "On Feminity" (1932) concludes in a decidedly ambiguous fashion: "That is all I had to say to you about femininity. It [theory? femininity?] is certainly incomplete and fragmentary and does not always sound friendly" (*SE* 22:135). No indeed.

"The Taboo of Virginity"

This brings me to "The Taboo of Virginity." Read in the light of Freud's account of the child's momentous discovery of sexual difference, his 1917 essay becomes an exemplary text. Its deployment of the Judith and Holofernes story, in particular, allows one to see not so much the archetype of penis envy Freud intended, as the double movement of menace and reassurance inherent in the notion of penis envy. The essay starts from the apparent contradiction between the high premium put on virginity in so-called civilized society and the taboo of virginity which leads primitive societies to institute elaborate prohibitions and defloration rituals. Of the reasons adduced by Freud to explain this taboo—the horror of shedding blood which connects defloration and menstruation, for instance, or a more generalized, lurking anxiety attending "threshold" situations such as the first act of sexual intercourse—only one is pursued with any interest. The fear of "something not understood or uncanny" may attach itself, he suggests, to sexual life as a whole, taking form as a "generalized dread of woman," perhaps "based on the fact that woman is different from man, for ever incomprehensible and mysterious, strange and therefore apparently hostile. The man is afraid of being weakened by the woman, infected with her femininity and of then showing himself incapable" (*SE* 11:198–99). Faced with sexual differences, the man sees it as unfriendly to his own narcissistically conceived identity; femininity is dangerous because, by "infecting" him, it might erase the distinction which buttresses his idea of masculinity. This is what Freud aptly calls the "narcissism of minor differences," a narcissism which he traces back to the influence of the castration complex. So far so good. But at this point the essay takes a strange tack. Freud has still not been able to account to his own satisfaction for the menace which apparently attends the first sexual encounter with a woman. In order to do so he introduces the notion of penis envy. Before elaborating its bearing on the taboo of virginity, however, he points out that primitive man doesn't distinguish between actual and psychic danger, "real" and imaginary threats to his integrity, but is simply "accustomed to project his own internal impulses of hostility on to the external world" (SE 11:200). The essay's procedure is the more bizarre because this distinction falls into abeyance for Freud himself. Having attributed the dread of woman to projected hostility, he produces penis envy to account for "a correctly sensed, although psychical, danger" (SE 11:201); having distinguished between a danger that really exists and "psychical" danger, he proposes the startling idea that women actually do pose a threat to men after sexual intercourse, and especially on the first occasion. For Freud himself, it seems, the projected danger is as real as for primitive man.[11]

The story of Judith and Holofernes is Freud's way of "realizing" this danger. Karen Horney, in her 1932 essay, "The Dread of Woman," astutely ventriloquizes the process: "'It is not,' he [the man] says, 'that I dread her; it is that she herself is malignant, capable of any crime, a beast of prey, a vampire, a witch, insatiable in her desires. She is the very personification of what is sinister.'" Alluding to Freud's essay, Horney implicated Freud himself: he too "objectifies this anxiety, contenting himself with a reference to the castration-impulses that actually do occur in women."[12] Characteristic of male efforts to disavow their dread, Horney continues, are the "objectifications" of artistic and scientific work. This is the role played by the Judith story in "The Taboo of Virginity," where "art" colludes with "science" in the guise of interpretation. Though Freud goes through the motions of searching elsewhere for the causes of female hostility toward men as a result of defloration (pain, narcissistic injury, disappointment, frigidity—a dismal litany), he fastens finally on the girl's desire to possess the penis. Citing the dream of a young woman whose unconscious wish was "to castrate her young husband and to keep his penis for herself" (SE 11:205), he invokes literature to back up his interpretation. Friedrich Hebbel's tragedy, Judith (1840), differs significantly from its apocryphal source in a number of ways. Judith is not only a widow, but a virgin whose first husband "was paralyzed on the bridal night by a mysterious anxiety"; she beheads

Holofernes after being raped by him instead of being able "to boast after her return that she has not been defiled" as she does in the Bible; and above all, the displacement of patriotic and religious motives by the sexual motive is central to her tragedy as Hebbel sees it (*SE* 11:207). For Freud, Hebbel's revision of the apocryphal narrative parallels his own reading of the young woman's dream: "with the fine perception of a poet, he sensed the ancient motive, which had been lost in the tendentious narrative, and has merely restored its earlier content to the material." By a reversal common in Freud's appeal to literature, it is not the Bible which provides the archetype—not "life," so to speak—but the psychoanalytic theory which always pre-cedes it and which literature embodies: "Judith is accordingly the woman who castrates the man who has deflowered her, which was just the wish of the newly-married woman ex-pressed in the dream I reported" (*SE* 11:207).

If the embodiment of theory involves the suppres-sion of hesitation, representation by the same token, could be said to involve the repression of difference.[13] A feminist read-ing of *Judith* might set out to undo that repression. For Sarah Kofman, whose *Quatre romans analytiques* remains among the most telling indictments of Freud's violence against literature, the deformations, mutilations, and disfigurements of the analy-tic method put an end to the indecision of the literary text by substituting a univocal meaning.[14] Her rereading of *Judith* in the light of Freud's own categories explains the source of its "power" for him, that of "condens[ing] in a single work the different motifs which [he] exposes in the form of detached and fragmentary pieces."[15] Literature makes theory whole, reflect-ing back a pleasing image of its own completion. Within the play, the casualty of this process is Judith, who must become (according to Freud's reading) mutilated and incomplete, only able to love herself in the man who completes her; or in the child, the penis substitute which the tragic irony of Hebbel's play leads her finally not to desire. In elaborating the Freudian reading which Freud's own partial and allusive account of the play omits, Kofman also rights the balance by restoring to it Holofernes' role. If Judith plays out Freud's explanation for the taboo of virginity, Holofernes plays out the castration anxiety which is the complement of her penis envy. Kofman's aim, however, is not simply to restore a text which Freud mutilates in his desire to make literature corroborate analytic "truth"; rather, it is to reveal the complicity of literature in sustaining Freud's version of the truth. *Judith,* she concludes at the end of her own reading, derives its power as a representation from allowing the spectator to come to terms with his fantasms of castration; moreover,

> If literature can, after reductive treatment, seem to bend itself to an analytic reading, isn't it because Freud's conceptions, here, for example, his conceptions of women, reinforce those of the literature he exploits?—an adequation between the literary and the analytic which, far from being an index of truth, is only that of the impress on both of the same cultural and ideological tradition, of the identity of prejudices whose constraining force imposes itself like that of the truth.[16]

Her conclusion provides the starting point for a different reading—one which not simply exposes the collusion of literature and psychoanalysis in calling their "identity of prejudices" the truth, but also brings to light the repressed indecision whose presence serves to call this ideology in question. What if, instead of reading *Judith* univocally, one read it, so to speak, as a knife that cuts both ways?

Hebbel himself had approached the biblical narrative with repugnance; he not only sexualized it, as Freud observes, but depoliticized it. The original Judith, he wrote, "was nothing more than a Charlotte Corday, a fanatic cunning monster" (*"ein fanatisch-listiges Ungeheuer"*; interestingly, a contemporary witness had called Charlotte Corday "this modern Judith").[17] The triumph of morality and innocence over force gives way to a psychomachia of a different kind. Instead of being a national and religious heroine, Judith kills to avenge her rape; but the man she kills is the man whom she has desired—desired because she cannot be him. Hebbel claimed to have created in *Judith* a play that harshly opposed the emancipation of women, and her overstepping of the limits of womanhood is designed to parallel Holofernes' overstepping of the limits of mortal power.[18] In Judith herself one sees, according to Hebbel, "the *deed* of a woman, i.e., the strongest contrast, this wanting and not being able to, this doing which is yet no action."[19] Hebbel wrote of this, his first tragedy, that "were it nothing, then I myself would be nothing"; and later, *Judith* "paralyzes my inner self."[20] Projecting his artistic uncertainties onto Judith, he simultaneously experiences the paralyzing anxiety of her husband Manasses on his wedding night.

The play must mirror back Hebbel's wholeness—his potency—or unman him. If impotence is what it reveals ("this doing which is yet no action"), then, like Manasses, or like Holofernes in dread of his mother—"The mirror of his impotence of yesterday and tomorrow!"[21]—Hebbel himself would be "a mistake": "Myself depends upon my poetry; if the latter is a mistake, then I am one myself."[22] The word used by Hebbel ("*Irrthum*" or "error") suggests the boy's panic and denial before the perception that woman lacks a penis as Freud ventriloquizes it in his essay "Fetishism" (1927): "No, that could not be true: for if a woman had been castrated, then his own possession of a penis was in danger" (*SE* 21:153). In order not to be a paralyzing threat, Judith must have phallic attributes, like the phallic woman fantasized by the boy as a defense against castration anxiety. Instead of being mutilated by a cut, woman has a sword in her hand; the mark of castration is replaced by the castrating instrument. In the imagery of *Judith*, sword and woman are closely identified. When Judith's weak-spirited lover, Ephraim, comes to urge his suit by emphasizing the threat posed by the beseiging Holofernes, he holds up a knife with which he intends to commit suicide if she refuses him: "Do you see this knife?" he asks; and she replies, taking it, "It's so shiny, I can see myself reflected in it" (p. 50). What she sees is her image made whole in the desire of another, the fantasized phallic woman whom the boy invents to reassure himself at the moment of doubt.

Judith is all reflections, all eyes. Soon after this incident, Judith imagines Holofernes to herself as a "face which is all eyes"; confronting her image in the mirror, she sees it consumed by his eyes ("Holofernes, all this is yours"). When Holofernes sees Judith, he says: "One becomes what one sees," and adds, "we received eyes so that we could swallow [the world] piecemeal!"[23] Becoming what one sees or incorporating what one sees: two ostensibly distinct yet closely linked ways of viewing one's relation to the world (world as self, self as world). This is the oscillation which marks the positioning of Judith and Holofernes in relation to each other. The reciprocity of their mutual gaze merely installs them, with fatal results, in the eye of the other's desire. What Judith sees is man-with-sword; the man she'd like to be ("When you see a man, don't you feel as though you were seeing what you'd like to be . . . ?" p. 55). What Holofernes sees is his own phallus, his own desire, mirrored in Judith. But the image is split—or rather, in mirroring the onlooker's identity, the image divides it. Judith prophecies of Holofernes' possession of her body: "tremble when you have it; I shall leap out of myself, like a sword out of a sheath, when you least expect it" (p. 54). Holofernes, imagining the fulfillment of his desire in the same imagery, turns the sword against its wielder:

> When I was a young man and encountered an enemy, I'd sometimes wrestle with him until I had his sword and would then slay him with it instead of drawing my own. That's how I'd like to slay her. She's to dissolve before me because of her own feeling, because of the faithlessness of her senses! (p. 78)

Slain by her own desire, Judith is to be Holofernes self-ravished. Earlier, Holofernes has dreamed of a threatened assassination, waking to find himself in the act of stabbing, not his assassin, but his own chest. The self-inflicted wound foretells the self-destruction of his relation to Judith; she is his cutting edge, and therefore irresistible, but so, by the same token, is he the sword in which she sees herself. Rape and decapitation, then, are the mirror image of each other in Hebbel's design. Freud's famous equation in "Medusa's Head" (1922), "To decapitate = to castrate" (*SE* 18:273) is reformulated by the play to read: "To rape = to be castrated" and "To castrate = to be raped."[24] Seeking to complete themselves in the other (Holofernes tells Judith, "I am destined to inflict wounds; you, to heal them," p. 74), each finds only a prior psychic division or "wound."

  Demanding restitution for "the destruction [she] experienced in his arms," Judith looks back to her virginity, after the rape, in a passage which must have confirmed Freud's association of the play with the taboo of virginity:

> A Virgin is a foolish creature who even trembles with fear before her own dreams because a dream can mortally wound her, and still, she lives in hopes of not always remaining a virgin. There is no greater moment for a virgin than the one when she stops being a virgin, and every sensation of her blood which she tried to fight, every sigh she choked back enhances the value of the sacrifice she has to make at that moment. (p. 86)

But the passage reveals what Freud's account represses, that the threat to the integrity of the self—to "virginity"—is always ("already") there. To be destroyed by Holofernes is on one level to admit the image of another, to submit to the desire of the other. But on another level, it is merely to experience a preexisting inner division as externally imposed. The shiny knife in which Judith first sees herself reflected recurs at the end of the play as "something shiny" which "struck [her] eye" at the moment of the rape itself. Possession of Holofernes' sword holds the promise of an illusory wholeness—"My fainting thoughts clung to that sword, and, if, in my humiliation, I've lost the right to live, I'll fight to regain that right with that very sword!" (p. 86)—and it is in the grip of this illusion that Judith beheads Holofernes.

The parallelism of the play's design makes it inevitable that she is as unable as Holofernes to fulfill her desire and reunify the divided self-image by the severed head. Since the cut preexists the sword, since the cut is what brings the sword into being in the first place, the sword can never put the head back on the body. The fantasy of a wound in the other which would restore one's own wholeness exactly parallels the structure of the boy's castration complex and the role of penis envy in Freud's theory of female sexuality. Hebbel's play uncovers this structure to reveal the split within the subject, the division within sexuality, which ideology—the "identity of prejudices" in literature and psychoanalysis—attempts to conceal under the cloak of wholeness and "truth." *Judith* allows us to see what Freud himself is blind to, or obscures, in "The Taboo of Virginity"; namely, that the phallus is an arbitrary and divisive mark around which sexuality is constructed.[25] To put it another way, it is not the possession of the phallus which brings the castration complex into being, but the castration complex which privileges the phallus. That the sword (the instrument of castration) can occupy the place of the cut (the mark of castration) returns us to the stick with two ends, or, if you like, the knife that cuts both ways—to the oscillation of meaning or "irresolution" which both Freudian theory and the little boy must repress in order to make sense of what they see.

The Phallic Woman

Hebbel records that the sight in Munich of a painting of Judith holding Holofernes' head was the starting point for his play; the theme of Judith, he writes, imposed itself on him of its own accord. This original picture by Giulio Romano (now reattributed to Domenichino) was later displaced by another.[26] Four years after writing his play, in Paris, he saw Horace Vernet's painting of Judith *en déshabille*, about to behead the sleeping and clearly postcoital Holofernes: "I remained a long time before the picture. If I could be French and Horace Vernet German, that would be something to look into; he has expressed in his picture the same motives that I set in action in the tragedy."[27] Hebbel had apparently known Vernet's painting previously in reproduction; strikingly, however, the image which first imposed itself on him has given way to another which seems to objectify the motives of his play (figure 4). A French art historian has pointed to its paradoxical role: "what we have taken for the putting into an image of a discourse has functioned here like the first image, the significant image, calling into being a reading—several readings—of which none exhausts it and all teach us something."[28] The picture, itself a "reading" or interpretation of the apocryphal narrative, gives rise in turn to still other readings by which it is interpreted. The image has a prehistory, and yet it can only tell its story by being installed in the narratives which reread it. Moreover, its inter-

Figure 4. Horace Vernet, *Judith and Holofernes* (1831):
Pau, Musée des Beaux Arts.

pretability depends on the onlooker's insertion into the same narrative. For Freud, this was the narrative—the theoretical construct—which he himself had brought to bear on Hebbel's play, just as for the boy his sight of the woman's genitals could only make sense in the light of his theory of castration. In other words, there can be no such thing as "innocent" seeing, only one that is already structured, already symbolic (as the boy's sight of sexual difference comes to be structured), or one that is not seeing at all (like the boy's initial sighting). What makes the image "significant"—what gives it the status of an objective truth—is not its visibility, but its legibility.

Hebbel may well have known the most memorable "reading" of Vernet's now largely forgotten painting, Heine's contemporary account of 1831. Heine's is just such an interpretative narrative, the story of a boudoire *crime passionelle* in which woman's voluptousness and man's abandonment to pleasure coexist with purity on one hand, and death on the other:

> The most outstanding picture of those exhibited [writes Heine] was a Judith on the point of killing Holofernes. A slender, blooming young girl has just risen from his very bed. A violet gown, knotted in haste about her hips, falls to her feet; above the hips she wears an undergarment of pale yellow whose sleeve falls off her right shoulder and which she pushes up over her left hand rather in the manner of a butcher, and yet at the same time with magical elegance, since with her right hand she has already drawn the curved sword destined for the sleeping Holofernes. She stands there, a charming figure, scarcely emerged from virginity, totally pure in the face of God and yet sullied by contact with the world, like a profaned Host. Her head is wonderfully elegant and uncannily amiable; black locks, like short snakes, not merely flutter down, but rather rear up with awful grace. Her face is partly in shadow, and a gentle savagery, a sombre softness, and a sentimental grimness permeate the noble features of the deadly beauty. In her eyes above all sparkles a sweet cruelty and the desire for vengeance; for she has her own violated body to avenge on the odious pagan. In fact, the latter is not particularly attractive but seems at bottom to be a *bon enfant*. He sleeps so at ease with the world in the after-

glow of his bliss; he snores, perhaps, or, as Luise says, he sleeps noisily; his lips are parted as if still in the act of kissing; he lay just a moment ago in the lap of happiness, or perhaps also happiness was lying in his lap; and drunk with happiness and certainly with wine too, without the interlude of anxiety and illness, Death sends him by the hand of a most beautiful angel into the white night of eternal oblivion. What an enviable end! If I should die one day, ye Gods, let me die like Holofernes![29]

This is as highly colored a reading as one could wish for, at once sentimental, sententious, and satiric. It is also an unwitting precursor of Freud's essay on the Medusa's head. Heine's Judith is the castrating woman—the virgin bearing the emblem of the mother's genitals—whose beauty brings with it contradictory associations of dread. Not desire, but she, becomes deadly. The displaced emphasis on Judith's head, and above all on her hair, signals the identification; its uncanny amiability is the uncanniness of something that has been repressed, a sight too terrible to tell. As Freud puts it, elaborating his equation ("To decapitate = to castrate"), "The terror of Medusa is . . . a terror of castration that is linked to the sight of something" (*SE* 18:273). But the "black locks, like short snakes" which seem to "rear up with awful grace" (not, incidentally, a particulaly accurate description of the coiffure Vernet gives his Judith) have another function in representations of the Medusa's head. Invoking "the technical rule according to which a multiplication of penis symbols signifies castration," Freud argues that the serpents which surround the Medusa's head serve to mitigate its horror by replacing and multiplying the penis whose very absence is the cause of the horror. There should be no surprise in finding that if Judith has become the castrating mother to Holofernes' blissfully sleeping *bon enfant* (in French in the German text), Holofernes himself has been lapped in protective happiness ("*Glück*"). A lucky boy, he doesn't know what's coming to him. It is as if Heine wishes on him the serenity which would come from the absence of castration anxiety—eternal oblivion from all that is envisioned by his reading of Vernet's picture.

Heine's wishful reading demonstrates the reversal by which images of castration can become images of reassurance against the very castration they represent. Even the most psychologically dramatic of the many depictions of the Judith and Holofernes story, Caravaggio's famous painting, contains the telltale multiplication of penis symbols in the gushing of scarlet blood that seems to create an image of the sword in motion as it slices through Holofernes' neck (figure 5). Here the drooping swag of crimson drapery above Holofernes' head, echoed in the diagonal drapery of Judith's skirt as it falls from her bodice, poses the riddle to which the sword is the answer. As in Vernet's painting, where the curve of the sword echoes the curving slash in the garment knotted round Judith's hips, the fetishistic sword both is and is not there, like the phallus. Caravaggio's painting also renders explicit the doubling of virgin and mother which we find in Heine's account of the Vernet painting. Judith's servant, obscenely aged and ferociously intent, displaces from the severely resolute and purified image of Judith herself all that Renaissance and seventeenth-century representations of a religious heroine could not admit.

Figure 5. Michelangelo Caravaggio, *Judith and Holofernes* (1599): Rome, Galleria Nazionale d'Arte Antica.

The psychological drama—Holofernes is the obverse of Heine's and Vernet's sleeping child in his vivid last moment of con- sciousness—is displaced from one head to another; the old woman's grimace, not Judith's severe composure, is what Holo- fernes "sees" as his eyes roll upward to the gaping swathe of drapery. The grotesque old woman's skull, her hair bound back in a cloth, points by contrast to the hairy encirclement of Holo- fernes' upturned head and the gaping wound already cut in his neck.[30] The figure of the old woman here is like the mother who hovers on the margin of Hebbel's drama. His Judith, poised between sexual innocence and sexual knowledge, is a virgin because Manasses was prevented from approaching her on their wedding night "as though the black earth had stretched forth a hand and seized him from below." What comes between them is "something strange and terrifying," "something dark and unknown" ("*etwas Fremdes und Ent- setzliches," "etwas Dunkles und Unbekanntes,*" pp. 47, 48); mean- while Manasses' mother whispers accusingly from her corner. Later it is Holofernes' mother in whom the son sees "a ghost . . . which brings him visions of old age and death and makes his own form, his flesh and blood, abhorrent to himself" ("My mother! I'd have as little desire to see her as to see my grave!", p. 71). The mother reminds Holofernes of being a little child again, as she reminds Heine of sleeping like a *bon enfant;* and with the thought of weakness comes the thought of death, the third form taken by the three mothers of Freud's "The Theme of the Three Caskets" (1913), "the Mother Earth who receives him once more" (*SE* 12:301).[31] Worst of all, to be unmanned means not simply to be impotent, childish, or dead; it means becom- ing like a woman.

If representations of castration can serve to protect the viewer against castration anxiety, it might by the same token be said that representations of the phallic woman protect the viewer against doubts about his masculinity. Making her like a man conserves the small boy's narcissism, his belief in the universal possession of the phallus. One might expect, there- fore, to find powerful representations of the phallic woman arising in the context of feminization. An obvious example comes to mind: Donatello's statue of Judith and Holofernes (fig-

ure 6). Freud claims that "The sight of Medusa's head makes
the spectator stiff with terror, turns him to stone"; and because
"becoming stiff means an erection," the image once more contains reassurance as well as horror (*SE* 18:273). One recalls
Hebbel's remark that his *Judith* "paralyzes" his inner self, and
the comment in his diary: "My Judith is paralyzed by her deed;
she is petrified [*erstarrt*, stiffens, becomes rigid] at the possibility that she might bear the son of Holofernes."[32] Becoming phallic, Judith embodies a fantasized creative potency. If
artistic anxieties can be figured as consoling petrification,
then Donatello's statue, not only designed as an interlocking,
columnlike form but erected on a tall column, may have served
just such a consoling function for its creator; indeed, Donatello
is on record as having been so delighted with it that he inscribed it (as he had not done with other works) *"Donatelli
opus."*[33] The most *ad hominem* reading of all would presumably
be to see the group as a companion piece to Donatello's David—
as a narcissistically invested, fetishistic "erection"; that is,
equating the feminized Holofernes with the markedly androgynous David, and associating the phallic Judith with
Donatello's supposed homosexuality.[34]

A less reductive "psychoanalytic" reading, however,
might install the statue in another narrative, seeing in it not a
medieval psychomachia involving the triumph of *Humilitas* or
Sanctimonia over *Superbia* or *Luxuria* (as Donatello's contempo-
raries may have done); nor a political allegory relating to the
Florentine Republic (as did those still close to his own times);
nor a Renaissance Christianizing of pagan forms and motifs (as
is the wont of contemporary art historians);[35] but seeing it
rather as a narrative of representation itself—that is, as an instance of the power of representation to structure, and hence
allay, the anxieties attending indeterminacy. Donatello's group
(it has been called "Janus-like") faces every which way; it may
in fact be the first without a fixed frontal viewpoint.[36] The
dynamic movement is not that of the figures themselves, but
that of the gaze that circles them, looking for a point on which
to fix. This point is provided by Judith's ritually upraised
sword, which, visible from all sides, seems frozen—"petrified,"
as it were—while Holofernes dissolves beneath her, his body, as

Figure 6. Donatello, *Judith and Holofernes* (c. 1455):
Florence, Piazza della Signoria.

one contemporary observer put it, "exhibit[ing] the effect of wine and sleep, with death in his cold and drooping limbs."[37] If Judith's sword were ever to descend, it would describe an arc that cut through Holofernes' neck to the point defined by her sash as it rises up to meet it; and as his forever to-be-severed head is positioned in the angle of her thighs, so she stands between his parted thighs, providing an upright counterthrust to his drooping limbs and the detumescent cushion from whose corners water was designed to flow. At once column and fountain, the statue stems the flow by fixing Judith fetishistically at the very midpoint of the design[38]—the point where uncertainty would otherwise set in.

Granted that it is not so much the unconscious of the artist we see at work here as the unconscious of representation, there can be no *ad feminam* interpretation of another famous, not to say notorious, Judith and Holofernes, this time created by a woman (figure 7). Artemisia Gentileschi's painting comes to us already installed in her own sensational and lamentable story, that of "repeated rape" by her art teacher when she was allegedly still only fifteen, and of her torture by means of the thumbscrew at his trial.[39] Ironically, a biographical interpretation would make her bloody and businesslike decapitation scene a confirmation of Freud's theory of the role of penis envy in giving rise to the taboo of virginity. Like Vernet's and Hebbel's Judith, she would be avenging in her own fashion the violence done to her body. But—leaving aside the question of who commissioned the picture and of the subject's popularity in Caravaggesque circles—there is another way to look at it; the way in which the girl looks at what the boy sees (or rather, comes to see) and adopts his view of the matter. Although for Freud the boy, seeing nothing, arrives at a theory, the girl, seeing something, is confronted by so-called fact. Perception follows from theory in his case, but in hers perception makes her jump to conclusions. Her refusal to accept them leads to penis envy. As Freud puts it in "Female Sexuality," "She acknowledges the *fact* of her castration, and with it, too, the superiority of the male and her own inferiority; but she rebels against this unwelcome state of affairs" (*SE* 21:229; my italics).[40]

Figure 7. Artemisia Gentileschi, *Judith Beheading Holofernes* (c. 1615–1620) Florence, Galleria della Uffizi.

Although one might argue that the girl's castration has psychic rather than actual reality for her ("the wound to her narcissism" that is "like a scar," *SE* 19:253), Freud's story skips over a decisive step, the girl's adoption of the boy's fiction as a matter of fact. Now, up until this point I've spoken of the viewer as "he." What difference would it make if the viewer was "she"? None at all; for what other "way of seeing" has she than to see through his eyes, since his are the terms of representation itself? In order to see herself, or be seen, she has to insert herself into a preexisting narrative. This is surely the moment to take up the implications of Kofman's comment about "the identity of prejudices" in the literary and psychoanalytic text which impose themselves as "truth." If femininity, psychoanalytically speaking, is constructed in relation to a representation, then we are dealing not with a truth, still less with an essence, but precisely that—with a representation; or rather, with the set of representations which imposes itself as reality. Gentileschi's picture is significant not for representing decapitation from a feminine, still less a feminist, viewpoint (where castration is concerned there can be no other view than the boy's), but for its reinscription of the violent fiction; the violence of fiction itself.

This reinscription can be seen by comparing two accounts—two "readings"—of Gentileschi's picture, one by a man, one by a woman; one scholarly and ostensibly neutral, the other avowedly feminist and polemical. Alfred Moir, historian of the Italian followers of Caravaggio, has this to say of a "violence" and "sensationalism" which he sees as surpassing those of Caravaggio's original:

> Artemisia's figures form a more compact group, in a semicircle; the arms of the two women radiate from Holofernes' head like spokes from the hub of a wheel. . . . Focus is concentrated on his head; the blood spurts out and flows down; and almost everything else in the painting, not only Holofernes' torso and the two women, but even the heavy velvet coverlet, seems to be bursting out from the center. The light, from a source beyond the left frame of the painting, throws Holofernes' head into shadow but picks out the drapery, the arms of all three figures, and the faces of the two women. . . . the whole effect of the painting is horrifyingly dramatic.[41]

And here is Germaine Greer in her study of women painters:

> The painting depicts an atrocity, the murder of a naked man
> in his bed by two young women. They could be two female
> cut-throats, a prostitute and her maid slaughtering her client
> whose up-turned face has not had time to register the change
> from lust to fear. The strong diagonals of the composition all
> lead to the focal point, the sword blade hacking at the man's
> neck from which gouts of blood spray out, mimicking the
> lines of the strong arms that hold him down, even as far as the
> rose-white bosom of the murderess.[42]

Moir's horrifying drama becomes Greer's lurid bordello melodrama; as her caption has it, "The apocryphal Jewish heroine
had been depicted in many ways but never as a brutal, cold-
blooded killer."

Once again, a representation has given rise to the
story that stabilizes its ambiguous meanings. Glossing the violent sensationalism seen by Moir, Greer's account of the painting becomes sensational itself; her women are cut-throat
prostitutes, her Judith "the murderess." Oddly, neither Moir
nor Greer mentions Holofernes' strangely foreshortened,
thighlike arms, and the ambiguity which results from this incomplete displacement from genitals to head.[43] Instead, the
two accounts are structured by a reciprocal dynamic, each mirroring the other. For Moir, the arms of the two women "radiate
like spokes" from Holofernes' head; it is on this "hub" that
"focus is concentrated," yet the movement is centrifugal ("the
blood spurts out and flows down . . . everything . . . seems to
be bursting out from the center"). But the center itself is not
light, but dark, as if marked by the horror of absence. What is
absent?—the sword, of course, which constitutes for Greer the
focal point emphasized by the "strong diagonals" ("The strong
diagonals of the composition all lead to the focal point, the
sword hacking at the man's neck"). The field of force surrounds
a site marked for Moir by absence and for Greer by a sword. If
in one account the eye moves away from the center, in the other
the act of looking returns to it and then rebounds on the
woman herself, like the accusing gouts of blood that "spray out
. . . even as far as [her] rose-white bosom." As Greer's account
parodies Moir's, and Gentileschi's picture "imitates" Caravag-

gio's, the paired readings and paintings mimic (like the blood "mimicking" the lines of the arms) Freud's fiction of the boy and the girl confronted by the absence and presence of what comes to mean for each, at once the same and unequally, the "fact" of castration.

I began with a footnote, and I want to end with a biographical pendant to this castration story. Freud's "The Taboo of Virginity" has referred in passing to "the woman's hostile bitterness against the man . . . which is clearly indicated in the strivings and in the literary productions of 'emancipated' women" (SE 11:205). When, in 1919, he sent his essay to Lou Andreas-Salomé—just such an emancipated woman—she responded with a Bachofen-derived speculation that the taboo might have been intensified "by the fact that at one time (in a matriarchal society) the woman may have been the dominant partner. In this way, like the defeated deities, she acquired demonic properties, and was feared as an agent of retribution."[44] Diplomatically, Freud replied that he had "long had unexpressed ideas on the question of matriarchy," which he was inclined to place "in the period after the fall of the primal father . . . [when] the dominant role now fell as a matter of course upon the shoulders of the woman, who had lost her master."[45] When the talk is of matriarchy, mastery, and historical priority, one can be sure that power-relations are at stake; here, the power of psychoanalytic theory.

In the same letter to Freud, Lou Andreas-Salomé, who was in the habit of supplying him with amusing tidbits about the "slips" of her everyday life, retailed an anecdote which duly found its way into the revised edition of *The Psychopathology of Everyday Life* (1919), where it becomes an instance of the way apparent clumsiness may serve "unavowed purposes in a far from clumsy way." She used, she tells Freud, regularly to allow milk to boil over ("*überkochen*") even at a time when it was expensive and scarce; oddly, she has ceased to do so since the death of her beloved terrier, "Friend" ("*Duzhok*," in Russian)—what a good thing, she adds, "for now there would be no more use for the milk which boiled over on to the hot plate or floor—and which the terrier had had the benefit of!" With that realization "all was clear, and in addition the fact that I had been even fonder of him than I had realized."[46] (When Freud later counseled her against overinvolvement in the custody squabble and impending divorce of one of her woman patients, she apologized in terms that echo her anecdote: "I am a cold old animal that takes to few people, that is why I am so grateful to be able to boil over within psychoanalysis").[47] What connections can one make between Lou Andreas-Salomé's comment on "The Taboo of Virginity" and her story of the little dog? One might guess that she was letting some psychoanalytic milk boil over for the benefit of her dear "Friend," Freud, who laps up the overspill. But perhaps the small animal imagery also domesticates some latent sexual sparring between them—a matter of cat and dog.

Not only Lou Andreas-Salomé's transference, but Freud's countertransference, had been cemented on her arrival in his psychoanalytic circle by an evening's talk in 1913 when he told her the story of the Narcissistic Cat—a cat whose intrusion into Freud's office had begun by arousing anxiety (might it break his precious collection of antique objects?) but which won him over in time so far as to extract from him the tribute of a daily bowl of milk, and of "increasing affection and admiration." In return "the cat paid him not a bit of attention and coldly turned its green eyes with their slanting pupils toward him as toward any other object," unless roused from its "egoistic-narcissistic purring" by the "enticement of his shoe-toe."[48] For Freud, of course, it was Lou Andreas-Salomé herself who displayed "all the peaceful and playful charm of true egoism," and whose beauty made her the type of the narcissistic woman whom he elsewhere compares to a cat.[49] If she retaliated by making him her little dog, so that she had lost, not her master (as Freud speculated of the origins of matriarchy) but her pet, Freud could recuperate her into his scheme by admiring her "skill in synthesis, which knits together the *disjecta membra* won through analysis and clothes them with living tissue."[50] Unscarred by castration anxiety, the narcissistic woman, far from breaking the analyst's "*disjecta membra*," makes them whole. In discipular fashion, she tells him "how little it is really a question of the fragmentary, and how the unifying factor emerges unsought and of itself."[51]

It's all the more curious that her biographer, Rudolph Binion, should see in Lou Andreas-Salomé a bad case of the Judiths—unable to overcome her infantile father complex, experiencing its revival in middle age in relation to Freud and psychoanalysis, and, not content with taking her stand against him on the ground of narcissism itself, even setting out to "make herself master" there in his stead; her "regression" is definitively signaled by the writing of an essay boldly entitled "What Follows from It Not Having Been the Woman Who Slew the Father" (1927).[52] For Binion, all this amounts to penis envy and a futile assertion of women's immunity from castration anxiety which only serves to prove his point. Binion's narrative of Lou and Freud reenacts the hazardous relations of Judith and Holofernes, as each sees in the other what s/he desires. I won't attempt to adjudicate. But at the risk of seeming overly discipular myself, I want to let Lou Andreas-Salomé have the last word in the controversy between analysts with feminist views and their opponents with which I began. Here is an entry from her Freud journal of 1913, endorsing "psychology's right to its own media and methods no matter what"—

> And that means to be allowed to write, with appropriate obscurity, its personal mark of X, even there where the psychic organization eludes it, instead of defecting into the alien clarity belonging to another side of existence called the "physical." It means to take seriously the principle stating that psychic and physical *stand for* each other ("represent" each other . . .) but neither *determine* nor *explain* the other and hence cannot substitute for each other.[53]

With that "personal mark of X," Lou Andreas-Salomé reinstates the "stick with two ends" of psychoanalysis—the mark at once of sexual difference and of indecidability; the "site" where something (the feminine) is hidden by what comes to stand for it.

3. *Dora* and the Pregnant Madonna

"**Now, let us remember** the pathetic moment when Dora spent two hours contemplating the Sixtine Madonna of Raphael in the museum of Dresden, a Madonna that is one of the images of beauty before which desire experiences itself in its intimate tenor of nostalgia and regret at the same time that its pain and sickness are veiled. In any case, this is not a reason for us in our turn to remain mute before it.

"Let us imagine that the stomach of the Madonna begins to inflate, to round out, advancing into the real space, and imagine the effect that this unusual miracle would produce in the one contemplating it. This helps us arrive at an idea of the strange convulsions that—every time that her discourse, and not her vain curiosity, puts her closer to the *reality* of maternity—transport the body of the hysteric and make of it, not a dispossessed body . . . but—unique condition of the hysteric— a possessed body: a body that spits, vomits, bleeds, grows fat, and symptomatizes. Of all that she understands nothing." (Moustapha Safouan, "In Praise of Hysteria")[1]

George Eliot experienced a premonition of this hysterical swelling on her arrival in Dresden in 1858. She found the Dresden art gallery "a proper climax, for all other art seems only a preparation for feeling the superiority of the Madonna di San Sisto the more." As she wrote in her journal,

> Three mornings in the week we went to the Picture Gallery from twelve till one. The first day we went was a Sunday, when there is always a crowd in the [Sistine] Madonna Cabinet. I sat down on the sofa opposite the picture for an instant; but a sort of awe, as if I were suddenly in the living presence of some glorious being, made my heart swell too much for

me to remain comfortably, and we hurried out of the room. On subsequent mornings we always came, in the last minutes of our stay, to look at this sublimest picture, and while the others . . . lost much of their first interest, this became harder and harder to leave.[2]

The swelling of George Eliot's heart (a pre-psychoanalytic age would have called it "the mother" in her) took place before an image thoroughly installed in the iconography of idealized maternity. When *"Mutter"* or *"Madonna"* (as George Eliot was known to her intimates) came face to face with the Sistine Madonna, maternal identification met its miraculous apotheosis. For Eliot as for Freud's Dora, the discourse of Christianity and that of art history would have combined to make the Sistine Madonna among the most sublimated representations of the mother in Western art. According to Freud's *Fragment of an Analysis of a Case of Hysteria* (1905), this was the painting in front of which Dora stationed herself for two hours, "rapt in silent admiration;" when Freud asked her what had pleased her so much about Raphael's picture, all she could answer was: "The Madonna" (*SE* 7:96)—as if the name was enough to explain her adoration of the only consecrated version of femininity available to her.

     Dora's phantom pregnancy, an episode recounted elsewhere in Freud's narrative, is a reminder that in the discourse of psychoanalysis to which hysteria belongs, the invention of the mother goes hand in hand with the invention of the neurotic woman. For Foucault, the mother is simply "the most visible form" of the hystericization of women's bodies during the nineteenth century.[3] But as Julia Kristeva argues in "Héréthique de l'amour," her essay on the cult of motherhood represented by the Virgin Mary, a prior discourse had already achieved this assimilation of femininity to maternity.[4] Christian tradition in Western art sanctifies the feminine body by making it a maternal body. The imaginary inflation of the Madonna's stomach before Dora's eyes seems profane not miraculous because it reminds us that the maternal body isn't virginal after all. Raphael's original, by contrast, offers us a Madonna who is still, as it were, *virgo intacta*. The painting makes us witnesses to a celestial vision; intensely humanized, his Madonna is at the same time removed from earthly taint (figure 8). She stands

Figure 8. Raphael, *Sistine Madonna* (c. 1512–1513): Dresden, Gemäldegalerie.

on billowing clouds, disclosed by the drawing back of a green curtain whose aperture leads our eyes to the picture's focal point, the doubled, meditative, and unseeing gaze of mother and child. Two putti seem to mirror our upward gaze, raptly contemplating the vision in a heavenly looking glass. By encircling mother and child in the flowing curve of the Madonna's veil, Raphael embraces them both in a cocoon of maternal symbiosis. The child rests weightlessly along his mother's arm, seeming to draw back the garment which swathes him, as if participating in the revelation. The naturalistically naked child and the mother with her naked gaze, at once disarmed and disarming, contrast with their formally dressed attendants. Beneath and in front, the figures of Saint Sixtus (the power of the church) and Saint Barbara (the power of the secular world) serve as privileged mediators of the vision—Saint Sixtus gesturing to it in his papal regalia, Saint Barbara, with her fashionable sleeves and carefully dressed hair, averting her eyes. The triangulated structure of the picture teaches us that the Madonna and her son only reveal themselves indirectly to their earthly adorers. The church is the instructor, its saints are the witnesses. A patriarch interprets while a female saint, her eyes lowered, seems to imply that where religion is concerned, mute testimony is woman's proper sphere.[5]

The Madonna's condition as depicted by Raphael images a maternity which is God's desire, not her own. The Christian dogma of the Immaculate Conception depends on the fantasy of the Madonna's unconsciousness; one might almost call it her hystericization. She must become a maternal body unawares in order to be sanctified as the mother of God. In this sense, the Christian Madonna is a sublimated version of the hysteric. Like Dora's, her body swells of its own accord; she knows nothing about it. "Of all that she understands nothing," writes Safouan—divesting Dora herself of understanding in order to celebrate hysteria, just as the Sistine Madonna is divested of knowledge in order to celebrate the miracle of the Incarnation. When Dora falls mute before Raphael's picture, she hystericizes the Madonna's muting by Christian motherhood and the innocence of carnal knowledge which makes hers a Virgin Birth. The hysterical identification denies Dora's own sexual knowledge, an aspect of her "case" to which Freud constantly draws attention. If Dora identified with the Madonna, it was in order to represent herself as the sexual innocent which her hysteria simultaneously acted out and betrayed. Unlike the Madonna, Dora had read up on sexual reproduction—conception, pregnancy, and childbirth—and had the information at her fingertips. One of the accusations made against her was her preoccupation with sexual matters. Freud's tactic in his analysis was to get Dora not only to admit her sexual knowledge, but to give up the role of hysterical ingénue which she had adopted. Safouan's Dora may understand nothing, but her problem is "knowing too much about maternity", and it is "this *too much*"—this excess of knowledge without understanding—which for him constitutes hysteria.[6] Safouan, in other words, praises Dora for the very quality which sanctifies Raphael's Madonna; that is, for being possessed of bodily knowledge which is beyond her. Hence Dora's phantom pregnancy; a virgin birth is the only birth she can admit to.

Without Safouan's profane fantasy of a miraculous or hysterical pregnancy, how might the Sistine Madonna have looked to Dora? Speculatively, one could say that the triangular structure would have allowed her to insert herself at its focal point, imagining herself as at once purified (virgin) and narcissistically completed (mother-and-child). From the spectator's point of view, however, Dora is placed at the center of an interpretive tableau featuring a man and two women. As told by Freud, Dora's story consists of a web of shifting triangular relationships. Each triangle ostensibly involves two men and the woman whom they exchange between them. Dora's father hands Dora over to Freud for treatment; Dora's father has an affair with his friend's wife, Frau K.; Dora's father hands Dora over to Herr K. as the price of his complicity in the affair. But as Freud's unraveling of the case proceeds, another triangle comes into view, the one represented by Raphael's picture—a man and two women. The second triangle looks like this: Dora loves Herr K. only as his wife's husband; Dora purports to be jealous of her father's affair, but the real object of her adoration is Frau K.; and (more speculatively) Dora's transferential relationship to Freud conceals her relation to the missing mother. The second triangle provides a glimpse of the archaic, pre-oedipal structure which underlies the oedipal. In this triangle, the privileged term is not the all-powerful father, but the (m)Other Woman whom Dora adores. Though Freud is alert to the multiple substitutions that make up the first triangle—stumbling only when it comes to Dora's transferential relationship to him—he is blinkered when it comes to dealing with a triangle in which a man mediates the relationship between two women. Relations between women, along with the question of mother, are relegated to the realm of the homosexual or "*gynaecophilic*" (Freud's term). Behind Freud's inquiry—whom (or who) does Dora truly desire (to be), Herr K. or Frau K.?—another question slides into view, Dora's own (and perhaps ours too): what does it mean to be a woman, at once desired and desiring? Above all, what does it mean to be a mother, when mothers are the waste product of a sexual system based on the exchange of women among men? Freud's question concerns hysteria: Dora's question, aimed at the blind spot of Freud's inquiry, concerns femininity; but it also implicates the mother who is strikingly absent from Freud's account.

Freud seems to have glimpsed in Dora's arrest before the Sistine Madonna an aspect of her hysterical predicament, the idealization of the feminine body, and especially the maternal body, which is the complement to its hystericization, denigration, and denial. Freud's own account stops here, unable to deal with the submerged presence of the (m)Other Woman. As the other of the missing mother, the Sistine Madonna becomes a symptom of the repressed maternal discourse which surfaces in the sublimated discourse of Christianity. Where Freud falls silent, the other woman in the picture hints at the existence of a rival source of instruction, secular rather than religious, unsanctioned rather than sanctified, maternal rather than paternal, oral rather than written. To revert to the Sistine Madonna: if Dora, in Safouan's words, "understands nothing" (like the Madonna herself), Saint Barbara clearly knows (as the ingenuous Madonna does not) the meaning of Christian Incarnation—the meaning of the (maternal) body. Hence her combination of sophistication and reticence. What she knows is not for the telling. Saint Sixtus is the interpreting patriarch: Saint

Barbara, the woman who defies her father for the sake of her faith. Had Dora known of her martyrdom, Saint Barbara might even have provided an unexpected role model for her resistance to Freud's analysis and to the oedipal law which her "case" inscribes. The distribution of knowledge figured by Raphael's picture provides an emblem for Dora's own epistemological confusion. Caught in the oscillation of the dilemma figured by sight without insight (the Madonna's lovely, unseeing gaze), or insight without authority (Saint Barbara's averted eyes), Dora can only be a hysterical subject. By definition, she is severed from her own desire, at once seeing and not seeing (or rather, in Safouan's terms, seeing "too much"); at once knowing everything and understanding nothing. In the last resort, the triangulation imaged by Raphael's painting renders all identification with the mother problematic because it must negotiate both the Law of the Father (the Oedipus complex) and the relations between women which Freud terms "gynaecophilic." Dora's hysterical dilemma, the dilemma of access to the mother and to the maternal body, could then be refigured as an impossible choice between the Father and the (m)Other Woman.

Freud's analysis of Dora allows us to glimpse the significance of the Madonna not only for Dora herself, but for his own theoretical scheme. What part does the mother play—whether by her presence or her absence—in sustaining Freudian theory? A feminist analysis might focus especially on uncovering what this theoretical scheme screens by relegating woman-to-woman relations (relations that threaten the father's installation as the regulating term of sexual arrangements) to the realm of the "gynaecophilic." A first step would be to privilege the maternal in place of the paternal as an alternative to Freud's oedipal perspective. To stress the pre-oedipal is to reverse the hierarchy which defines the mother's role as secondary, insisting on her primacy in the prehistory of the gendered subject. A second step might be to install mother-daughter relations in place of the mother-son relations which provide the paradigm for both patriarchal Christianity (as the mother of God-the-Father, the Madonna is assimilated to paternal law) and motherhood according to Freud; based on the premise of the woman's desire for the phallus, Freudian theory makes the mother conceive her child (all the better if a boy) through desire of and for the father, compensating for her felt deficiency as a woman. In feminist theory, the bond between mother and daughter offers an alternative, becoming the model for relations between women and giving rise to the pervasive maternal metaphor in literary as well as psychoanalytic theory—matrilineality, the (m)other tongue, lost literary foremothers, the herstory of our grandmothers. But—as in the concept of a female literary tradition or feminist literary history—the term "motherhood" (like "tradition" or "history") often remains quite unexamined, either an ideological or a biological given. What part does the mother play in current feminist theory? What does she sustain, and what serve to screen? I want to indicate one direction for feminist self-inquiry by examining the "case" of Julia Kristeva.[7]

Feminist theories of the mother generally have two (overlapping) tendencies: psychosocial and psychobiological. The first tendency stresses the politics of mothering. Analysis of the representation and ideology of motherhood reveals the system it buttresses and the institutions which make mothering itself the basis of women's oppression—whether as "institution" (in Adrienne Rich's terms) or "reproduction" (in Chodorow's terms).[8] The conditions of maternity both create and emblematize the condition of women ("confinement," sexual subordination). The revaluation and social reorganization of mothering would lead (so the argument runs) to an ecologially improved, less homophobic, more nurturant and peaceloving environment (Rich) and to restructured sex roles in which women's exclusive association with mothering would cease to have its present social and psychic ill effects (Chodorow). But current feminist concern with the mother also arises from a contradictory impulse to recognize and celebrate difference. When the sociologizing tendency turns biological, motherhood is privileged as unique to women, implicating the female body and the feminine subject in primary processes, and permeating even women's writing (*écriture féminine*). From this point of view, maternity is not only a visible emblem of sexual difference but one aspect of an essentially feminine libidinal economy.

Regarded as the case in which psychoanalysis must recognize the implication of the subject in biological processes, maternity becomes either the last refuge of essentialism or else, by a more subtle psychoanalytic move, the confrontation between the subject and the species—the point where the subject emerges as such. This is the move made by Kristeva's writing about the mother, surely the most formidable literary and psychoanalytic elaboration of maternity currently available to feminists. Setting out to redress the imbalance in Freudian and Lacanian theory, Kristeva's focus is the site of the pre-oedipal, the maternal body. Her uniqueness lies in attempting to link "maternity" and "discourse"—arguing, in effect, that the discourse of maternity abuts on the origin of discourse itself. Kristeva provides the most promising avenue for attempts to destabilize the commanding position previously held by the father in psychoanalytic theories (whether Freudian or Lacanian) of the subject-in-language. I want to explore and juxtapose two influential theoretical discourses, Freud's and Kristeva's—one masculinist, the other feminist; one privileging the father, the other privileging the mother—in order to ask: what are the theoretical stakes in their respective representations of the mother? Above all, what can Kristeva tell us about Freud, and how does her attempt to theorize a discourse of maternity help us to understand why it is the mother who is missing from *Dora*?

But before turning to Kristeva, I'd like to offer a fantasy of my own. Imagine Dora confronting, not the Sistine Madonna, but Piero della Francesca's "Madonna del Parto," or "Pregnant Madonna" (figure 9). The fresco makes outrageously visible what Raphael's painting represses, the Madonna's corporeal implication in the Virgin Birth. Here the curtain is drawn aside by two angelic figures, but their gesture is repeated by the mother herself as she opens the already gaping split in her dress to show us her swelling stomach. Her lugubrious, slightly preoccupied expression is that of a woman in the early stages of labor, closer to the strenuous exertion than to the miracle of childbirth. Contained as she is within a kind of pavilion, her body (or rather her dress) becomes the pavilion which will in turn be split open. The repetition of the design

Figure 9. Piero della Francesca, *Pregnant Madonna* (c. 1460):
Monterchi, Arezzo, Capella del Cimitero.

containing her seems almost to suggest that, like a Russian doll, she will give birth only to other and smaller versions of herself—more and yet more pregnant madonnas, the last no bigger than a pip—in a parturitive *mise en abyme.* While Raphael's Madonna is an emblem of unity, mother and child enfolded by the Virgin's seamless garment, the split dress of Piero della Francesca's Pregnant Madonna creates an emblem of division. The root meaning of "parturition" comes from a verb of separation. Raphael's painting makes one out of two (mother-and-child): Piero della Francesca's design makes two out of one—figuring the condition of maternity, not as symbiosis, or as completion by divine desire, but as internal separation. To what does the mother gives birth? Surely (to vary a feminist catchphrase of the seventies) at once to herself and to an other, in a movement of differentiation imaging the movement which gives birth to meaning. To figure maternity as division is to acknowledge the process of separation which gives rise both to the subject and to language. If to imagine maternity as unity is to fantasize the possibility of wholeness, making the Madonna the guarantee of a masculine representational and sexual economy, her role in an alternative, feminist economy might be to provide an emblem of the subject's difference from itself and its division by, and in, both language and the unconscious. Superimposing the Pregnant Madonna on Raphael's Sistine Madonna swells the maternal body until it splits open to reveal, not the (Christ-man-)child but the mother as the site of an originary, constitutive splitting. In Kristevan terms, the discourse of maternity is another name for the movement of parturition which (re)produces the subject in, and of, representation.

Motherhood According to Kristeva

Kristeva's most intriguing but (in some respects) bafflingly opaque essay on the mother, "Motherhood According to Giovanni Bellini," identifies Bellini's painting as the site of a hidden maternal discourse. The tradition of pictorial representation practiced by Bellini—Christian, incipiently humanist—intersects, Kristeva argues, with a unique biographical experience which can be traced in his changing depiction of the Madonna. Her essay opens by evoking the split maternal body; or rather, the process of splitting which takes place at conception: "Cells fuse, split, and proliferate; volumes grow, tissues stretch, and body fluids change rhythm, speeding up or slowing down. Within the body, growing as a graft, indomitable, there is an other." Within the (m)other—"that simultaneously dual and alien space"—is the other; a "graft" which Christianity establishes as "a sort of subject at the point where the subject and its speech split apart, fragment, and vanish."[9] For Kristeva, the point where the subject comes into being enacts the first splitting, the first differentiation. During the mother's initial, intimate connection with the child in the pre-oedipal phase, when the body—the oral, anal, and instinctual drives—constitute a signifying process of sorts, full differentiation is yet to come; the "I" only emerges later, with the child's entry into signification and the symbolic order. In another essay, "Place Names," Kristeva draws on Winnicott's concept of the transitional object as the "potential space" or "hypothetical area that exists (but cannot exist) between the baby and the object (mother or part of mother)" to define the marginal space of the maternal body in relation to which language acquisition occurs.[10] Or, to invoke the terms of a more recent book, the mother will come to constitute an archaic pseudo-object, which Kristeva calls the "abject" (as distinct from the object), by way of the child's first attempts at separation—in Winnicott's terms "repudiation of the object as not-me"—en route for, but prior to, its constitution as a fully signifying subject. This earliest intimation of difference is mapped in the archaic language of the pre-oedipal, termed by Kristeva (to distinguish it from the symbolic order) the "semiotic." These are the maternal rhythms, melodies, and bodily movements which precede and prepare the way for the language of signification. Although the symbolic dimension of language (which Kristeva, like Lacan, associates with the paternal) works to repress the semiotic, the maternal nonetheless persists in oral and instinctual aspects of language which punctuate, evade, or disrupt the symbolic order—in prosody, intonation, puns, verbal slips, even silences; a site of meaning counter to, though inscribed within, the sym-

bolic. The pre-oedipal continues to structure the speaking subject, making itself heard in the "unconscious" of linguistic
practice.

If for Kristeva, as for Christianity, "the maternal
body is the place of a splitting," this is because the mother is
neither the subject of gestation—in command of a process prior
to the social, symbolic, and linguistic systems which create the
subject—nor is she precisely its object. To imagine the mother
as coherent and whole is to attempt to maintain the illusion of
unity, creating a "phallic mother" who defends against the
threat to identity, mastery, and stability in the face of instinctual drives which elude and precede symbolization. Placed
at the intersection of "nature" and "culture," the maternal
body becomes a filter, a thoroughfare, or a threshold that unsettles the paternal and symbolic order ("this unsettling of
the symbolic stratum, this nature/culture threshold, this instilling the subjectless biological program into the very body of
the symbolizing subject, this event called motherhood," pp.
238–42). Simultaneously traversed by paternal desire (whether
desire of, or for, the father) and impelled by "a nonsymbolic,
nonpaternal causality," the maternal body can either be imagined (like Raphael's Sistine Madonna) as a source of religious
mystification, "an impossible elsewhere, a sacred beyond, a
vessel of divinity," or, alternatively, be experienced fantas-
matically by the woman herself as a return to the body of her
own mother: "By giving birth, the woman enters into contact
with her mother; she becomes, she is her own mother; they are
the same continuity differentiating itself."

The oedipal, incestuous dimension of maternal desire has as its other face this refusal of the symbolic which
Kristeva calls "the homosexual facet of motherhood." In its
"symbolic-paternal facet," motherhood is characterized by "the
feminine, verbal scarcity so prevalent in our culture;" in its
"homosexual-maternal facet," by "a whirl of words, a complete
absence of meaning and seeing; it is feeling, displacement,
rhythm, sound, flashes, and fantasied clinging to the maternal
body" (pp. 239–40). These alternating versions of the mother—
whether the "symbolic-paternal" (the woman's desire to bear
the father's child or the masculine fantasy of hidden godhead)

or "homosexual-maternal" (the woman's fantasy of a paradisal maternal origin)—oscillate to define the space of the maternal body, enclosing the mother herself in what Kristeva, playing on the different meanings of the word, calls an *"enceinte"* or pregnant space. Elsewhere she calls this "dual and alien space," this "strange space" or nonspace "where drives hold sway," (after Plato) "a *chora,* a receptacle."[11]

Through and in her marginal space—"the strange form of split symbolization (threshold of language and instinctual drive, of the 'symbolic' and the 'semiotic') of which the act of giving birth consists"—the mother experiences her unique maternal jouissance. The threshold or meeting point of the symbolic and the semiotic, maternal jouissance can be reached (Kristeva writes) "only by virtue of a particular, discursive practice called 'art'" which requires the same powerful sublimation, the same minute, archaic, uncertain differences, the same "indwelling of the symbolic within instinctual drives" (p. 242). Outside the realm of art or what Kristeva elsewhere privileges as "poetic language," jouissance remains only an intimation, a residue within the symbolic dimension of language of the child's fantasied clinging to the maternal body. The surfacing of this repressed residue in aesthetic practice returns "the unsettled and questioned subject" to an earlier dependence on the body of the mother.

From the point of view of what Kristeva calls "social coherence" (the symbolic organization of culture), motherhood can only be understood as a defense against instinctual chaos. But from the point of view of art, motherhood according to Kristeva implicates "the other aspect of maternal jouissance, the sublimation taking place at the very moment of primal repression within the mother's body" (p. 242). In its secondary repression (the founding of signs), aesthetic practice borders on primal repression (the founding of the species). Hence the importance for Kristeva of an antifigural modernism. Maternal jouissance, she argues, can be heard or glimpsed not only in marginal aspects of literary or poetic language such as sound and rhythm, but in twentieth-century painting, where the part of the semiotic is played by color, tone, volume—by minute, nonrepresentational differences which correspond, in Kristeva's account, to the child's earliest experience of differentiation; as she writes in "Giotto's Joy," "the chromatic apparatus, like rhythm for language . . . involves a shattering of meaning and its subject into a scale of differences" (p. 221).[12] This surfacing of instinctual semiotic processes, at once prior to symbolization and sublimated within it, creates the half-heard meaning beyond signification and beyond figuration which Kristeva calls jouissance (*"j'ouis sens,"* or, "I hear meaning").

The transfer or crossing of archaic destiny into the symbolic realm creates maternal jouissance: its investigation in and by pictorial representation (which Kristeva equates with primary narcissism, or the subject's identification with the world of images) causes jouissance in the beholder. Bellini's Madonnas, Kristeva argues, "retain the traces of a marginal experience, through and across which a maternal body might recognize its own, otherwise inexpressible in our culture" (p. 243). The image of the Madonna developed in Western art, and specifically in Bellini's painting, provides access to this marginalized maternal experience—the border where sublimation takes place: "At the intersection of sign and rhythm, of representation and light, of the symbolic and the semiotic, the artist speaks from a place where she is not, where she knows not. He delineates what, in her, is a body rejoicing [*jouissant*]" (p. 242). By means of his own identifications with the mother (whether fetishistic or incestuous), the artist, Kristeva writes, lodges in his work "his own specific jouissance, thus traversing both sign and object." Her account of Western art reveals two attitudes to the maternal body, one represented by Leonardo (fetishistic in its emphasis on figurative representation), and the other by Bellini, in whose work she finds "a predominance of luminous, chromatic differences beyond and despite corporeal representation."

The eclipse of figure and fracturing of coherent images in Bellini's painting assimilate it, Kristeva argues, to the modernist aesthetic practice of Cezanne, Rothko, and Matisse. The point of departure for her reading of Bellini's "specific jouissance" is Freud's reading of Leonardo as a fetishistic artist whose homosexuality arose from precocious maternal seduction. The "humanist realism" of Leonardo's painting, with its emphasis on the body and its refinement of representational technique, contrasts in Kristeva's account with Bellini's chromatic luminousness and artistic experimentation. On one hand, "worship of the figurable, representable man"; on the other, "integration of the image . . . within the luminous serenity of the unrepresentable." Unlike Leonardo, Bellini left nothing but his paintings for the psychoanalytic reader. But for Kristeva (in conjunction with the known facts of Bellini's life) they tell a very different story. For the first five years of his life, according to Freud, Leonardo seems to have had a mother but no legitimate father. Bellini, by contrast, was a son who bore his father's name, worked in his studio, and carried on his painterly tradition. "But the mother is absent—the mother has been lost," Kristeva asserts; she remains an enigma.

The mother in Bellini's painting is enigmatic, not in the manner of the Mona Lisa (whose smile, according to Freud, is that of the child's first seductress), but rather through the inscription of her absence—"the very space of the lost-unrepresentable-forbidden jouissance of a hidden mother" (p. 248). Paradoxically, Kristeva finds the mother in Bellini's paintings because the maternal space is empty—or rather, because she is associated with the movement beyond representation into chromatic difference which Kristeva privileges in modernist aesthetic practice. In Kristeva's reading of Bellini, the biographical obscurity surrounding his mother is confirmed by "the distance, if not hostility, separating the bodies of infant and mother in his paintings." What Kristeva calls "maternal space" is there, "fascinating, attracting and puzzling. But we have no direct access to it." Whereas the mother's solicitude in Leonardo's paintings insists that the child is the sole object of maternal desire—that she exists only to confirm the child as subject—the mother in Bellini's painting is represented as inaccessible. Her face is characteristically turned away, so that "the body not covered by draperies—head, face, and eyes—flees the painting, is gripped by something other than its object. And the painter as baby can never reach this elsewhere." The maternal is figured as "ineffable jouissance, beyond discourse, beyond narrative, beyond psychology, beyond lived experience and biography—in short, beyond figuration." Traces of the maternal space, a "presumed jouissance" which remains untouchable and invisible, are to be glimpsed only in the interplay of color, tone, and volume.

The true subject of Bellini's painting, for Kristeva, is the quest for this unrepresentable maternal jouissance—a quest which becomes apparent "wherever color, constructed volume, and light break away from the theme . . . [of the Madonna and child], implying that they are the real, objectless goal of the painting." Kristeva admits that a fetishized image of mother and child is as present in Bellini's painting as in Leonardo's; the difference, for her, is that the image seems to be "floating over a luminous background," delineating the threshold of repression and primal narcissism which is also the threshold of the child's experience of the maternal. Infinitesimally present in the non-representational aspects of Bellini's painting are encoded the traces of the earliest splitting, the process by which separation from the mother first occurs, yielding a glimpse of the pre-oedipal structuring of the subject in relation to the maternal body. Thus, although he followed in his father's footsteps as a painter (Kristeva argues), Bellini aspired to "a space of funda-mental unrepresentability towards which all glances . . . con-verge"; using the symbolic language of the father, he gestures at "the place where the mother could have been reached." In doing so, he "provides motherhood, that mute border, with a language" (pp. 247–48).

As Kristeva charts its progress, Bellini's painting in-volves a movement away from the loss of the mother to her triumphant "surrogation," a journey said to lead from "the 'iconographic' mother to the fascinating mother-seductress, and then passing through a threatening and fleeing mother to the luminous space where she surrogates herself" (pp. 262–63). Somewhat puzzlingly (at first sight), Kristeva focuses initially on an early group of paintings (c. 1455–65) which seem to accent the maternal hands. They testify, in her words, to "a maternal appropriation of the child. There is a crushing hug, a tussle between a possessive mother and her child, who tries in vain to loosen her grip" (p. 254). These, rather than the later triumphs of luminous space, are the paintings which she chooses to reproduce in her essay. In one, the child seems to

Kristeva to grip its mother's thumb, as if in anguish and fear. Stressing the mother's "precocious, already sexual caresses," Kristeva traces a drama of maternal seduction that threatens the child rather than comforts him. What she terms "this miniature drama" comes into the open in paintings such as the Correr and Bergamo Madonnas, where the mother's hands shift toward the child's buttocks. In these paintings, she writes, "we have a striking cleavage of the maternal body. On one side the mother's hands hold their object tightly . . . on the other, we see the softened, dreamy peasant faces."

The Correr Madonna (figure 10) gazes abstractedly away from her child, while her hands half hold, half display his body. Once more the child grips her thumb, but (it seems to me, at any rate) almost casually, as the palm of one hand cradles his buttock. The other hand, spread across the baby's chest, ritualizes the gesture of holding into one of merest indication. Kristeva writes of the mother's hands holding their object tightly; yet the pair—mother and child—could be seen as folded loosely together in a formalized pattern which emphasizes, not her grip, but the interlacing of hands and legs, the repeated folds of sleeve and veil, the crinkles and curls of mother's and child's hair. The heart-shaped jewel (a ruby set in pearls) which gathers the Madonna's veil at her throat repeats the curves and color of her mouth, as if to provide an emblem of Bellini's non-naturalistic art. Resting on a stone balustrade, the figures seem to float slightly beyond it, almost in a different plane. Light glimmering on the Madonna's arm and shoulder, sky melting behind her, colors at once soft and glowing (aquamarine sky, rose red drapery, the milky, greenish pallor of the baby's flesh) reinforce the mother's expression of dreamy abstraction. Figuration has been abstracted into translucence, making Madonna and child a formalized design like the jewel she wears. The composition gestures beyond figural representation to chromatic and formal values; in other words, what it draws attention to, in Kristevan terms, is the sublimation of, and in, art.

The same preoccupation with the tension and separation between mother and child structures Kristeva's account

Figure 10. Giovanni Bellini, *Madonna and Child* (c. 1465–1470):
Venice, Civico Museo Correr.

of the Bergamo Madonna (figure 11), which for her constitutes the climax of the series, "a spotlight thrown on a dramatic narrative:"

> Aggressive hands prod the stomach and penis of the frightened baby, who, alone of all his peers, frees himself violently, taking his mother's hands along on his body. All the while, the folds of the virginal gown separate this little dramatic theater from the maternal body, whose illuminated face alone is revealed. Her characterless gaze fleeting under her downcast eyelids, her nonetheless definite pleasure, unshakable in its intimacy, and her cheeks radiating peace, all constitute a strange modesty. This split character of the maternal body has rarely been so clearly brought forward. (p. 254)

Kristeva offers a specular, and spectacular, observation ("Aggressive hands prod the stomach and penis of the frightened baby"). Here too however, the dynamic between mother and child could be viewed as energized not so much by a struggle against constraint, but by the premature maturity of the robust, bucolic child—surely about to spring to his feet. The mother's supporting arms proffer him rather than restrain him. Kristeva makes no mention of the vivid, highlighted expanse of the mother's blue robe against the child's white shirt, or the elaborately finished marble sill on which the child sits—marble whose veining contrasts with the almost Byzantine regularity and two-dimensional moulding of the mother's face and the child's chubbiness. In this light, the iconographic formalization which Kristeva emphasizes elsewhere once more usurps on psychological drama.

The mother's hands could be made to tell a quite different story if the picture is installed in the tradition of iconographic display for which Leo Steinberg argues in *The Sexuality of Christ in Renaissance Art and in Modern Oblivion* (1983). For Steinberg this story is not manual (or maternal) in focus, but genital (or paternal). Bellini's Bergamo Madonna—reproduced, incidentally, on the cover of his book—joins other paintings whose emphasis on the infant's genitals is intended, Steinberg argues, to reveal the two natures, human and divine, united in the Incarnation. As Steinberg puts it, the Bergamo Madonna's gesture belongs to the genre of "the calculated

Figure 11. Giovanni Bellini, *Madonna and Child* (c. 1470):
Bergamo, Accademia Carrara.

near-miss," the tactful display by the mother's hand and half-veiling drapery that her baby is a Man-child; the goal of such pictures is to "confess the mystery of the dual nature of Christ."[13] Like Kristeva, who tries to uncover a pre-oedipal story beneath the oedipal emphasis of Freudian theory, Steinberg inserts the Bergamo Madonna into a forgotten narrative in order to uncover the Renaissance concern with Christ's sexuality. Steinberg's emphasis on the theological meaning of such displays threatens to expose Kristeva's reading as anachronistic in its importation of modern, psychologistic concerns. What Kristeva dramatizes as the child's attempted strangulation of the guilty mother in the Sao Paulo Madonna, for instance, is for Steinberg the erotic "chin-chuck" given by the baby to his mother-bride in Christian iconography.[14] But Steinberg too has his *idée fixe*; piling illustration on illustration, his book not only testifies to the Christian and cultural drama of Manhood, but seems, delightedly, to fetishize it.[15] For him genitality (masculine genitality) is everywhere strikingly visible—whether draped or undraped, erect or detumescent; one recalls that for Freud the founding moment of sexual difference depends precisely on this drama, the visibility of the penis.

Kristeva attempts on the contrary to explore what Steinberg renders invisible—the meaning of the maternal body, arguably more important than Christ's in Renaissance iconography. How then can we account for Kristeva's own emphasis on the visible drama of separation?—and, more strangely, for her reproduction of paintings which seem only to depict the struggle of child against mother, while other, later paintings revealing (in her words) "the greatest blossoming of luminous space" remain unillustrated? One explanation, I think, lies in what might be called the desire of the theorist (by definition, a looker-on). It is as if, in the midst of her theoretical concern with the unrepresentable, Kristeva finds herself trapped in the object-invested, fetishistic economy of representation itself; like Steinberg, she must illustrate. "Giotto's Joy" locates her strategy "somewhere between an immediate and subjective deciphering and a still incoherent, heteroclitic theoretical apparatus yet to be worked out" (p. 211). Kristeva's emphasis on the struggle of maternal hands and infant bodies in Bellini's early paintings has the air of "immediate and subjective deciphering"; but its significance for her can only be explained by a theoretical apparatus not yet in place. Subjective deciphering on one hand, theory-in-process on the other, make "Motherhood According to Giovanni Bellini" a sketch for the theoretical elaboration of the maternal which has been the focus of Kristeva's more recent writing on "abjection."

Another way to understand Kristeva's emphasis on the drama of separation in Bellini's painting is to read it in the light of a passage from her book *Powers of Horror* (1980), subtitled "An Essay on Abjection." "Abjection" is Kristeva's term for the precarious casting out or primal repression which marks the emergence of the signifying subject (a subject which is self-differentiating, self-representing, and therefore narcissistic). The "abject," in Kristeva's definition, is the most fragile, most archaic sublimation of an "object" (i.e., the mother) at the point where it is still inseparable from instinctual drives. If primal repression is "the ability of the speaking being, always already haunted by the Other, to divide, reject, repeat," the abject confronts us "within our personal archeology, with our earliest attempts to release the hold of *maternal* entity even before ex-isting outside of her." This is the very struggle for release which Kristeva locates in the archeology of Bellini's painting—"a violent, clumsy breaking away, with the constant risk of falling back under the sway of a power as securing as it is stifling." The precarious emergence of subjectivity takes place in a "close combat" between a sort of subject that is not yet a subject and a mother who is not yet an object—"a reluctant struggle against what, having been the mother, will turn into an abject. Repelling, rejecting; repelling itself, rejecting itself. Ab-jecting."[16]

Only by this self-differentiating movement which installs boundaries, difference, and at the same time narcissism, can instinctual chaos be confined and kept at bay. Otherwise a confusion of bodily limits would result, preventing the not-yet-subject's installation into signification. For Kristeva's pre-oedipal (and somewhat Kleinian) infant, not only is there already an ego and an object of sorts, with drives and defenses present from the start; there is also already a third term—the mother's (fantasized) desire for the phallus. Although division in the pre-oedipal is not yet structured by the phallus (as in

Lacanian accounts of the child's entry into the symbolic and into language), the child's own identification with the mother's imaginary desire means that an archaic form of the paternal is present, permitting the opening of a gap between child and mother. The blankness or "*vide*" (Kristeva's term) sensed in the mother's place—her abstraction, her focus on something other than the child—is a necessary emptiness. Winnicott's "good-enough" mother is for Kristeva a mother who desires something other than her child; call it the father, or simply a necessary third term (her work, perhaps).[17] By a kind of collusion, the child chooses narcissism as a defense against, and as a way of maintaining, the necessary space of "*vide*" which will enable it to enter into the realm of images (Lacan's "imaginary") and ultimately into the symbolic realm.

In "Motherhood According to Giovanni Bellini," Kristevan theory seems to be trapped in an insurmountable primal narcissism at the very moment of delineating its borders. Identifying the first differentiating movement in the infant with the minute differences which constitute nonrepresentational and prelinguistic modes of signification, Kristeva turns to representation. An image must close off the "*vide*," even for the theorist of the modernist crisis in figuration. This is the very trajectory traced by Kristeva in Bellini's art, whose evolution becomes the mirror for her own investigation of the threshold of primal narcissism. Transformations in Bellini's representation of motherhood can be tied, she argues, to his own discovery of paternity—"as if *paternity* were necessary in order to relive the archaic impact of the maternal body on man; in order to complete the investigation of a ravishing maternal jouissance but also of its terrorizing aggressivity" (p. 263). The archaic struggle with a reencountered mother freed Bellini for his greatest artistic experiments, and according to Kristeva allowed him to find in the mother "an increasingly appropriate language, capable of capturing her specific imaginary jouissance, the jouissance on the border of primal repression." Bellini's identification with the maternal body brings him to the border where the loss of signs occurs, and with it "a loss of the seducing figure (the compassionate or laughing mother)" which similarly haunts Leonardo's painting. Earlier in her essay, Kristeva has invoked Dante's *Paradiso* to gesture toward this loss of signs—

> "And tell why the sweet symphony of Paradise
>   Which below sounds so devoutly
>   Is silent in this heaven."
> "Your hearing is mortal, like your vision,"
>   He answered me, "therefore there is no song here,
>   For the same reason Beatrice has no smile."
>   (*Paradiso*, XXI:58–63)

Later in Kristeva's essay, the allusion to Dante recurs when she turns to Bellini's "Madonna, Child, Saints, and Angelic Musicians" as the place where "music can henceforth be heard; the shout has burst through, and it is orchestrated following the greatest blossoming of luminous space" (p. 262).

The bursting through of maternal jouissance beyond figuration—"therefore . . . Beatrice has no smile"—coincides with the movement in Kristeva's own text away from pictorial representation toward an increasingly abstract mode of analysis in the service of what she celebrates in Bellini's own art, "a shattering of figuration and form in a space of graphic lines and colors, differentiated until they disappear in pure light" (p. 269). In a final movement, the "luminous, colored imprint, devoid of object, figure, or spectacle" becomes the rediscovery of the female form—still an emblem of splitting rather than unity—in Bellini's late "Venus," evidence of the old master's entry into the "sex shop" of his humanist age, but also a revelation of "the nude and passably erotic body" (p. 266) hidden behind the Madonna's veils. Here the Madonna's averted gaze returns nakedly to her mirror, the first pseudo-object, and "the mirror can do nothing more than to return the gaze" (pp. 264–65). For Kristeva, this entrapment by the image marks the insurmountable limits of primary narcissism while intimating "a jouissance at the far limits of repression, whence bodies, identities, and signs are begotten"—the minute space opened between a body and the images to which it gives rise; the space where the subject finds itself both mirrored and split.

Motherhood, then, provides a language for Bellini's artistic provocation and investigation of this narcissistic threshold—in Kristeva's terms, both the threshold of maternal jouissance and the cause of jouissance in his painting. But what of Freud's Leonardo?—an essay to which Kristeva herself does no more than allude, but which bears intriguingly both on the mother and on the imbricated relations of narcissism and theory. The study of Leonardo contains one of Freud's earliest published references to narcissism, first mentioned in a similar context (the etiology of homosexuality) a few months before in a footnote to the second edition of his *Three Essays on Sexuality* (*SE* 7:145*n.*). *Leonardo da Vinci and a Memory of his Childhood* (1910) traces the sublimations of Leonardo's art back to their pre-oedipal origins in the relationship between mother and child—a relationship simultaneously idealized as the complete satisfaction of infantile and maternal desire, and viewed as the premature seduction leading to Leonardo's later homosexuality and "narcissistic" object choice. Identifying with the mother's desire for him, Leonardo (according to Freud) "takes his own person as a model in whose likeness he chooses the new objects of his love. In this way he has become a homosexual" (*SE* 11:100).

Freud bases his theory of infantile seduction by the mother on Leonardo's famous memory (and his own notorious mistranslation) of the vulture that came down to him in his cradle "and opened [his] mouth with its tail, and struck [him] many times with its tail against [his] lips" (*SE* 11:82). Interpreting this "memory" as an erotic fantasy of fellatio transposed to the period of infantile sucking, Freud installs it in the pictorial tradition of Christian art: "What the phantasy conceals," he writes, "is merely a reminiscence of sucking—or being suckled—at his mother's breast, a scene of human beauty that he, like so many artists, undertook to depict with his brush, in the guise of the mother of God and her child" (*SE* 11:87). Painting the Madonna and child sublimates the homosexual structure of Leonardo's fantasy. The vulture leads Freud to the phallic mother whom the child endows with a "tail" or penis, and to the vulture-headed Egyptian Mother Goddess, *Mut* (whose name recalls the German *Mutter* or mother). *Mut*, Freud re-

minds us, was regularly depicted with a phallus, just as infantile sexual theories give the mother a penis to fend off castration
anxiety. The vulture became a symbol of motherhood, Freud
goes on, because there were thought to be no males of the
species; the fable of the vulture (impregnated by the wind)
provided the Church Fathers with evidence that the Virgin
Birth of sacred history was compatible with natural history.
Thus Leonardo, Freud speculates, was himself "such a vulture-
child—he had a mother, but no father" (*SE* 11:90 and *n.*). In
this way he could identify himself with the fatherless Christ
child in his own paintings, seeing himself as the object of his
phallic mothers's undivided love.

The connection between Leonardo's relationship
with his mother in early childhood and his later homosexuality
lies, for Freud, in the intense, erotic attachment encouraged or
evoked by "too much tenderness" on the mother's part and by
the absence of the father. Yet Freud's text at one point celebrates
the bond of mother and infant in terms that seem strangely
complicit with Leonardo's sublimation, as well as providing an
unwitting commentary on the motif of Madonna and child in
Christian iconography:

> A mother's love for the infant she suckles and cares for is
> something far more profound than her later affection for the
> growing child. It is in the nature of a completely satisfying
> love-relation, which not only fulfils every mental wish but
> also every physical need; and if it represents one of the forms
> of attainable human happiness, that is in no little measure
> due to the possibility it offers of satisfying, without reproach,
> wishful impulses which have long been repressed and which
> must be called perverse. (*SE* 11:117)

This is the model on which Christianity can subsume feminine
desire into maternity (and, more covertly, polymorphous perversity into what Kristeva calls "*pèreversion*" or submission to
the Law of the Father). "Like all unsatisfied mothers," Freud
speculates, Leonardo's mother "took her little son in place of
her husband, and by the too early maturing of his eroticism
robbed him of a part of his masculinity." Loving boys, as
Leonardo did, is simply a way of repressing this early love for a
too seductive mother by identifying with her, and then choos-

ing his own love objects on the model of hers. Although his is the narcissistic solution, it paradoxically allows him to be faithful to the mother, his first love, by turning away from all other women. Freud's account of the etiology of Leonardo's homosexuality at once enshrines the mother's love for her child as "completely satisfying" and locates in this "too-good" mothering a threat so great that even in "the happiest young marriage," the father may feel marginalized. Complete maternal satisfaction—Freud's version of maternal jouissance—does not merely threaten the child with homosexuality; it ousts the father and unbalances the oedipal triangle, rendering separation impossible. Although Freud himself participates in the narcissistic fantasy of the mother's absorption in her child, he does so only at the price of an accompanying movement of rejection. The child must cease to desire the mother, the mother her child, by way of the oedipal triangle which makes the father the regulator of sexual desire.

Freud comes close to suggesting that Leonardo's repressed homosexuality and sublimated narcissism—the product of maternal rather than paternal identification—are the source of his artistic representations; the enigmatically smiling Madonnas and androgynous youths of his mature painting are seen as corresponding to the laughing mothers and beautiful children of his earliest productions. But as the essay draws to its close, the figure who intrigues Freud most is the failed creative artist—the investigative genius Leonardo later became. Without a father, Leonardo "at a tender age became a researcher, tormented as he was by the great question of where babies come from and what the father has to do with their origin" (SE 11:92). The sublimation of this infantile desire to look and to know—researches that have their origin in the child's sexual curiousity—leads (Freud argues) to Leonardo's later scientific investigations. This is the basis, surely, of Freud's own identification with the subject of his psychoanalytic biography. Investigating the origins of artistic creation by way of the techniques of psychoanalysis ("penetrating the most fascinating secrets of human nature") could be compared with investigating the origins of life, as Leonardo had done both in his childish researches and as an adult.[18] Indeed, writes Freud, "Leonardo himself, with his love of truth and his thirst for knowledge, would not have discouraged an attempt to take the trivial peculiarities and riddles in his nature as a starting-point" (*SE* 11:130–31). Because he lacked a father, Leonardo could press his investigations unusually far without fear of authority; Freud too has risked provoking criticism, "even from friends of psycho-analysis," for having written a psychoanalytic novel which abandons science for fiction.

"Biographers," Freud asserts in the final section of his essay, "are fixated on their heroes in a quite special way. In many cases they have chosen their hero as the subject of their studies because—for reasons of their personal emotional life—they have felt a special affection for him from the first" (*SE* 11:130). Perhaps they idealize their subject along the lines of their infantile image of the father; or perhaps (though Freud is silent on this point) they choose an object who resembles themselves—the child imaged in the mother's desire—like Leonardo. Freud concedes that he too may have "succumbed to the attraction of this great and mysterious man" and made a narcissistic object choice in choosing Leonardo as the subject of his biographical study. But at precisely the moment when he implicates his own narcissism, Freud turns away to inquire into the theoretical achievements and limits of psychoanalytic biography. I want to linger on this displacement from narcissism to theory. Freud's account of Leonardo's too great investigative sublimation puts his own theoretical investigation on the line. Pausing to stake out the proper domain of psychoanalytic biography, he discerns it in "instincts and their transformations;" the limits of this domain are the most minimal of original and individuating differences—the accident of "our origin out of the meeting of spermatazoon and ovum" which gives rise to the individual (*SE* 11:136–37). Biography stops here. Narcissism leads, by way of theory, to the point where Kristeva begins her essay on Bellini: "Cells fuse, split, and proliferate; volumes grow, tissues stretch, and body fluids change rhythm. . . . Within the body . . . there is an other" (p. 236). The Mona Lisa returns Leonardo to "the oldest of all his erotic impulses," his love for the enigmatically smiling mother: the enigma of theory returns Freud to the maternal body or fundamental space of differentiation as the place where theoretical mastery must recognize its limits.

It is tempting to link this simultaneously self-limit-
ing and self-defining moment in Freud's *Leonardo* with a similar moment in Kristeva's account of the pre-oedipal in "L'abjet
de l'amour," an essay which crystalizes many of the ideas developed in her book-length "Essay on Abjection." For Freud, the
myth of Narcissus ("a youth who preferred his own reflection
to everything else and who was changed into the lovely flower
of that name," *SE* 11:100) emerges in the context of too great
identification with the mother. But for Kristeva, narcissism can
only emerge in the child's identification with the space opened
up by the paternal, the imaginary or archaic father of infantile
prehistory—the space which implies the possibility of maternal
absence. In a long passage added to "L'abjet d'amour" for its
republication in her most recent book, *Histoires d'amour* (1983),
Kristeva, like Freud, breaks off to reflect on narcissism and its
relation to theory. The interruption occurs at precisely the point
where she alludes to the constitutive gap or void, the *"vide,"*
which she regards as equivalent to the arbitrariness of the sign
in Saussure or the *"béance"* or gaping in Lacan's mirror phase—
the universal psychic space which makes signification possible.
For Kristeva, narcissism is (in) this gap, from and against which
the machinery of imagery, representations, identification and
projections is a conjuration. But if separation offers us the
chance to become narcissists—that is, subjects of and in representation—the void which it opens is also the abyss in which
our identities and images risk being swallowed up.

Narcissus thus becomes the hero of theory, and (by
the same token), narcissism becomes the heroism of theoretical
reflection itself:

> In the last analysis, the mythical Narcissus is heroic in gazing
> into this void [*"vide"*] in order to seek in the aquatic maternal
> element a possibility of self-representation or the representa-
> tion of an other: of someone to love. Since Plotinus at least,
> theoretical reflection has forgotten that it functions in the
> void [*"roulait sur le vide"*], and instead has projected itself
> lovingly towards the solar source of representation, the light
> which makes us see and which we aspire to equal in idealiza-
> tion on idealization, perfection on perfection: *In lumine tuo
> videbimus lumen.*[19]

At this moment, narcissism and theory (a theory about narcissism and the narcissism involved in theory) become mutually constitutive, mirroring each other in Kristeva's self-reflexive and self-reflecting text. An image at once thrown up by and covering over the void, theory simultaneously closes off and is sustained by the abyss; the progression from narcissism to sublimation follows with seeming inevitability. Kristeva's writing ends, it seems, by locating the production of images and of theory in one and the same place—the pre-oedipal, the space of the maternal body which is also the space of primal narcissism.

In a recent interview, Kristeva spoke of the theorist, and especially the psychoanalytic theorist, as posited on the site of a scar: "we are holding a knowing discourse, a discourse which pretends to some objectivity, and at the same time we elaborate this discourse through what is often painful involvement in the observation. We have to exhibit this contradiction, this pain."[20] Maternal love, she specifies, is one of the personal points of departure for *Histoires d'amour*; in particular for the only dated chapter in the book, *"Stabat Mater."* Originally published in *Tel Quel* in 1977 as "Héréthique de l'amour," the essay reflects (on) her own experience of the birth of a child. She tried, she says, to provide an image of this contradiction between theory and painful involvement by the device of a printed text in which analytic discourse and "poetic" or literary discourse literally diverge on the page: "I didn't want to give an impression of coherence, on the contrary I wanted to give an impression of a sort of wound, a scar."[21] Here the *"vide"* or gap becomes a wound (both the wound to and the wound of narcissism) which theory at once covers and opens. Like the maternal body, the text is divided. On one hand, Kristeva provides an account of the history and symbolic meaning of the cult of the Virgin Mary, showing how Christianity constructs femininity as the maternal; Christian humanism, she reminds us (*pace* Steinberg) can only be maternalism in its emphasis on the mother as the guarantee of Christ's humanity, the Word made flesh. On the other hand, an intertext in a different typeface questions the coherence of this analytic account with lyrical outbursts, fragments, and reflections which evoke the physical and emotional dimensions of maternity—conception, child-

birth, breastfeeding, infantile memories, mother-daughter relations—as subjectively experienced by Kristeva herself. This is
the flesh made Word.

Poetic language in Kristeva's text mimes the presence of the semiotic within the symbolic in an attempt to unfold a maternal discourse unconstructed by the discourse of
Christianity. When the two columns come parallel and their
modes converge, we are reminded that maternal jouissance
makes itself heard even in the passionate play of theory. Typo-
graphically, the split columns of "Héréthique de l'amour" represent the split in the maternal speaking subject, divided
between the singleness of the symbolic or paternal discourse
and the doubleness of her position as mother. Conceptually,
and indeed theoretically, Kristeva attempts to rehabilitate the
discourse of maternity for a secular era which has rejected the
discourse provided by Christianity, whether through unrespon-
siveness to the cult of the Virgin Mary or through experiencing
its construction of feminity as coercive. Basing her account on
Marina Warner's *Alone of All Her Sex: The Myth and the Cult of the
Virgin Mary* (1976), she traces the changing historical forms of
the Marian heresy and of its evolution in Christian dogma as
the Virgin Mary became successively homologized with her son
(freed of sin), then Mother or Queen of the Church, and finally
the prototype of all love relations. The doctrines and representation of the Virgin Mother, the Immaculate Conception, Dormition and Assumption, the Mater Dolorosa, all provide a
copious Marian discourse which contrasts strikingly with the
little that (for instance) Freud has to say about the mother.
Kristeva's own contribution is to speculate that the Virgin
Mary's function in social formations was to maintain equi-
librium between the sexes, simultaneously providing a means
of dealing with feminine paranoia and a response to male paranoia about women.

Although the Virgin Mother appears to deny the
opposite sex, Kristeva argues, she is actually subordinated to
God. Although woman's envy of power is satisfied by making
her regal, she is placed on her knees before her child. Her
desire to kill is obliterated by the oral investment which makes
her the source of all (lactatory) satisfaction, while her associa-

tion with death is transformed into the valorization of sorrow (the Mater Dolorosa) and her sexual body into the ear of tenderness with which she listens. Her exclusion from time and death is ensured by putting her to sleep (Dormition). Above all, the Virgin Mother's unique status ("Alone of all her sex") effects the exclusion of other women, or else enforces their adoption of extreme forms of masochism and self-abnegation (physical martyrdom and the alienating sublimation of the feminine body within marriage). For Kristeva, the maternal body itself is the "not-said" of this highly developed Marian discourse. The strange wrinkle, difficulty, or crease, the *"pli"* (Kristeva's term), is that of a body in which biology speaks, declaring its heterogeneity most violently in pregnancy and in childbirth. The specificity of the maternal body provides a point of resistance, making woman a divided being—*"un être de plis"*—which the dialectic of Christianity is finally unable to subsume.

Kristeva's Marian heresy is to rewrite Christian morality as an ethics of otherness, or love, emphasizing the difficult access to a radical Other demanded by maternity. She never ceases (contrary to popular misunderstanding) to dwell on the abyss separating mother and child even in the pre-oedipal.[22] What rapport can there be, she asks, between her, or rather her body, and *"ce pli-greffe interne"* (this internal fold which is also a graft), once the umbilical cord is cut? But Kristevan ethics are nothing if not (her)esthetics. The function of the Virgin Mother in Western symbolic economy, she argues, is to provide an anchor for the nonverbal and for modes of signification closer to primary processes. In the face of the fascinated fear of the powerlessness of language which sustains all belief, the Mother is a necessary pendant to the Word in Christian theology—just as the fantasized preverbal mother is a means of attempting to heal the split in language, providing an image of undivided signs, plenitude, and imaginary fullness to compensate for the actual poverty of language and its inability to situate or articulate the (maternal) speaking subject.

For Kristeva, division is the condition of all signifying processes. No pre-oedipal language, no maternal discourse, can be free of this split. We live (Kristeva writes) on the frontier, in a permanent parting, a division of the flesh which is also a division of language. The biological processes of conception and parturition are at once metaphor, analogue, and foundation for this originating difference. But, one is bound to ask, what function does the mother serve in Kristeva's own theoretical (heretical-herethical-heresthetic) economy? Like Christianity, she could be accused of attempting to recuperate heterogeneity for the Word. For Kristeva, there is only one way to traverse the religion of the Word and its supporting pendant, the mother; that is, the way of the artist, whose oversaturation of sign-systems (in her terms) compensates for the poverty of signs themselves. The "drama of the word/body separation whose flash-spasm the poet alone can hear" (p. 196) is the same drama enacted by Kristeva's discourse of maternity. The mother in Kristevan theory can be redefined as a metaphor for the symbolic crisis brought about by the disunited, multifold differences and engraftings of poetic language. The discourse of maternity, like the Madonna in Christian art, veils what (for Kristeva) Bellini's late, nude "Venus" unveils—the wish to hear more, and yet subtler differentiations of meaning in and beyond the jouissance of the literary text, the unheard meaning or senses at its margins. The function of the mother in Kristeva's theory is to sustain this sense of the literary or "poetic" text as the privileged site of jouissance ("*j'ouis sens*"). The discourse of maternity gives birth to Kristevan poetics.

The Missing Mother

Lacan's essay on *Dora*, "Intervention on Transference," defines the problem of Dora's condition as "that of accepting herself as an object of desire for the man." Christianity comes to her rescue with the Sistine Madonna; "in her long meditation before the Madonna, and in her recourse to the role of distant worshipper, Dora is driven toward the solution which Christianity has given to this subjective impasse, by making woman the object of a divine desire, or else, a transcendent object of desire, which amounts to the same thing."[23] Freud's famous self-reproach on the score of his failure to master the transference in his analytical relationship to Dora—a failure which he believed led to her breaking off the analysis—is accompanied by a contradictory self-accusation. He had failed, a footnote tells us, "to discover in time and to inform [Dora] that her homosexual (gynaecophilic) love for Frau K. was the strongest unconscious current in her mental life" (*SE* 7:120*n.*). His first reproach belongs to the oedipal triangle, the second to the pre-oedipal. Freud's failure to master Dora's transference only makes sense in the context of the multiple substitution by which all men, himself included, occupy the place of the father. As Freud outlines the oedipal triangle, Dora's tender attachment to her father prefigures and determines her relations both to Herr K. (her would-be seducer) and to Freud (her analyst). Her anger at her father for his affair with Frau K., observes Freud, is that of a jealous wife, while her attachment to him is a form of flight from her unacknowledged love for Herr K. Similarly, her rejection of Freud reenacts her anger at her father while echoing her chagrined rejection of Herr K.

Freud's second self-reproach, however—his failure to register Dora's "gynaecophilia"—only makes sense in the context of his discovery that it is her relation to the (m)Other Woman, not the father, that matters; or, as he puts it, his discovery of the "masculine or, more properly speaking, *gynaecophilic* currents of feeling . . . typical of the unconscious erotic life of hysterical girls" (*SE* 7:63). As the second layer of Freud's story comes into view, Dora's jealousy is revealed not as that of a wife, but "a jealousy such as might have been felt by a man" (*SE* 7:63). The secret object of her adoration is not Herr K., but Frau K. ("she used to praise her 'adorable white body' in accents more appropriate to a lover than to a defeated rival," *SE* 7:61). Frau K., Dora's traducer and betrayer, is the only person spared by Dora in the quest for revenge that includes her father, Herr K. and Freud himself. In effect, then, Freud tells two stories—the first narrated openly in the text, the second developed as a subtext in his retrospective comments and footnotes. The mediating or third term between the two stories, and between Freud's connected but incompatible self-reproaches, proves to be none other than the Sistine Madonna, Raphael's sublimated representation of the mother.

Freud's account of Dora provides a paradigm of the circulation of women, goods, and desire. Dora's father tells Freud that he "get[s] nothing out of [his] own wife" (*SE* 7:26)—in German, *"Ich habe nichts an meiner Frau"* ("I have nothing in my wife"). His investment is elsewhere, in Frau K., from whom Herr K., in turn, "gets nothing." To buy Herr K.'s silence about the affair, Dora's father hands Dora over to him in exchange for his wife—but this fails to silence Dora herself; and so she is "handed over" to Freud (as both Freud and Dora perceive it) in exchange for Freud's assumption of the role of father. Dora, her father claims, is making it all up; Freud will cure her, since he can't shut her up himself (unlike Saint Barbara's father). Meanwhile, Herr K., according to Dora, has made two attempts to seduce her, once when she was only fourteen (she reacts with disgust), and once more recently, during a lakeside outing (she slaps him). When confronted by her father with Dora's accusation, Herr K. claims, like Dora's father, that she is making it all up. As the arbiter of fantasies, Freud believes both Dora's accusations but suspects that they conceal a self-reproach; the two families are engaged in an adulterous quadrille which includes Dora herself (she secretly loves Herr K. and has dreamed of acting the part of wife and mother in Frau K.'s place). For Freud, Dora's father is the dominant figure in the family circle. A "man of means" (*"ein vermögender Mann"*), his money and sexual attractions turn the merry-go-round despite his impotence (he is also *"ein unvermögender Mann,"* *SE* 7:47).

Dora's mother, on the other hand, whom Dora herself devalues, equals "nothing" to Freud either. Though he questions Dora's version of almost everything else, he accepts her denigration of the mother at face value ("From the accounts given me by the girl and her father I was led to imagine her as an uncultivated woman and above all as a foolish one," *SE* 7:20). As Jane Gallop points out, "wife" and "nothing" tend to converge in Freud's own account.[24] By contrast, Frau K. is really something, and gets given more. Though Frau K., like Dora's syphilitic father, has her share of ill health, the affair with Dora's father makes her bloom; she only relapses strategically when her husband returns from his periodic absences. Moreover, she is something (has something) for Dora as well. The

two turn out to have been intimates, confidantes, even confede-
rates in the interfamilial intrigue. According to one story, the
father is the source and object of all desire; according to the
other, Frau K., the (m)Other Woman, is the desiring subject
who, in Lacan's terms, accepts herself as the object of desire
without benefit of Christian sublimation. Hers, Lacan suggests,
is the mystery of bodily femininity. In this reading, the story
turns, not on Dora's father (whether with or without means),
but on Frau K., who has ways and means of her own.

Freud reproaches himself on the score of failing to
master Dora's transference. But the question of countertransference goes unasked. Lacan suggests that Freud went wrong in
identifying with Herr K., and hence, in effect, overurged his
suit. But did the "*gynaecophilic* currents of feeling" run both
ways?—the term, by Freud's own definition, means loving a
woman as a man might do. Just as Dora desires the father
through her identification with Frau K. (in one scheme), Freud
may desire the (m)Other Woman, who both is and has something, through his identification with Dora's father—or even (in
another scheme) through the more threatening identification
with Dora's own "gynaecophilic" stance. Freud's oversight
about Dora's homosexual love for Frau K. might then be suspected of screening an unuttered self-reproach—that of having
fallen into the pattern of Leonardo's homosexual relation to the
mother (i.e., loving the mother as a man might do). Dora's
desire for Frau K. is represented by Freud as male identified ("a
jealousy such as might have been felt by a man"). Herr K. is
nothing to Dora if his wife is nothing to him, as he makes the
blunder of telling her in words he had earlier used when attempting to seduce a governess; hence the rejection put into
Dora's mouth by Lacan: "If she is nothing to you, then what are
you to me?"[25]

Freud's insight (that Dora's desire for Frau K. is male
identified) and the meaning of his blindness (his inability to
figure her relation to the (m)Other Woman as anything but
modeled on a man's love for a woman) coincide. Freud may be
right that relations to the maternal are inevitably triangulated
by the father—that access to the mother is always (as Kristeva
would argue) mediated by an archaic paternal space—but if

that is so, the unmediated maternal identification later posited in Leonardo's case can never exist; the too good mother-child relationship is not after all to blame for Leonardo's homosexuality. It follows that Dora's alleged homosexuality or "gynaecophilia" becomes the norm for women's relations to the mother. To put it in terms of the Sistine Madonna, Dora's perspective can only ever be that of a masculine adorer once the oedipal has been installed as the governing structure or main story. The hysterical predicament—Dora's identification with her father and with Herr K. in relation to Frau K.—turns out to be unavoidable for a woman looking at the mother from the point of view of Freud's oedipal triangle. Access to the pre-oedipal is always mediated by the oedipal.

This question of perspective (Dora's on the Sistine Madonna) provides the focus both for Freud's interpretation of her rapt two-hour vigil in the Dresden art gallery and for his analysis of the dream which gives rise to the association. Freud interprets the dream, the second of two designed to develop his earlier "clinical picture" of Dora's family situation and hysterical symptoms, in the light of Dora's feelings for Herr K., and especially the scene by the lake when Herr K. had unsuccessfully propositioned her. In the course of analyzing the dream, Freud uncovers an episode which he construes as a hysterical pregnancy and childbirth exactly nine months after Dora had delivered her decisive slap to Herr K. The hysterical fantasy confirms his view that Dora secretly wished for a different upshot. Freud's interpretation of the dream is resolutely oedipal; it proves the persistence of Dora's love for Herr K., and so persuasive is he that in the end "Dora disputed the fact no longer" (*SE* 7:104), bringing the analysis to a satisfactory point of closure. But a footnote reopens his open-and-shut case with the dis-closure of "Dora's deep-rooted homosexual love for Frau K." (*SE* 7:105*n*.)—a conclusion broached by way of a lengthy supplementary interpretation of the Sistine Madonna.

Dora's dream begins: *"I was walking about in a town which I did not know. I saw streets and squares which were strange to me"* (*SE* 7:94). Both she and Freud connect the strange town with an album containing pictures of a German health resort sent her by a would-be lover, and with her earlier visit to the

Dresden art gallery. Dora recounts that later in the dream she goes to the station and sees a thick wood before her. Freud returns to the scene by the lake with Herr K., suggesting that the wood in the dream and the wood by the lake are the same. But, Dora objects "she had seen precisely the same thick wood the day before, in a picture at the Secessionist exhibition. In the background of the picture there were *nymphs*" (*SE* 7:99). As Freud observes, "pictures" constitute a junction point (what he elsewhere calls a "switch-word") in the network of the dream thoughts. Or, as he notes, the dream involves three kinds of picture or "*Bild*": views of towns, Raphael's Sistine Madonna, and now one containing nymphs. What, he asks, is depicted by these pictures?

The views sent her by the young man whom Freud elsewhere refers to in his footnote on the Madonna as an "adorer" (*SE* 7:104*n*.), the Sistine Madonna which had been the object of Dora's adoration in the Dresden art gallery, and now a picture of wood nymphs from the Secessionist exhibition—the picture collection reveals (Freud argues) a concealed "phantasy of defloration, the phantasy of a man seeking to force an entrance into the female genitals" (*SE* 7:100). The words for station ("*Bahnhof,*" literally "railway court") and cemetery ("*Friedhof,*" literally "peace court"), both of which occur in the dream text, direct what Freud calls his "awakened curiosity" to "the similarly formed '*Vorhof*'—['*vestibulum*'; literally, 'fore-court']—an anatomical term for a particular region of the female genitals" (*SE* 7:99). The nymphs visible in the background of a thick wood are none other than the "*Nymphae*" ("*Nymphen*" in German), the physician's technical term for the labia minora which lie, as Freud puts it quaintly, "in the background of the 'thick wood' of the pubic hair." Since anyone using this latinate vocabulary must have derived such knowledge from books, Freud plausibly suggests that Dora's own awakened curiosity has lead her to an anatomical textbook or an encyclopedia (as he notes, "the common refuge of youth when it is devoured by sexual curiosity," *SE* 7:99). With scarcely veiled triumph, Freud exclaims: "Here was a symbolic geography of sex!" Behind a Secessionist painting lies a symbolic landscape depicting the female genitals: behind the Sistine Madonna ("*Bild*") lies a "*Weibsbild*," as Freud tells us, "literally, 'picture of a woman'—a somewhat derogatory expression for 'woman'" (*SE* 7:99*n*.). The most sublimated representation of femininity (a Madonna) veils a venereal landscape (a "nude and passably erotic" Venus).

As Freud points out, Dora identifies herself with a young man in the first part of her dream, adoring the Sistine Madonna from the perspective of her own distant adorer; she is at once lover and ideal beloved. She also identifies with a man in her concealed defloration fantasy; here she is at once seducer (this time, Herr K.) and seduced. Her perspective on the symbolic geography mapped by medical terminology is also masculine, by virtue of being identified with Freud's. With a remarkable demonstration of linguistic acuity, Freud traces her terminology to a source of information which replicates (and implicates) his own professionally gynecological, or gyne-philological, stance in relation to Dora. To whom, then, does the concealed fantasy of defloration belong? Is feminine desire bound hysterically to imitate the forms of masculine fantasy? But perhaps one should ask instead: what economy produces the fantasy? If the fantasy is Dora's, and not simply that of (respectively) her adorer, her seducer, or her analyst, then she imagines herself a deflowered virgin—revising or screening the fantasy by identifying with Raphael's virgin mother—from a point of view that is "masculine" precisely because specular. Unless, of course, as Freud later suggests, it is "gynaecophilic"; i.e., involves loving a woman as a man might do. But loving women and looking at them turn out to be implicated in the same specular economy. The hysteric may be characterized by her confused sexual identifications; but in this scenario, Dora has no alternative to her confusion since neither sexual ideology nor sexual representation (neither the construction of loving nor the structure of looking) can be anything but male identified. One way to read *Dora* might therefore be to rethink Lacan's "subjective impasse" (Dora's need to accept herself as the object of male desire) in terms of the route leading from "*Bild*" to "*Weibsbild*"; in terms, that is, of the related impasse which Jacqueline Rose calls "this question of woman *as* representation."[26] The politics of visibility which render feminine desire invisible to Freud (and Dora too) except as a reflection of masculine desire can be unsettled by provoking (as for Kristeva, Bellini's paintings do) what eludes a specular economy, its invisible margin.[27] In the blankness or *"vide"* which structures the pre-oedipal, Freud's missing mother may yet be glimpsed.

At this point I want to turn to Kristeva in an attempt to refigure "this question of woman *as* representation" as it bears on Freud's representation of the mother. Kristeva's theory of the pre-oedipal refines Lacan's "mirror phase" by pushing further back the moment of accession to the world of reflecting images and objects (whether seen, heard, or felt) which bring the infant into being as a subject. Lacan's rereading of *Dora* refers in passing to Dora's need to gain access to her femininity—that is, to her genital nature, as opposed to the mis-recognition of the body and "functional fragmentation" which link the mirror phase with the fragmented conversion symptoms of hysteria. In their reading of the scene of the Sistine Madonna, the authors of the collective "Dora Archive" suggest that Dora's immobilization before the image of the mother recalls the fascination of the mirror phase. Dora's deepest desire would be not so much identification with the mother, as (imagined) fusion with her in the imaginary, prior to its rupture by entry into the symbolic.[28] For Lacan, the subject first comes into being as a fiction or mis-recognition. The child held up to the mirror in its mother's arms gains a necessary but illusory sense of coherent identity, an image bounding its fragmented and incoherent drives. The mother grants the image to the child, but this image is at once alienated (exterior) and fractured (doubled or split). Language will come to symbolize the process of alienation and splitting through which the "I" or subject is constituted by and in an order outside itself, and therefore both in and as division.[29] Or, to recapitulate Kristeva's account, it is not so much the mother's look that guarantees the child's image, founding its narcissism and therefore its subjecthood, as her looking away—her imaginary focus on something other than the child (call it the phallus). In its identification with the mother, the child identifies also with this desire for and of the other; hence with the absence or *"vide"* which the child simultaneously preserves (in order to preserve its emerging identity) and covers over (as a defence against separation or absence). Primary narcissism—in Kristeva's terms, "the whole machinery of images, representations, identifications and projections" to which it gives rise—is a conjuration from and against this originating "*vide.*" As she puts it, "Separation is our chance to become subjects of representation."[30] But becoming a subject of representation means casting out or "abjecting" the mother.

Kristeva's refinement of the mirror stage in terms of the pre-oedipal origins of the representing subject could be reformulated in terms of yet another origin, that of sexuality. In "Fantasy and the Origins of Sexuality," Laplanche and Pontalis (the subtlest as well as the most authoritative interpreters of a post-Lacanian Freud) redefine the moment when the subject becomes the subject of representation as the birth of sexual fantasy. Autoeroticism, they argue, begins in "the moment when sexuality, disengaged from any natural object, moves into the field of fantasy and by that very fact becomes sexuality." Or, if you like, it is "the breaking in of fantasy which occasions the disjunction of sexuality and need." Fantasy disjoins sexuality from any natural function; it is "the first manifestation of desire," and although desire may be created by the lack of an object, it can never be appeased. Sucking, the most primal source of instinctual pleasure, becomes autoerotic, and hence sexual, at the point when it is disengaged from the fulfillment of need: "sexuality lies in its difference from the function: in this sense its prototype is not the act of sucking, but the enjoyment of going through the motions of sucking . . . the moment when the external object is abandoned."[31]

By the very fact of being detached from a natural object (i.e., the mother) and handed over to fantasy, sexuality as such can come into existence. This approximates to Kristeva's moment of abjection—the process by which a not-yet-subject constitutes itself in relation to a not-yet-object through the opening of a functional gap (call it desire or lack), as distinct from the prior merging of subject and object in a form of instinctual satisfaction impelled by need. The ideal of autoeroticism, suggest Laplanche and Pontalis, is "lips that kiss themselves"—minimal difference or division within the subject which is not yet constituted in relation to a genuine other.[32] Pursuing the relation between autoeroticism and fantasy, or the staging of erotic scenarios, Laplanche and Pontalis distinguish fantasy itself from the object of desire; rather, fantasy is the setting for desire: "In fantasy the subject does not pursue the object or its sign: he appears caught up himself in the sequence of images. He forms no representation of the desired object, but is himself represented as participating in the scene although, in the earliest forms of fantasy, he cannot be assigned any fixed place in it."[33] That is to say, the subject may be present in the original fantasy only in a desubjectivized form—as a not-yet-subject, located only in the syntax or structure of the autoerotic fantasy itself.

To return to Freud, Dora's earliest memory is a memory of sucking; the sexual fantasy later grafted onto it is a scene of imagined fellatio involving her father and Frau K. Freud convincingly makes the connection between the memory and the fantasy; but for us the parallel is triangulated (so to speak) by the picture of the sublimated Madonna and its concealed "*Weibsbild.*" Freud defines a hysterical symptom as "the representation—the realization—of a phantasy with a sexual content . . . signif[ying] a sexual situation" (*SE* 7:47). Dora's collection of hysterical symptoms are specifically oral: disgust (she is mildly anorexic); a nervous cough or *tussis nervosa;* loss of voice. Freud early on refers Dora's disgust (provoked by Herr K.'s attempt to kiss her) to "repression in the erotogenic oral zone, which, as we shall hear . . . had been over-indulged in Dora's infancy by the habit of sensual sucking" (*SE* 7:46). Later, in the context of Dora's nervous cough, Freud elicits from her an unconscious fantasy of fellatio to which she gives "expression by an irritation of her throat and by coughing." In her case, Freud tells us, "a noteworthy fact afforded the necessary somatic prerequisite for this independent creation of a phantasy:"

> She remembered very well that in her childhood she had been a thumb-sucker. Her father, too, recollected breaking her of the habit after it had persisted into her fourth or fifth year. Dora herself had a clear picture of a scene from her early

childhood in which she was sitting on the floor in a corner sucking her left thumb and at the same time tugging with her right hand at the lobe of her brother's ear as he sat quietly beside her. Here we have an instance of the complete form of self-gratification by sucking . . . (*SE* 7:51)

For Laplanche and Pontalis, this early recollection would be the originating scene of autoerotic fantasy; pleasure is fantasized in relation to a function that has lost its object. Dora sucks her thumb but the breast has gone. The mother is absent. (Freud's analysis, it might be noted, makes much of the "secret" of Dora's childhood masturbation, tying its origins to her infant thumb sucking.)

In his Leonardo essay, Freud writes that it's not necessary to have read Krafft-Ebing's *Psychopathia Sexualis* or any other source of information to have the fantasy of fellatio which he attributes both to Leonardo and to Dora; "Women it seems, find no difficulty in producing this kind of wishful phantasy spontaneously" (*SE* 11:86–87). It comes straight from the nipple. In Dora's case, Freud comments that "this excessively repulsive and perverted fantasy of sucking at a penis has the most innocent origin," the substitution of penis for nipple or thumb; it is simply "a new version of what may be described as a prehistoric impression of sucking at the mother's or nurse's breast" (*SE* 7:52). But the obvious substitution (penis for breast) explains neither the scene of autoerotic activity as Dora recollects its "syntax" nor why it should come to structure her later fantasy of fellatio—not to mention her entire constitution as a desiring and representing subject. Here Lacan's reading of *Dora* provides a shrewd interpretation. For him "the image . . . of Dora, probably still an *infans*, sucking her left thumb, while with her right hand she tugs at the ear of her brother, her elder by a year and a half" provides what he calls "the imaginary matrix in which all the situations developed by Dora during her life have since come to be cast. . . . It gives us the measure of what woman and man signify for her now." In other words (Lacan's), "her only opening to the [maternal] object was through the intermediary of the masculine partner, with whom . . . she was able to identify, in that primordial identification through which the subject recognizes itself as *I.*"[34] Dora's fantasized, autoerotic relation to the maternal body is structured from infancy by a masculine mediator, and it is through this structure that she arrives at her first "primordial identification" as a not-yet-subject.

Dora's elder brother simultaneously marks Kristeva's pre-oedipal paternal space and the absence of the mother; later, the oedipal father takes over in her fantasy of fellatio or sexual sucking involving Frau K. Like the missing mother, Dora herself is only to be seen in the fantasy's syntax. Lacan is famous for pointing out, with the knowingness of a connoisseur, the illogicality of Dora's fantasy taking this form in view of her knowledge of her father's impotence; one might expect the fantasy of cunnilingus to arise as the more likely mode of lovemaking between an impotent man and a sexually active woman. Dora, writes Lacan, fantasizes a scene of fellatio because of her inability to detach woman from primitive oral desire (her own for her mother). Her triangulated relation to Frau K.—in Freud's terms, her "gynaecophilia"—similarly involves a masculine intermediary because her infantile autoerotic fantasy, and with it her earliest differentiation as a subject, had been structured by the third term which Kristeva equates with the archaic paternal space. The point is not that Freud inexplicably detects the wrong pages of Krafft-Ebing in Dora's unconscious, but that he missed what the transposition could tell him about Dora's relation to the (missing) mother. The effect of this blind spot for both Dora and Freud is to make the mother either "nothing" or something to be trashed ("abjected").

In Kristeva's terms, Dora constitutes herself as a representing (fantasizing and desiring) subject by identifying herself with the imaginary phallic object instead of the mother. The consequence is the casting out or abjecting of the mother, the radical exclusion of what threatens to collapse all distinctions between self and other, and with them, meaning. As Kristeva puts it epigrammatically, "To each ego its object, to each superego its abject"—to each "*Bild*" its "*Weibsbild*"; for if the "abject is edged with the sublime," by the same token sublimation verges on abjecting the mother.[35] In Freud's *Dora*, the female genitals are the unclean "abject" of desire which disturb identity and system by their ambiguity and must therefore be cast out. Defilement, according to Mary Douglas, relates to margins and to what must be jettisoned in order to maintain them. The most obvious form of marginality is matter issuing from the body—spittle, blood, milk, feces.[36] Dora's mother, with whom Dora is on bad terms, is reported as having what Freud calls "housewife's neurosis" (*SE* 7:20), an obsession with domestic cleanliness which she tries (unsuccessfully) to pass on to Dora. In a footnote, Freud raises the question of the hereditary etiology of neurosis, speculating that an unusually high number of neurotics are the children of syphilitic parents. Dora's father is syphilitic. Though Freud makes no mention of it here, he later reveals that Dora's mother suffered, not from syphilis, but from a gonorrhoeal discharge or "catarrh" transmitted by her husband.

Dora on some level understands that her mother's genitals, which ought to have been clean, have been dirtied by this "disgusting catarrh" and that, in Freud's words, "her mother's mania for cleanliness was a reaction against this dirtying" (*SE* 7:90). Dora, herself, it transpires, is also afflicted with a "common catarrh" which not only provides the basis for her nervous cough but represents the upward displacement of a "a catarrh (leucorrhoea) whose beginning, she said, she could not remember" (*SE* 7:76). On the evidence of her catarrh, Freud accuses Dora of childhood masturbation—a confession which she refuses to make orally, but which (to Freud's evident satisfaction) she makes with her fingers by playing with a little reticule at her waist. "Dora's reticule," writes Freud, "was nothing but a representation of the genitals, and her playing with it, her opening it and putting her finger in it, was an entirely unembarrassed yet unmistakeable pantomimic announcement of what she would like to do with them—namely, to masturbate" (*SE* 7:95). This is the secret that Dora has kept from her other physicians. Like another lady, who symbolically hands Freud a small ivory box to open, Dora carries about her person a representation of the female genitals, or *"Weibsbild,"* for him who has eyes to see.

As Freud puts it, Dora's fingertips chatter; "betrayal

oozes out of [her] at every pore" (*SE* 7:78). His analysis of Dora's first dream turns these treacherous female oozings to good account; here too, they betray the presence of the missing mother. Dora dreams that the house is on fire and her father wakes her; the dream continues: *"Mother wanted to stop and save her jewel-case; but Father said: 'I refuse to let myself and my two children be burnt for the sake of your jewel-case' "* (*SE* 7:64). Like the reticule and the little ivory box, the jewel case is another *"Weibsbild"*—for Freud, more than any other element in the dream "a product of condensation and displacement," combining infantile anxieties about masturbation (which Freud links with bed wetting and so, by reversal, with fire) and Dora's current anxieties about Herr K. (who had both given her a jewel case and entered her room while she was asleep). One meaning of the dream, Freud tells her, is simply "My 'jewel-case' is in danger, and if anything happens it will be Father's fault." But, he goes on, "the mystery turns upon your mother" (*SE* 7:69–70). How does the missing mother get into Dora's dream?

Dora shares not only her father with her mother, but her discharge—and her jewels. When Dora recalls an episode in which her father had given her mother a bracelet, instead of the pearl drops she really wanted, Freud suggests that she herself would have been glad to accept the gift. In the circulation of gifts and women which her very name inscribes, Dora is handed from man to man—enacting the age-old exchange of women under patriarchy. But she is also a receiver of gifts, caught up in what Lacan calls "a subtle circulation of precious gifts, serving to compensate the deficiency in sexual services, a circulation which starts with her father in relation to Frau K., and then comes back to the patient through the liberality which it releases in Herr K." Along with her mother, she also receives lavish gifts of reparation from her father—in Lacan's words, again, "the classic form of honorable redress through which the bourgeois male has managed to combine the reparation due to the legitimate wife with concern for the patrimony."[37] Dora's father gives Frau K. jewels to make up for his impotence; Herr K. gives Dora a jewel case, since he gets nothing from his wife, in return for which Dora fears she may have to give up her

own "jewel-case"; meanwhile, Dora's father gives jewels to his
wife and daughter to disguise his liberality to Frau K. while re-
compensing them for his infidelity . In both kinds of circulation, what goes round are "jewels" or "drops"—whether se-
men ("something liquid *in the form of drops,*" *SE* 7:90) or the
(con)genital discharge which Dora thinks she has inherited
from her father.

　　　For Dora, then, the hidden thought is "Mother got
both things from father: the sexual wetness and the dirtying
discharge" (*SE* 7:90). Her father is "a man of means," a man
with the wherewithal to make lavish gifts (*"ein vermögender
Mann"*); but he is also, she knows, a man without means (*"ein
unvermögender Mann"*). For Freud, however, mother rather than
father is the source of dirty liquidity. Dora gets her dirtying
discharge, not, as she supposes, from her syphilitic father (she
mistakes both her mother's gonorrhoeal infection and her own
leucorrhoea for inheritable venereal disease), but from her
masturbation; autoeroticism begins at the mother's breast. Orality and the mother represent the real source of sexual contamination, the leak in the oedipal cistern.

　　　Freud's reading of the first dream ends with a highly
condensed recapitulation of its overdetermined imagery. The
episode of the "drops" or jewelry (*"Schmuck"*) gets linked to
thoughts about sexual wetness and being dirtied by a series of
verbal connections of a largely oral or colloquial kind. Pointing
out that the word "drops" functions ambiguously as a "switch-
word" (just as "pictures" form a point of junction in the dream
thoughts), Freud locates in this bodily excretion nothing other
than the principle of ambiguity which the process of "abjection"
tries to cast out. The junction "jewel-drops" brings together
both sexual intercourse and the transmitted venereal disease
which contaminates it; the associated term "jewel-case"
(*"Schmuckkästchen"*) similarly functions, Freud says, as "an innocent word" and, because "a term commonly used to describe
female genitals that are immaculate and intact," as a word "ad-
mirably calculated both to betray and to conceal the sexual
thoughts that lie behind the dream" (*SE* 7:91). The lips of the
jewel case chatter; betrayal oozes from it. One might go a step
further than Freud. The derogatory Yiddish term *Schmuck,*

adopted from the German word for jewel, is commonly held to mean "penis" (as in the expression, "you schmuck" = "you prick"). But at least one dictionary of slang—Eric Partridge's—defines the term latinately as "female pudend" (i.e., "you schmuck" = "you cunt"). The figurative word for flowers or "jewels" of speech, *Schmuck* drops into the vernacular not only as a dirty discharge, but as dirty talk (conversely, Freud points out, a throat irritation forms the basis for a hysterical symptom "like the grain of sand around which an oyster forms its pearl," *SE* 7:83). Moreover, the treacherous ambiguity lurking within orality not only turns jewel to dirt, but man into woman, threatening as it does so to abolish difference itself, and with it the most precarious of all, in psychic terms—sexual difference.

Throughout his analysis of Dora, Freud is at pains to show that the woman—ambiguous orality—talks dirty, but not the doctor. Although he announces near the start that "sexual questions will be discussed with all possible frankness, [and] the organs and functions of sexual life will be called by their proper names" (*SE* 7:9), he anxiously parades the gyneco-philological propriety of his sex talk with Dora. "Why, after all, your treatment is far more respectable than Mr X.'s conversation!" (*SE* 7:49)—so one of his women patients gratifyingly exclaims. Eschewing bawdy talk, Freud is like the gynecologist who maps the female sexual landscape in latinate terms (*Nymphae, vestibulum*), or the taxonomist of sexual practices who refers to cocksucking as fellatio. At all times he shows himself mindful—too mindful—of Dora's innocence, insisting that he never imparted his own sexual knowledge to her until it became clear that (as always proves the case) she already knew. Where hysteria is, "innocence of mind" is not; the therapist's role is simply "to translate into conscious ideas what was already known in the unconscious" (*SE* 7:49). If Dora is no innocent, Freud can converse on sexual topics without risk: "I did not call a thing by its name until her allusions to it had become so unambiguous that there seemed very slight risk in translating them into direct speech" (*SE* 7:31).

But translation, or naming, is never innocently un-ambiguous; never risk free. The "scene of sexual gratification *per os*" imagined between Dora's father and Frau K. provides

Freud with his opportunity to call a spade a spade only to find his tools already dirty. *Per os,* he recommends a sanitizing dryness: "The best way of speaking about such things is to be dry and direct" (*SE* 7:48). Yet the conversation veers riskily (excitingly?) toward impropriety just as, in his essay on the uncanny, Freud describes himself being drawn back repeatedly to the red light district of a strange city. Defending himself against the horror that his risqué talk "may perhaps have excited in the medical reader," Freud insists: "I call bodily organs and processes by their technical names, and I tell these to the patient if they—the names, I mean—happen to be unknown to her. *J'appelle un chat un chat*" (*SE* 7:48). Or, as Jane Gallop translates Freud's pussyfooting, "I call a pussy a pussy."[38] The vernacular is always contaminated, always at risk from the punning ambiguity which Kristeva identifies with the semiotic or maternal. Regressive orality can't be rinsed out of the mouth since it sullies the symbolic as a trace or taste of originating pre-oedipal difference. All Freud can do is mouth dry technical names in the face of an impropriety which constantly risks making him a sucker. The name of that impropriety is mother.

Freud's footnote of "supplementary interpretations" to the Madonna leads, via Dora herself (for whom the Madonna functions as a counter-idea against imputations of sexual guilt), to the books she has read in her quest for sexual knowledge, and thence to Dora's surname, whose repressed presence Freud detects in her second dream. The reason for its repression, Freud suggests, "lay in her surname itself, which also denoted an object and in fact more than one kind of object, and which could therefore be regarded as an 'ambiguous' word." For obvious reasons, Freud was unable to disclose Dora's surname in order to "show how well designed it was to indicate something 'ambiguous' and 'improper'"(*SE* 7:104–5*n.*). Dora's real name was Ida Bauer. Although "*Bauer*" means "peasant," it can also denote yet another feminine container, a birdcage. Freud doesn't specify whether this was a slang term for the female genitals, but simply continues: "These improper words seemed to point to a second and *oral* source of information, since the encyclopaedia would not cover them" (*SE* 7:105*n.*). This second, oral source, he suspects, is none other than Frau

K., the woman who had originally calumniated Dora—as reported by Herr K. to Dora's father—by saying "that she took no interest in anything but sexual matters, and that she used to read Mantegazza's *Physiology of Love* and books of that sort in their house on the lake" (*SE* 7:26). Freud's note concludes, triumphantly: "Behind the almost limitless series of displacements . . . it was possible to divine the operation of a single simple factor—Dora's deep-rooted homosexual love for Frau K." (*SE* 7:105*n*.). The ambiguity is cleared up; or rather, attributed unambiguously to Frau K. ("a single simple factor").

The series of displacements that leads by way of the Madonna to the literature of sexology, and from there to improper words and orality, tends inexorably toward female homosexuality. Throughout *Dora*, Freud uses a liquid metaphor of tendency to image the regressive current associated with Frau K. Unconscious sexual thoughts become "a current . . . pouring into the symptom, in the words of the Gospel, like new wine into an old bottle" (*SE* 7:54). Although "the homosexual current of feeling often runs completely dry" it is "often set flowing again by the libido in later years" (*SE* 7:60); "*gynae-cophilic* currents of feeling are to be regarded as typical of the unconscious erotic life of hysterical girls" (*SE* 7:63); and finally, Freud's last footnote insists not only that "[Dora's] homosexual (gynaecophilic) love for Frau K. was the strongest unconscious current in her mental life" but that "the current of feeling" which ran contrary to her craving for revenge was her love for the woman who had betrayed her (*SE* 7:120). Frau K., betrayer and gossip, is at once the ultimate source of all orality—she who sets flowing the gynaecophilic current—and the object to which its regressive flow returns.

Freud's last footnote reverts to Frau K. specifically in connection with Dora's sexual knowledge. Ostensibly reproaching himself for his failure to inform Dora of her homosexual love for Frau K., Freud raises his earlier question. What, or who, is the source of Dora's sexual knowledge? "I ought to have guessed," Freud writes, "that the main source of her knowledge of sexual matters could have been no one but Frau K.—the very person who later on charged her with being interested in those same subjects" (*SE* 7:120*n*.). Previously, Freud has identified a former governess of Dora's ("well-read and of educated views") as "the source of all Dora's secret knowledge" (*SE* 7:52*n*.). Just as Dora turns out to have "lived for years on a footing of the closest intimacy" with Frau K. ("There was nothing they had not talked about," *SE* 7:61), so "This governess used to read every sort of book on sexual life and similar subjects, and talked to the girl about them" (*SE* 7:36*n*.). Like Frau K. herself, the governess turns out to have been making use of Dora with an eye to her father; once Dora discovers her motives, she has the governess sacked. But Dora too has behaved like the governess in her motherly attentions to Herr K.'s children; hence the violence of her rejection of Herr K.—fueled by the knowledge that he propositions her with the same words which he had successfully used to seduce the K.'s own governess ("he got nothing from his wife").

The pair of governesses, one in each household, reveal a parallel pair of subplots—on one hand, covert desire for the father of the house (a plot which implicates Dora); and on the other hand, the covert transmission of sexual knowledge (a plot which implicates Frau K.). As Jane Gallop points out, "The family never was, in any of Freud's texts, completely closed off from questions of economic class. And the most insistent locus of that intrusion into the family circle . . . is the maid/governess/nurse."[39] At once the hole through which sexual, social, and economic oppression leaks into the family and the source of contaminating sexual knowledge, the governess proves in the last resort to be only ambiguously differentiated from Dora or Frau K., or even from Dora's mother (whose role is that of a domestic). Despite appearances, all women are mutually substitutable, whether governesses or daughters, maids or mothers. But it is the governess who gets sacked—cast out in order to maintain the fiction of Dora's purity—and the mother who counts for nothing so that Frau K. can have it all (or have it off) with impunity.

Freud renamed Dora after a maid who had herself been renamed because her own too flowery name (Rosa) was that of the lady of the house, Freud's sister.[40] A gift between men, Dora is also called after a domestic servant; although her function is dignified by classical learning (the language of books), she is domesticated and subordinated by word of mouth. Dora famously revenged herself on Freud and on all men by terminating her analysis, giving Freud himself two weeks' notice as if he were the maidservant. As Gallop puts it, "Dora and Freud cannot bear to identify with the governess because they think there is still some place where one can escape the structural exchange of women."[41] For Freud, identifying himself with the governess has an additional risk, since it brings home to himself, or domesticates, the question of sexual knowledge. The source of knowledge is at issue not only in Freud's dealings with Dora, but in his relation to knowledge generally. If the prior source of Dora's sexual knowledge is Frau K., and before that her governess, then Freud himself has always been anticipated in what he discloses to Dora; just as there is always an oral source as well as Dora's book-derived information. In this scheme, Frau K. not only forestalls Freud (clearing him of the imputation of improper talk); she also becomes his rival—the feminine other or (m)Other Woman who unsettles the oedipal triangle, and with it the authority of Freudian theory to instruct and interpret.

The relation between Freud and Frau K. (ultimately the relation between Freud and the missing mother) can be formulated in terms of Freudian theory. Gallop points out that Freud was forced to revise his original theory of hysteria (that hysterics had undergone actual seduction by their fathers), substituting for it the hysterical seduction fantasy (a screen for the hysteric's own wish to seduce). But when it came to the mother, he later let slip the crucial distinction between actual and fantasized seduction. In "On Femininity" (1932), seduction fantasy is pressed back into service to illuminate the pre-oedipal phase, where it turns out to have an actual basis in the mother's relation to the little girl's body ("by her activities over the child's bodily hygiene [the mother] inevitably stimulated, and perhaps even aroused for the first time, pleasurable sensations in her genitals," *SE* 22:120). In "Female Sexuality" (1931), Freud writes of the common fantasy that makes mother or nurse into a seducer: "Actual seduction, too, is common enough; it is initiated either by other children or someone in charge of the child who wants to soothe it" (*SE* 21:232). As in

Dora, there is a split between mother and nursemaid. The mother may unwittingly arouse the child's body in the course of tending it, but the nurse does so deliberately; in Gallop's words, only "The servant, member of a lower class . . . is capable of a perversion."[42] Why does Freud save the mother by calumniating the nurse?

The answer, I think, is to be found in the same minimal difference which structures the distinction between book language and improper oral sources. In *"Mater* and Nannie: Freud's Two Mothers and the Discovery of the Oedipus Complex,"* Jim Swan links the emergence of Freud's theory of the Oedipus complex with a series of dreams related to Wilhelm Fleiss during Freud's period of self-analysis in 1897, involving recollections of the old nursemaid who had looked after him as a small child. Freud calls her his "prime originator;" in German, his *"Urheberin"*—his upbringer, or rather, his first seducer, since she was also his "teacher in sexual matters" (*SE* 1:262).[43] The old woman at once arouses him and shames him; she is unattractive but humiliating. By contrast, Freud refers to his mother, latinately, as the *"matrem"* toward whom his sexual feelings were awakened after spending the night with her during a journey and probably seeing her *"nudam"* (*SE* 1:262). He is guiltily aroused toward his (linguistically purified) mother, whereas the old nannie shamefully arouses him. Swan argues that the early split (pure mother, sexually shaming nannie) gets redistributed in the later relationship between pure mother and humiliating father figure of the oedipal triangle; but this argument seems less compelling than his examination of the pre-oedipal split itself—or rather, its formulation in terms of purity and danger.

The naked *"mater"* and the old nannie (it scarcely needs saying) are one and the same, like Dora and the sacked governess, or Frau K. and the neurotic housewife. But the means by which Freud effects the split between mother and nurse are worth noticing, as is the curious fact of his own identification with the nannie. Freud recalls two "ancient" (and therefore, by implication, reliable) memories of "bad treatment" by his nurse—that "she washed [him] in reddish water, in which she had previously washed herself" and that "she made [him] carry off *'zehners'* (ten kreuzer pieces) and give them to her" (*SE* 1:263). If the reddish tinge of the water is attributed to menstrual blood, this is strange, since his nurse was an old woman; only "*mater*" could have mistreated him so. As for the coins, it turns out (and here Freud's revered mother was his informer) that far from making Freud steal coins for her, his nannie actually stole them from him; for this she was subsequently sacked and imprisoned—swelling the ranks of dismissed domestics. On one hand, Freud purifies the mother by defiling his nurse with menstrual blood, and so (to use Kristeva's term) abjects her; on the other hand, he accuses himself of her crime toward him, abjecting himself. Hers, after all, is the peculiarly abject and identity-disturbing crime of betraying the innocent whose welfare is her charge. This would be Freud's crime if he took Dora's money only to seduce her mind.[44]

The function of rituals of defilement and pollution—the "abjection" which accompanies all religious structurings—is for Kristeva "to ward off the subject's fear of his very own identity sinking irretrievably into the mother."[45] The purity of Madonna or "*mater*" is ensured by abjecting menstrual blood, a sign at once of her ability to conceive and of the fragility of the symbolic order: the process which wards off fear of sinking irretrievably into the maternal body consists in abjecting the maternal body itself. This is the process encoded in the configuration of ideas surrounding the composite figure, at once "*mater,*" nannie, and the nannie-identified infant Sigmund, of Freud's "ancient" memories. Ultimately at stake here is nothing less than sexual identity; "Menstrual blood," writes Kristeva, "stands for the danger issuing from within the identity (social or sexual); it threatens the relationship between the sexes . . . and . . . the identity of each sex in the face of sexual difference."[46] If Freud is like nannie, what is to stop him being like mother? Only the taboo of menstruation. The signifying order which inscribes limits and distinctions in language—rejecting the oral as "improper" and instituting the latinate language of gynecology as the language of sexual propriety—repeats the same process, abjecting the oral as defilement or contamination. Just as Freud displaces menstrual blood from *"mater"* to nannie, so he displaces dirty talk from his own conversation (and writing) to oral exchanges between women.

In *The Interpretation of Dreams* (1900), Freud himself records that it was the mother who had taught him his first lesson about the relation between knowledge and dirt, with a piece of "ocular demonstration:"

> When I was six years old and was given my first lessons by my mother, I was expected to believe that we were all made of earth and must therefore return to earth. This did not suit me and I expressed doubts of the doctrine. My mother thereupon rubbed the palms of her hands together—just as she did in making dumplings, except that there was no dough between them—and showed me the blackish scales of epidermis produced by the friction as a proof that we were made of earth. My astonishment at this ocular demonstration knew no bounds . . .(*SE* 4:205)

Here the latinate *mater* turns out, by a punning effect of the semiotic, to contain the "matter" to which all life returns, and all knowledge too. The identity of the lesson (the body is material) and the teacher (the maternal body) constitutes a similar epistemological pun. *Mater* is matter; or, as Freud will formulate it, what is the matter with mother is precisely her materiality. As Sarah Kofman points out in *The Enigma of Woman*, the mother's visual demonstration "anticipates the science to come, in which men merely formulate, formalize, what women have always known though they have been unable to say it, only to show it." The attempt (in Kofman's terms) to "suspend" the mother (in Kristeva's, to "abject" her) "amounts in effect to wishing for self-conception, and thus to cause the mother to die before giving birth, or else to cause the son to be born before the mother."[47] This is the theorist's ruse in *Dora*. By suspending or abjecting the mother, Freud authors the immaculately self-conceived speculations of theory which always anticipate (by abjecting) the ocular demonstrations of the earthy maternal body.

Kristeva's theory of "abjection" helps us to see why the mother is missing when minimal but crucial linguistic differences or epistemological boundaries are at stake.[48] The mother must be absent in order for a self-conceived Freud to authorize a clean break between psychoanalytic theory and practice, on one hand, and women's knowledge and women's talk, on the other. But the unclean matter in *mater*—the semiotic in the symbolic—always turns out to be the prior source of his own sexual knowledge, as well as the source of the treacherous impropriety that makes all language risky. Language can never be cleansed of orality, any more than knowledge can be rinsed of grubbiness; betrayal oozes from its puns. Like the distinction between oral and written language, or *mater* and nannie, the distinction between what Freud knows and what Dora knows (between Freud and the mother in whose identity he fears to lose his own) is based on the fiction which abjection sustains. Both Freud and Dora have the same first seducer, the same first sexual teacher or "*Urheberin,*" and the same (masculine) identification with the mother which for Freud makes Leonardo at once homosexual and his investigative precursor.

In *Dora*, the virgin's immaculate (self-)conception provides an image for Freud's own attempted theoretical self-conception, his abjection of the mother, and his installation of the oedipal perspective as the only angle on the pre-oedipal. Freud makes Dora's mother a neurotic housewife obsessed with cleanliness; but his obsession with keeping his own talk and text pure makes her a figure for a haunting theoretical anxiety. Getting rid of the mother is a way of cleaning up before himself (establishing oedipal priorities), but also, perhaps, a way of denying the materiality of signs. "The mother"—Kristeva's term for the unauthorized (jouis) sense heard in signification—generates the treacherous signs of what is missing. The "*Weibsbild*" in the "*Bild,*" the linguistic impropriety or epistemological blurring of boundaries which unsettles Freud's mastery of language and contests his monopoly on knowledge, the missing mother in Freud's text leaves her traces in its hysterical pregnancy—in its unconsciously embodied "sense" or "matter." Despite its masculine identification, the phantom pregnancy of *Dora* discloses the pre-oedipal whenever it throws up or gives birth to ("spits, vomits, bleeds, grows fat, and symptomizes") the impropriety which is the material of language, or the material basis of life which is the property of knowledge. To put it another way, what hatches when the mother goes missing in Freudian theory is the *couvade*.[49]

IV. ANNA (WH)O.'S *ABSENCES:* READINGS IN HYSTERIA

Preface

"**I have not** always been a psychotherapist . . . it still strikes me myself as strange that the case histories I write should read like short stories and that, as one might say, they lack the serious stamp of science. I must console myself with the reflection that the nature of the subject is evidently responsible for this, rather than any preference of my own. The fact is that . . . a detailed description of mental processes such as we are accustomed to find in the works of imaginative writers enables me, with the use of a few psychological formulas, to obtain at least some kind of insight into the course of [hysteria]. Case histories of this kind . . . have . . . an intimate connection between the story of the patient's sufferings and the symptoms of his illness—a connection for which we still search in vain in the biographies of other psychoses" (*SE* 2:160–61).

Freud's literary confession opens his discussion of "Fräulein Elisabeth von R.," the last of the five case histories included in *Studies on Hysteria* (1895). Declaring himself an estranged scientist ("I have not always been a psychotherapist"), Freud also places himself in a strange relation to his own writing ("it still strikes me myself as strange [*eigentümlich*]"). The author of case histories that read like literary texts—short stories—he experiences their literariness as peculiar or alien, as if imposed on him by the nature of his subject; almost as a form of hysterical utterance. The story of the patient's sufferings, he discovers, is intimately connected with the patient's symptoms. As hysteria produces symptoms, so symptoms produce stories. The body of the hysteric becomes her text: the body of Freud's text becomes a short story. The hysterical "conversion" from mind to body and from body to text—from hysteria, via symptom, to narrative—implicates the narrator himself in the "splitting of consciousness" or hysterical estrangement which (in Breuer and Freud's own terms) characterizes the original illness. Hysteria, Freud seems to say, generates hysterical narrative, and hysterical narrative makes strange reading.

Studies on Hysteria, the collaborative collection of case histories and theoretical papers published by Breuer and Freud between 1893 and 1895, marks the beginning of the psychoanalytic discourse that has come to be known as Freudian. From the start, there was "an intimate connection" (like the connection between the patient's story and her symptoms) between psychoanalysis, hysteria, and the telling of stories—stories which by definition "lack the serious stamp of science." If science is knowledge, literature is the knowledge that knows more than it knows, just as the hysteric's story remembers what its teller has forgotten. Like the "Hysterics [who] suffer mainly from reminiscences" (in Breuer's famous definition, SE 2:7), literature too suffers from reminiscences, forever repeating stories or prior texts whose meaning has been lost. The significance of Breuer and Freud's discovery—that the symptom (reminiscences) and the cure (reminiscing) were related—led to the institutionalization of "the talking cure" as the defining therapeutic mode of psychoanalysis. Psychotherapy has been called "the listening cure"; unlike Charcot, Breuer and Freud listened to their patients instead of merely looking at them. But they were also the first systematic close readers.

The characteristic literary form of psychoanalysis is a narrative that resembles "the works of imaginative writers," not only in its representation of mental processes, but in constituting itself as what contemporary criticism would call "a reading" (a reading of the tale told by the hysteric's body). The tales which Breuer and Freud retold and reread (reminisced and repeated) compel them to reenact the hysterical processes they describe; forgetting the meaning of the stories they tell, analytic listeners are themselves turned into hysterical tellers—"turned," that is, by the transferences of hysteria, the "intimate connection" that seems inescapable, even uncanny. The founding text of psychoanalysis, in other words, tells a double story. The case histories included in Studies on Hysteria are at once narratives generated by hysteria, and narratives that generate hysterical reading—a form of reading which might even be called theoretical. Hysterical or psychoanalytic theory is the shadow-image of hysteria; the one constitutes and is constituted by a reading of the other. The literariness that strikes Freud as strange is the symptom of this doubling or rereading. Analytic reading reactivates passive desire and returns blindness to insight. Like the literary text, the psychoanalytic text knows more than it knows; the difference between it and "science" is its implication, at once knowing and unknowing, in the transferential processes that constitute knowledge.

This uncanny turn in the literature of psychoanalysis—the turn toward literature—can be traced, not simply to hysteria, but to women. The strangeness of hysterical desire is inseparable from femininity. Freud acknowledged that hysteria was not specific to women, and with easy hindsight we can say that the prevalence of hysteria in Freud's women patients had its social origins in the oppressive and domestically confined lives of middle-class wives and daughters at the end of the nineteenth century. Still, the very name of the illness inscribes the specificity of the female body, and in doing so, repeats a characteristic aspect of the hysteric's relation to language; that is, her translation of psychic metaphors into the language of the body. Naming a disease of the uterus, language produces a metaphoric "conversion symptom" of its own. Breuer, in his "theoretical" contribution to *Studies on Hysteria*, warns against "the danger of allowing ourselves to be tricked by our own figures of speech" (*SE* 2:228)—against taking figures literally—when we resort to metaphor. Figures of speech, like hysterical narratives, impose themselves on those who repeat them. To the extent that both Breuer and Freud were tricked by their own figures of speech—to the extent that they consciously or unconsciously participated in the transferential and countertransferential turns of analysis (as Breuer did in the case of Anna O., and Freud, most famously, in the case of Dora)—they too fell victim to this trickery of tropes. To the extent that they recognized the incompleteness of their stories, the limits of their knowledge, and the seductive power of language, they also acknowledged in themselves the presence of hysterical desire.

For feminist readers, the accusation is not so much

that Freud and Breuer themselves were capable of hysterical blindness in relation to hysteria (or femininity, for that matter), but that hysteria itself is seen by them as the specifically, almost normatively, feminine neurosis; Freud's theory of bisexuality ensures that this is so, since the confused sexual identifications which for him produce hysteria are themselves constitutive of femininity. As hysteria generates narrative, so femininity generates hysteria. In its anxiety to rehabilitate the hysteric, contemporary feminist criticism has tended to view her as a form of psychoanalytic heroine; Freud's case history of Dora is by now a canonical feminist text, in which Dora's resistance to taking up the position assigned to her under patriarchy makes her the first feminist critic of Freud. Hysteria, according to this reading, is the product not of femininity but of patriarchy. But there is another way to approach the intimate connection between women and hysteria in psychoanalytic theory; that is, by way of literature—or rather, by way of the turns and counterturns, the repetitions and reproductions, of the reading process itself.

Freud treats hysteria as the special case which establishes the general category of the unconscious, along with the role of sexuality, in the psychic life of all desiring subjects. Breuer excuses himself for his "extensive report" on Anna O. by citing the importance for embryology of the sea urchin's eggs—important not because sea urchins are particularly interesting but because their eggs are transparent. Similarly, woman is treated by Freud as a special case of man, her lopsided bisexual constitution at once illustrating and reproducing the structure of his, while apparently predisposing her alone to neurosis. In the same way, the study of hysteria provides the basis for psychoanalytic theory because hysterical processes lend themselves to the analytic reading process. But what is specific to femininity and what is specific to hysteria in each case turns out to provide the defining characteristics of the class to which they belong. "Femininity" and "hysteria" name the otherness or strangeness which inhabits psychoanalytic theory (and literature) and which psychoanalysis must marginalize in order to found itself as a theoretical body of knowlege.

The same could be said about the role of the uncanny in narrative. Like "romance," all forms of the improbable must be cast out in order that narrative—"realist" narrative, at least—may bear the weight of representational truth; fictionality is repressed so that realism can become a mode of knowledge authorized by "the serious stamp of science." That the construction of psychoanalytic theory, theories of sexual difference, and realist narrative resemble one another in needing to marginalize the terms which constitute them (respectively hysteria, femininity, and fictionality) perhaps tells us no more than that theory needs a victim—an error—against which to pose itself as true. Hysteria, women, and the uncanny are the points of instability which threaten to expose theory, sexual difference, and "reality" as themselves the product of representation; as constructs. The hysteria that is femininity must be repressed in the interests of a masculinist psychoanalytic theory: the uncanny that is narrative must be repressed in order to sustain a realist view of fiction (and vice versa, given the association of women and the uncanny in psychoanalysis). Hysteria provides a thread by which to unravel the enmeshed relations or "intimate connection" between theory and fiction, femininity and the uncanny, in the short stories which read (like) psychoanalysis.

In the interface between psychoanalysis and feminism, the question which arises for feminists—"Can psychoanalytic theory ever be anything but masculinist?"—might be reformulated as the different but related question which arises for feminist literary critics: "Can women's writing ever be anything other than hysterical?" More particularly, what is the literary status of that version of the uncanny known to feminist critics as "female Gothic"? Apropos of Julia Kristeva's assertion that women's writing is "the discourse of the hysteric," Juliet Mitchell has written: "The woman novelist must be an hysteric. Hysteria . . . is simultaneously what a woman can do both to be feminine and to refuse femininity, within patriarchal discourse";[1] simultaneously *what* a woman can do, and *all* a woman can do. But how can we tell a woman's writing from a man's? What is the relation between female hysteria—femininity—and the male hysteria which haunts patriarchal discourse, including the discourse of psychoanalysis, as its mirror image? As Mitchell says, "I do not believe there is such a thing as female writing, a 'woman's voice' " but only that "there is the hysteric's voice which is *the woman's masculine language"* (Mitchell's italics). But what if the special case, hysterical (women's) writing, once more turns out to define the characteristics of writing itself (just as femininity turns out to define masculinity)? And what if the features of hysterical narrative—narratives both by and about "hysterical" women, reenacting the hysterical disorders they present—turn out to embody the repressed (because disruptive, unassimilable, and contradictory) aspects of all narrative? What if they inscribe a hysteria that might as well be called masculine? Both the hysterics figured in, and the hysteria embodied by, women's writing ("the woman's masculine language") might then prove to be the shadow of male hysteria about women; hysterical narrative would expose the repressive assumptions of all narrative; and the so-called "hysterical" readings generated by women's writing would expose normative readings as themselves hysterically, unavoidably, implicated in the very stories they retell.

To test these speculations, I want to offer a reading, first of Breuer's "Fräulein Anna O.," the earliest and most celebrated of the case histories included in *Studies on Hysteria,* and then of two short stories by women writers which not only lend themselves to being read in the light of Freud's theory of hysteria, but offer their own "hysterical" readings of that theory. Charlotte Perkins Gilman's "The Yellow Wallpaper," published in 1892, thematizes hysterical reading as well as apparently fictionalizing Gilman's own breakdown in the late 1880s. George Eliot's "The Lifted Veil," published anonymously in 1859, rehearses the uncanny aspect of hysterical reminiscence while apparently fictionalizing Eliot's own melancholy fears about authorship. But both stories might also be said to know more than their authors knew, and perhaps more than their biographical readers too; in their gaps, incompleteness, and *"absences"*—their hysterical splitting of consciousness—the ghostly presence of the uncanny and of woman can be glimpsed. They are the short stories which Freud's case histories read like.

Because such stories (like Freud's own) by definition "lack the serious stamp of science," reading them next to, into, and against "Fräulein Anna O." has the effect of hystericizing both psychoanalysis and feminist criticism. The literariness or strangeness of this hysterical reading has its own "intimate connection" with a similar lack (or feminization) in the protagonists of each short story, each "case" or biography. Like Breuer's "Fräulein Anna O.," Gilman's "The Yellow Wallpaper" and Eliot's "The Lifted Veil" make the failed imaginative writer their central figure. Bertha Pappenheim (the real-life Anna O.), Charlotte Perkins Gilman, and George Eliot resemble their fictional counterparts in possessing unusual literary gifts. The difference is that while each lived to tell the tale, their stories appear to have internalized Breuer's secondhand verdict: "The overflowing productivity of their minds has led one of my friends to assert that hysterics are the flower of mankind, as sterile, no doubt, but as beautiful as double flowers" (*SE* 2:240). Not just flowers (as women should be), but double flowers, hysterics are represented as being at once more decorative than other women, and reproductively sterile; at best they can hope to resemble, like George Eliot's Dorothea Brooke, the woman whom Breuer calls "the patron saint of hysteria"— Saint Theresa, a woman of good deeds.

Literary production as well as social doing actually distinguished Pappenheim, Gilman, and Eliot themselves from the feminized figures of their "hysterical" imaginings, as if such flowers of fiction were not simply a metaphor for their own condition as nineteenth-century women, but as women writers. The woman writer's desire to produce rhetorical flowers as well as figure them—to represent or (in a different sense) to "reproduce" as well as adorn—makes her hysterically double in the field of masculine representation. But the hystericization of the woman writer is not only an aspect of the hystericization of women: it is a symptom of the hystericization of writing. Women become a metaphor for the singleness that writing itself has lost, so that the woman writer comes to figure both for herself and for her readers the hysterical doubleness and incompleteness which representation must repress in order to figure as true, unified, and whole—as masculine, or bearing "the serious stamp of science." Freud puts it rather differently from Breuer's (fictive?) friend when he writes that "hysteria of the severest type can exist in conjunction with gifts of the richest and most original kind—a conclusion which is, in any case, made plain beyond a doubt in the biographies of women eminent in history and literature" (*SE* 2:103).

Modern readers know now, as Breuer's contemporary readers did not, that Bertha Pappenheim later became a pioneering organizer and activist in the Jewish women's movement in Germany, cofounder in 1904 of the *Judischer Fräuenbund* or League of Jewish Women, and, in 1899, the translator of Mary Wollstonecraft's *A Vindication of the Rights of Woman* as well as the author of a play called *Women's Rights*.[2] Charlotte Perkins Gilman, once she had left her disabling marriage behind her, became a pioneering feminist writer, lecturer, and spokeswoman for the American women's movement. George Eliot (Mary Ann or Marian Evans) emerged from her pseudonymity to become George Eliot, the memorializer of frustrated feminine and feminist aspiration, the Saint Theresa of the nineteenth-century novel. What enabled these women (all, incidentally, deeply attached to their fathers, all overshadowed in the family hierarchy by less gifted and better educated brothers, and all in revolt against their assigned roles as women in nineteenth-century society) to accomplish so much despite the mourning, melancholia, and hysteria which afflicted them as young women? And what made them mournful, melancholy, and hysterical in the first place, given that as adolescents they were, to quote Breuer, "lively, gifted and full of intellectual interest"? (*SE* 2:240) The answers to questions like these are to be found in the history of women's oppression. The biographies of Bertha Pappenheim, Charlotte Perkins Gilman, and George Eliot ("women eminent in history and literature") are moving in their own right, but the readings that follow are not primarily biographical or historical. Rather, they are readings of three stories told by and about hysteria, by men and women, masculinists and feminists; readings designed to trace the "intimate connection" between hysteria, femininity, and literature. Their strangeness will tell—if not "all," at any rate what incompleteness or "lack" they embody; what (and whose) is the absence figured by "Anna (Wh)O.'s '*Absences*.'"

1. Taking Liberties with Words

It is an irony of the history of psychoanalysis that the patient credited with the invention of "the talking cure" (Anna O.'s English phrase for the therapeutic technique which she evolved with Breuer) should have had as her major hysterical symptom the inability to talk. Afflicted by "a deep-going functional disorganization of her speech," Anna O. took refuge in a speaking dumbness. Initially at a loss for words, and eventually almost completely deprived of them, she successively lost "her command of grammar and syntax; she no longer conjugated verbs, and eventually she used only infinitives, for the most part incorrectly formed from weak past participles; and she omitted both the definite and indefinite article" (*SE* 2:25). This loss of herself as a speaking subject is nowhere more clearly enunciated than in her tormented refrain: "tormenting." As Breuer relates, she tended to wake up with the complaint that "something was tormenting her—or rather, she would keep repeating the impersonal form, 'tormenting, tormenting'" (*SE* 2:25). Anna O.'s torment might be called the pains of thinking, and perhaps associated even with the torment of theory invoked by Freud himself in connection with *Studies on Hysteria*—a torment in the last resort connected with representation. In a letter to Breuer apropos of their joint volume, Freud writes of "the uneasiness which is apt to go along with the unremitted pains of thinking. I am *tormented* by the problem of how it will be possible to give a two-dimensional picture of anything that is so much of a solid as our theory of hysteria" (*SE* 1:147; my italics). "Torment" means (in some sense) "twisted teaching," the tor-mentor here being Breuer himself, for whom the sexual etiology of hysteria remained, literally, unthinkable. The pains of this unthinkable thought make themselves felt in the hysterical turn finally taken by Breuer's "Fräulein Anna O."—a turn in which Freud has a hand.

Language breaks down for Anna O. not only because she is haunted by tormenting thoughts but because the very process of representation involves self-estrangement, fracturing into two dimensions the unity which the hysteric yearns to recreate on the site of her body. Freud himself resorts to such hysterical thinking when he suggests that what seem now to be merely figurative expressions were once literal descriptions of physical sensations: "In taking a verbal expression literally and in feeling the 'stab in the heart' or the 'slap in the face' after some slighting remark as a real event, the hysteric is not taking liberties with words, but is simply reviving once more the sensations to which the verbal expression owes its justification." Darwin in "The Expression of the Emotions," according to Freud, has taught us that "hysteria is right in restoring the original meaning of the words" (SE 2:181). Because the hysteric seeks to restore the original meaning of words, discourse itself—conversation—can mean intercourse for Anna O. Given her familiarity with Shakespeare in the original, she may even have been conscious of the bawdy association surrounding the term "conversation" (from the Latin conversari, "to keep company with") in Elizabethan English. Anna O.'s other phrase for "the talking cure" was (again in English) "chimney sweeping"—as Freud noted wryly in a letter to Jung, "an action symbolic of coitus, something Breuer certainly never dreamed of."[1] If Breuer had dreamed in this fashion, Freud implies, he too might have woken with the word "tormenting" on his lips; or else, like Anna O., tried to keep them shut.

Unlike Breuer, Anna O. seems to have known that neither talk nor language (nor talk about language) are ever innocent. Her silence is a speaking symptom, a conversational matter (one connected with sexuality) as well as a symptom of hysterical conversion. Dumbness might be viewed as an instance of the symptom (in Freud's phrase) "joining in the conversation" (SE 2:296), just as deafness at one point joins in the conversation during her analysis. Breuer writes that this deafness had its origin in "some oversight"—a metonymic shift (from not-seeing to not-hearing) which discloses that his text knew more than he did. On the analogy with "overhearing," "oversight" can be read other-wise; as the sight of what is not supposed to be seen rather than the hysterical blindness which screens the sight from view. Anna O., we know, was haunted by an array of visual hallucinations such as death's-heads and snakes which may be suspected of screening sights at once less gothic and less innocent. The oversight is both a sight of the forbidden and its covering over or repression.

Breuer primly locates the origins of Anna O.'s hysterical silence in her having "felt very much offended over something and [having] determined not to speak about it" (*SE* 2:25). But nothing he suggests adequately accounts for either her tight-lippedness or her torment (any more than her later refusal to drink is accounted for by disgust at seeing the English lady-companion's little dog drinking out of a glass). Perhaps some critical free association is called for. Anna O. read English fluently and she copied the roman printed letters in which she wrote from her edition of Shakespeare. If she read Milton too, like this feminist critic, she might have recalled Satan's envious outburst in *Paradise Lost*, Book IV, at the sight of Adam and Eve (our first parents) engaged in the erotic dalliance which Adam later refers to as "converse sweet":

> Sight hateful, sight *tormenting*! Thus these two
> Imparadised in one another's arms
> The happier Eden, shall enjoy their fill
> Of bliss on bliss, while I to hell am thrust,
> Where neither joy nor love, but fierce desire,
> Among our other *torments* not the least,
> Still unfulfilled with pain of longing pines . . .
>   (*Paradise Lost* IV:505–11; my italics)

For the literary reader, this primal scene and the unspeakable sight of incestuous desire which it screens (Satan couples with his daughter Sin) form the forgotten story or literary pre-text of Anna O.'s tormenting thoughts.

More tormenting for the hysteric than even unfulfilled oedipal desire is the question, "Am I a man or a woman?" Satan (himself androgynously seductive) may envy both Adam his Eve and Eve her beauty, or, for that matter, her

Adam. With whom did Anna O. identify—her mother, whose place she took in her father's sickroom when he fell ill in 1880, or the father of whom she was so passionately fond, and whose death the following year precipitated a new phase in her illness? Throughout his "theoretical" contribution to *Studies on Hysteria*, Breuer links being in love and sick-nursing as "the two great pathogenic factors" in hysteria (*SE* 2:219), as if, for women at least, they were almost interchangeable—the bed equally the site (or sight) of pleasure and of pathology. "These things," Breuer told Freud, "are always *secrets d'alcove.*"[2] Perhaps Anna O. wanted not only to take her mother's place at (or in) her father's bed, but also to be her father. (The English lady-companion may even have seemed to her desirable, or desirous, whether as rival, as mother, or as seen through her father's eyes—a complication in keeping with the role played by governesses in other Freudian case histories such as Dora's). It was her father, after all whose fatal lung disease she imitated with her nervous cough, whose doctor (Breuer) became hers, and at whose bedside she experienced her first and most terrifying hallucination. Later—another "particularly terrifying hallucination"—she mistakes her own reflection in a mirror for "her father with a death's head" (*SE* 2:37), surely a revelation of morbid identification with the dead or dying father. Yet Anna O. also fantasized giving life. Breuer wrote that although her "life became known to [him] to an extent to which one person's life is seldom known to another," she had never been in love ("The element of sexuality was astonishingly undeveloped in her," *SE* 2:21–22). Events proved him wrong, exposing his knowlege as a form of denial. When sexuality finally found its way out of Anna O.'s body, it made her for Breuer himself what he most feared to find her—not only an embodiment of unspeakable feminine desire, but a mother; and at that, the mother of his own child.[3]

In the realm of sexuality, Breuer imposes on his text a silence as complete as Anna O.'s own. But language is eloquent about the confused sexual identity which he refused to recognize. Breuer tells us that Anna O. became almost completely deprived of words; or rather, he tells us that "She put them together laboriously out of four or five languages and became almost unintelligible" (*SE* 2:25). The same polyglot medley or "jargon" (Breuer's term) appeared when she wrote. Her "jargon" may figure as a euphemism for Yiddish—a language that Bertha Pappenheim in later life referred to as "the women's German," a sign at once of the Jewish woman's alienation from her heritage and her incomplete assimilation (like Anna O.'s own) into a bilingual or even trilingual culture.[4] Breuer records that he successfully removed both Anna O.'s speechlessness and this linguistic scrambling or "jargon" after diagnosing its origins in her resolution to keep her mouth shut. But curing one symptom produced another, still more startling linguistic disorder—not assimilation but internal exile: "thenceforward she spoke only in English." Regressing by way of "the women's German," she loses the woman altogether. As Breuer puts it in his summary of the successive phases of her illness, "an inhibition of speech" was succeeded by "loss of her mother-tongue" (*SE* 2:42). Loss of her *what*? According to Ernest Jones, Anna O.'s mother was "somewhat of a dragon" (the mother in her familiar role as patriarchy's housekeeper?).[5] Losing the mother tongue serves a double function, at once banishing the mother and getting rid of a powerful censor. Breuer and Freud observe again and again that hysterical language attempts to recover a lost, literal dimension in language (as if literalness too were not a metaphor); they compare hysterical symptoms to "a pictographic script which has become intelligible after the discovery of a few bilingual inscriptions. In that alphabet being sick means disgust" (*SE* 2:129). Facial neuralgia may result (so to speak) from a "slap in the face;" a "piercing look" may produce a headache; difficulty in standing may enact such phrases as "not being able to take a single step forward" and "not having anything to lean upon;" pain in walking may reproduce the fear of not finding oneself "on a right footing;" and so on (*SE* 2:176–80). As the absence of speech acquires new meaning in the pictographic script of hysteria, so the carryover into another language (translation) means what it says, to the letter.

"Fräulein Anna O." can be read not only as a case of hysterically confused sexual identity but as a case of confused cultural identity—of repressed Jewishness as well as repressed sexuality, serving as a reminder that the Jewish woman's legacy may have been as problematic for Anna O. as it was for Daniel Deronda's mother. Tellingly, Breuer (himself, like Freud, a provincial Jew who had become a Viennese doctor) suppressed aspects of her case recorded in his notes which connect Anna O.'s unacknowledged sexuality and her lost faith. If indeed the hysteric identifies with both parents, then Anna O.'s faith—or rather, the complete loss of it which Breuer's case notes record—would have been identified with her dying father.[6] The loss of her mother tongue would then become a simultaneous attempt to lose the mother and evade the Law of the Father. Breuer traces the failure of language to a founding moment of her hysterical illness (an episode she later reenacts for Breuer's benefit as the analysis draws to its close). While sitting up one night with her father, by then fatally ill, "She fell into a waking dream and saw a black snake coming towards the sick man from the wall to bite him." As she tried to fend the snake off, her arm was paralyzed (it had gone to sleep, Breuer suggests), and "when she looked at it the fingers turned into little snakes with death's heads." After the snake vanished, "in her terror she tried to pray. But language failed her: she could find no tongue in which to speak, till at last she thought of some children's verses in English and then found herself able to think and pray in that language" (*SE* 2:38–39).

Anna O.'s prayer has a double function. On one hand, the language of childhood is surely exempt from the inhibition placed on speech ("she could find no tongue in which to speak")—at least before Freud exposed this prelapsarian view of childhood by installing infant sexuality in the nursery. Just as hysterical body language (paralysis, for instance) converts forbidden desire into loss of movement, hysterical translation converts forbidden desire into loss of tongue—and then recovers it, purified, in a children's prayer ("Matthew, Mark, Luke and John,/Bless the bed that I lie on"?). But the prayer that would most naturally have come to Anna O. at a time of crisis would surely have been in Hebrew rather than English. It was not only words that failed Anna O., but her dying father—and not only childhood that released the inhibition on speech, but a language whose purely literary associations were at the farthest remove from either Yiddish (the women's German) or Hebrew (the language of her forefathers).

Language did not fail Anna O. after all, since it spoke eloquently both of her denial of sexuality and of her alienation, female and cultural, while enacting the contradictory identifications which make all gender identity (like cultural identity) at once multiple and divided.[7] Bilinguality, as much as bisexuality, might after all be said to be the condition of every speaking and desiring subject. By hysterically losing her tongue, Anna O. translates herself into another text; escaping both home and family (typically the site of women's confinement), she enters the realm of literary discourse which was later to effect her "cure." Going abroad in the nineteenth century symbolized social freedom for women; specifically, sexual freedom. It also allowed writing—deviant, undomesticated, feminist writing—to replace hysterical malaise or unspoken revolt. One has only to think of George Eliot's departure for the Continent with George Henry Lewes, or even Charlotte Perkins Gilman's abandonment of home life on the East Coast for communal living in the West.

In Victorian literature, among the most famous examples of the liberating effects of travel for the woman writer is Charlotte Brontë's *Villette*. Translation also plays a crucial role in Bronte's novel. A scene from Chapter 35 of *Villette* at once anticipates Breuer's account and provides a subtext for the scene of Anna O.'s hysterical bilinguality. At one point in Anna O.'s treatment, Breuer stages a demonstration, for a colleague's benefit, of her remarkable ability to produce fluent extempore translation into English when asked to read aloud from French. Not surprisingly, Anna O. laughingly remarks (in English), "That's like an examination" (*SE* 2:27)—the performance is a cross between an exam and a physical. She takes no notice, however, of Breuer's colleague until, with a gesture which still makes the text reek with traces of masculine aggression, he blows smoke in her face: "She suddenly saw a stranger before her, rushed to the door . . . and fell unconscious to the ground" (*SE* 2:27).[8] The scene is reminiscent of Charcot's demonstrations of the hysteric's poses before audiences at the Salpêtrière. Anna O. becomes a spectacle, the silent woman whose hysterical symptom is the gift of tongues. By triangulating Anna O.'s discourse of desire—the labour of love involved in her translation—Breuer transforms Anna O. from a speaking subject into a senseless body; in his scenario, she falls unconscious between two medical men, no longer an actress in her own drama, but a patient bearing mute testimony to psychoanalytic theory. For Anna O. herself, such scenes were not spectacles but communications—passionate avowals of love.[9] Translation becomes a metaphor for transference, as well as a metaphor for metaphor itself.

In *Villette*, M. Paul (Lucy Snowe's mentor and teacher) stages a similarly impromptu demonstration of his pupil's scholastic and literary abilities in order to disprove the charge that he has signed her name to his own literary productions. Lucy calls it a "show-trial" and thinks she recognizes in her bewhiskered, cigar smoking examiners—"Pious mentors!"—the two men who harrassed her in the dark streets of Villette on the night of her first arrival. The effect of their examination is to make her fall silent. *"Je n'en sais rien,"* she replies to all their questions (in a parody of her own hysterical denial throughout the novel), and tells us: "I either *could* not, or *would* not speak—I am not sure which" (p. 493). Finally they dictate to her a theme on which to compose in French: "Human Justice." Here Lucy, whose mother tongue is English, must demonstrate her fluency in a foreign language in order to vindicate the demanding teacher who frequently figures as her tormentor. The chapter has begun with the advice given to Lucy by Mme. Beck, the jealous mother-rival who stands between her and M. Paul in the novel's phantasmagoric inner theater: *"Oubliez les Professeurs"*—words intended as a warning ("Hands off!"), but only intensifying Lucy's transferential love for her teacher. Now Lucy seizes her opportunity to settle the score, not only with her "examiners" but with Mme. Beck: "'Human Justice' rushed before me in novel guise, a red, random beldame with arms akimbo. I saw her in her house, the den of confusion . . . a swarm of children, sick and quarrelsome, crawled around her feet. . . . The honest woman cared for none of these things . . . whenever a cry of the suffering souls about her pierced her ears too keenly—my jolly dame seized the poker . . . "; and so on (pp. 495–96). Lucy's tormentors are male, but in this vivid, Gilray-inspired caricature, she belabors a female personification, the Bad Mother. As in the Freudian scenario, hatred of the mother is the dark underside of oedipal desire for the father. The resources of another language allow Lucy to cast out the mother as dragon (Mme. Beck's watchword is the "surveillance" which she exercises over her often "sick and quarrelsome" family, her school, and her staff) by portraying patriarchy's housekeeper as at once termagant and slut, while also allowing her to court the love of her teacher-father. The double function of Lucy's undutiful *"devoir"* serves as a gloss on the scene of interpretation in "Fräulein Anna O.," where the relation of analyst to patient similarly resembles that of mentor to pupil—giving birth not only to "the talking cure" but to an untoward turn of events named transference.

The case of Miss Lucy Snowe, who at one point invokes the story of Jael driving a nail into Sisera's head as a metaphor for her self-torment, might well have provoked Freud's diagnosis in *Studies on Hysteria:* "The pain that occurs in hysteria of nails being driven into the head [is] without any doubt to be explained . . . as a pain related to thinking. ('Something's come into my head.')" (*SE* 2:180). Lucy Snowe (who is neither lucid nor chilly) can only name the estranged thoughts that come into her head by means of translation, the realm *par excellence* of metaphor. French—traditionally the language of love—allows her to utter the erotic fury repressed by her role as English lady governess. Breuer tells us that when most at her ease, Anna O. spoke only French or Italian. French was also the language that came most easily to Breuer and Freud themselves when they wrote of hysteria; Freud's own major work of translation during this period was his heavily annotated edition of Charcot's famous *Leçons du Mardi (1887–88)*, published during 1892–93.[10] Charcot, in Ernest Jones' phrase, had "'put hysteria on the map,'" and Freud in turn transformed the map of thinking about hysteria in his native Germany by importing ideas from France. From the beginning, translation has constituted an important means of intervention—sometimes, inevitably, of domestication—in psychoanalytic theory. Psychoanalysis itself could be termed (in Lacan's phrase) "the repatriation of alien

signifiers," while Breuer and Freud saw themselves as the bilingual translators of the pictographic texts presented by their
hysterics.[11] If the cure for hysteria (reminiscence) is reminiscing, the cure for Anna O.'s hysterical language (translation)
was perhaps translation itself. As well as translating Mary
Wollstonecraft's *The Rights of Woman* from English, Bertha Pappenheim later translated from Yiddish into German (the language symbolizing assimilation into the dominant culture) the
Ze'enah U'Ree'nah or Jewish women's Bible. In Breuer's
"Fräulein Anna O.," bilinguality represents a trace of the otherness of hysteria. The text is spoored with Anna O.'s English
phrases; but to describe the symptom that most clearly labels
her a hysteric, Breuer himself has to have recourse to a foreign
language, French.

What Breuer calls Anna O.'s *"absences"*—elsewhere
glossed as her *"condition seconde"* or *"double conscience"* (*SE*
2:31, 42)—mean for him the state of consciousness in which
she hallucinates and sometimes misbehaves; the place where
she is when she is foreign to herself. For Anna O., these "absences" are "lost" time and constitute a "gap in her train of
conscious thoughts" (*SE* 2:24). Her "absences" first manifest
themselves as pauses while speaking ("she used then to stop in
the middle of a sentence, repeat her last words and after a short
pause go on talking," *SE* 2:24). Mere "absence of mind," they
mark her preoccupation with the stock of images or unthinkable thoughts which later become hallucinations. *"Absences"*
characteristically occur while she is in her *"condition seconde"*—
a condition that is not synonymous with *"absence"* but continuous with it (later, Breuer says, her *"absences"* are "organized
into a *'double conscience'* ").

"Absences" have an indeterminate epistemological
status in the hysterical text. Breuer equivocates over whether
they occur, like pauses, in the middle of a sentence, or whether
they constitute the hysterical text itself, making it a tissue not of
words or presence, but of gaps, absence, and silence. The term
"absence" itself has an interesting range of dictionary meanings,
spanning both nonpresence, lack (*"manque"*), and (figuratively) *"perte de connaissance, d'esprit, etc."* Reformulated like
this, hysteria means that instead of going mad, Anna O. loses (a

part of) her mind; but it is precisely the unified status of mind that Freudian theory challenges most radically. In its dreamlike "wealth of imaginative products and hallucinations, its large gaps of memory and the lack of inhibition and control in its association" (*SE* 2:45), Anna O.'s *"double conscience"* or *"condition seconde"* is simply another name for the paradoxical coexistence of wealth and lack, gaps and productivity, characterizing unconscious processes. Breuer places *"absences"*—the sign of hysteria—over the mind's internal division. Attempting to heal the split and repatriate the alien signifiers of feminine desire, psychoanalysis can only resort to Anna O.'s own linguistic patchwork, her "jargon."

Lamenting the incompleteness of his attempts at a theoretical representation of hysteria, Breuer concludes: "With what uncertain strokes have its outlines been drawn in these pages, with what clumsy hypotheses have the gaping lacunas been concealed rather than bridged!" (*SE* 2:250). Theory—"clumsy hypotheses," in Breuer's phrase—attempts to make whole or patch up what is incomplete. The lacunas of the theoretical text mark the site of gaps in the text of hysteria. Breuer himself viewed hysterical processes as continuous with those of the theorist. Anna O., he explains, was in the habit of compensating for the monotony of her existence and her lack of intellectual outlet by "indulging in systematic day-dreaming," an activity she called her "private theatre" (*SE* 2:22). Elsewhere, Breuer writes that such daydreaming not only falls within the bounds of normality, but characterizes the analyst: "An investigator who is deep in a problem is also no doubt anaesthetic to a certain degree, and he has large groups of sensations of which he forms no conscious perception; and the same is true of anyone who is using his creative imagination actively" (*SE* 2:218). The analytical daydreamer—a creator of characters and narrator of fictions—himself possesses (or is possessed by) a double or even divided consciousness. As Juliet Mitchell has written, "a characteristic element of the illness is taken up and repeated first in the treatment and then, in its turn, finds a place at the centre of the theoretical construction."[12] Hysteria and theory resemble one another in being acts of self-division or (self-)representation. The difference is that in the case of Anna O., "habitual day-dreaming while she was well passed over into illness without a break" (*SE* 2:22). Gaps in consciousness like those experienced by the creative writer are here opposed to hysterical *"absences,"* reformulating the difference between investigator and daydreamer, theorist and hysteric in terms not of gaps but the lack of gaps—the paradoxical absence of *"absences."* The hysteric lacks "lack"; instead of recognizing division within the subject, she becomes the subject of her divisions.

Like Alice James, the hysteric can only "abandon" her body—"the pit of [her] stomach, the palms of [her] hands, the soles of [her] feet"[13]—to the fragmentation of hysterical representation. Anna O. is a creative writer manqué who lives her own texts instead of writing them. According to Breuer, she was a young woman of penetrating intuition, powerful intellect, and exceptional poetic and imaginative gifts which she was unable to realize except in her daydreams. We are told that during her "absences" she was "obviously creating some situation or episode to which she gave a clue with a few muttered words" (*SE* 2:28–29)—telling stories to herself. If cued with her mutterings, "She at once joined in and began to paint some situation or tell some story, hesitatingly at first and in her paraphasic jargon," but then with increasing fluency in correct German (this was before her shift to English). Though her stories had other topics, they usually concerned a young girl sitting anxiously, as Anna O. herself had sat, by a sickbed; their pathetic and charming style resembled, says Breuer, Hans Andersen's *Picture-Book Without Pictures*, on which they were probably modeled. After her father's death, Anna O.'s stories became more tragic and eventually, as her mental condition worsened, "her evening narratives ceased to have the character of more or less freely-created poetical compositions and changed into a string of frightful and terrifying hallucinations" (*SE* 2:29). Anna O. tells herself stories about herself, but is unable to distinguish storyteller from the story. She falls into her own text, no longer experiencing herself as a writer, but only as written; no longer as figuring, but only as a figure. Dissociated from her imaginative activity, she can only view it as a series of blinding and fragmented hallucinations.

The hysteric takes metaphor literally and so arrives at an instructive misreading. A writer manqué, she attempts to deny that the condition of writing—the condition of language itself—is one of lack. Throughout *Studies on Hysteria*, Freud draws attention to the phenomenon of hysterical reading as a specular relation to the self: "It was as though [Fräulein Elisabeth von R.] were reading a lengthy book of pictures, whose pages were being turned over before her eyes" (*SE* 2:153). Or, apropos of Frau Cäcilie's hysterical attacks, "They were like a series of pictures with explanatory texts" (*SE* 2:177). A picture book without pictures, a lengthy book of pictures, a series of pictures with explanatory texts: the string of analogies illustrates the "intimate connection" between hysteria and (picto)graphic representation—a form of representation in which the sign is fetishized as a defense against absence. Rereading her own text, the hysteric is put in illusory possession of an apparently unified version of her forgotten story; the specular relation at once doubles and stabilizes the inner division which she denies. The analyst's task is to offer a critique (a "reading") of hysterical reading, supplying the explanatory text which translates pictographs into signs and body language into metaphor. Just as it is the fate of writers to fall into their own texts, experiencing themselves no longer as figuring but as figures, so the writer continually risks (mis)taking metaphors for pictures. One might say that the fetishizing of signs is the occupational hazard of writing. What the analyst learns from the hysteric's misreading is how to be a good (that is, a metaphoric) reader; how to disembody the text and discover what the picture covers.

The analyst also learns from the hysteric how to tell a story backwards (as all stories are told), submitting to the contradictory condition of knowing and not knowing—authorial omniscience and authorial irony—at one and the same time. The analyst must pretend to know as little, and as much, as the hysteric in order to retell her story. Breuer's formulation, *"Hysterics suffer mainly from reminiscences"* (*SE* 2:7), means more than a random return of the past or a compulsion to repeat which disfigures the present. Hysterical narrative instructs the reader about the crucial role of sequence, at once foreseen and unforeseeable, in analytic interpretation. A story derives its meaning from the temporal order which constitutes it; narrative exists in the time of its telling rather than the order of its events. Throughout their case histories, Breuer and Freud emphasize the role of strict chronology not only in the etiology of hysteria (at times their quest for origins seem to be a displacement for sexual etiology) but in hysterical narrative, and in the therapeutic process itself.

Fräulein Elisabeth von R., for instance, turns the pages one after the other: "it was surprising with what promptitude the different scenes relating to a given theme emerged in strictly chronological order" (*SE* 2:153). And again: "To my astonishment the patient produced a whole number of scenes, without hesitation and in chronological order, beginning with her early childhood" (*SE* 2:172). Or this, of a lady who had nursed a number of close relatives in their final illnesses: "Shortly after her patient's death . . . there would begin in her a work of reproduction which once more brought up before her eyes the scenes of the illness and death. . . . The whole thing would pass through her mind in chronological sequence . . . this lady celebrated annual festivals of remembrance at the periods of her various catastrophes, and on these occasions her vivid visual reproduction and expressions of feeling kept to the date precisely" (*SE* 2:162–63). For Freud and Breuer, the analytical task is to reconstruct chronological sequence, facilitating the "work of reproduction," and imposing on the hysteric's rehearsal of the past a (con)sequentiality necessary both for the satisfactory therapeutic outcome of the analysis and for its subsequent literary re-presentation—which in the end amount to the same thing; the case history, after all, is a form of *Tendenzroman* in which the elimination of gaps leads simultaneously to closure and cure.[14]

Hence the formal peculiarity of hysterical narrative, its reversal of chronology in the process of retelling. Freud records that he learned from hysterical narrative "what was confirmed on countless later occasions, that when one is resolving a current hysterical delirium, the patient's communications are given in a reverse chronological order, beginning with the most recent and least important impressions and connections of thought and only at the end reaching the primary impression, which is in all probability the most important one causally" (*SE* 2:75*n*.). In the beginning of hysteria lies its end. Hysterical narrative comes full circle until, with the reproduction of its founding moment, reminiscence loses its grip on the present and life can begin again. Anna O.'s own sense of an ending informs Breuer's narrative, at once bringing her treatment to a telling close and providing Breuer himself with the formal and therapeutic re-solution which his case history calls for.

Anna O.'s "inner theatre" is really a form of re-hearsal—at once a repetition of the past and a reenactment of unarticulated desire. In the strangest development of her "talking cure," she relived for Breuer's benefit, day by day, the events of the previous year, during which first her father and then she herself had fallen ill. During her *"absences"* (now characterized by a temporal lapse or gap rather than a split in consciousness) she lives in the previous winter. Like a Proustian *madeleine*, an orange can carry her back to the time of her first collapse, when she lived almost entirely on fruit—except that the effect is less one of memory than of uncanny déjà vu. She mistakes the color of her dress, hallucinating the color of the dressing gown she had been making for her father a year before. She confuses the layout of her room in a new flat with her old room in the house where she had lived before her father's death. Finally, each of the psychic events from what Breuer terms the incubation period of her illness reappear in reverse order; and one by one, each symptom is talked away. This reverse chronology (instead of the patient living in the past, the past seems to relive the present) creates the characteristic passive voice of hysterical narrative; the story she tells, tells her. Because the hysteric always already "knows" (like the text) what has gone before, her story has an uncanny element of prevision. Its climax is an anticlimax; like the omniscient analyst, she has always seen it coming. There are no surprises after all—no secrets to unlock or mysteries to unravel—but only the repetition which Freud elsewhere defines as the secret of uncanny effects.

The culminating—or rather, originating—revelation puts an end both to the hysteric's illness and to the analyst's story by putting hysteric and reader in possession of what they have deliberately forgotten. For the analyst, too, resolution is only achieved at the price of having deliberately withheld or denied prior knowledge—a form of analytic irony close to hysterical duplicity. Remembering and forgetting, omniscience and irony, double one another in analytical and hysterical narrative. The moment of revelation only functions simultaneously as cure and conclusion because the analytic narrative has successfully reproduced the hysteric's own blindness and its transformation into insight. Knowing that her time with Breuer is drawing to a close, Anna O. uses their last session together to reenact the episode at her father's bedside when words had first failed her. After rearranging the furniture in her room to correspond to the arrangement of her father's sickroom, "she reproduced the terrifying hallucination which . . . constituted the root of her whole illness. During the original scene she had only been able to think and pray in English; but immediately after its reproduction she was able to speak German" (*SE* 2:40). The "cathartic method" is credited by both Anna O. and, more strangely, Breuer himself with almost magical curative power; as if saying the spell backwards could exorcize it. In the original episode, Anna O. had warded off evil with the magic of prayer, which permitted her to utter once more: now she wards off hysteria with cathartic utterance, the premise on which "the talking cure" is based. Reenactment leads to release. In a word, "reproduction" frees her from the compulsion to repeat.

Breuer gives the impression that with this "solution" to her case Anna became "free from the inumerable disturbances which she had previously exhibited. After this she left Vienna and travelled for a while . . ." (*SE* 2:40). But there was another act still to be played out between hysteric and analyst—one which Breuer himself felt compelled to omit from his account. Anna O.'s final performance turns on a hysterical misreading of the reproductive metaphor. For Freud, an "incomplete therapeutic result correspond[s] to an incompleteness in the analysis" (*SE* 2:154). Both Anna O., who remained seriously ill for a number of years, and Breuer, who was unable to get the story out of his head, were haunted by the hysterical aftereffects of this incompleteness. In the end, hysteria makes its presence most strongly felt, not in Anna O.'s final disclosure, but in the false closure of Breuer's narrative. His crucial omission, the gap, *"absence,"* lacuna, or (Freud's term) "hiatus" that marks the text, transforms Breuer's own narrative into a form of hysterical forgetting. The discourse of the hysteric, according to Freud, is characterized by such "gaps and imperfections" (*SE* 2:293). Confronted by sexuality, Breuer himself falls hysterically silent, enacting a censorship which Freud—taking on in relation to Breuer the role played by Breuer in relation to Anna O.—was later to lift.

The penultimate act in Anna O.'s "private theatre," the reenactment of her first hallucination, took place on the anniversary of the day on which Anna had been transferred, against her will, to a country nursing home where she saw Breuer less often and immediately became suicidal. It was her own decision to terminate her analysis with Breuer on the anniversary of this day. Immediately after Breuer's claim that Anna O. was thenceforward freed from her innumerable disturbances, Strachey inserts a footnote: "At this point (so Freud once told the present editor, with his finger on an open copy of the book), there is a hiatus in the text." The "hiatus" marks the surfacing of what Breuer systematically repressed from his account of Anna O., as she repressed it from her account of herself: the fact that Anna O. was in love with him; the fact of transference. In other words, sexuality—or rather (in the familiar biologized euphemism) "human reproduction." Anna O.'s body became the site of a reproductive or "untoward" event (as Freud later called it)[15] which not only acts out her desire to be a mother but represents in an uncanny form the work involved in both hysterical narrative and its "cure"—the work of reproduction.

The "untoward event" which marked the end of Anna O.'s treatment silenced Breuer. It also caused him to draw back from the whole enterprise represented by *Studies on Hysteria* and ultimately to dissociate himself from Freud's theory about the role of sexuality in the etiology of hysteria; or rather (in the term used by Alice James to describe hysterical dissociation) it led to his "abandonment"—Strachey's word—of their joint researches. Strachey's footnote elaborating the "hiatus" in Breuer's account is scrupulously reticent:

> It is enough to say here that, when the treatment had apparently reached a successful end, the patient suddenly made manifest to Breuer the presence of a strong unanalysed positive transference of an unmistakably sexual nature. It was this occurrence, Freud believed, that caused Breuer to hold back the publication of the case history for so many years and that led ultimately to his abandonment of all further collaboration in Freud's researches. (*SE* 2:41*n*.)

Here is Freud's own account, given in a letter of 1932 to Stefan Zweig, of the hysterical pregnancy which (unbeknownst to Breuer himself) Anna O. had been gestating as a result of their "chimney-sweeping":

> What really happened with Breuer's patient I was able to guess later on, long after the break in our relations, when I suddenly remembered something Breuer had once told me in another context before we had begun to collaborate and which he never repeated. On the evening of the day when all her symptoms had been disposed of, he was summoned to the patient again, found her confused and writhing in abdominal cramps. Asked what was wrong with her, she replied: "Now Dr. B's child is coming!"

Anna O., in other words, gave birth to the unspeakable.

But Freud does not stop with this allusion to a phantom pregnancy; the key to Anna O.'s case was also the key that unlocked his own theory of hysteria:

> At this moment [Breuer] held in his hand the key that would have opened the "doors to the Mothers," but he let it drop. With all his great intellectual gifts there was nothing Faustian in his nature. Seized by conventional horror he took flight and abandoned the patient to a colleague. For months afterwards she struggled to regain her health in a sanatorium.[16]

Breuer apparently confirmed this reconstruction before his death when his youngest daughter ("born shortly after the above treatment," Freud notes, a fact "not without significance for the deeper connections!") asked him about it. Ernest Jones writes that Freud related to him an even fuller account "of the peculiar circumstances surrounding the end of this novel treatment." According to Freud, Breuer had developed a strong countertransference, and—in a reaction "compounded of love and guilt"—brought the treatment to a close when the cause of his wife's increasing jealousy finally dawned on him.[17] One might almost say that if the case of Anna O. gave birth to "the talking cure," her hysterical pregnancy gave birth to psychoanalysis; it was she who played Mother. But psychoanalysis was to be Freud's baby, not Dr. B's.

The wording of Freud's letter is doubly significant— at once self-congratulatory (a Faustian Freud did not flee with conventional horror from the secrets of the unconscious) and apt in its use of an image from Goethe's *Faust*; when the mysteries of feminine desire were finally revealed to him, Breuer had fled from a woman giving birth (if only to herself) as Mother. Freud's later allusion echoes a moment in Breuer's "theoretical" contribution to *Studies on Hysteria* when he apologizes "for taking the reader back to the basic problems of the nervous system" with these words: "A feeling of oppression is bound to accompany any such descent to the 'Mothers' [i.e., exploration of the depths]" (*SE* 2:192). Breuer's recoil from hysteria, his recoil from femininity itself, is at bottom a recoil from the Mother—"the depths" from which all life proceeds. The revelation of Breuer's male hysteria and its speaking silence, its "oversight," clearly places Freud himself in a position of omniscience. His subtext bridges the gaping lacuna which Breuer had merely tried to conceal. Read as an unfolding sequence of revelations, Breuer's story becomes a tale-within-a-tale told by Freud, whose finger marks the hiatus in the text and turns it against Breuer himself. The all-seeing narrator proves to have a blind spot; ironized beyond his powers of prevision by an unexpected turn of events, Breuer falls through the gap and becomes a character or figure for hysteria in his own story.

But what of Anna O.? Though Freud stands in relation to Breuer's narrative as Breuer had stood in relation to his hysterical patient (that is, in a relation of knowledge), the rivalry between Freud and Breuer is the one that matters in the history of psychoanalysis. Anna O. ends up marginal to a history not her own; first on the stand as a historical witness, she testifies at a trial which is really a trial of strength between men and which, because man-to-man, excludes her. We know that the story of Anna O., as first told to Freud in late 1882 soon after Breuer had broken off the analysis, played an important part in conversations between the two men—ostensibly pupil and mentor, or junior and senior colleagues. According to Jones, Freud was so fascinated with the case that "he would discuss the details of it with Breuer over and over again."[18] But while Anna O. drew Freud to Breuer, the theoretical differences which later caused them to break off relations can already be glimpsed between the lines. In the last resort, "Fräulein Anna O." proved less important to the history of psychoanalysis than the power struggle between male theorists confronting each other over her case. Fainting on the floor between two doctors (Freud himself was a smoker), she figures as nothing but an unconscious body after all.

The hiatus marked by Freud's accusing finger points to other gaps—other signs of the future split—indicated in Freud's original contribution to *Studies on Hysteria*. Freud already knew that he knew better than Breuer (though not necessarily better than Breuer's text). His closing remarks in the final essay of the joint volume, on "Psychotherapy of Hysteria," concern no less a subject than the hysteric's erotic transferences. At first, Freud tells us, he "was greatly annoyed at this increase in [his] psychological work," until he came to see that the phenomenon of transference could be dealt with along with his patients' other symptoms. But, he ends up, if he neglected to subject the transference itself to analysis, "I should simply have given them a new hysterical symptom . . . in exchange for another" (*SE* 2:304). This new hysterical symptom was just what Breuer had given to Anna O. (" 'Now Dr. B's child is coming!' ") and Freud knew it and knew that Breuer had concealed it (according to Jones it was only when Freud told him about a similar experience of his own that Breuer allowed the story to be published.)[19]

The positioning of Freud's crucial discussion of the

mechanisms of transference gives the last word on her case, not to Breuer (and not to Anna O. either), but to him. Transference becomes the ground for a theoretical difference whose ostensible issue is the role of sexuality in psychoanalytic theory; but this issue turns out to screen one of psychoanalytic priority. Who fathered psychoanalysis, Breuer or Freud? Elsewhere, Freud consistently stresses his astonishment at discovering the sexual etiology of hysteria. But how surprised was he? And how far was his display of surprise merely a replay of Breuer's resistance—a feint (or faint) of unconsciousness? Freud's 1932 letter to Zweig corrects him for saying that Anna O. had "under hypnosis made the confession of having experienced and suppressed certain 'sentimenti illeciti (i.e., of a sexual nature) while sitting at her father's sickbed." If this had been the case, he goes on, "then everything else would have taken a different turn. I would not have been surprised by the discovery of sexual etiology, [and] Breuer would have found it more difficult to refute this theory."[20] By his own account, Freud had initially "regarded the linking of hysteria with the topic of sexuality as a sort of insult—just as the women patients themselves do" (*SE* 2:260). Where sexuality is concerned, he represents himself as playing a role not unlike that of the hysteric, surprised to discover what she has known all along.

Freud writes of "Fräulein Anna O." that the case "was not considered at all by its observer from the point of view of a sexual neurosis, and is now quite useless for this purpose" (*SE* 2:259). But his fascination with it surely came from having glimpsed in it the oversight of its blind "observer," Breuer. In Freud's terms, Breuer was afflicted by "blindness of the seeing eye" (*SE* 2:117*n.*)—a hysterical condition to which Freud disarmingly draws attention in himself. This blindness of the seeing eye, or "strange state of mind in which one knows and does not know a thing at the same time," corresponds to the splitting of the mind that defines hysteria for Breuer, and for Freud comes to structure the mind into conscious and unconscious. If Freud and Breuer are alike in their hysterical oversights, the difference between them is Freud's knowledge of just how far he can't see—which is to say that he claims to be only as omniscient as the narrator can be in a post-Freudian age. While he looks back on his own case histories as similarly unseeing, what he altered or suppressed suggests that, like his hysterical patients, he himself always (already) "knew everything that was of pathogenic significance" (*SE* 2:110). The essential condition for hysteria, after all, is that "an idea must be *intentionally repressed from consciousness*" (*SE* 2:116; Freud's italics). In its own way, *Studies on Hysteria* can be read as a psychoanalytic instance of this intentional repression on Freud's part—a split maintained in the interests of theoretical unity. With the last case history of the five included in *Studies on Hysteria*, "Fräulein Elisabeth von R.," Freud openly abandons the stance of the all-knowing scientist for the more ambiguous half-knowledge of the man of letters ("it still strikes me myself as strange that the case histories I write should read like short stories," *SE* 2:160). Read as a short story, "Fräulein Elisabeth von R." rereads Anna O.'s absences while seeming to turn a knowingly blind eye to them.

Like the case of Anna O., "Fräulein Elisabeth von R." had special significance for Freud himself since it was both "the first full-length analysis of a hysteria" which he had undertaken and the one in which he arrived at the analytic technique he liked to compare to archeological excavation, free association. Fräulein Elisabeth resembles Anna O. in being "greatly discontented with being a girl"; and with good reason: "She was full of ambitious plans. She wanted to study or to have a musical training, and she was indignant at the idea of having to sacrifice her inclinations and her freedom of judgement by marriage" (*SE* 2:140). Like Anna O., she was also deeply attached to her father, and the onset of her hysterical symptoms was similarly bound up with an anxious period of sick-nursing when he fell ill of a fatal heart disease. Her illness too was an affliction of the heart—Fräulein Elisabeth is secretly in love with her brother-in-law. "Here, then," writes Freud, "was the unhappy story of this proud girl with her longing for love" (*SE* 2:143).

Using romance as his screen, Freud creates in Fräulein Elisabeth a heroine whose very normality argues convincingly for the sexual etiology of hysteria. Though he nowhere links the death of her father and her secret (but not incestuous) love for her brother-in-law, Freud introduces a telling subtext into her story. Fräulein Rosalia (Rosalie, as Freud calls her) shares Fräulein Elisabeth's musical ambitions and is training to be a singer. But she falls ill in circumstances that are far from romantic. Instead of being in love with her brother-in-law, she has been sexually harrassed by her "uncle"—or rather, as a footnote added in 1924 reveals, by her father. Once more the scene is a sickbed: "Her bad uncle, who was suffering from rheumatism, had asked her to massage his back, and she did not dare to refuse. He was lying in bed at the time, and suddenly threw off the bedclothes, sprang up and tried to catch hold of her and throw her down. Massage, of course, was at an end . . . " (SE 2:172). Why should Freud have thought it necessary to censor the motif of father-daughter incest in Rosalie's story?[21] And why does the story of Fräulein Elisabeth rely so heavily, by contrast, on the romantic smoke screen of her doomed love for her brother-in-law? Breuer does not tell us that Anna O.'s nervous cough mimics her father's fatal lung disease. But Freud reveals that Fräulein Elisabeth develops a pain in her thigh (just as she had developed a pain in her heart) where her father's swollen leg had once lain while his bandages were being changed. The name Freud himself gave to such phenomena was displacement. In "Fräulein Elisabeth von R.," Freud displaces displacement itself from one story to another, smuggling the incestuous oedipal plot ("sentimenti illeciti") into the sickroom without risking an open break with Breuer.

"Fräulein Elisabeth von R." closes with Freud's defense of hysterical linguistic processes ("It is my opinion . . . that when a hysteric creates a somatic expression for an emotionally-coloured idea by symbolization . . . [she] is not taking liberties with words," SE 2:180–81). If hysteria is right in restoring the original (i.e., bodily) meaning of figurative expressions, the analyst too can defend himself against the accusation of taking liberties with words. The speaking body cries out to be read as a metaphor. Freud's "reading" of the text of hysteria differs from Breuer's in being a metaphorical reading—a literary reading rather than a "scientific" one. In a strategically placed footnote to the closing words of "Fräulein Elisabeth von R.," Freud turns the collaboration with Breuer to his own account, relating an anecdote in which they are comically paired. Ostensibly, his footnote illustrates the way in which symbolic translations of "artificial turns of speech" (the turns of art?) give rise to concrete or embodied images. Frau Cäcilie M., one of Freud's and Breuer's joint patients, was troubled by "a hallucination that her two doctors—Breuer and [Freud]—were hanging on two trees next each other in the garden" (*SE* 2:181*n*.). Freud's explanation is both comical and deceptively innocent. Breuer had refused to give her a drug she had asked for and so, despite her hopes to the contrary, had his junior colleague, Freud: "She was furious with us over this, and in her anger she thought to herself: 'There's nothing to choose between the two of them; one's the *pendant* [match] of the other'" (*SE* 2:181*n*.). Pendant—or match? The vignette is amusing, even mildly self-satirizing, and the word play droll; but its meaning is left ambiguously hanging—a joke, clearly, though on whom? Freud's anecdote cries out to be read in the light of his relation to Breuer, hinting, perhaps, that he is not so much Breuer's assistant as his equal; or even, when it comes to psychoanalytic reading, his superior. Is Freud simply Breuer's collaborator (a good match), or has Breuer met his match at last? Leaving their partnership hanging in the balance, Freud's footnote hangs up a sign announcing his own skills as reader of the hysterical processes on which psychoanalytic theory itself has come to hang, as if to say: "And now read on . . . "

2. An Unnecessary Maze of Sign-Reading

"I may here be giving an impression of laying too much emphasis on the details of the symptoms and of becoming lost in an unnecessary maze of sign-reading. But I have come to learn that the determination of hysterical symptoms does in fact extend to their subtlest manifestations and that it is difficult to attribute too much sense to them"(*SE* 2:93*n*.).

Freud's footnote to *Studies on Hysteria* amounts to saying that where hysteria is concerned it is impossible to over-read. The maze of signs, his metaphor for the hysterical text, invokes not only labyrinthine intricacy but the risk of self-loss. What would it be like to become lost in the subtleties of sign reading? Charlotte Perkins Gilman's short story, "The Yellow Wallpaper," provides an answer of sorts. It would be like finding one's own figure replicated everywhere in the text; like going mad. This tale of hysterical confinement—a fictionalized account of Gilman's own breakdown in 1887 and the treatment she underwent at the hands of Freud's and Breuer's American contemporary, Weir Mitchell—could almost be read as Anna O.'s own version of "Fräulein Anna O." The flower of fiction reproduces herself, hysterically doubled, in the form of a short story whose treatment by feminist readers raises questions not only about psychoanalysis, but about feminist reading.

Freud had favorably reviewed a German translation of Weir Mitchell's *The Treatment of Certain Forms of Neurasthenia and Hysteria* in 1887, the year of Gilman's breakdown, and himself continued to make use of the Weir Mitchell rest-cure alongside Breuer's "cathartic treatment." Gilman later wrote that after a month of the Weir Mitchell regimen ("I was put to

bed and kept there. I was fed, bathed, rubbed, and responded
with the vigorous body of twenty-six") she was sent home to
her husband and child with the following prescription: "'Live
as domestic a life as possible. Have your child with you all the
time. . . . Lie down an hour after each meal. Have but two
hours' intellectual life a day. And never touch pen, brush or
pencil as long as you live.'" Not surprisingly, she "came per-
ilously near to losing [her] mind" as a result.[1] Mitchell, who
apparently believed that intellectual, literary, and artistic pur-
suits were destructive both to women's mental health and to
family life, had prescribed what might be called the Philadel-
phian treatment (a good dose of domestication) rather than the
Viennese treatment famously invoked by Chrobak in Freud's
hearing (*"Penis normalis dosim repetatur"*).[2]

Gilman, by contrast, believed that she only regained
her sanity when she quit family life—specifically, married life—
altogether and resumed her literary career. "The real purpose of
the story," according to Gilman herself, "was to reach Dr. S.
Weir Mitchell, and convince him of the error of his ways."
Hearsay has it that he was duly converted: "I sent him a copy as
soon as it came out, but got no response. However, many years
later, I met someone who knew close friends of Dr. Mitchell's
who said he had told them that he had changed his treatment
of nervous prostration since reading 'The Yellow Wallpaper.' If
that is a fact, I have not lived in vain."[3] Weir Mitchell figures in
this autobiographical account from *The Living of Charlotte Perkins Gilman* (1935) as a surrogate for the absent father whom
Gilman also tried to "convert" through her writing.[4] As Juliet
Mitchell puts it, "Hysterics tell tales and fabricate stories—particularly for doctors who will listen."[5] But to read "The Yellow
Wallpaper" as a literary manifestation of transference reduces
the figure in the text to Gilman herself; recuperating text as life,
the diagnostic reading represses its literariness. Gilman's is a
story that has forgotten its "real purpose" (conversion), becoming instead a conversion narrative of a different kind—one
whose major hysterical symptom is an unneccessary (or should
one say "hysterical"?) reading of the maze of signs.

John, the rationalist physician-husband in "The
Yellow Wallpaper," diagnoses his wife as suffering from

"temporary nervous depression—a slight hysterical tendency" and threatens to send her to Weir Mitchell.[6] This hysterical tendency is shared not only by a story whose informing metaphor is the maze of sign reading figured in the wallpaper, but by the readings which the story generates. If Gilman creates a literary double for herself in the domestic confinement of her hysterical narrator, her narrator too engages in a fantastic form of re-presentation, a doubling like that of Anna O.'s "private theatre." Just as we read the text, so she reads the patterns on the wallpaper; and like Freud she finds that "it is difficult to attribute too much sense to them." Hers is a case of hysterical (over-)reading. Lost in the text, she finds her own madness written there. But how does her reading of the wallpaper differ from readings of the story itself by contemporary feminist critics?

Two pioneering accounts of the assumptions involved in feminist reading have used as their example "The Yellow Wallpaper"—by now as much part of the feminist literary canon as Freud's *Dora*. Both Annette Kolodny's "A Map for Rereading: Or, Gender and the Interpretation of Literary Texts" and Jean E. Kennard's "Convention Coverage or How to Read Your Own Life" focus on the feminist deciphering of texts which are seen as having deeper, perhaps unacceptable meanings hidden beneath their palimpsestic surfaces. Kolodny's argument—that interpretative strategies are not only learned, but gender inflected—emphasizes the unreadability of texts by women embedded in a textual system which is controlled by men. Her own reading of "The Yellow Wallpaper" repeats the gesture of Gilman's narrator, finding in Gilman's story an emblem of women's dilemma within an interpretive community from which they are excluded as both readers and writers. For Kolodny, the doctor-husband's diagnosis anticipates the story's contemporary reception; male readers thought it merely chilling, while female readers were as yet apparently unable to see its relevance to their own situation. The "slight hysterical tendency" turns out to be, not that of Gilman's narrator or even of her story, but the hysterical blindness of Gilman's contemporary readers.

As Kolodny points out, John (the husband) "not

only appropriates the interpretive processes of reading," determining the meaning of his wife's symptoms ("reading to her, rather than allowing her to read for herself"); he also forbids her to write. Kolodny's retelling of the story involves the selective emphasis and repression which she views as normative in any attempt to make meaning out of a complex literary text:

> From that point on, the narrator progressively gives up the attempt to *record* her reality and instead begins to *read* it—as symbolically adumbrated in her compulsion to discover a consistent and coherent pattern [in the wallpaper]. Selectively emphasizing one section of the pattern while repressing others, reorganizing and regrouping past impressions into newer, more fully realized configurations—as one might with any complex formal text—the speaking voice becomes obsessed with her quest for meaning . . . .[8]

"What [the narrator] is watching . . . is her own psyche writ large," Kolodny concludes. But whose obsessive quest for meaning is this? Surely that of the feminist critic as she watches her interpretive processes writ small, finding a figure for feminist reading within the text. The result is a strange (that is, hysterical) literalization; the narrator, we are told, "comes more and more to experience herself as a text," and ends by being "totally surrendered to what is quite *literally* her own text."[9] The literalization of figure (a symptom of the protagonist's hysteria) infects the interpretive process itself. Read as the case which exemplifies feminist reading, just as "Fraulein Anna O.," exemplifies hysterical processes for Breuer and Freud, "The Yellow Wallpaper" becomes, not the basis for theory, but the model on which it is constructed. Ostensibly, Kolodny emphasizes the need to re-learn interpretive strategies. But her reading ends by suggesting that re-vision is really pre-vision—that we can only see what we have already read into the text. Meaning is pre-determined by the story we know; there is no room for the one we have forgotten.

As Kennard points out, surveying approaches such as Kolodny's, or Gilbert and Gubar's in *The Madwoman in the Attic*, readings that stress the social message of "The Yellow Wallpaper" (assuming both that the narrator's madness is so-

cially induced and that her situation is common to all women)
have become possible only as a result of "a series of conventions available to readers of the 1970s which were not available
to those of 1892."[10] Kennard summarizes the concepts associated with these conventions as: *patriarchy, madness, space,* and
quest. Feminist interpretations of "The Yellow Wallpaper" have
tended, inevitably, to see the story as an updated fictional treatment of Mary Wollstonecraft's theme in her novel, *The Wrongs of
Woman: or, Maria* ("Was not the world a vast prison, and
women born slaves?");[11] mental illness replaces imprisonment
as the sign of women's social and sexual oppression. But how
justifiable is it to read into Gilman's story a specifically feminist
tendency of this kind? And what is the tendency of such thematic readings anyway? We have learned not only to symbolize
(reading the narrator's confinement in a former nursery as
symbolic of her infantilization) but to read confinement itself
as symbolic of women's situation under patriarchy, and to see
in madness not only the result of patriarchal attitudes but a
kind of sanity—indeed, a perverse triumph; the commonsen-
sical physician-husband is literally floored by his wife at the
end of the story. As he loses consciousness, she finds herself in
the madness whose existence he has denied.

The "feminist" reading contradicts the tendency to
see women as basically unstable or hysterical, simultaneously
(and contradictorily) claiming that women are not mad and
that their madness is not their fault. But a thematic reading
cannot account for the Gothic and uncanny elements present in
the text. The assumption of what Jacqueline Rose calls "an
unproblematic and one-to-one causality between psychic life
and social reality" not only does away with the unconscious; it
also does away with language.[12] In the same way, the assumption of a one-to-one causality between the text and social reality does away with the unconscious of the text—specifically,
with its literariness, the way in which it knows more than it
knows (and more than the author intended). Formal features
have no place in interpretations that simply substitute latent
content for manifest content, bringing the hidden story upper-
most. A kind of re-telling, feminist reading as Kennard defines
it ends by translating the text into a cryptograph (or picto-

graph) representing either women in patriarchal society or the woman as writer and reader. If we come to "The Yellow Wallpaper" with this story already in mind, we are likely to read it with what Freud calls "that blindness of the seeing eye" which relegates what doesn't fit in with our expectations to the realm of the un-known or unknowable.

The "feminist" reading turns out to be the rationalist reading after all ("the narrator is driven mad by confinement"). By contrast, signs that might point to an irrationalist, Gothic reading ("the narrator is driven mad by the wallpaper") are ignored or repressed. Kennard admits that although the "feminist" reading is the one she teaches her students, "Much is made in the novella of the color yellow; feminist readings do little with this."[13] The color of sickness ("old foul, bad yellow things" p. 28), yellow is also the color of decay and, in a literary context, of Decadence (although the *Yellow Book* was not to appear until 1894). In America, it gives its name to "the yellow press" and to the sensationalism ushered in during the mid-1890s by color printing. Gilman's wallpaper is at once lurid, angry, dirty, sickly, and old: "The color is repellent, almost revolting; a smouldering unclean yellow, strangely faded by the slow-turning sunlight . . . a dull yet lurid orange . . . a sickly sulphur tint" (p. 13). The sensational ugliness of yellow is an unexplained given in Gilman's story. Yet the adjectival excess seems to signal not just the narrator's state of mind, but an inexplicable, perhaps repressed element in the text itself.

If feminist readings do little with the color of Gilman's title, they do even less with the creepiness of her story. Both Kolodny and Kennard ignore the uncanny altogether. Like the yellowness of the wallpaper, it is unaccountable, exceeding meaning; or rather, suggesting a meaning which resides only in the letter. The uncanny resists thematization, making itself felt as a "how" not a "what"—not as an entity, but rather as a phenomenon, like repetition.[14] A symptom of this uncanny repetition in the letter of the text is the word "creepy," which recurs with a spectrum of meanings spanning both metaphorical and literal senses (seeming to remind us, along with Freud, that figurative expressions have their origin in bodily sensations). Gilman's contemporary readers (to a man) found the story strange, if not ghostly. Her own husband thought it "the most ghastly tale he ever read."[15] The editor of *The Atlantic Monthly*, rejecting it, wrote that "I could not forgive myself if I made others as miserable as I have made myself!" and when he reprinted it in 1920, William Dean Howells called it a story to "freeze . . . our blood."[16] The *OED* reveals that the word "creepy" starts as "characterized by creeping or moving slowly," only later taking on the sense of chill associated with the uncanny ("creeping of the flesh, or chill shuddering feeling, caused by horror or repugnance"). Toward the end of the nineteenth century, the term came to be used especially in a literary context (*OED:* "A really effective romance of the creepy order"; 1892—the year in which "The Yellow Wallpaper" was finally published in the *New England Magazine*). If Gilman wrote a minor classic of female Gothic, hers is not only a tale of female hysteria but a version of Gothic that successfully tapped male hysteria about women. What but femininity is so calculated to induce "horror or repugnance" in its male readers?

The story's stealthy uncanniness—its sidelong approach both to the condition of women and to the unspeakably repugnant female body—emerges most clearly in the oscillation of the word "creepy" from figurative to literal. The link between female oppression, hysteria, and the uncanny occurs in the letter of the text; in a word whose meaning sketches the repressed connection between women's social situation, their sickness, and their bodies. A reading of the "slight hysterical tendency" displayed by "The Yellow Wallpaper" involves tracing the repression whereby the female body itself becomes a figure for the uncanny and the subjection of women can surface only in the form of linguistic repetition. A necessary first move would be to recover its lost literary and political "unconscious." The setting for Gilman's story is "a colonial mansion, a hereditary estate, I would say a haunted house, and reach the height of romantic felicity—but that would be asking too much of fate!" (p. 9). The trouble with the narrator is that her husband doesn't believe she's sick: the trouble with the text is its refusal of "romantic felicity." The narrator is no Jane Eyre (though the sister-in-law who is her "keeper," or "housekeeper," is named Jane) and her husband no Rochester ("John is practical in the extreme," p. 9); yet she must play the role of both Jane Eyre, who at once scents and represses a mystery, and Bertha Mason, who explodes it while refusing all attempts at sublimation—"I thought seriously of burning the house" (p. 29), the narrator confesses at one point.

In this prosaic present, romance can only take the form of hallucination (like Anna O.'s daydreaming); or perhaps, the form of a woman deranged by confinement. Female oppression has been de-eroticized, making the woman's story at best merely creepy and at worst sensational, just as the colonial mansion has been emptied of its romantic past. The empty house evokes romantic reading ("It makes me think of English places that you read about," p. 11), with its hedges and walls and gates that lock, its shady garden, paths, and arbors, and its derelict greenhouses. The rationalist explanation ("some legal trouble . . . something about the heirs and co-heirs," p. 11) "spoils my ghostliness," writes the narrator; "but I don't care—there is something strange about the house—I can feel it. I even said so to John one moonlight evening, but he said what I felt was a *draught,* and shut the window" (p. 11). Like the coolly rational Dr. John in *Villette,* who diagnoses Lucy's hysteria as "a case of spectral illusion . . . resulting from long-continued mental conflict" (p. 330), John comes to stand not only for unbelief ("He has no patience with faith," p. 9), but for the repression of romantic reading. His *"draught"* is a literary breeze from *Wuthering Heights* ("the *height* of romantic felicity"?), and his gesture a repetition of Lockwood's in the nightmare that opens Emily Brontë's book. Indeed, like Lockwood confronted with the ghost of Cathy in his dream, John has "an intense horror of superstition" (p. 9) and scoffs at intangible presences ("things not to be felt and seen") as a way of shutting them out of house and mind. Hence his horrified loss of consciousness at the end of the story, when the narrator confronts him in all her feminine otherness.

Madness—the irrational—is what Doctor John's philosophy cannot dream of, and his repressive refusal of the unconscious makes itself felt in the narrator's inconsequential style and her stealthy confidences to the written page. But the same rationalist censorship also makes itself felt in Gilman's authorial relation to the uncanny. An age of doctors had made the tale of supernatural haunting a story about hysteria; no one dreamed of taking Anna O.'s death-head hallucinations seriously or believed that her *"absences"* or "split-off mind" were a form of demonic possession.[17] As Freud points out, literature provides a much more fertile province for the uncanny than real life. A deranged narrator is licensed to think irrational thoughts and confide the unsayable to her journal ("I would not say it to a living soul, of course, but this is dead paper and a great relief to my mind," pp. 9–10). Gilman herself only differs from the insane, in the words used by Alice James to describe the recollected torments of her own hysteria, in having imposed on her "not only all the horrors and sufferings of insanity but the duties of doctor, nurse, and straight-jacket."[18] Medical knowledge, in other words, straight-jackets Gilman's text as well as her narrator: "I am a doctor, dear, and I know," John tells his wife (p. 23). It is as if Gilman's story has had to repress its own ancestry in nineteenth-century female Gothic, along with the entire history of feminist protest. The house in "The Yellow Wallpaper" is strange because empty. An image of dispossession, it points to what Gilman can't say about the subjection of women, not only in literary terms, but politically— imaging the disinherited state of women in general, and also, perhaps, the symptomatic dispossession which had made Gilman herself feel that she had to take her stand against marriage alone, without the benefit of feminist forebears.[19] Lacking a past, privatized by the family, all she had to go on was her personal feeling. *"Personally,"* the narrator opines near the start of the story ("Personally, I disagree with their ideas. Personally, I believe that congenial work . . . would do me good," p. 10)— the subjection of women is also the enforced "subjectivity" of women, their constitution as subjects within an economy which defines knowledge as power and gives to women the disenfranchizing privilege of personal feeling uninformed by knowledge ("I am a doctor, dear, and I know"). In other words, an economy which defines female subjectivity as madness and debases the literature of the uncanny to the level of the merely creepy.

Mary Wollstonecraft's invective against the infantilization of women through sensibility and ignorance in *The Rights of Woman* becomes Gilman's depiction of marriage in terms of a disused attic room that has formerly been a nursery ("It was nursery first and then play-room and gymnasium, I should judge; for the windows are barred for little children, and there are rings and things in the walls," p. 12). But where Wollstonecraft had taken an enlightenment stance in her polemic (if not in her novel), Gilman is compelled to assume an irrationalist stance which she has no means of articulating directly; in her story, the irrational inhabits or haunts the rational as its ghostly other, hidden within it like the figure of a mad woman hidden in the nursery wallpaper. The site of repression, above all, the family is also the place that contains both strangeness and enslavement (as Engels reminds us in *The Origin of the Family, Private Property and the State*, the word "family", derives from "famulus," or household slave). For Freud, *"Heimlich"* and *"Unheimlich"* are never far apart; what is familiar returns as strange because it has been repressed. John may shut out the "draught," but the strangeness he fears is already within the home and creeps into the most intimate place of all, the marital bedroom—creeps in as both woman's estate and woman's body; at once timorous, stealthy, and abject; and then, because split off from consciousness, as alien.

The figure whom the narrator first glimpses in the wallpaper "is like a woman stooping down and *creeping* about behind that pattern," and by the light of the moon which *"creeps* so slowly" she watches "that undulating wall-paper till I felt *creepy"* (pp. 22–23; my italics). The meaning of the word "creep," according to the *OED*, like that of "creepy," starts from the body; and it too ends by encompassing a figurative sense: "1. To move with the body prone and close to the ground . . . a human being on hands and feet, or in a crouching posture"; "2. To move slowly, cautiously, timorously, or slowly; to move quietly or stealthily so as to elude observation"; and "3. *fig.* (of persons and things) a. To advance or come on slowly, stealthily, or by imperceptible degrees . . . . b. To move timidly or diffidently; to proceed humbly, abjectly, or servilely, to cringe." As "creepy" becomes "creep" we are reminded of Freud's formulation about the language of hysteria: "In taking a verbal expression literally . . . the hysteric is not taking liberties with words, but is simply reviving once more the sensations to which the verbal expression owes its justification" (*SE* 2:181). "Creepy" and "creep"—the female uncanny, the subjection of women, and the body—are linked by a semantic thread in the textual patterning of Gilman's story; only by letting ourselves become "lost in an unnecessary maze of sign-reading" like the narrator herself (and like Freud) can we trace the connection between female subjection and the repression of femininity; between the literature and the politics of women's oppression.

The narrator of "The Yellow Wallpaper" enacts her abject state first by timorousness and stealth (her acquiescence in her own "treatment," and her secret writing), then by creeping, and finally by going on all fours over the supine body of her husband. If she was Anna O., her creeping would be read as hysterical conversion, like a limp or facial neuralgia. At this point one can begin to articulate the relationship between the "feminist" reading, the hysterical reading, and the uncanny. The story is susceptible to what Kennard calls the "feminist" reading partly because the narrator herself glimpses not one but many women creeping both in and out of the wallpaper. But like the inconsequential, maddening pattern in the wallpaper—like a hysterical symptom—the repressed "creeping" figure begins to proliferate all over Gilman's text:

> It is the same woman, I know, for she is always creeping, and most women do not creep by daylight.
> I see her on that long road under the trees, creeping along, and when a carriage comes she hides under the blackberry vines.
> I don't blame her a bit. It must be very humiliating to be caught creeping by daylight!
>
> .   .   .
>
> I often wonder if I could see her out of all the windows at once.
> But, turn as fast as I can, I can only see out of one at one time.
> And though I always see her, she *may* be able to creep faster than I can turn!
> I have watched her sometimes away off in the

open country, creeping as fast as a cloud shadow in a high
wind. (pp. 30–31)

And finally: "I don't like to *look* out of the windows even—
there are so many of those creeping women, and they creep so
fast" (p. 35).

As the creeping women imprisoned both in and out
of the wallpaper become the creeping woman liberated from
domestic secrecy ("I always lock the door when I creep by
daylight," p. 31) into overt madness ("It is so pleasant to be out
in this great room and creep around as I please," p. 35)—as the
"creeping" figure is embodied in the narrator's hysterical acting
out—there emerges also a creeping sense that the text knows
more than she; perhaps more than Gilman herself. At the culmination of the story, the rationalist husband tries to break in
on his wife's madness, threatening to take an axe to her self-
enclosure in the repetitions of delusion and language. The
story's punchline has all the violence of his attempted break-in:

> "What is the matter?" he cried. "For God's sake,
> what are you doing!"
> I kept on creeping just the same, but I looked at
> him over my shoulder.
> "I've got out at last," said I, "in spite of you and
> Jane. And I've pulled off most of the paper, so you can't put
> me back!"
> Now why should that man have fainted? But he
> did, and right across my path by the wall, so that I had to
> creep over him every time! (p. 36)

The docile wife and compliant patient returns as a defiant apparition, her rebellious strength revealed as the other of domesticated invalidism. This time it is the doctor who faints on the
floor. But the story leaves us asking a creepy question. Did she
tear and score the wallpaper round her bed herself, or has her
madness been pre-enacted in the "haunted" house? Who bit
and gnawed at the heavy wooden bed, gouged at the plaster,
splintered the floor? What former inmate of the attic nursery
was confined by those sinister rings in the wall? As readers
versed in female gothic we know that Bertha Mason haunts this
text; as readers of the feminist tradition from Wollstonecraft

on, we know that the rights of women have long been denied by treating them as children. The uncanny makes itself felt as the return of a repressed past, a history at once literary and political—here, the history of women's reading.

"Now why should that man have fainted?" The narrator's question returns us to male hysteria. The body of woman is hystericized as the uncanny—defined by Freud as the sight of something that should remain hidden; typically, the sight of the female genitals. The woman on all fours is like Bertha Mason, an embodiment of the animality of woman unredeemed by (masculine) reason. Her creeping can only be physical—it is the story that assumes her displaced psychic uncanniness to become "creepy"—since by the end she is all body, an incarnation not only of hysteria but of male fears about women. The female hysteric displaces her thoughts onto her body: the male hysteric displaces his fear of castration, his anxiety, onto her genitals. Seemingly absent from "The Yellow Wallpaper," both the female body (female sexuality) and male hysteria leave their traces on the paper in a stain or a whiff—in a yellow "smooch" and a yellow smell that first appear in metonymic proximity to one another in Gilman's text:

> But there is something else about that paper—the smell! I noticed it the moment we came into the room. . . .
> It creeps all over the house.
> I find it hovering in the dining-room, skulking in the parlor, hiding in the hall, lying in wait for me on the stairs.
> It gets into my hair.
> Even when I go to ride, if I turn my head suddenly and surprise it—there is that smell!
> Such a peculiar odor, too! I have spent hours in trying to analyze it, to find what it smelled like.
> It is not bad—at first, and very gentle, but quite the subtlest, most enduring odor I ever met.
> In this damp weather it is awful, I wake up in the night and find it hanging over me.
> It used to disturb me at first. I thought seriously of burning the house—to reach the smell.
> But now I am used to it. The only thing I can think of is that it is like the *color* of the paper! A yellow smell.

> There is a very funny mark on this wall, low
> down, near the mopboard. A streak that runs round the
> room. It goes behind every piece of furniture, except the bed,
> a long, straight, even *smooch*, as if it had been rubbed over
> and over. (pp. 28–29)

At the end of the story, the narrator's own shoulder "just fits in
that long smooch around the wall" (p. 35). The mark of repetition, the uncanny trace made by the present stuck in the groove
of the past, the "smooch" is also a smudge or smear, a reciprocal dirtying, perhaps (the wallpaper leaves "yellow smooches
on all my clothes and John's" p. 27). In the 1890s, "smooch"
had not taken on its slangy mid-twentieth-century meaning
(as in "I'd rather have hooch/And a bit of a smooch" [1945]).[20]
The "smooch" on the yellow wallpaper cannot yet be a sexual
caress, although dirty rubbing might be both Doctor John's medical verdict on sexuality and the story's hysterical literalization
of it. As such, the dirty stain of smooching would constitute not
just the unmentionable aspect of the narrator's genteel marital
incapacity, but the unsayable in Gilman's story—the sexual
etiology of hysteria, certainly (repressed in Gilman's as in
Breuer's text); but also the repression imposed by the 1890s on
the representation of female sexuality and, in particular, the
repression imposed on women's writing.

And what of the "yellow smell"?—a smell that
creeps, like the figure in the text; presumably the smell of decay, of "old foul, bad yellow things." *Studies on Hysteria*
provides a comparable instance of a woman "tormented by
subjective sensations of smell" (*SE* 2:106), the case of "Miss
Lucy R.," an English governess secretly in love with the wid-
owed father of her charges. Since, in Freud's words, "the subjective olfactory sensations . . . were recurrent hallucinations,"
he interprets them as hysterical symptoms. Miss Lucy R. is
troubled first by "a smell of burnt pudding," and then, when
the hallucination has been traced back to its originating episode, by the smell of cigar smoke. The episode of the burnt
pudding turns out to be associated not only with her tender
feelings for her employer's children but with tenderness for her
employer ("I believe," Freud informs her, "that really you are
in love with your employer . . . and that you have a secret hope

of taking their mother's place," *SE* 2:117). The smell of cigar smoke proves to be a mnemonic symbol for a still earlier scene associated with the disappointing realization that her employer doesn't share her feelings. Here, hysterical smells function as a trace of something that has been intentionally forgotten—marking the place where unconscious knowledge has forced itself into consciousness, then been forcibly repressed once more. Freud does not pursue the question of smell any further in this context, although he does so elsewhere.

Jane Gallop's *The Daughter's Seduction* intriguingly suggests not only that smell is repressed by Freud's organization of sexual difference around a specular image ("sight of a phallic presence in the boy, sight of a phallic absence in the girl") but that smell in the Freudian text may have a privileged relation to female sexuality.[21] The female stench, after all, is the unmentionable of misogynist scatology. Two disturbing or "smelly" footnotes in *Civilization and Its Discontents* seem to argue, according to Gallop, that prior to the privileging of sight over smell, "the menstrual process produced an effect on the male psyche by means of olfactory stimuli" (*SE* 21:99*n*.) and that "with the depreciation of his sense of smell . . . the whole of [man's] sexuality" fell victim to repression, since when "the sexual function has been accompanied by a repugnance which cannot further be accounted for" (*SE* 21:106*n*.). In other words (Gallop's own), "The penis may be more visible, but female genitalia have a stronger smell"; and that smell becomes identified with the smell of sexuality itself.

Gallop connects Freud's footnotes with an essay by Michèle Montrelay associating the immediacy of feminine speech and what she terms, italianately, the *"odor di femina"* emanating from it. Montrelay is reviewing *Recherches psycho-analytiques nouvelles sur la sexualité féminine*—a book which, combining theory with case histories like *Studies on Hysteria,* "take[s] us to the analyst's: there where the one who speaks is no longer the mouth-piece of a school, but the patient on the couch. . . . Here we have the freedom to follow the discourse of female patients in analysis in its rhythm, its style and its meanderings." "This book," Montrelay concludes, "not only talks of femininity according to Freud, but it also makes it speak in an immediate way. . . . An *odor di femina* arises from it."[22] For Montrelay, feminine immediacy—predicated on the notion of an incompletely mediated relation between the female body, language, and the unconscious—produces anxiety which must be managed by representation; that is, by the privileging of visual representations in psychic organization. Or, as Gallop explicates Montrelay, "The *'odor di femina'* becomes odious, nauseous, because it threatens to undo the achievements of repression and sublimation, threatens to return the subject to the powerlessness, intensity, and anxiety of an immediate, un-mediated connection with the body of the mother."[23] The bad smell that haunts the narrator in "The Yellow Wallpaper" is both the one she makes and the smell of male hysteria emanat-ing from her husband—that is, fear of femininity as the body of the mother ("old, foul, bad yellow things") which simul-taneously threatens the boy with a return to the powerlessness of infancy and with anxiety about the castration she embodies.

"The Yellow Wallpaper," like the Freudian case his-tory or the speech whose immediacy Montrelay scents, offers only the illusion of feminine discourse. What confronts us in the text is not the female body, but a figure for it. The figure in the text of "The Yellow Wallpaper" is "a strange, provoking, formless sort of figure, that seems to skulk about behind that silly and conspicuous front design" (p. 18). A formless figure? "*Absences*" could scarcely be more provoking. Produced by a specular system as nothing, as lack or absence, woman's form is by definition formless. Yet both for the hysteric and for Freud, figuration originates in the body—in "sensations and innerva-tions . . . now for the most part . . . so much weakened that the expression of them in words seems to us only to be a figurative picture of them . . . hysteria is right in restoring the original meaning of the words and depicting its unusually strong inner-vations" (*SE* 2:181). The hysterical symptom (a smell, a paraly-sis, a cough) serves as just such a trace of "original" bodily meaning. Figuration itself comes to be seen as a linguistic trace, a "smooch" that marks the body's unsuccessful attempt to evade the repressiveness of representation.

What is infuriating (literally, maddening—"a lack of sequence, a defiance of law, that is a constant irritant to a

normal mind," p. 25) about the yellow wallpaper is its resistance to being read: "It is dull enough to confuse the eye in
following, pronounced enough to constantly irritate and
provoke study, and when you follow the lame uncertain curves
for a little distance they suddenly commit suicide—plunge off
at outrageous angles, destroy themselves in unheard-of contradictions" (p. 13). A hideous enigma, the pattern has all the
violence of nightmares ("It slaps you in the face, knocks you
down, and tramples upon you. It is like a bad dream," p. 25).
But perhaps the violence is really that of interpretation. The
"figure" in the text is at once a repressed figure (that of a
woman behind bars) and repressive figuration. Shoshana Felman asks, "what, indeed, is the unconscious if not—in every
sense of the word— a *reader*?"[24] Like the examinations undergone by Lucy Snowe and Anna O., interpretive reading involves the specular appropriation or silencing of the text. Only
the insistence of the letter resists forcible translation.

In Gilman's story, the narrator-as-unconscious embarks on a reading process remarkably like Freud's painstaking
attempts, not simply to unravel, but, more aggressively, to
wrest meaning from the hysterical text in *Studies on Hysteria*:
"by detecting lacunas in the patient's first description . . . we
get hold of a piece of the logical thread at the periphery . . . . In
doing this, we very seldom succeed in making our way right
into the interior along one and the same thread. As a rule it
breaks off half-way . . ."; and finally, "We drop it and take up
another thread, which we may perhaps follow equally far.
When we have . . . discovered the entanglements on account of
which the separate threads could not be followed any further in
isolation, we can think of attacking the resistance before us
afresh" (*SE* 2:294). The language of attack entangles Freud
himself in a Thesean fantasy about penetrating the maze to its
center ("I *will* follow that pointless pattern to some sort of a
conclusion," writes Gilman's narrator, with similarly obsessional persistence; p. 19).

The meaningless pattern in the yellow wallpaper
not only refuses interpretation; it refuses to be read as a text—
as anything but sheer, meaningless repetition ("this thing was
not arranged on any laws of radiation, or alternation, or repeti-

tion, or symmetry, or anything else that I ever heard of," p. 20).
Attempts to read it therefore involve the (repressive) substitution of something—a figure—for nothing. At first the pattern
serves simply to mirror the narrator's own specular reading,
endlessly repeated in the figure of eyes ("the pattern lolls like a
broken neck and two bulbous eyes stare at you upside
down. . . . Up and down and sideways they crawl, and those
absurd, unblinking eyes are everywhere," p. 16). But as the
process of figuration begins to sprout its own autonomous rep-
ertoire of metaphors ("bloated curves and flourishes—a kind of
'debased Romanesque' with *delirium tremens*"; "great slanting
waves of optic horror, like a lot of wallowing seaweeds in full
chase," p. 20), it becomes clear that figures feed parasitically on
resistance to meaning; the pattern "remind[s] one of a fungus.
If you can imagine a toadstool in joints, an interminable string
of toadstools, budding and sprouting in endless convolutions—
why, that is something like it" (p. 25). The function of figuration is to manage anxiety; any figuration is better than none—
even a fungoid growth is more consoling than sheer absence.

Learning to read might be called a hysterical process, since it involves substituting a bodily figure for the self-
reproducing repetitions of textuality. Significantly, the narrator's sighting of a figure in the text—her own—inscribes her
madness most graphically. As the "dim shape" becomes clearer,
the pattern "becomes bars! The outside pattern, I mean, and
the woman behind as plain as can be. I didn't realize for a long
time what the thing was that showed behind, that dim sub-
pattern, but now I am quite sure it is a woman" (p. 26). The
figure of bars functions in Gilman's text to make the narrator's
final embodiment as mad woman look like a successful prison
break from the tyranny of a meaningless pattern: "The woman
behind shakes it! . . . she crawls around fast, and her crawling
shakes it all over . . . she just takes hold of the bars and shakes
them hard. And she is all the time trying to climb through" (p.
30). The climax of Gilman's story has her narrator setting to
work to strip off the paper and liberate the figure which by now
both she and we—hysterically identified with her reading—
recognize as her specular double: "As soon as it was moonlight
and that poor thing began to crawl and shake the pattern, I got

up and ran to help her. I pulled and she shook, I shook and she pulled, and before morning we had peeled off yards of that paper" (p. 32). And finally, "I've got out at last . . . so you can't put me back!" (p. 36).

The figure here is the grammatical figure of chiasmus, or crossing (*OED*: "The order of words in one of two parallel clauses is inverted in the other"). "I pulled and she shook, I shook and she pulled" prepares us for the exchange of roles at the end, where the woman reading (and writing) the text becomes the figure of madness within it. Gilman's story hysterically embodies the formal or grammatical figure; but the same process of figuration dimly underlies (like the "dim shape" or "dim sub-pattern") our own reading. By the very fact of reading it as narrative, hysterical or otherwise, we posit the speaking or writing subject called "the narrator." "*Figure*" also means face, and face implies a speaking voice. In this sense, figure becomes the trace of the bodily presence without which it would be impossible to read "The Yellow Wallpaper" as a first-person narrative, or even as a displaced form of autobiography.

The chiastic figure provides a metaphor for the hysterical reading which we engage in whenever the disembodied text takes on the aspect of a textual body. Since chiasmus is at once a specular figure and a figure of symmetrical inversion, it could be regarded as the structure of phallogocentrism itself, where word and woman mirror only the presence of the (masculine) body, reinforcing the hierarchy man/woman, presence/absence. Is there a way out of the prison? The bars shaken and mistaken by the madwoman might, in a different linguistic narrative, be taken for the constitutive bar between signifier and signified. The gap between sign and meaning is the absence that the hysteric attempts to abolish or conceal by textualizing the body itself. Montrelay writes of the analyst's discourse as "not reflexive, but different. As such it is a *metaphor*, not a mirror, of the patient's discourse."[25] For Montrelay, metaphor engenders a pleasure which is that of *"putting the dimension of repression into play on the level of the text itself"*—of articulating or designating what is not spoken, what is unspeakable, yet incompletely repressed, about the feminine body. The ultimate form of this unmentionable pleasure would be feminine jouissance, or meaning that exceeds the repressive effects of interpretation and figuration. Montrelay's formulation risks its own literalness, that of (hysterically) assuming an unmediated relation between feminine body and word. But her story follows the same trajectory as Gilman's. The end of "The Yellow Wallpaper" is climactic because Doctor John, previously the censor of women's writing (as Felman demands, "how can one write *for* the very figure who signifies the suppression of what one has to say *to* him?"),[26] catches the text, as it were, *in flagrante delicto*. The return of the repressed, in Freud's scenario, always figures the sight of the castrated female body. What we glimpse in this moment of figuration is the return of the letter in all its uncanny literalness to overwhelm us with the absence which both male and female hysteria attempt to repress in the name of woman.

3. Hysterics Suffer Mainly from Reminiscences

"**What a lifeless,** diseased, self-conscious being [George Eliot] must have been! Not one burst of joy, not one ray of humor, not one living breath in one of her letters or journals. . . . Whether it is that her dank, moaning features haunt and pursue one thro' the book, or not, but she makes upon me the impression, morally and physically, of mildew, of some morbid growth—a fungus of a pendulous shape, or as of something damp to the touch. I never had a stronger impression" (Alice James, *Diary*).[1]

Alice James' response to reading the third and last volume of George Eliot's posthumous *Life, Letters and Journals,* in 1889, was to see Eliot as the buried self of her own hysteria. Like the fungoid pattern in Gilman's wallpaper, George Eliot's moaning features "haunt" Alice James' journal as a reminder of the parasitic morbidity masked by her elaborate self-mockeries and fantastic ironies. Herself a noted invalid, she objects especially to George Eliot's chronicling of headaches, diseases, and "depressions" (what Eliot refers to as *"malaise"*); "they seem simply cherished as the vehicule [*sic*] for a moan," (p. 42). Alice James, by contrast, assumed an antic disposition or a Yorick-like vein of sickroom humor in relation to her own malaise (it is George Eliot's humorlessness that she can't forgive). She writes always with her own death in view, epitaphically ("when I am gone, pray don't think of me simply as a creature who might have been something else, had neurotic science been born").[2] Seeing herself as by turns all body and all mind—a "poor old carcass" on one hand, a frustrated artist on the other—she imagines participating in her own death as both audience and lead actress ("a creature who has been denied all dramatic episodes might be allowed, I think, to assist at her extinction," p. 135). Death is a means of acting out which "seems to double the value of the event, for one becomes suddenly picturesque to oneself" (p. 208); embodied pathos assumes a hysterical pose: "I might pose to myself before the footlights of my last obscure little scene, as a delectably pathetic figure" (p. 222). When the doctors finally diagnose a "palpable disease," the breast cancer which killed her in 1892 (by chance, the year in which Gilman published "The Yellow Wallpaper"), she greets it with enthusiasm: "To him who waits, all things come! My aspirations may have been eccentric, but I cannot complain now, that they have not been brilliantly fulfilled" (p. 206). Perhaps cancer, in Freud's famous phrase, finally transformed James' "hysterical misery into common unhappiness" (*SE* 2:305).

Confronting her death, Alice James writes of "the enormous relief of [the] uncompromising verdict, lifting us out of the formless vague and setting us within the very heart of the sustaining concrete" (p. 207). Representation comes to her rescue, creating a body language ("the sustaining concrete") for the formless disease which Weir Mitchell had nicknamed "mysteria."[3] Like Anna O., Alice James writes stories in which she is the central figure, vindicating her hysterical career by creating a "private theatre" of her own while displacing onto "the shape of the British Doctor" the paralyzing symptoms of hysteria ("the spectacle of impotent paralysis that he presents is truly pitiful," p. 225). In a comic story at his expense, an eminent but unpunctual specialist becomes "the *late* Sir Andrew Clark!" (p. 225)—a walking *bon mot* who assists at his own extinction, like Alice James herself. Experiencing hysteria as an innocent bystander caught in the agon between body and mind ("it was a fight simply between my body and my will, a battle in which the former was to be triumphant to the end"), James saves her mind by giving up her body to illness: "'tis a never-ending fight . . . . So, with the rest, you abandon the pit of your stomach, the palms of your hands, the soles of your feet, and refuse to keep them sane" (pp. 149–50). But the hysterical dilemma is also figured as an artistic one, the mingled joy and despair of those "made up of chords which vibrate at every zephyr." The horns of this writer-hysteric's dilemma are dumbness and impotence; which of the two orders, artists manqués or failed artists, she wonders, "know the least misery, those who are always dumb and never lose the stifled sense, or the others who ever find expression impotent to express!" (p. 31). Measuring herself against the great nineteenth-century women writers, James recognized in them her own unacted part. By the same token, she acts theirs. In Alice James we can recognize, not just an articulate and literary Anna O., but the plight of the woman writer whose imagination clung defiantly to the sickroom.

According to Alice James' biographer, Jean Strouse, George Sand represented "one path not taken" by Alice James and George Eliot the other; Eliot's heroines—Maggie Tulliver, Dorothea Brooke—depicted the fates of intelligent women in conflict with the limitations imposed on them by society and especially by their sex. As Strouse points out, James resembles both Eliot and Maggie Tulliver (not to mention Anna O. and Charlotte Perkins Gilman) in being the sister of privileged, well-educated boys; she was also the sister of two powerful thinkers and writers, William and Henry James.[4] The question of writing would inevitably have presented itself to her as one of gender, just as it did to George Eliot, whose choice of male pseudonym betrays her ambiguous view of the woman writer. In the mid-1880s, Alice James' commonplace book contains a revealing quotation from Eliot's letters: "There is something more piteous almost than soapless poverty in this application of feminine incapacity to literature."[5] Strouse speculates that for James, "the anomalous literary realm occupied by the diary lay safely within the feminine province of the personal" (similarly, the narrator of "The Yellow Wallpaper" is driven to secret writing by her physician husband). By keeping a private diary, James avoided the risk of competition either with her brothers or with an androgynously named woman writer like George Eliot. But her journal reveals that she wrote with one eye on an imaginary audience, even if that audience represented her own divided consciousness. The "private theatre" always has a spectator; if not her doctor (as in Anna O.'s case) then "the benignant pater" himself, or else an idealized masculine (br)other—"dear Inconnu (please note the sex! pale shadow of Romance still surviving even in the most rejected and despised of Man)" (p. 129). The erotic paternal or fraternal dimension brings with it rivalry both with and for the mother. Alice James would have known that George Eliot was affectionately nicknamed "*Mutter*" and "Madonna" by her intimates. Casting out the morbid solemnity of the mother, Alice James gives birth to the hysterically funny diarist who was occupied in "making sentences" until the day she died.

Writing and self-consciousness—the diseased self-consciousness which James identifies with Eliot—are never far apart. If James' verdict on Eliot represents an attempt to exorcize the ghost of morbidity from her writing, Eliot's attempt to lay her own gloom to rest can be seen in her relation to a younger self named Mary Wollstonecraft. In a famous letter of 1871, Eliot writes:

> Hopelessness has been to me, all through my life, but especially in painful years of my youth, the chief source of wasted energy with all the consequent bitterness of regret. Remember, it has happened to many to be glad they did not commit suicide, though they once ran for the final leap, or as Mary Wollstonecraft did, wetted their garments well in the rain hoping to sink the better when they plunged. She tells how it occurred to her as she was walking in this damp shroud, that she might live to be glad that she had not put an end to herself—and so it turned out.[6]

The hopelessness of this literary and feminist foremother haunts George Eliot with the damp shroud of her encumbering skirts, just as Eliot's dank, moaning features pursued Alice James. Women's literary genealogies threaten them with the story that they have tried to forget—the hysteric's story; the story of hopeless desire. The past can provide a source of strength and attachment in George Eliot's writing, but equally it can be a parasitic legacy, the inheritance that Wollstonecraft (in an earlier sense than ours) named women's "depression." Though Eliot knew Wollstonecraft had been saved from death by drowning, Maggie Tulliver, another younger self, must go under for Eliot to assume her own freedom.

George Eliot's other recovery of Wollstonecraft (as she points out, an under-read author in the 1850s) occurs in her 1855 review of Margaret Fuller's *Woman in the Nineteenth Century*; here Wollstonecraft's *Rights of Woman* figures (like Eliot's letters and journals in Alice James's journal) as the humorless pre-text which her own surpasses in liveliness and wit ("she has no erudition, and her grave pages are lit up by no ray of fancy").[7] A writer who "wrote not at all for writing's sake," Wollstonecraft becomes a common voice raised against what Eliot calls, quoting Tennyson's *Princess*, the "Parasitic forms/ That seem to keep [woman] up, but drag her down."[8] These parasitic forms are social. The "fungus of a pendulous shape" which Eliot represents for James, and which figures hysteria for Gilman, is a psychic fungus. Externalized as women's oppression, it becomes more manageable. The parasite without—the social parasite—is easier to cast out than the one within. The managed threat in Eliot's review is not the depression of the past but the caricatured, socially formed woman "who is fit for nothing but to sit in her drawing-room like a doll-Madonna in her shrine"—the power-hungry child-woman anatomized by Wollstonecraft as the product of women's subjection: "When, therefore, I call women slaves, I mean in a political and civil sense; for indirectly they obtain too much power, and are debased by their exertions to obtain illicit sway." Or, as Eliot glosses Wollstonecraft, "Wherever weakness is not harshly controlled it must *govern*, as you may see when a strong man holds a little child by the hand, how he is pulled hither and thither."[9] Who is the mother here—the doll-Madonna, or George Eliot playing the Dr. Spock of marital relations?

In a world of male hysteria, the woman writer is as likely to identify with her father as her mother. Like Wollstonecraft, Eliot castigates the face of woman most visible to male misanthropy; only "cultured women"—educated literary women—escape censure since the rest (in Wollstonecraft's phrase) are "depressed from their cradles." Another review, written in 1856 at the moment when George Eliot herself was emerging as a woman writer, elaborates on the verdict recorded in Alice James' commonplace book ("this application of feminine incapacity to literature"). Honing a fine but necessary distinction between Eliot herself and other contemporary women writers, "Silly Novels by Lady Novelists" singles out for attack the incompletely educated literary woman who can never be assimilated to male culture: "If . . . a very great amount of instruction will not make a wise man, still less will a very mediocre amount of instruction make a wise woman. And the most mischievous form of feminine silliness is the literary form, because it tends to confirm the popular prejudice against the more solid education of women." The unmistakable voice of male misogyny speaks through Eliot:

> After a few hours' conversation with an oracular literary woman, or a few hours' reading of her books, [men] are likely enough to say, "After all, when a woman gets some knowledge, see what use she makes of it! Her knowledge remains acquisition, instead of passing into culture . . . she keeps a sort of mental pocket-mirror, and is continually looking in it at her own 'intellectuality' . . . she struts on one page, rolls her eyes on another, grimaces in a third, and is hysterical in a fourth. . . . "No—the average nature of women is too shallow and feeble a soil to bear much tillage; it is only fit for the very lightest crops."[10]

This strutting, theatrical, self-representing, and above all hysterical puppet is cast out, like the doll-Madonna, in order that the "really cultured woman" may be assimilated into masculine culture. Though Eliot invokes "a cluster of great names, both living and dead" (names such as Harriet Martineau, Currer Bell, and Elizabeth Gaskell) as evidence that "fiction is a department of literature in which women can, after their kind, fully equal men,"[11] she was to give herself a name which could not be distinguished from a man's. Eliot knew what the legacy of Wollstonecraft and Fuller meant for her; but she had forgotten the legacy of female self-hatred and masculine misogyny which every "cultured" woman writer internalizes.

Eliot's view of the impotent tyranny and murderous commonplaceness of women is fictionalized in a story which has also been read as her most tormented account of the woman writer's self-mistrust. In "The Lifted Veil," written in 1859 between the successful publication of *Adam Bede* and the beginnings of *The Mill on the Floss*, women play a killing role.

George Eliot called the story a *"jeu de mélancolie"* (a melancholy version of self, perhaps—the suicidal *"je"* she saw in Mary Wollstonecraft). It portrays a consciousness so diseased, so bent on suicide, as to inscribe its own death. Writing and death come together as they do in Alice James' diary to create a hysterical text whose hysteria, in the last resort, can be read as that of the woman writer trapped in male prevision. "The Lifted Veil" may also be read autobiographically, as a fictional expression of Eliot's chronic self-mistrust; but formally at least, it is a deliberately dissociated version of female gothic told from the man's point of view. The story is not only a *"jeu de mélancolie"*— Blackwood thought that Eliot "must have been worrying and disturbing [herself] about something when [she] wrote"[12]— but a tale of uncanny (dis)possession. Like the haunted house in "The Yellow Wallpaper," the haunted consciousness of the narrator can be read as a symptom of social disinheritance; in this case, the disinherited mind or cultural exclusion that is one symptom of women's oppression. Eliot did not acknowledge the story as hers until near the end of her life, in the Cabinet edition of 1877, and its anonymity dissociates it still further from the culturally integrated George Eliot of the successful "realist" novels, whether pastoral or European. The cultural dispossession that George Eliot successfully repressed in these novels returns as alien in the hystericized "case" of the artist manqué whose state is one of incomplete manhood, i.e., "feminine incapacity."

In 1873, George Eliot equipped "The Lifted Veil" with a motto designed to throw light on its informing idea:

> Give me no light, great heaven, but such as turns
> To energy of human fellowship;
> No powers save the growing heritage
> That makes completer manhood.[13]

Here Eliot, the woman writer, asks only for powers that will make her more of a man. To dissent from the great onward movement ("the growing heritage") is to be either neurotically disinherited (like Latimer, the narrator of "The Lifted Veil") or impotently feminine (as Latimer also is). In this masculinist cultural hegemony, Marianne Evans is doomed to experience

her powers either as demonic possession or as feminine dispossession unless her incapacitating femininity can be erased
under the masculine name of George Eliot. It is not so much
that female creativity is demonic or satanic, as Gilbert and
Gubar argue in their reading of "The Lifted Veil," but that it is
threatened by the dumbness and impotence which Anna O.
enacts and Alice James articulates as the dilemma of the artist-
hysteric.

Confessing her lack of "confidence in the work to be
done" in a letter of 1874, Eliot relates that "the other day,
having a bad headache, I did what I have sometimes done
before at intervals of five or six years—looked into three of
four novels to see what the world was reading. The effect was
paralyzing."[14] Paralysis (and a bad headache) symptomize a
writer's block whose cause is the wish to be different rather
than in-different; that is, as she puts it in the same letter, the
fear of writing "indifferently after having written well." The
following year, Eliot wrote of *Daniel Deronda* (1876) that "as
usual I am suffering much from doubt as to the worth of what I
am doing and fear lest I may not be able to complete it so as to
make it a contribution to literature and not a mere addition to
the heap of books"[15]—a heap she had surveyed scornfully
twenty years before in "Silly Novels by Lady Novelists" at a
moment of originating literary self-differentiation.

Readings of "The Lifted Veil" have inevitably
stressed its relation to George Eliot's "paralyzing" authorial
anxieties, whether or not they are viewed as specifically female.
Gillian Beer, for instance, writes percipiently of the way in
which Latimer's fatal powers of prevision "express the determinism and solipsism latent in the act of writing fiction";
Latimer's hyperaesthesia—an inversion of the hysteric's
anaesthesia—is diagnosed as "the particular disease of the Victorian consciousness."[16] As Gilbert and Gubar point out in *The
Madwoman in the Attic,* both Latimer and Eliot identify imaginative vision with illness (Latimer speculates that his insight into
the minds of others is "a disease—a sort of intermittent delirium"),[17] while Eliot's own authorial omniscience becomes for
Latimer a curse. Hysterical paralysis is one symptom of this
disease. Latimer experiences sensations of numbness at the

touch of his future wife after viewing a picture of Lucrezia Borgia—a vision that (strangely enough) takes place in Vienna. Later "his constitutional timidity and distrust . . . benumb [him]" (p. 310); significantly, his father dies of paralysis. Later still, Latimer looks back on the fading of marital joy "as a man might look back on the last pains in a paralyzed limb" (p. 322). Finally, the sight of Bertha when she is revealed as a would-be poisoner "paralyze[s]" Latimer's scientific friend, Meunier, in the culminating scene of the story.

   "The Lifted Veil" replicates its terms in the largely biographical readings it has generated. Ruby Redinger's psychoanalytic biography, for instance, refers Latimer's symptoms ("the underlying psychic paralysis which robs him of the power of artistic creation") to the effects on Eliot's creative processes of her own fear and guilt—"both of which, singly or together, could have produced paralysis." Read like this, the motto Eliot later attached to her story becomes "a hymnlike expression of thankfulness for deliverance from the sense of guilt which the story dramatizes and which had almost paralyzed her creativity."[18] Gilbert and Gubar, however, were the first to raise the issue of gender, reading "The Lifted Veil" as an expression of Eliot's divided identity as a woman writer split "between a misogynist male and a misandrist female." The struggle between Latimer and his hateful wife, they write, "dramatizes Eliot's sense of paralysis, her guilt at having internalized attitudes at once debilitating and degrading to her sex"; her paralysis is "the paralysis of self-loathing . . . initiated by acceptance of patriarchal values."[19] Their diagnosis ("the depth of her need to evade identification with her own sex") accords well with the classic hysterical dilemma of confused and conflicted sexual identity as it emerges from Freud's theory of hysteria. Viewed as the "case" of George Eliot, "The Lifted Veil" brings hysteria back to George Eliot herself.

   But what would a less biographical reading look like? *Look* may be the operative word here. Omniscience and insight are a kind of seeing—in Latimer's "case," too much seeing for his own good. The touch of a woman (after looking at a portrait of the cruel-eyed Lucrezia Borgia) benumbs: the sight of her paralyzes. We might suspect here the hidden touch or sight of that emblem of male castration, the Medusa's head. Whatever George Eliot's own confused or divided sexual identification (can sexual identity ever be anything but split?), the lifted veil of the story's title conceals a view of woman—of female sexuality—which is hysterical precisely because masculine. Shelley's "painted veil" ("Lift not the painted veil which those who live/Call Life") conceals the horror of prevision: "Fear/And Hope, twin Destinies; who ever weave/Their shadows, o'er the chasm . . . " ("Sonnet," 1818, 11.1–6). The omniscient or visionary author might well view the twin powers of premonition as "sightless and drear," in Shelley's words—as paradoxically blinding, since what they reveal is nothing; the nothingness or chasm of death.

In his childhood, Latimer suffers from an episode of blindness which he remembers, with "a slight trace of sensation," spending on his mother's knee, as if the mother was still the phallic mother who did not threaten castration. Later he experiences the seer's curse—his uncanny previsions—as episodes not unlike Alice James' agonizing bouts of hysteria ("presentiments that spring from an insight at war with passion . . . the powerlessness of ideas before the might of impulse," p. 307). As Freud points out, the uncanny images the sight of something "that ought to have remained secret and hidden but has come to light" (SE 17:225); classically, the sight of the apparently castrated female genitals. Eliot's authorial anxieties can certainly be linked to creative processes. But in a specular system, to see all and know all is to run the risk of seeing what should remain hidden from view, the shadowy chasm of female "absence" or what is lacking in the mother. Paralysis, whether in the text itself or in the readings generated by it, could be read as a symptom of the privileging of sight and its consequences in the moment of specular differentiation which for Freud constitutes the gendered subject. Vision and prevision bring with them as their complement the terror of what can't be seen; of what appears, in the case of women, to be absent—that is, a reassuring reflection of masculinity.

"*Hysterics suffer mainly from reminiscences*" (SE 2:7): Breuer's formulation alludes to the hysteric's forgotten story. The story sketched by Freud's theory of sexual differentiation is the one that the female hysteric must forget as she oscillates between masculine and feminine and the one that the male hysteric is continually compelled to recall. In "The Lifted Veil," Latimer's powers of prevision are a form of fatal déjà vu—"my visions were only like presentiments intensified to horror" (p. 307). The presentiment is at once a prepossession and a preconception; a form of vague anticipation or foreboding, and precise foreknowledge. As Freud points out in "The Uncanny," obsessional neurotics are especially afflicted with "presentiments": "They are in the habit of referring to this state of affairs in the most modest manner, saying that they have 'presentiments' which 'usually' come true" (*SE* 17:239–40). The male hysteric's preconception of woman spells impotence and death. Seeing into the enigmatic Bertha, Latimer has a prevision that "urge[s] itself perpetually on [his] unwilling sight" (p. 307); the presentiment not of a secret but of "a measured fact," her castrating ordinariness. In Latimer's case, knowledge brings, not power, but powerlessness and uncanny repetition. Doomed not only to see into the minds of others, but to foresee the critical events of his own life and the date and manner of his death, he can only reinscribe them. His story begins: "The time of my end approaches. . . . I foresee when I shall die, and everything that will happen in my last moments." Being prepossessed of the facts of his own story merely intensifies his presentiments to the pitch of horror: "Just a month from this day, on the 20th of September 1850, I shall be sitting in this chair, in this study, at ten o'clock at night, longing to die, weary of incessant insight and foresight, without delusions and without hope" (p. 277). To be without delusions and without hope is to be already dead; Latimer has inscribed his own death sentence from the start ("Darkness—darkness—no pain—nothing but darkness"). By the end of the story, all that is left is the sheerest repetition: "It is the 20th of September 1850. I know these figures I have just written, as if they were a long familiar inscription. I have seen them on this page in my desk unnumbered times, when the scene of my dying struggle has opened upon me . . . " (p. 341). Reminiscence in "The Lifted Veil" takes the form of purgatorial circularity; nothing is resolved, nothing renewed. Writing is death.

If Latimer's end is death by writing, a woman delivers the coup de grâce. Eliot's model for "The Lifted Veil" seems to have been a short story by Mary Shelley called "The Mortal Immortal" about a man who cannot die after drinking the elixir of life. Like Latimer, he marries a woman named Bertha in whom the process of physical aging reveals, by contrast, the curse of his own immortality. While she grows jealous, bedridden, and paralytic, he longs only for death.[20] Woman comes to image the condition of being a corpse. But unlike Mary Shelley's narrator, Latimer dies a little more each time he sets pen to paper. At the climax of the story, he learns from a dead woman's lips that to be recalled from beyond the grave is merely to reenact the automatism and compulsion of one's life: "Great God! Is this what it is to live again . . . to wake up with our unstilled thirst upon us, with our unuttered curses rising to our lips, with our muscles ready to act out their half-committed sins?" (p. 339). Freud reminds us that one source of uncanny effects are "the impression of automatic, mechanical processes at work behind the ordinary appearance of mental activity" (*SE* 17:226). Because woman images "a measured fact," the limitations of corporeal existence, she images also what must be repressed and what always returns as uncannily previewed—the fact of one's implication in processes beyond one's control; the fact of one's own mortality. This is the forgotten story which confronts Latimer in the form of a woman's speaking corpse.

The date of "The Lifted Veil" places Latimer's death in 1850, the year after George Eliot's own father had died. We know that this was a troubled period for George Eliot herself. The parallel with Anna O., while it might seem to return us to the "case" of George Eliot, also suggests a reading whose implications are formal rather than biographical, tied to the literary uncanny rather than to the author's life. Anna O.'s rehearsal of the events of the preceding year, including the death of her much loved father, is a form of repetition compulsion which ends by freeing her from the compulsion to repeat and from her morbid identification with death and death's-heads. By contrast, Latimer (whose father also dies in the course of the narrative) hysterically reenacts the death of the father in his own continual dying, but is unable to free himself from the cycle of reminiscence. Like the case of Anna O., his narrative is closely tied to chronology—in his case, however, the reverse chronology which transforms hindsight into foresight.

Latimer's powers of prevision first manifest themselves in Geneva during his convalescence from an unspecified "terrible illness." This first vision, anticipating a later visit to Prague, is of a city arrested in time and "a people doomed to live on in the stale repetition of memories, like deposed and superannuated kings" (p. 287). Caught in the unseeing gaze of blackened medieval statues, its modern inhabitants are diminished to "a swarm of ephemeral visitants infesting it for a day":

> It is such grim, stony beings as these, I thought, who are the fathers of ancient faded children, in those tanned time-fretted dwellings that crowd the steep before me; who pay their court in the worn and crumbling pomp of the palace which stretches its monotonous length on the height; who worship wearily in the stifling air of the churches, urged by no fear or hope, but compelled by their doom to be ever old and undying, to live on in the rigidity of habit, as they live on in perpetual mid-day, without the repose of night or the new birth of morning. (p. 287)

Dead fathers create children doomed to live on without the solace even of the "twin Destinies," Fear and Hope, which lurk behind the painted veil called Life in Shelley's sonnet. Time stands still for them, in a hysterical paralysis which freezes the onward movement of narrative. Eliot's story, in effect, refuses the future tense despite being predicated on foresight. Latimer is locked into the narrative tense of hysteria, a reenactment which turns all futures to the inescapability of the past.

Immediately after the death of her father, in April 1881, Anna O. suffered a disturbance of vision and complained of not being able to recognize people: "Normally, she said, she had been able to recognize faces without having to make any deliberate effort; now she was obliged to do laborious 'recognizing work.' . . . All the people she saw seemed like wax figures without any connection with her" (*SE* 2:26). Sight kills what it looks on. As the child of a dead father, she can only see with the eyes of the dead; later, her hallucinations are filled with emblems of death ("terrifying figures, death's heads and skeletons," *SE* 2:27). This is death-in-life, the nightmare experienced by Latimer and embodied in the "surviving withered remnant of mediaeval Judaism" which he shudders at when, with all the uncanniness of repetition, he visits Prague in the flesh—finding only "a more shrivelled death in life" than that even of the blackened Christian statues of his prevision. The death of the father fractures representation and renders living forms unrecognizable. The body itself is revealed only as a wax figure, the *locus classicus* of uncanny effects. The unfathered seer, Eliot seems to suggest, can only uncreate, like Milton's Satan, a world of death. This world of death is the world of the uncanny, in which the animated figures of story are no more than phantoms or puppets; "recognizing work" is an attempt to read significance back into the fixity of characters who have been divested of life and meaning by the father's paralyzing gaze.

Latimer at first hopes that his vision of Prague is a symptom, not of a diseased imagination, but of "the poet's nature . . . manifesting itself suddenly as spontaneous creation": "Surely it was in this way that Homer saw the plain of Troy, that Dante saw the abodes of the departed, that Milton saw the earthward flight of the Tempter" (p. 289). Strong fathers that they are, Homer, Dante, and Milton seem more likely to induce a sense of "feminine incapacity" in the aspiring poet than a sense of manliness. Latimer is in any case dogged by feeling like a girl. His elder brother—"a handsome, self-confident man"—provides "a thorough contrast to [his] fragile, nervous, ineffectual self" and "half-womanish, half-ghostly beauty" ("I thoroughly disliked my own *physique*, and nothing but the belief that it was a condition of poetic genius would have reconciled me to it," p. 295). Like Nathanael in Freud's reading of "The Sandman," Latimer has early dealings with castration anxiety; one recalls his childhood eye complaint and the "unequalled love" represented by his dead mother (as Freud reminds us, "anxiety about one's eyes, the fear of going blind, is often enough a substitute for the dread of being castrated," *SE* 17:231). As a child, he experiences "the agitation of [his] first hatred" when his head is read by a phrenologist who "stared at [him] with glittering spectacles" and prescribes a scientific education to remedy the "deficiency" he diagnoses. "This big bespectacled man"—clearly the bad father—doubles the role of the lawyer Coppelius and the oculist Coppola in Freud's reading of "The Sandman"; one might speculate that Latimer has wished the death of his kindly but unbending father, or at any rate feared him (in Freud's words) as "the dreaded father at whose hands castration is expected" (*SE* 17:232)—the jealous father who is responsible for the mother's castration.

Latimer, we are told, "had no desire to be this improved man" (pp. 282–83) envisaged by his father, and, like Nathanael, remains fixed in what Freud calls his "feminine attitude towards his father." He wants to be a poet, not a scientist; "but my lot was not so happy as that. A poet pours forth his song and *believes* in the listening ear and answering soul. . . . But the poet's sensibility without his voice—the poet's sensibility that finds no vent but in silent tears . . . —this dumb passion brings with it a fatal solitude of soul in the society of one's fellow-men" (p. 284). Dumbness in Freud's reading of "The Three Caskets" is equated with feminine concealment and duplicity, and read as a sign of death—an equation which may shed light on Anna O.'s silence too.[21] Feminized by poetic sensibility, Latimer is doubly consigned to the realm of those who identify with the dead. As his "feminine incapacity [for] literature" becomes clear, Latimer sees on his own face (or "*figure*") "nothing but the stamp of a morbid organisation, framed for passive suffering—too feeble for the sublime resistance of poetic production" (p. 295). Dumb passion in his case can only lead (like Anna O.'s daydreaming) to hysterical hallucinations which portend his sterility, feminization, and death rather than becoming the sign of poetic manhood or life-engendering powers.

As Peggy Kamuf puts it, "What gives the hysterical fantasy its specific structure is the use of the passive voice as a fictional device to hide an active desire." Seduction fantasies typically involve a reversal of subject and object and a false accusation ("for 'I was violated' one reads 'I [wished to] violate'").[22] Hysterically speaking, Latimer denies his forbidden desire for the father by representing himself as the passive victim of the figure who replaces the father in his story—the poisonous and castrating figure of the woman ushered in by his second vision. As Freud puts it of Nathanael, "the young man, fixated upon his father by his castration complex, becomes incapable of loving a woman" (*SE* 17:232). While waiting for his father one day, Latimer has the prevision of a neighbor and her orphan niece, a young woman named Bertha whom he has never seen:

> . . . a tall, slim, willowy figure, with luxuriant blond hair, arranged in cunning braids and folds that looked almost too massive for the slight figure and the small-featured, thin-lipped face they crowned. But the face had not a girlish expression: the features were sharp, the pale gray eyes at once acute, restless, and sarcastic. They were fixed on me in half-smiling curiosity, and I felt a painful sensation as if a sharp wind were cutting me. The pale-green dress and the green leaves that seemed to form a border about her blond hair, made me think of a Water-Nixie—for my mind was full of German lyrics, and this pale, fatal-eyed woman, with the green weeds, looked like a birth from some cold, sedgy stream, the daughter of an aged river. (p. 291)

The look of "this pale, fatal-eyed woman" is "cutting," the features "sharp."

Later, Bertha is compared to "Giorgione's picture of the cruel-eyed woman" with her "cunning, relentless face," whose gaze produces "a strange intoxicating numbness" (p. 303). In his third and final preview of their marriage, she is "my wife—with cruel eyes," an emblem of his own castration anxiety: "I saw the great emerald brooch on her bosom, a studded serpent with diamond eyes. . . . I felt helpless before her, as if she clutched my bleeding heart, and would clutch it till the last drop of life-blood ebbed away" (p. 304). Latimer's powers of prevision (unlike those George Eliot wishes for herself in her motto for "The Lifted Veil") are unmanning; his vision of a cruel-eyed woman castrates him. Bertha is Latimer's Olympia, the doll-woman whom he loves with senseless obsession (since she is a dissociated aspect of himself—that is, his enslavement to the castration complex) and yet must destroy. She has what he wants; in Freud's words, "Whoever possesses something that is at once valuable and fragile is afraid of other people's envy. . . . A feeling like this betrays itself by a look" (*SE* 17:240). Like Olympia, she has his eyes—his manhood (in a blind trust, perhaps).

U. C. Knoepflmacher reads "The Lifted Veil" in terms strangely complicitous with Latimer's own: "Latimer is essentially guiltless. He is betrayed by his blonde wife and by his extraordinary capacities of insight and foresight."[23] Blonde, elaborately coifed serpent women are familiar agents of male castration in George Eliot's novels. Is Eliot too in complicity with this masculine vision? After all, it is not the blonde wife who betrays Latimer by clutching his bleeding heart but George Eliot who makes Bertha a Germanic Medusa, the water-nixie bearing the sign of a serpent—a serpent which is turned against her own breast in "the white marble medallion of the dying Cleopatra" decorating the chimneypiece in the library, the scene of Latimer's third vision. The "plot" in "The Lifted Veil" is a plot by two women to poison the narrator; but the hidden plot is the plot of one woman against another—a double plot unmasked at the story's climax. Bertha's character is far more thoroughly assassinated by Eliot's own plot than Latimer himself, or even the brother who becomes "an object of intense hatred to [him]" as they vie for Bertha's love. Caught between two men in a Girardian triangle, Bertha is desirable to Latimer only because desired by another man. Rather than his love for Bertha causing him to hate his brother, mimetic rivalry with his brother causes him to love Bertha; though the brother dies, leaving Bertha free for Latimer, it is really (as usual) the woman who has been eliminated in the homoerotic face-off between two men.

Bertha is never credited with desire on her own account, whether by Latimer or by Eliot; in Girard's misogynist scheme, feminine desire is unthinkable except as it mimics the man's love for her—except, that is, as narcissistic self-love.[24] Her attraction lies in her narcissism, her apparent self-sufficiency. As Eliot puts it, "there is no tyranny more complete than that which a self-centered negative nature exercises over a morbidly sensitive nature" (p. 297). The complete tyranny is the tyranny of imagined completeness. Bertha is the woman who possesses the fantasized phallus, the imaginary wholeness which endows her for Latimer with her mysterious allure. All Latimer's self-knowledge is impotent in the face of this fantasy: "I created the unknown thought before which I trembled as if it were hers" (p. 324). Tormented by his ability to see into the deficient minds of others (as the bespectacled phrenologist had seen into the deficiencies of his own mind), Latimer is baffled only by Bertha, whose consciousness remains veiled: "she had for me the fascination of an unravelled destiny"; "She was my oasis of mystery in the dreary desert of knowledge" (pp. 297, 301). Though we are told that she is "keen, sarcastic, unimaginative, prematurely cynical," Latimer "wait[s] before the closed secret of [her] face, as if it were the shrine of the doubtfully benignant deity who ruled his destiny" (pp. 297–98). Even when the cruel-eyed woman of their future married life has been revealed to him, "Bertha, the *girl*, was a fascinating secret to [him] still" (p. 305). "An unravelled destiny," "an oasis of mystery," "a closed secret," "a fascinating secret," Bertha becomes the enigma of woman which Freudian theory at once fails to unravel and unveils as castrating lack or absence. For Eliot, as for Latimer, there is only a death-dealing nothingness behind the veil.

Latimer's narrative simultaneously discloses the shrine as vacant and holds up the veil that makes it mysterious—"no matter how empty the adytum, so that the veil be thick enough" (p. 318). The name Freud gives to this story is fetishism. Bertha's uncanny secret is not her propensity for becoming Lucrezia Borgia, but the private parts she conceals behind the veil. In "The Uncanny," Freud explores the dictionary meanings of "*Heimlich*" and finds an oscillation in the direction of the opposite meaning, "*Unheimlich*"—"*Heimlich* is used in conjunction with a verb expressing the act of concealing: 'In the secret of his tabernacle he shall hide me *heimlich*' (Psalm 27:5) . . . *Heimlich* parts of the human body, *pudenda*" (*SE* 17:225). "Probably," writes Freud in his essay "Fetishism" (1927), "no male human being is spared the fright of castration at the sight of a female genital." The veil of the story's title is like the fetishist's undergarments which "crystallize the moment of undressing, the last moment in which the woman could still be regarded as phallic" (*SE* 21:154, 155). The fetish can even become a vehicle for simultaneously denying and admitting the "fact" of (woman's) castration, like the fig leaf on a statue, making her castrated and phallic at the same time. Latimer's "double consciousness," his vision of Bertha as both girl and woman, mystery and "measured fact," similarly allows him to entertain two contradictory ideas:

> Behind the slim girl Bertha, whose words and looks I watched for, whose touch was bliss, there stood continually that Bertha with the fuller form, the harder eyes, the more rigid mouth,—with the barren, selfish soul laid bare; no longer a fascinating secret, but a measured fact, urging itself perpetually on my unwilling sight. (pp. 306–7)

Here the unwilling sight at once encounters and denies the lack veiled by the fetish.

Gilbert and Gubar point out that fictional characters named Bertha seem always to be associated with dangerous female sexuality; besides deriving her name from the coquettish girl and jealous wife in Shelley's "The Mortal Immortal," Bertha shares it with the mad wife in *Jane Eyre*.[25] But the Teutonic associations of the name "Bertha" (which means "bright") would not have been lost on a German-speaking George Eliot. Early on in his essay on fetishism, Freud refers to "the case of a young man who had exalted a certain kind of 'shine on the nose' into a fetishistic condition." Freud's patient, he reveals, had been brought up in an English nursery: "The fetish, which originated from his earliest childhood, had to be understood in English, not German. The 'shine on the nose' [in German '*Glanz auf der Nase*']—was in reality a '*glance* at the nose.' The nose was thus the fetish, which . . . he endowed . . . with the luminous shine" (*SE* 21:152). The fetish is based on a metonymic substitution (nose instead of missing penis); but the phrase metaphorically mis-translates a look as a shine, or brightness—as if it is not the nose that constitutes the fetish, but rather the veil of words. In the specular scheme which "The Lifted Veil" shares with Freudian theory, Bertha's brightness is bestowed on her by Latimer's look, then translated into a fetishistic veil of metaphor.

Illumination puts blankness in place of brilliance:

"The terrible moment of complete illumination had come to me, and I saw that the darkness had hidden no landscape from me, but only a blank prosaic wall" (p. 323). Confronted by the girl's or mother's genitals, the boy at first sees nothing (struck, as it were, with hysterical blindness) then concludes that there is nothing to see, erecting his castration theory as a fetish in place of perceived absence. Like the little boy, Freudian theory posits an absence where we might prefer to locate its own blind spot, or inability to solve an enigma of its own making. The unveiling or castration of Bertha is the necessary complement to Latimer's blind worship at the empty shrine of feminine mystery. Latimer's "terrible moment of complete illumination" (a moment revealing Bertha's incompleteness) is precipitated in "The Lifted Veil" by the death of the father. After Latimer's brother dies, the father grudgingly transfers to Latimer himself "the inheritance of an eldest son" and even his "anxious regard" ("There is hardly any neglected child for whom death has made vacant a more favoured place, who will not understand what I mean," p. 317). Freud's family romance comes to the rescue, promoting the feminized sibling to the position of favored son—only for the father to become the impossible object of desire once more; for hysteria to flourish, the object of desire must remain forever lost. The second part of "The Lifted Veil" completes the unveiling of the woman—or rather, it unveils the hidden face of male hysteria as the face of the most castrating woman of all, death. Bertha's lack puts Latimer's "deficiencies" in a glaring light: "I saw myself in Bertha's thought as she lifted her cutting grey eyes, and looked at me: a miserable ghost-seer, surrounded by phantoms in the noonday . . . pining after the moonbeams" (p. 323). A blank prosaic wall, she reflects nothing back; neither sun to his moon, nor moon to his sun, she becomes merely an impediment to the specular system in which her brightness can no longer signify, thus signifying only the end or extinction of all figures.

Bertha stands for the death of desire—instilling a poison that leaves the victim "without appetite for the common objects of desire" and so preventing the circulation of desire itself. The previsioned scene in which Bertha appears to Latimer "with her cruel, contemptuous eyes fixed on [him], and the glittering serpent, like a familiar demon, on her breast" (p. 327) ushers in a second woman who is to play the part of Bertha's familiar demon or double. The new maid—"a tall, wiry, dark-eyed woman . . . with a face handsome enough to give her coarse hard nature the odious finish of bold, self-confident coquetry" (p. 328)—is the antithesis of Bertha, the blonde, slight water-nixie. Mrs. Archer (an Amazon, perhaps?) forces Latimer to avert his gaze lest he should "be obliged to see what had been breeding about two unloving women's hearts" (p. 338). Like the doubling of women in Caravaggio's and Gentileschi's paintings of Judith accompanied by her maid, the doubling here allows the chilling fantasy of the phallic woman to take on its reassuring (and homophobic) function; such women are really men, it seems to say, and the model for homosexual love is really heterosexual.[26]

In the sensational culmination of Eliot's story, Bertha is exposed as the would-be poisoner of her husband, the maid as her accomplice. The two women quarrel, the maid falls ill and dies, and Latimer's scientific friend, Meunier, performs an experiment on the dead woman which momentarily revivifies her and allows her to denounce Bertha before she falls silent once more. In this lurid scene, Bertha's "cutting eyes" no longer chill Latimer. Instead, the two women engage each other's gaze in "the recognition of hate," or the "look of hideous meaning" which Mrs. Archer turns on Bertha. That love might breed about the hearts of two unloving (i.e. homosexual) women is proved after all to be impossible, or at least to bring about only a monstrous birth. Women hate each other. The scene presents as self-evident the proposition that women are murderously commonplace, morally debased, loving neither men nor each other, but only themselves; and that this essential, unredeemably carnal feminine nature persists even beyond death—residing in the body itself—since Mrs. Archer returns from the dead only to reenact her part in life as the puppet or automaton of passion.

Blackwood disliked "the revivifying experiment" and advised George Eliot to delete the scene; later, a painting called *"La Transfusion du Sang"* by H. E. Blanchon, exhibited in the Paris Salon of 1879, provided a lurid Continental translation.[27] But was "the dominant French taste" (George Eliot's phrase) so far from the mark in singling out this aspect of her writing as the revelation of something better kept hidden? The scene of the blood transfusion makes woman at once all body and all representation. Bertha has hoped for "the moment of death as the sealing of her secret" (p. 338)—a secret that is duplicity, imposture, masquerade. A reanimated corpse is at the center of the tableau, "the chamber where death was hovering" (p. 336). The pinched and ghastly face of Mrs. Archer becomes interchangeable with Bertha's "preternaturally sharp" features and hard eyes: "I asked myself how that face of hers could ever have seemed to me the face of a woman born of woman . . . she looked like a cruel immortal, finding her spiritual feast in the agonies of a dying race" (p. 337). Preyed on or preying, the faces of a dying woman and a cruel immortal double each other; they are death's-heads. When Mrs. Archer breathes her last, the onlookers "all felt that the dark veil had completely fallen" and Latimer turns his eyes from Bertha "with a horrible dread lest [his] insight should return" (pp. 337–38). What he sees is the third woman, the hovering figure of Death.

By this stage, Latimer's "delirium" has taken the form of an odyssey through a series of strange yet familiar visionary landscapes (the scene of his future wanderings), in all of which "one presence seemed to weigh on [him] . . . the presence of something unknown and pitiless" (p. 329). This "presence" is the prevision of his own death, later figured as "the one Unknown Presence revealed and yet hidden by the moving curtain of the earth and sky" (p. 340). The unknown presence has Bertha's face ("she looked like a cruel immortal"). Latimer's wanderings bring him home to his place of origin. "There is a joking saying that 'Love is homesickness,'" writes Freud; "whenever a man dreams of a place or a country and says to himself, while he is still dreaming: 'this place is familiar to me, I've been here before,' we may interpret the place as being his mother's genitals or her body" (*SE* 17:245). Freud's "beautiful confirmation of [his] theory of the uncanny" is clinched by this equation of the uncanny, death, and the mother. Bertha, whose face seems not to be "the face of a woman born of woman," neither mothered (she is an orphan) nor capable of mothering, figures for Latimer the third of the three forms taken by the figure of the mother in "The Theme of the Three Caskets"—first the mother herself, then "the beloved one who is chosen after her pattern, and lastly the Mother Earth who receives him once more" (*SE* 12:301). Replacing the Goddess of Love in Latimer's narrative, the Goddess of Death (Atropos) cannot be stayed.

The uncanny twist to the narrative thread of "The Lifted Veil" is not that death cuts it off, but rather that it goes on forever. The veil lifted by Mrs. Archer's reanimated corpse reveals only the horror of endless familiarity: "this scene seemed of one texture with the rest of my existence: horror was my familiar, and this new revelation was only like an old pain recurring with new circumstances" (p. 340). The culminating vision of "The Lifted Veil" spells for Latimer, and perhaps for George Eliot too, the reduction of the textual body to a figure of recurrence. The closing words of the story ("I know these figures I have just written, as if they were a long-familiar inscription. I have seen them on this page in my desk unnumbered times, when the scene of my dying struggle has opened upon me . . . ," p. 341) reduce the body not simply to a wax figure, but to mere characters, mere "figures," or writing. The body of a woman defends against the death or absence (or rather, in Eliot's terms, "Presence") which writing represents. The feminine body veils lack in language. Any representation, however castrating—even a Medusa's or death's-head—is better than none at all. Earlier, Bertha has tantalized Latimer by seeming to signify ("out of the subtlest web of scarcely perceptible signs, she set me weaving"). Mrs. Archer reveals the body to be a signifying system like any other from which meaning may be absent; as Latimer discovers, "We learn *words* by rote, but not their meaning; *that* must be paid for with our life-blood, and printed in the subtle fibres of our nerves" (p. 326). "The Lifted Veil" tells us that there is no other way to learn words; that the price of signification—language—is indeed the loss of "our life-blood."

Memory itself, the narrative mode adopted in "The Lifted Veil" (where recollection and presentiment amount to the same thing) is merely another form of hieroglyphic or pic-

tographic writing: "The recollections of the past become con-
tracted in the rapidity of thought till they sometimes bear
hardly a more distinct resemblance to the external reality than
the forms of an oriental alphabet to the objects that suggested
them" (pp. 328–29). Passages like these do more than unveil
the fiction of referentiality which must be maintained in the
interests of realist narrative. They spell a paralyzingly contradictory self-consciousness, making a disease out of the writer's
relation to language and (self)-representation. Latimer's
"double consciousness" is analogous to Anna O.'s impotent
"private theatre" or the dumbness-inducing dilemma of the
writer-hysteric described by Alice James: "My self-consciousness was heightened to that pitch of intensity in which our own
emotions take the form of a drama which urges itself imper-
atively on our contemplation, and we begin to weep less under
the sense of our suffering than at the thought of it" (p. 311). The
hysteric's drama is the drama of self-representation, the acting
out or doubling which allows us to contemplate, not only our
thoughts, but ourselves. Without representation, there could be
no "self," and therefore no meaning. The words we learn by
rote and repeat to dramatize our (forgotten) stories are all that
stands between us and the unraveling of identity.

Why should anxieties about representation take the
form of anxiety about the mother—figured as the recurrence in
male hysteria of a fantasy about the castrating and castrated
woman? Why should the central motif of "The Lifted Veil," a
story written by a woman yet hysterically identified with the
vision of the father, be the treacherous incarnation of a woman,
that sign of death whose absence renders her paradoxically
corporeal and all body, all signifier but no signified? Latimer's
"double consciousness" has often been linked with "the sincere acting" or habitual self-dramatization of Daniel Deronda's
mother, the Princess Halm-Eberstein:

> This woman's nature was one in which all feeling—and all
> the more when it was tragic as well as real—immediately
> became matter of conscious representation: experience im-
> mediately passed into drama, and she acted her own emo-
> tions. In a minor degree this is nothing uncommon, but in
> the Princess the acting had a rare perfection of physiognomy,

voice, and gesture. It would not be true to say that she felt less because of this double consciousness: she felt—that is, her mind went through—all the more, but with a difference: each nucleus of pain or pleasure had a deep atmosphere of the excitement or spiritual intoxication which at once exalts and deadens.[28]

For Deronda himself, this confrontation with his origins might well be thought to have a touch of the uncanny (something familiar that has been forgotten); unsurprisingly, the Princess is associated with a serpent woman: "Her worn beauty had a strangeness in it as if she were not quite a human mother, but a Melusina" (pp. 687–88). The chapter has opened with a motto that seems to identify the Princess with Erinna, the spinner-poetess (author of *The Distaff*), as if to make her one of the Spinners—an embodiment of Deronda's hidden destiny ("It seemed as if he were in the presence of a mysterious Fate rather than of the longed-for mother," p. 688). A figure with "piercing eyes" which make Deronda "chang[e] colour like a girl" and expressions which constitute "a tacit language," she images an unspeakable foreignness ("He could not even conjecture in what language she would speak to him. He imagined it would not be English," p. 687). Though she has a foreign accent, her true language is the body language of the artist-hysteric: "I was a great singer, and I acted as well as I sang." The Princess is also Jewish, and (like Anna O., whose hysteria Breuer ascribes in part to the same cause), she has refused her prescribed place as a woman in the faith of her forefathers. Her rejection of this Jewish female identity initiates the self-divisive struggle which at once makes her an artist and a moral outcast—or rather, the cast-out of George Eliot's representational system.

It's no accident, then, that Eliot's figure for the artist should be a woman, and at that a mother. The Princess' father, we learn, had wanted a son, but he "had no other child than his daughter, and she was like himself" (p. 694). Though she is like her father, the Princess has had to play the part of his daughter. She marries in accordance with her father's wishes ("I was to be what he called 'the Jewish woman' under pain of his curse," p. 692), but she attempts to secure for her son another legacy—to break the paternal line and its hold on her identity. Paternal law returns in George Eliot's novel as the son's wrathful resumption of his inheritance, a humanized version of Jewish didacticism ("Teaching, teaching for everlasting—'this you must be,' 'that you must not be'—" p. 693). The father's curse is the Princess' illness, her lovelessness, and, above all, her dissociation or "double consciousness." The Princess allows us to reformulate the artist-hysteric's dilemma as Alice James had stated it, and perhaps also to redefine the relation between hysteria and the father. The woman under patriarchy is caught in an unavoidably hysterical dilemma. She can either submit to the desire of the father, identifying herself with it so completely that she becomes what he desires her to be; that is, all body, the fetish who veils the horror of absence in the male hysterical fantasy which (as Freud admits) afflicts all men in the face of their mothers. This is why, for the hysteric, the death of the father fractures the system of representations in which she has taken up her assigned position. Alternatively, a woman can break with the desire of the father by choosing to be "like himself" instead of what he likes. This means, for the writer and actress, being at once self-authoring and self-estranged, haunted by the father's repressed castration anxiety, for ever retelling his forgotten story. George Eliot must cast out the Princess's "double consciousness" as diseased, just as Latimer is consigned to the purgatory of repetition, or else own up to it as the condition of the woman writer under patriarchy—owning, that is, to the *double conscience* or *absences* which figure hysteria, femininity, and writing (the threefold forms of death) as the matter of her reminiscent story.

V. READING CORRESPONDENCES

"Addressing these memoirs to you, my child, uncertain whether I shall ever have an opportunity of instructing you, many observations will probably flow from my heart, which only a mother—a mother schooled in misery, could make.

"The tenderness of a father who knew the world, might be great; but could it equal that of a mother—of a mother, labouring under a portion of the misery, which the constitution of society seems to have entailed on all her kind? It is, my child, my dearest daughter, only such a mother, who will dare to break through all restraint to provide for your happiness—who will voluntarily brave censure herself, to ward off sorrow from your bosom. From my narrative, my dear girl, you may gather the instruction, the counsel, which is meant rather to exercise than influence your mind.—Death may snatch me from you, before you can weigh my advice, or enter into my reasoning: I would then, with fond anxiety, lead you very early in life to form your grand principle of action, to save you from the vain regret of having, through irresolution, let the spring-tide of existence pass away, unimproved, unenjoyed.—Gain experience—ah! gain it— while experience is worth having, and acquire sufficient fortitude to pursue your own happiness; it includes your utility, by a direct path. What is wisdom too often, but the owl of the goddess, who sits moping in a desolated heart; around me she shrieks, but I would invite all the gay warblers of spring to nestle in your blooming bosom.—Had I not wasted years in deliberating, after I ceased to doubt, how I ought to have acted—I might now be useful and happy.—For my sake, warned by my example, always appear what you are, and you will not pass through existence without enjoying its genuine blessings, love and respect."

—Mary Wollstonecraft[1]

With your milk, Mother, I swallowed ice. And here I am now, my insides frozen. And I walk with even more difficulty than you do, and I move even less. You flowed into me, and that hot liquid became poison, paralyzing me. My blood no longer circulates to my feet or my hands, or as far as my head. It is immobilized, thickened by the cold. Obstructed by icy chunks which resist its flow. My blood coagulates, remains in and near my heart.

And I can no longer race toward what I love. And the more I love, the more I become captive, held back by a weightiness that immobilizes me. And I grow angry, I struggle, I scream—I want out of this prison.

But what prison? Where am I cloistered? I see nothing confining me. The prison is within myself, and it is I who am its captive.

How to get out? And why am I thus detained?

You take care of me, you keep watch over me. You want me always in your sight in order to protect me. You fear that something will happen to me. Do you fear that something will happen? But what could happen that would be worse than the fact of my lying supine day and night? Already full-grown and still in the cradle. Still dependent upon someone who carries me, who nurses me. Who *carries* me? Who *nurses* me?

A little light enters me. Something inside me begins to stir. Barely. Something new has moved me. As though I'd taken a first step inside myself. As if a breath of air had penetrated a completely petrified being, unsticking its mass. Waking me from a long sleep. From an ancient dream. A dream which must not have been my own, but in which I was captive. Was I a participant, or was I the dream itself—another's dream, a dream about another?

—Luce Irigaray[2]

Reading Correspondences

Mary Wollstonecraft's Maria, to her infant daughter: Luce Irigaray, to her infantilizing mother. Two addresses, two letters; a correspondence between a mothering text, *The Wrongs of Woman,* and the smothered daughter's reply, "And the One Doesn't Stir Without the Other."

Wollstonecraft's Maria: "Addressing these memoirs to you, my child . . . many observations will probably flow from my heart, which only a mother . . . could make." Luce Irigaray: "With your milk, Mother, I swallowed ice. . . . You flowed into me, and that hot liquid became poison, paralyzing me." The flow of maternal misery ("a mother schooled in misery") becomes liquid poison in the daughter's mouth. Maria is her child's would-be guardian and protector, but also Minerva's owl—her warning: "my child, my dearest daughter, only such a mother . . . will voluntarily brave censure herself, to ward off suffering from your bosom. . . . For my sake, [be] warned by my example." Irigaray is her mother's reproach and her prisoner: "I want out of this prison. . . . You take care of me, you keep watch over me. You want me always in your sight in order to protect me. You fear that something will happen to me." Maria writes of separation (foremost among *The Wrongs of Woman* is the loss of maternal rights); Irigaray, of too much closeness. Wollstonecraft makes milk a figure for writing ("many observations will . . . flow from my heart") and writing a substitute for the milk which flows from Maria's engorged breasts ("her burning bosom—a bosom bursting with the nutriment for which . . . [her] child might now be pining in vain," p. 75). Irigaray makes mothering a kind of force-feeding, a metaphor for the suffocating absence of boundaries between mother and child: "You put yourself in my mouth, and I suffocate" (p. 61). The distance which generates both desire and narrative in Maria's story ("her soul flowed into it," p. 82) is the "blind assimilation" which for Irigaray drives the daughter into the arms of the father, with the threat, "I'll leave us. . . . I'll live my life, my story" (p. 63).

What is this life story? And whose?

A mother's instructions to her daughter: a daughter's denunciation of the mother. Wollstonecraft's adaptation of an eighteenth-century didactic form to the needs of her feminist novel, Irigaray's harnessing of twentieth-century feminism's rage at the mother and at the daughter's own complicity in her oppression, answer one another across two centuries, seeming to enforce resemblance as much as correspondence. As Frances Ferguson writes, "the letter has long functioned as a long arm of education . . . the letter, precisely because it lays claim to a reply, registers an attempt both to generate and to enforce resemblance between the correspondents."[3]

The story both letters tell is the daughter's abduction (not seduction); her loss of self (*abduct*: "To lead or take away improperly, whether by force or fraud; to carry off, to kidnap. Applied especially to the carrying off of a woman or child"; *OED*). For Maria, "Was not the world a vast prison, and women born slaves?" (p. 79.) The abduction of the daughter lands the mother in prison. The life story which Maria narrates for the benefit of her infant daughter tells of her imprisonment, both as a metaphor for women's confinement (a subjection at once social and subjective) and as the literalization of that metaphor in society's actual treatment of women. Whether as mothers, as subjects, or as social beings, women are confined. As soon as her story is told, Maria finds herself miraculously free; she walks out of her prison, leaving behind the petrifying forms that haunt and imprison her imagination ("You have nothing to do with me," p. 190).

"I, too," writes Irigaray, "am abducted from myself"—immobilized in masculine reflections. "My paralysis signif[ies] your abduction in the mirror," she tells her mother (p. 66). The mother's abduction in the glass of a specular economy takes the daughter away from herself. She exclaims: "I want out of this prison. But what prison? . . . The prison is

within myself, and it is I who am my captive." Which is the
mother, which the daughter? Feeling the stirrings of "petrified
being," the daughter asks (the question Wollstonecraft's readers ask of her fictional Maria), "Was I a participant, or was I the
dream itself—another's dream. A dream about another?" Reading Irigaray through Wollstonecraft, her reader asks in turn:
whose is the dream? Is Irigaray Maria's (Mary Wollstonecraft's)
daughter? Is Wollstonecraft the abducted mother dreamed by
Irigaray? To whom are these letters addressed, and by whom
read? What meaning can we, as feminist readers—as mothers
and daughters (daughters who also are, or have, mothers)—
give to this unhappy feminist correspondence?

   Irigaray figures the relation between mother and
daughter as one of specular entrapment: "I look at myself in
you, you look at yourself in me" (p. 61). Frozen in the mirror
(*"glace"*) of resemblance ("I look like you, you look like me"),
the daughter can only see the mother as a petrifying image of
in-difference. Without difference there is nothing but freezing
identity; call it hysterical maternal identification, as maternal
desire speaks through and in the daughter—the daughter who
assumes her assigned place in the eye of the mother's desire.
Wollstonecraft's Maria "still wished, for [her] own consolation,
to be the mother of a daughter" (p. 160). Irigaray accuses her
mother: "You desired me, such is this love of yours"—such is
this love of yourself (*"tel cet amour de toi"*). "Imprisoned by your
desire for a reflection, I became a statue" (p. 64); a petrified
form. Maria makes her daughter the privileged reader of the
maternal text: "To them I write not—my feelings are not for
them to analyze; and may you, my child, never be able to ascer-
tain . . . what your mother felt" (p. 163)—except through maternal identification; except in the act of reading her address.
Whether as reader of the text or as swallower of (swallowed up
by) the flow of maternal feeling, the daughter inherits, drinks
in, the mother's story. She is read by it; the letter engulfs her,
making her resentfully (on Irigaray's side of the exchange) her
mother's reflection: "Here is she who I shall be, or was, or
would like to be—was that not your response to my birth?"
demands Irigaray-as-daughter (p. 66). Yet if as feminist readers
(both mothers and daughters) we construct a mother-daughter

dialogue (each positioned in the eye of the other's desire), it is surely not so that the two letters, in reading one another, should kill each other off with their mutual, petrifying resemblance.[4]

Maria's daughter—abducted, presumed dead—provides Wollstonecraft with her feminist, matrilineal fiction of a life worth living after all ("I will live for my child!", p. 203); in the fragmentary sketch which survives of the novel's post-suicidal (biographically, posthumous, or rather, postpartum) ending, the daughter is restored to her mother. Irigaray too sees herself as the guarantor of her mother's life ("if I leave, you lose the reflection of life, of your life") but also of her death ("And if I remain, am I not the guarantor of your death?" p. 66). How can the correspondence continue if the life of the daughter images the death of the mother? How can it ever end if it provides the only image available for the (m)other's continued life?—making this mothering of the text either a stillbirth, or a solipsistic nightmare (a hall of mirrors in which each acts her part in the other's dream). Yet the continuity of letters in the maternal line is the continuity of feminist reading itself, backward from Irigaray's French feminism, forward from Wollstonecraft's French (Revolutionary) feminism. If the daughter reads the mother's abduction, the founding mother reads her daughter's abduction as already read. Crossing the fixed lines of chronological reading, the correspondence puts matrilinear structures in question, allowing meaning (and difference) to emerge from the knot of daughterly (af)filiation.

Irigaray glimpses an alternative to the glassy mirror imaging of mother and daughter texts: "I would like us to play together at being the same and different. You/I exchanging selves endlessly. . . . We would play catch, you and I. . . . I throw an image of you, to you, you throw it back, catch it again" (pp. 61–62). The textual interchange or dialogue refuses the specular structure of frozen resemblance, turning the unending argument into a game, a play of difference or a liberating exchange; a correspondence: "The action or fact of corresponding or answering to each other in fitness or mutual adaptation; congruity, harmony, agreement"; but also, "Relation of agreement, similarity, or analogy"; "Concordant or sympathetic response"; "Relations between persons or communities"; "Intercourse, communication (between persons)"; and finally, *"Intercourse or communication by letters" (OED;* my italics). This answering fitness, mutuality, and sympathetic response accords with Irigaray's definition of the ideal play of possibility between mother and daughter, between an image and its difference, between what passes from one feminist text to another, between feminist writer and feminist reader.

"Intercourse or communication by letters" is a woman of letters' (Wollstonecraft's/Maria's) answer to the problem of narrative form/the abduction of the daughter. The model of reciprocity and correspondence becomes a metaphor for relations between persons; but also a model for textual relations and for reading itself. By "relation of agreement, similarity, or analogy"? No; rather by an answering correspondence. Letters address both the structure of feminist exchange and the process of feminist reading. For feminist readers, the life stories of Wollstonecraft and Irigaray are the stories of women of letters. Their letters (like their correspondences) are what makes them readable—readable as feminist texts; their letters read us, narrate us, free us from the imprisoning glass of a specular history. Fractured, multiplied, and dispersed, the images glassed in the mirror of resemblance become neither Mary Wollstonecraft's, nor Irigaray's, nor our own, but those shifting and composite differences which at once make up and discompose readerly identity. If we find ourselves mirrored in their correspondence, in other words, it is because their specular relations petrify and freeze ours. If instead we find in their answering address a play of difference, it is because the letter of the text (not the figure in it) undoes the specular imprisonment which keeps us captive as readers, opening the gates to a liberating intertextuality and refusing even that imaginary unity, the "we" of feminist reading, as an imprisoning image.

In *The Daughter's Seduction,* Jane Gallop writes about Irigaray writing about Freud; Irigaray's close reading of "On Femininity" (1932) is called "The Blind Spot of an Old Dream of Symmetry." Has Freud perhaps led Irigaray astray? asks Gallop. Has Irigaray been, not abducted, but seduced—flinging herself into the father's arms in order to escape the mother? (*Seduction*: "The action or an act of seducing (a person) to err in conduct or belief. . . . The condition of being led astray. . . . The action of tempting (a female child) to leave her parents for marriage or otherwise. . . . The action of inducing (a woman) to surrender her chastity"; *OED*). Who is the dreamer? Freud, or Irigaray herself—a participant in the old dream of hysterical, oedipal seduction? "Symmetry," writes Gallop, "is appropriating two things to like measure, measure by the same standard: for example the feminine judged by masculine standards" (i.e., judged as inadequate or castrated).[5] Nothing to see is the "oculocentrism" of phallocentricity; woman is "nothing" in Freud's old dream of symmetry. Both "theory" and its "blind spot" (the ocular shadow of theory) invoke the visual register, or the oculocentricity of speculation. The specular figure of symmetry ("like measure") is the error that Freud (Gallop points out) refers to as "the error of superimposition" ("*Über-deckungsfehler*"); in French, "*l'erreur de raisonnement analogique*" (the error of analogical reasoning). Elsewhere, Gallop points out, Freud writes of "yield[ing] to the temptation" of analogy; and again, "I have not been able to resist the seduction of an analogy."[6] The seduction of analogy makes man the measure of woman, the little boy's constitution as a gendered subject the model for the little girl's. Analogy is the blind spot of the old dream. The ana-logue is the same old logic, the sameness of a phallogocentric economy; sameness, identity, or analogical reasoning—the error of superimposition—elides or represses difference as the mirror image of resemblance (woman reflects man, denying sexual difference just as the phallic mother is assimilated to the father, the bisexual daughter to the oedipal son).

Analogy sustains and screens the defining of difference as sameness. Analogy is a means of denying difference; since it really works to superimpose likeness, difference becomes the blind spot of analogy. But here is K. K. Ruthven in *Feminist Literary Studies: An Introduction* (1984): " 'Homology' is the name given to similarities of relationship."[7] For Lévi-Strauss, Ruthven argues, regulations and kinship systems constitute (analogically) a kind of language; but the relation between women (circulated between clans) and words (circulated between individuals) is that of homology. This is the similarity of structural relation rather than the resemblance of analogy (the same again). *Vive la différence féministe,* Ruthven seems to say, in privileging homology like-wise. "In feminist discourse," writes Ruthven, "it is common to encounter homological equations between sexual practices and cultural formations, most often by way of protest against oppressively phallocratic homologies" (e.g. "the husband is the head of the wife, even as Christ is the head of the Church").[8] The weapons of phallocracy are turned against phallocracy itself. Homology, in Ruthven's diagnosis, licenses "a good deal of homological freeplay" (a good deal for feminist discourse?) in feminist word play on the subject of masculine erection—getting it up, keeping it up; the replication of coital postures in power structures (men on top, the missionary position). Ruthven—a missionary among masculinist critics—is on top of feminist discourse here; but as feminist readers, should we take his position lying down? From his vantage point (above and beyond), Ruthven can see that clitoridectomy (for instance) allows feminist semiotics "to link the microstructure of sexual practices to the macrostructure of sexual politics." He instances other visual excisions, other spectacular homologies; Gayatri Spivak writes (homologically) that repression of the clitoris as a feminine signifier "operates the specific repression of women."[9] Freud has to repress the clitoris for the phallic little girl to become the measure of masculine phallocentricity. Intrigued by the excision of the clitoris from lexicography and literature, Ruthven views in this unseeable "blind spot"—this feminine castration—the rationale for feminist homology or freeplay. Perhaps there is something in it after all (the clitoris, or little penis) for male feminists to get their fingers on.

But is homology really free of phallocentric (androcentric) sameness? Is it so different from analogy? The same word (homo-logy), it seems rather to repeat the structure of analogy—to replicate the seduction of symmetry (an agreeable coherence) which leads to the leading away or abduction of both mother and daughter. *"Pour faire une omelette il faut casser des oeufs"* ("you can't make an omelette without breaking eggs"), writes Freud apropos of his naming of sexual parts and acts to Dora (*SE* 7:49). Lacan's homonymic usage (omelette = *hommelette* or little man) is a homological reminder that here too masculine punning may be viewed as the agreeable measure for feminist freeplay. For Ruthven, "The advantage of a homological method of investigation is that it avoids problems associated with that 'specular' model of literary enquiry which treats art as some sort of mirror to life and expects literature to reflect what goes on around it."[10] That is, for Ruthven the homological method refuses the reflectionist model whose dream of symmetrical blindness is Irigaray's nightmare. Yet it is through this reflectionist glass that Ruthven obtains his own overview of feminist critical difference. Which amounts to this: there are separatist feminists; and then there are nonseparatist feminists. Togetherness or agreement—binary opposition—becomes the measure both of feminist difference and of male-female critical relations. In Ruthven's text, homology works to restore the old dream of symmetry (*homme*-ology) whereby the feminist text only reflects or measures up to what has been seen by a masculine viewer. You can't make a masculinist critic (*hommelette*) without breaking a few feminist eggs. Ruthven places himself *hors de combat*, outside the place where textual breakage (rupture) occurs; his own discourse on feminist criticism retains its imaginary mastery of the discourse of feminism. The measure is separation (feminist criticism as castration) or a reassuring image of wholeness (feminist criticism as the imaginary, narcissistic completion of critical lack): the phallic woman, in short, has something to offer the institution of criticism after all.

If homology won't do, or does nothing but the same old thing (enacts only an old dream of symmetry), could "correspondence" effect a break with *homme*-ology by allowing the woman of letters at least the letter of her difference? The readings in this book move between one text and another as if they were mutually constituting—as if they "correspond," not in the sense of sameness, but in the sense of answering to the preoccupations of the feminism that receives them. The differences between these feminist "letters"—historical (Revo-

lutionary Mary Wollstonecraft, twentieth-century Irigaray)
or national (Anglo-French, Franco-American) or philosophical
(rationalist/reforming, anti-rationalist/deconstructive)—are not
so much elided as re-marked in the context of their meaning for
the receiver. Reading such correspondences in the texts of feminism, I risk, as a feminist critic, making them my mirror. But
these self-reflexive readings are not imprisoningly specular
(unlike the mother-daughter relations immobilizing Irigaray) if
they allow for the self-dispersing shattering of figure (*figure* or
face) which breaks the glass into different pieces, refusing to
replicate the same little feminist (*femmelette*) in every text.
Though reading is an unavoidably specular activity, reading
itself can be "read" as a diacritical rather than specular process—one that puts the reader, as well as reading itself, in question. So long as the letter is read as a letter, and not as a
reflection, the text of feminism reads me even as I read it.
Women of letters like Wollstonecraft and Irigaray situate their
feminist readers, making me (for instance) one of their textual
effects. The feminist letter "reads" (feminist) reading. The end
in view would be the blind spot of reading, the discomposition
of the literal in order to reveal what reading represses in the
interests of *homme*-ology or phallogocentric sameness. Abduction—the improper leading away of meaning—might then become an apt metaphor for feminist reading as well as for
women's sequestration or invisibility in patriarchal and phallocentric systems.

　　　The abduction of correspondences leads away from
the seduction of analogy to the otherness of the letter. The
alterity of feminist reading is posited, not simply in opposition
to masculinist reading, not simply as a move that carries off
familiar readings and puts them to strange uses, but rather as a
move that installs strangeness (femininity) within reading itself.
Femininity can be defined as the uncanny difference of masculinity within and from itself: feminist reading (correspon-
dingly) can be defined as the uncanny internal difference or
division—the ambiguity—by which reading refuses phallogocentric identity as the measure of available meanings. The letter
of reading is always abducted; if not lost, at any rate, carried off,
carried over, or metaphorically translated—purloined, like the

letter of Poe's text. In Barbara Johnson's reading of Derrida's reading of Lacan's reading of Poe's "The Purloined Letter," Lacan insists on the intersubjectivity which gives meaning to the circulation and substitution of one letter for another.[11] The structural positioning of the letter for each reader (not its contents) determines how it is read. Less a locus of meaning than a producer of reading effects, the letter can be taken not in one way as opposed to another, but differently.

What Johnson calls Lacan's *"allegory of the signifier"* might also signify the circulation of desire, of meaning, and of letters as they travel along differing critical itineraries (p. 115). Lacan would argue that the letter lacks meaning; this lack is its meaning. Accusing Lacan of installing absence of meaning (lack) as *the* meaning of the letter, Derrida (as read by Johnson) sees in this ambiguous double movement, at once veiling and unveiling, the installation of the truth that is woman (castration): "a hole." Johnson points out that Derrida thereby repeats the move for which he had criticized Lacan—installing woman in place of a blank. The (ana)logic of the purloined letter is that it confounds all attempts to read, turning reading itself into a series of dialectical moves in an unfolding series of readings. In seeking to "find" woman—to read woman— in the gaps and absences of the literary text, feminist criticism might be criticized for its (*homme*-ological) repetition of the Derridean reading. Unless, that is, "woman" is posited, not as content, but as a reading effect—as a definition produced by textual relations, whether the relations between texts or within them. To unveil woman within the text would be to reinstall the phallic woman—to replicate the imaginary wholeness which is the boy's and the fetishist's defense against castration anxiety. To analyze the textual production of woman-as-nothing (or woman as man-mirroring) is, by contrast, to read the discomposing letter of the letter, and not its unifying, idealizing "spirit" or meaning.

Feminist reading of woman might, for a start, want to insert itself there—where Lacan and Derrida, in the very process of establishing difference (between themselves, and from themselves), turn their rivalrous face-off into mirror-imaging resemblance. Or, to paraphrase Johnson's "Frame of

Reference" once more, it is not where Lacan and Derrida look alike but where they look away (not where they hit but where they miss) that opens a space for feminist criticism.[12] Of course, the feminist critic risks being seen (like Dupin in Lacan's reading of the Poe story) as merely getting even, and therefore as implicating herself in the repetition of critically interested misreading. The feminist critic's interest—her lack of disinterestedness, her desire—could be described as the wish to get even; but only at the cost of invoking the old dream of symmetry. Evenness is the seduction of analogy ("like measure"). Though (for instance) moves such as installing the pre-oedipal in place of the oedipal may be one way for the mother to get even with the Law of the Father, still, it could be argued, the triangulation of the familiar Freudian paradigm is replicated even as it is turned. A further move must follow if this overturning of hierarchy is to mean a changed dynamic for feminism.

That feminist move would mean a putting in play (a reading) of the structures which produce and reproduce meaning, whether sexual or textual. For feminist criticism, femininity itself comes to a be a figure for this meaning that is a difference—both sexual and textual—rather than a content. But another figure is necessarily installed within and by the reproduction of meaning involved in (re)reading textual correspondences. This figure for breaking or interruption (the figure which remains invisible in Ruthven's phallocritical text) is the figure of the feminist reader. Feminist reading represents a critical rupture (breaking eggs to unmake the *hommelette*) as the feminist critic intervenes in the face-off between Lacan and Derrida, or the mirror play between mother and daughter. Her function is to open the gap between petrifying sameness and repeated identity, installing herself as the reader-in-between; her feminist reading is the reading of correspondences which are always near misses (Mss.). Less a triangulation than an internal differentiation, the feminist reader holds open a gap which would otherwise render her invisible in the seamless continuum of masculinist critical and theoretical reading, whether such masculinist reading takes the form of the duality of narcissistic reflection or the imaginary unity (identity) of two-in-one.

For Derrida, the lack which Lacan fills with the letter (as a substitute for the woman's missing phallus) risks idealizing the truth of the signifier as that which (in Lacan's phrase) "always arrives at its destination."[13] Derrida's contrary assumption of the infinitely disseminating, transgressive, and ultimately unreadable character of writing reinstates castration in the place of the veiled, transcendental phallic signifier. But it does so, as Johnson points out, by repressing a certain ambiguity in the Lacanian text itself. Johnson's own reading occupies the space of this ambiguity, pointing to the ways in which Derrida's reading of Lacan is (as it were) a "Lacanian" reading—a reading of what "they" ("*ils*") read Lacan as saying. Johnson herself, however, does not (or not here) go further, to ask how "*elles*" might read either Lacan, or Derrida, or even Johnson herself as a differential feminist reader—a reader self-admittedly "framed" by two powerful discourses, psychoanalytic and deconstructive, and whose own reading frays the edges of that frame by being at once inside and outside (at once content and frame of reference). The powerful (but not univocal) feminist "frame of reference" and its ability to dissolve the edges of other, seemingly impermeable frames goes largely unremarked, though it is surely implicit, in Johnson's subtle demarcations of the terrain across which Lacan and Derrida vie for textual mastery. It is, after all, the special mark of feminist reading that it differentiates between "*ils*" and "*elles*" as readers and undoes the unifying or homologizing assumption which identifies all reading as masculine. Gender—sexual difference—as an aspect of the frame of reference or scene of writing (reading) doesn't get a look-in, not for Lacan, not for Derrida, and not for Johnson either, even though it is the Queen in Poe's story whose letter has been purloined; even though this frame of reference (reading gender or the discourse of feminism) is both outside and inside the question of reading the letter itself—enfolded, as it were, within its "*pli*" like the repeated story of a Queen's adulterous betrayal of a King which Poe's story (un)enfolds.

If restoring the letter to its rightful owner isn't quite the point of a feminist reading (whose would be the property, whose the propriety, when the letter itself inscribes an illicit relation and the Law is that of the Father?), still, a feminist reading would seem to call for some acknowledgment of feminist deictics (to whom is Poe's letter addressed? by whom read?)—as well as calling for a feminist intervention in the dispute over the itinerary of the letter of the text between two competing male theorists. A feminist reading might also bring into play that principle of treacherous, unstable feminine sexuality which generates not only Poe's story, but the readings supplied in unfolding this vertiginous feminine *"pli"* by Lacan, Derrida, and Johnson herself. Ultimately unveiled as the myth of Oedipus, an enigma or riddle of sexual difference, the story still serves to privilege both a Freudian reading and an obligatory textual indeterminacy. Privileging indeterminacy, however, risks ignoring powerful determinants on the readings which a text may generate, one of these determinants being the question of sexual difference (whether signaled by its presence or its absence).

Inevitably, the Freudian reading tries to fix the answer to this undecidable question as the one *"ils"* have always given ("woman is castrated"). It is to Johnson's credit that she detects this maneuver on the part of Poe/Lacan/Derrida (the inscription of difference as castration). But significantly, Johnson's reader here remains *"il"* rather than *"elle"*—"The text's 'truth' puts the status of the reader in question, 'performs' *him* as its 'address'" (pp. 143–44; my italics). For a feminist reading, what is put in question is not only the text's "truth," not only the equivocal status of the reader, but that undifferentiated "him." If (to quote Johnson), "The letter's destination is thus *wherever it is read* . . . the receiver is the sender, and the receiver is whoever receives the letter" (p. 144), then the meaning of the letter (however ambiguous) undergoes a differential change according to the position of the reader vis-à-vis sexual difference. And if, as Johnson concludes, "the sender again receives his own message backward from the receiver" (p. 146), one topsy-turvy effect would be that the reader could only be read as a reversed image or reflection of masculinity ("his own message"). Which, as it happens, is just the case with a Freudian reading of femininity (a reversed mirror image of masculinity). A feminist reading of sexual difference puts the status of Freudian reading in question by providing a rereading of the self-mirroring discourse of psychoanalysis which defines the reading subject, *faut de mieux*, as agreeably, *homme*-ologically, masculine.

"A letter always arrives at its destination": Lacan argues that the letter is always received, always reversed; Derrida argues that Lacan's epistolary law can miss its destination, go astray; Johnson, that its received meaning is always missing, always performed by the reader. Each reading is at once an intervention and an effect of the letter. The woman reader turns the letter a little further. One could say that Charlotte Brontë's *Villette* "reads" Breuer's "Fräulein Anna O."; George Eliot's "The Lifted Veil" both reads and is read by *Studies on Hysteria*; reading "The Yellow Wallpaper" through Wollstonecraft, Wollstonecraft becomes its political unconscious; Irigaray reads George Eliot's *Mill on the Floss*; Kristeva reads Freud's "abjection" of the mother; and so on. But that's not quite all. Feminist reading means reading back into these correspondences the elided *"elle(s)"*; *"elle(s)"* is installed, differentially, between these feminist correspondences, or between feminist and Freudian theory. The system of textual relations or "readings" sketched here is an aspect of a feminist intertextuality which (too easily) gets subsumed under the misleading title of "the female literary tradition" (which tradition, and whose? in what sense literary? in what sense traditional?). The concept of a female literary tradition depends on a linear reading of the relations (usually chronologically conceived) between texts or "letters." Reading back through our mothers and grandmothers (Woolf's model of a female literary tradition) places the feminist reader at the end of a line. Only from this imaginary vantage point (hers) can the feminist literary tradition—the handing on or over of a feminist "address"—be perceived as a signifying chain.

Yet the existence of these chain letters is what makes it possible for the feminist reader to create (and read) her "tradition." She is its reading effect. Matrilinear models of textual relations (relations between texts authored by women) depend on two assumptions—that texts are mothered (what of the father? or, can feminist theory do without Freud?) and that linear descent is constitutive of meaning. To question both assumptions is not to dissolve the (political) category of "women's writing," nor to refuse history, treating all texts as unauthored and existing in an imaginary, chronologically undifferentiated present. Rather, it is to insist that the feminist letter derives its meaning (and its refusal of meaning—its unreadability) from the feminist "plot" or narrative in which it is installed. Feminist literary herstory tells one story, "gynocritics" another, to which post-Lacanian feminist psychoanalysis gives yet a different turn. These feminist discourses argue and interrogate the status claimed for each by their practitioners. Feminist criticism is situated within the exchange that constitutes it, within the differences which divide it from any self or essence, any unified position. Feminist reading thus becomes a reading of the internal difference by which the letter refuses any univocal meaning; but it is also a reading that puts the feminist reader's own position as reader on the line. Taking issue with (as well as from) the mother, the daughter may take a line of her own.

Reading correspondences acknowledges that drawing the line, or closure, can only be an arbitrary and temporary gesture, the placing of an accent here rather than there in the continuing exchange—the movement—of feminist literary criticism which I have chosen to call "Reading Woman." Or, as Irigaray has it, "the one doesn't stir without the other. But we do not move together" ("*Mais ce n'est ensemble que nous mouvons*"). "We" don't make the same moves, but as feminist critics we move only by getting together and by getting across (each other). The correspondence between Wollstonecraft and Irigaray remains unfinished, its itinerary incomplete and its destination deferred. Reading woman goes on from—moves in between—where these women of letters leave off.

Notes

I. Reading Woman (Reading)

1. Virginia Woolf, *Orlando, A Biography* (New York and London: Harcourt Brace Jovanovich, 1928), pp. 188–89.

2. Shoshana Felman, "Rereading Femininity," *Yale French Studies* (1981), 62:28.

3. See the introductions to Mitchell and Rose, eds., *Feminine Sexuality,* pp. 1–57 *passim* for the evolution of Freudian and Lacanian theories of the gendered subject.

4. "Defined by man, the conventional polarity of masculine and feminine names woman as a *metaphor of man.* Sexuality . . . functions . . . as the sign of a rhetorical convention, of which woman is the *signifier* and man the *signified.* Man alone has thus the privilege of proper meaning"; Felman, "Rereading Femininity," p. 25.

5. Virginia Woolf, "George Eliot," *Collected Essays of Virginia Woolf,* 4 vols. Leonard Woolf, ed., (London: Hogarth Press, 1966–67), 1:204.

6. See, for instance, Annette Kolodny, "A Map for Rereading: Or, Gender and the Interpretation of Literary Texts," *New Literary History* (Spring 1980), 11(3):451–67, and Jean E. Kennard, "Convention Coverage or How to Read Your Own Life," *New Literary History* (Autumn 1981), 13(1):69–88, as well as Judith Fetterley, *The Resisting Reader: A Feminist Approach to American Fiction* (Bloomington: Indiana University Press, 1978).

7. Culler, *On Deconstruction,* p. 64; cf. Peggy Kamuf, "Writing Like a Woman," in Sally McConnell-Ginet, Ruth Borker, and Nelly Furman, eds., *Women and Language in Literature and Society,* p. 298 (New York: Praeger, 1980).

8. Sandra Gilbert's essay was first published in *Critical Inquiry* (Winter 1980), 7(2):391–417 and republished in Abel, ed., *Writing and Sexual Difference,* pp. 193–219; Elaine Showalter's review article appeared in *Raritan* (Fall 1983), 3(2):130–49; and Shoshana Felman's essay appeared in *Yale French Studies* (1981), 62:19–44.

9. Gilbert, "Costumes of the Mind," p. 218.

10. Robert J. Stoller, "A Contribution to the Study of Gender Identity," *International Journal of Psycho-Analysis* (April–July 1964), 45(2–3):223. Stoller's concept of "core gender identity" is also elaborated in "Facts and Fancies: An Examination of Freud's Concept of Bisexuality," in Jean Strouse, ed., *Woman and Analysis,* pp. 343–64 (New York: Grossman, 1974). Cf. Gilbert, "Costumes of the Mind," pp. 199–200 and *n.* for citation of Stoller's work on transvestism.

11. See Nancy Chodorow, *The Reproduction of Mothering: Psychoanalysis and the Sociology of Gender* (Berkeley: University of California Press, 1978), p. 158, and cf. Mitchell and Rose, *Feminine Sexuality,* p. 37n. for a brief analysis of Chodorow's displacement of "the concepts of the unconscous and bisexuality in favour of a notion of gender imprinting . . . which is compatible with a sociological conception of role."

12. Gilbert, "Costumes of the Mind," p. 214.

13. *Ibid.,* pp. 207, 214.

14. Showalter, "Critical Cross-Dressing," p. 134.

15. See Robert J. Stoller, *Sex and Gender,* 2 vols. (New York: Jason Aronson, 1975), 1:177, and cf. Showalter, "Critical Cross-Dressing," p. 138, and Gilbert, "Costumes of the Mind," p. 199.

16. Showalter, "Critical Cross-Dressing," p. 146.

17. *Ibid.,* p. 149; cf. the debate between Peggy Kamuf, "Replacing Feminist Criticism" and Nancy Miller, "The Text's Heroine: A Feminist Critic and Her Fictions," in *Diacritics* (Summer 1982), 12(2):42–47, 48–53.

18. Showalter, "Critical Cross-Dressing," p. 149.

19. Cf. the subtitle of Felman's "Literature and Psychoanalysis," special issue of *Yale French Studies* (1977), 55/56, "The Question of Reading: Otherwise."

20. Felman, "Rereading Femininity," pp. 21, 22.

21. Honoré de Balzac, "The Girl with the Golden Eyes," *The Thirteen*, Ellen Marriage and Ernest Dowson, trans. (London: Society of English Bibliophiles, 1901), pp. 308–9.

22. Henri Latouche, *Fragoletta: Naples et Paris en 1789* (Paris: Pour la Societé des Médecins Bibliophiles, 1929), p. 42.

23. Honoré de Balzac, "Du roman historique et de *Fragoletta* (1831)," *Oeuvres Complètes de Honoré de Balzac: Oeuvres Diverses*, 3 vols., Marcel Bouteron and Henri Longnon, eds. (Paris: Louis Conard, 1935–40), 1:207.

24. See, for instance, Honoré de Balzac, *Peau de chagrin* (Paris: Editions Gallimard, 1974), p. 204, and for another chimera in Balzac's *Sarrasine*, cf. Roland Barthes, *S/Z*, Richard Miller, trans. (New York: Hill and Wang, 1974), pp. 63–64.

25. Balzac, "The Girl with the Golden Eyes," p. 356.

26. Felman, "Rereading Femininity," p. 21.

27. See Jane Gallop, *The Daughter's Seduction*, pp. 59–62, for a reading of the role played by these lines in Freud's text.

28. See, for instance, Luce Irigaray, *Speculum of the Other Woman*, Gillian C. Gill, trans. (Ithaca: Cornell University Press, 1985), pp. 13–129, for an extended reading of "On Femininity"; cf. also Jane Gallop's reading of Irigaray in *The Daughter's Seduction*, pp. 56–79; and Part Two of Sarah Kofman's *The Enigma of Woman: Women in Freud's Writings*, Catherine Porter, trans. (Ithaca: Cornell University Press, 1985), pp. 101–225; Kofman's reading of Freud also takes issue with Irigaray's.

29. Mitchell and Rose, *Feminine Sexuality*, pp. 12, 29. Mitchell and Rose's book should be read in the context of Gallop's less sanitized, more diacritical reading of Lacan on femininity; see *The Daughter's Seduction*, pp. 1–42, where Gallop's point of departure is Mitchell's earlier reading of Freud in her *Psychoanalysis and Feminism* (Harmondsworth: Penguin, 1974).

30. Mitchell and Rose, *Feminine Sexuality*, p. 49 and note. Cf. also the discussion in Parveen Adams and Elizabeth Cowie, "Feminine Sexuality: Interview with Juliet Mitchell and Jacqueline Rose," *m/f* (1983), 8:13.

31. Stephen Heath, *The Sexual Fix* (New York: Schocken Books, 1984), p. 142.

32. See Kofman, *The Enigma of Woman*, pp. 122–42, 202–10.

33. See Culler, *On Deconstruction*, p. 171.

34. Mitchell and Rose, *Feminine Sexuality*, p. 43.

35. *Ibid.*, p. 57.

36. Woolf, *Orlando*, p. 139.

37. *Ibid.*, pp. 226, 267.

38. *Ibid.*, p. 269.

39. Gilbert, "Costumes of the Mind," p. 208.

40. Nigel Nicholson and Joanne Trautman, eds., *The Letters of Virginia Woolf*, 4 vols. (New York and London: Harcourt Brace Jovanovich, 1975–79), 3:429.

41. Virginia Woolf, "The New Biography," *Collected Essays*, 4:233–34.

42. Woolf, *Orlando*, pp. 310, 312. Cf. the later, more explicit text, with its reference to "this culmination to which the whole book moved, this peroration with which the book was to end"; *Orlando: A Biography* (Harmondsworth: Penguin, 1963), p. 220.

43. Barbara Johnson, "My Monster/My Self," *Diacritics* (Summer 1982), 12(2):10.

II. Feminist Readings

1. THE DIFFERENCE OF VIEW

1. Virginia Woolf, "George Eliot," *Collected Essays of Virginia Woolf,* 4 vols., Leonard Woolf, ed. (London: Hogarth Press, 1966–67), 1:204; my italics.

2. *Ibid.*, p. 204.

3. See, for instance, Julia Kristeva, "Phonetics, Phonology and Impulsional Bases," Caren Greenberg, trans., *Diacritics* (Fall 1974), 4:33–37.

4. See D. H. Lawrence, "Study of Thomas Hardy," *Phoenix: The Posthumous Papers of D. H. Lawrence,* E. D. McDonald, ed. (New York: Viking, 1936), p. 496.

5. Thomas Hardy, *Tess of the D'Urbervilles,* Juliet Grindle and Simon Gatrell, eds. (Oxford: Clarendon Press, 1983), pp. 242–43.

6. Mary Wollstonecraft, *A Vindication of the Rights of Woman,* Carol H. Poston, ed. (New York and London: Norton, 1975), p. 10.

7. Mary Wollstonecraft, *Mary, A Fiction and the Wrongs of Woman,* Gary Kelly, ed. (London and New York: Oxford University Press, 1976), pp. 83–84; my italics.

8. Virginia Woolf, *A Room of One's Own* (New York and London: Harcourt Brace Jovanovich, 1957), p. 72; my italics.

9. George Eliot, *Middlemarch,* 4 vols. (Edinburgh and London: 1971–72), 4:369–70.

10. Eliot, *Middlemarch,* W. J. Harvey, ed. (Harmondsworth: Penguin, 1965), p. 896.

11. Woolf, *A Room of One's Own,* p. 4.

2. THE BURIED LETTER: *VILLETTE*

1. Charlotte Brontë, *Shirley,* Andrew and Judith Hook, eds. (Harmondsworth: Penguin, 1974, p. 190).

2. Charlotte Brontë, *Villette,* Mark Lilly, ed. (Harmondsworth: Penguin, 1979), p. 334. Subsequent page references in the text are to this edition.

3. Sigmund Freud, "The 'Uncanny'" (1919), *SE* 17:241. See Hélène Cixous' seminal "Fiction and Its Phantoms: A Reading of Freud's *"Das Unheimliche* (The 'Uncanny')," *New Literary History* (Spring 1976), 7(3):525–48.

4. Matthew Arnold to Mrs. Foster, April 14, 1853, in Miriam Allott, ed., *The Brontës: The Critical Heritage* (London: Routledge & Kegan Paul, 1974), p. 201.

5. Kate Millett, *Sexual Politics* (Garden City, N.Y.: Doubleday, 1970), p. 146.

6. Charlotte Brontë to W. S. Williams, November 6, 1852, and George Smith, November 3, 1852, in T. Wise and J. A. Symington, ed. *The Shakespeare Head Brontë: The Brontës: Their Lives, Friendships and Correspondence,* 4 vols., (Oxford: Blackwell, 1932), 4:16, 18.

7. See Elizabeth Sewell, *Principles of Education,* 2 vols. (London: Longman, Green, 1865), 2:240. See also M. J. Peterson, "The Victorian Governess: Status Incongruence in Family and Society," *Victorian Studies* (September 1970), 14(1):7–26.

8. Charlotte Brontë to W. S. Williams, May 12, 1848, in Wise and Symington, *The Shakespeare Head Brontë,* 2:216.

9. See Millett, *Sexual Politics,* pp. 140–47, and Terry Eagleton, *Myths of Power: A Marxist Study of the Brontës* (London: MacMillan, 1975), pp. 61–73.

10. See Jacques Lacan, *Ecrits,* Alan Sheridan, trans. (New York: Norton, 1977), pp. 1–7.

11. Jacques Lacan, "Seminar on 'The Purloined Letter,'" Jeffrey Mehlman, trans., *Yale French Studies* (1972), 48:38–72.

12. See Harold Bloom, *Poetry and Repression* (New Haven: Yale University Press, 1976), pp. 147–54.

13. Charlotte Brontë, "Farewell to Angria" (c. 1839) in F. E. Ratchford and W. C. DeVane, eds., *Legends of Angria* (New Haven: Yale University Press, 1933), p. 316.

14. Charlotte Brontë to G. H. Lewes, November 6, 1847, in Wise and Symington, *The Shakespeare Head Brontë*, 2:152.

15. Emily Brontë, "The Prisoner," ll. 85–86, *The Complete Poems of Emily Jane Brontë*, C. W. Hatfield, ed. (New York: Columbia University Press, 1941), no. 190, p. 239.

16. Emily Brontë, "To Imagination," *ibid.*, no. 174, pp. 205–6.

17. See Mary Wollstonecraft, *Mary, A Fiction and the Wrongs of Woman*, Gary Kelly, ed. (London and New York: Oxford University Press, 1976), pp. vii–xxi, and Margaret Walters, "The Rights and Wrongs of Women," in Juliet Mitchell and Ann Oakley, eds., *The Rights and Wrongs of Women*, pp. 304–29 (Harmondsworth: Penguin, 1976).

18. Millett, *Sexual Politics*, p. 147. The most sustained recent reading of *Villette* is that of Gilbert and Gubar in *The Madwoman in the Attic*, pp. 339–440.

3. MEN OF MAXIMS AND *THE MILL ON THE FLOSS*

1. Luce Irigaray, "The Power of Discourse and the Subordination of the Feminine," *This Sex Which Is Not One*, Catherine Porter, trans., p. 81.

2. See Hélène Cixous, "The Laugh of the Medusa," Elaine Marks and Isabelle de Courtivron, eds., *New French Feminisms*, pp. 245–64 (Amherst: University of Massachusetts Press, 1980). The implications of such definitions of *"écriture feminine"* are discussed briefly in "The Difference of View," section II.1, and by Nancy K. Miller, "Emphasis Added: Plots and Plausibilities in Women's Fiction," *PMLA* (January 1981), 96(1):37; my own essay is indebted to Miller's account of *The Mill on the Floss* in the context of "women's fiction."

3. See Irigaray, *This Sex Which Is Not One*, pp. 68–85 *passim*, and her *Speculum of The Other Woman*, pp. 133–46. See also Carolyn Burke, "Introduction to Luce Irigaray's 'When Our Lips Speak Together,'" *Signs* (Autumn 1980), 6(1):71.

4. Miller, "Emphasis Added," p. 38.

5. *Ibid.*, p. 46.

6. See Irigaray, *This Sex Which Is Not One*, pp. 74–80 *passim*.

7. Irigaray, *This Sex Which Is Not One*, p. 76.

8. See, for instance, Gilbert and Gubar, "Toward a Feminist Poetics," Part I of *The Madwoman in the Attic*, pp. 3–104; Gilbert and Gubar's is above all a work of literary (her)story.

9. George Eliot, *The Mill on the Floss*, A. S. Byatt, ed. (Harmondsworth: Penguin, 1979), p. 628; subsequent page references in the text are to this edition. I am especially indebted to Byatt's helpful annotations.

10. See Gilbert and Gubar, *The Madwoman in the Attic*, who succinctly state that Maggie seems "at her most monstrous when she tries to turn herself into an angel of renunciation" (p. 491), and Gillian Beer, "Beyond Determinism: George Eliot and Virginia Woolf," in Mary Jacobus, ed., *Women Writing and Writing About Women*, p. 88, on an ending that "lacks bleakness, is even lubricious" in its realization of "confused and passionate needs."

11. *"Mors omnibus est communis* would have been jejune, only [Maggie] liked to know the Latin"; Eliot, *The Mill on the Floss,* pp. 217–18; see below.

12. *"Astronomer: ut—*'as,' *astronomus—*'an astronomer,' *exosus—*'hating,' *mulieres—*'women,' *ad unum* [mulierem]—'to one' [that is, in general]. (*Eton Grammar,* 1831 edition, p. 279)"; Eliot, *The Mill on the Floss,* p. 676 *n.*55.

13. See Virginia Woolf, "George Eliot," *Collected Essays of Virginia Woolf,* 4 vols., Leonard Woolf, ed. (London: Hogarth Press, 1966–67), 1:204: "With every obstacle against her—sex and health and convention—she sought more knowledge and more freedom till the body, weighted with its double burden, sank worn out."

14. See Eliot, *The Mill on the Floss,* pp. 675–76, *n.*44.

15. Aristotle, *Poetics,* 22:16 (my italics); see Eliot, *The Mill on the Floss,* p. 676 *n.*46. J. Hillis Miller notes apropos of this passage that it "is followed almost immediately by an ostentatious and forceful metaphor [that of a shrewmouse imprisoned in a split tree (p. 209)], as if Eliot were compelled . . . to demonstrate that we cannot say what a thing is except by saying it is something else"; "The Worlds of Victorian Fiction," *Harvard English Studies* (1975), 6:145*n.*

16. See Carol Christ, "Aggression and Providential Death in George Eliot's Fiction," *Novel* (Winter 1976), 9(2):130–40, for a somewhat different interpretation.

17. See Eliot, *The Mill on the Floss,* p. 676 *n.*53.

18. Luce Irigaray, "When Our Lips Speak Together," *This Sex Which Is Not One,* p. 212.

19. Miller, "Emphasis Added," p. 46.

20. Johnson, *The Critical Difference,* pp. 4, 5.

21. See Miller, "Emphasis Added," p. 38.

22. Cf. Gillian Beer, "Beyond Determinism," in Jacobus, ed., *Women Writing and Writing About Women,* p. 88: "Eliot is fascinated by the unassuageable longings of her heroine. She allows them fulfillment in a form of plot which simply glides out of the channelled sequence of social growth and makes literal the expansion of desire. The river loses its form in the flood."

III. Women and Theory

1. IS THERE A WOMAN IN THIS TEXT?

1. See *Jokes and Their Relation to the Unconscious* (1905), *SE* 8:97–101, and see also Jeffrey Mehlman, "How to Read Freud on Jokes: The Critic as Schadchen," *New Literary History* (Winter 1975), 6(2):439–61, for the suggestion that the interfering third party is the oedipal father.

2. Stanley Fish, *Is There a Text in This Class? The Authority of Interpretive Communities* (Cambridge, Mass.: Harvard University Press, 1980), p. 305.

3. See *The Interpretation of Dreams* (1900), *SE* 4:106–21. This was the dream apropos of which Freud wrote to Fliess in 1900, fantasizing that the house where he had dreamed it might one day bear a marble tablet with the words: "In This House, on July 24th, 1895, the Secret of Dreams was Revealed to Dr. Sigm. Freud." See Jeffrey Mehlman, "Trimethylamin: Notes on Freud's Specimen Dream," *Diacritics* (Spring 1976), 6(1):42–45: "Freud . . . make[s] her cough up (his) truth."

4. Kofman, *Quatre romans analytiques,* p. 133: "L'inconscient de l'analyse, comme celui de tout homme, est inéliminable."

5. As the editor of the *Standard Edition* notes, *Delusions and Dreams* contains "not only a summary of Freud's explanation of dreams but also what is perhaps the first of his semi-popular accounts of his theory of the neuroses and of the therapeutic action of psycho-analysis" (*SE* 9:5).

6. Compare Freud's own remark, in "Construction in Analysis," that "the delusions of patients appear to me to be the equivalents of the constructions which we build up in the course of analytic treatment" (*SE* 23:268).

7. Kofman, *Quatre romans analytiques,* p. 16: "Un appât pour mieux attraper la carpe vérité: celle du texte littéraire qui doit confirmer celle de la psychanalyse."

8. A copy of the bas-relief (figure 1)—which Freud saw in the Vatican in 1907 as "a dear familiar face"—hung in his consulting room; see Ernst L. Freud, ed., *Letters of Sigmund Freud* (New York: Basic Books, 1960), p. 267.

9. Sarah Kofman, "Narcissistic Woman," *The Enigma of Woman,* Catherine Porter, trans. (Ithaca: Cornell University Press, 1985), p. 56. See "On Narcissism: An Introduction," *SE* 14:73–102, esp. pp. 88–89.

10. As Kofman suggests in *Quatre romans analytiques,* p. 124, stone is at once a symbol of castration and a defense against castration; Hanold's foot fetishism might be related to the obsessive question, Does Gradiva, or does she not, have a penis?

11. Jacques Lacan, "Le rêve de l'injection d'Irma," *Le Seminaire, Livre II: Le moi dans la théorie de Freud et dans la technique de la psychanalyse—1954–55* (Paris: Seuil, 1978), p. 203: "Car c'est toujours être coupable que de transgresser une limite jusque-là imposée à l'activité humaine."

12. See Mary Shelley's 1831 "Introduction" to her *Frankenstein or the Modern Prometheus,* M. K. Joseph, ed. (London and New York: Oxford University Press, 1969), p. 8. Subsequent page references in the text are to this edition.

13. James Watson, *The Double Helix: A Personal Account of the Discovery of the Structure of DNA* (New York: Atheneum, 1968), p. 18. Subsequent page references in the text are to this edition.

14. Quoted by Horace Judson, *The Eighth Day of Creation: Makers of the Revolution in Biology* (New York: Simon and Schuster, 1979), p. 194. Judson's is perhaps the most balanced account of the relations between Watson, Crick, Wilkins, Franklin, and especially of the work of the latter.

15. See Anne Sayre, *Rosalind Franklin and DNA* (New York: Norton, 1975), p. 21.

16. Francis Crick, *Life Itself: Its Origin and Nature* (New York: Simon and Schuster, 1981), p. 72. Crick has interesting things to say about theory apropos of his own theory of "Directed Panspermia" as the origin of life on earth, which his wife objects to as "not a real theory but merely science fiction" (p. 148).

17. See Toril Moi, "The Missing Mother: The Oedipal Rivalries of René Girard," *Diacritics* (Summer 1982), 12(2):21–31, for an excellent critique of Girard.

18. See also Mary Poovey, "My Hideous Progeny: The Lady and The Monster," *The Proper Lady and the Woman Writer* (Chicago and London: University of Chicago Press, 1984), pp. 114–42, for a reading of Frankenstein in the light of its relation to Romantic egotism.

19. The film versions of Frankenstein, including Whale's, are discussed by Albert J. Lavalley, "The Stage and Film Children of Frankenstein: A Survey," in George Levine and U. C. Knoepflmacher, eds., *The Endurance of Frankenstein: Essays on Mary Shelley's Novel,* pp. 243–89, esp. p. 273 (Berkeley: University of California Press, 1979); see also Donald F. Glut, *The Frankenstein Legend: A Tribute to Mary Shelley and Boris Karloff* (Metuchen, N.J.: Scarecrow Press, 1973).

20. See Lacan's "Le rêve de l'injection d'Irma," p. 186: "Tout se mêle et

associe dans cette image, de la bouche à l'organe sexuel féminin. . . . Il y a là une horrible découverte, celle de la chair qu'on ne voit jamais, le fond des choses, l'envers de la face, du visage, les sécretats par excellence, la chair dont tout sort, au plus profond même du mystère, la chair en tant qu'elle est souffrante, qu'elle est informe, que sa forme par soi-même est quelque chose qui provoque l'angoisse."

21. See, for instance, the paintings by Masolino, Pseudo Met de Bles, and Raphael reproduced in Roland M. Frye, *Milton's Imagery and the Visual Arts: Iconographic Tradition in the Epic Poems* (Princeton: Princeton University Press, 1978).

22. Kofman's "Narcissistic Woman," in *The Enigma of Woman*, pp. 50–65, debates René Girard's "Le Narcissisme: le désir de Freud," in *Des choses cachées depuis la fondation du monde*, pp. 391–414 (Paris: B. Grasset, 1978), recast as "Narcissism: The Freudian Myth Demythified by Proust," in Alan Roland, ed., *Psychoanalysis, Creativity, and Literature*, pp. 293–311 (New York: Columbia University Press, 1978). For a related discussion of the narcissistic woman and her role in Kofman's writing, see Elizabeth Berg, "The Third Woman," *Diacritics* (Summer 1982), 12(2):11–20.

23. Kofman, "Narcissistic Woman," pp. 61–62.

24. Girard, "Le Narcissisme: le désir de Freud," pp. 393–94: "Ce qu'il appelle l'auto-suffisance de la coquette, c'est en réalité la transfiguration métaphysique du modèle-rival."

25. Girard, "Narcissism: The Freudian Myth," pp. 308, 309.

26. See Raimo Tuomela, *Theoretical Concepts* (New York: Springer-Verlag, 1973), pp. 3–4, and Nathan Rotenstreich, *Theory and Practice: An Essay in Human Intentionalities* (The Hague: Martinus Nijhoff, 1977), pp. 58–59; see also Clark Glymour, *Theory and Evidence* (Princeton: Princeton University Press, 1980).

27. See Jonathan Culler's discussion of the concept of "the woman reader" in *On Deconstruction*, pp. 44–64.

28. See the respective readings of Frankenstein by Ellen Moers, "Female Gothic," in Levine and Knoepflmacher, *The Endurance of Frankenstein*, pp. 77–87, and by Gilbert and Gubar, "Horror's Twin: Mary Shelley's Monstrous Eve," *The Madwoman in the Attic*, pp. 213–47.

29. See, for instance, Hélène Cixous, "The Laugh of the Medusa," in Marks and de Courtivron, *New French Feminisms*, pp. 245–64, and "Castration or Decapitation," Annette Kuhn, trans., *Signs* (Autumn 1981), 7(1):41–55; Luce Irigaray, "When Our Lips Speak Together," and "The Power of Discourse and the Subordination of the Feminine," in *This Sex Which Is Not One*, Catherine Porter, trans. (Ithaca: Cornell University Press, 1985), pp. 205–18, 68–85. For a recent critique of *écriture féminine*, see also Ann Rosalind Jones, "Writing the Body: Toward an Understanding of *L'Écriture Féminine*," *Feminist Studies* (Summer 1981), 7(2):247–63, reprinted in Elaine Showalter, ed., *The New Feminist Criticism: Essays on Women, Literature, and Theory* (New York: Pantheon Books, 1985), pp. 361–77.

2. JUDITH, HOLOFERNES, AND THE PHALLIC WOMAN

1. See *SE* 21:189 and Book XII, ch. 10, of *The Brothers Karamazov*; the "knife that cuts both ways" in Strachey's translation of Freud is derived from Constance Garnett's translation of Dostoevsky.

2. See Mitchell and Rose, eds., *Feminine Sexuality*, p. 13 for this shift; I am indebted here to their lucid accounts of the development of Freudian theory and its Lacanian revision.

3. Sigmund Freud, *Gesammelte Werke*, 18 vols. (London: Imago, 1940–68), 14:523.

4. See Karen Horney's "The Flight from Womanhood" (1926), *Feminine Psychology* (New York: Norton, 1967), pp. 57–58; and, for a summary of the "great debate," see Mitchell and Rose, *Feminine Sexuality,* p. 20.

5. Jean Laplanche, *Problématiques II: Castration-Symbolisations* (Paris: Presses Universitaires de France, 1980), p. 88; unless otherwise indicated, subsequent translations from French and German are my own. I am indebted to Laplanche's commentary on Freud's theory of castration and penis envy in what follows.

6. Cf. Laplanche's useful formula, that castration means "perception + menace" for the boy, and "perception + envy" for the girl; *ibid.*, p. 81. The asymmetry in Freud's account is also touched on by Juliet Mitchell, in Mitchell and Rose, *Feminine Sexuality,* pp. 16–17.

7. Laplanche, *Problématiques II,* p. 84: "le moment où la théorie prend corps, où les hésitations sont supprimées et où les démarches passées s'éclairent: le moment du 'c'était donc ça!' "

8. See the discussion that follows Sarah Kofman's "Ça cloche," in Phillipe Lacoue-Labarthe and Jean-Luc Nancy, eds., *Les fins de l'homme: à partir du travail de Jacques Derrida,* pp. 114–16 (Paris: Galilée, 1981); Kofman's telling feminist critique of Freudian theory has informed and stimulated my own account of "The Taboo of Virginity."

9. Cf. also "On Femininity," *New Introductory Lectures* (1932), *SE* 22:129: "feminists are not pleased when we point out to them the effects of this factor upon the average feminine character."

10. The phrase "*idée fixe*" is Freud's in "On Femininity," *SE* 22:132: "If you . . . regard my belief in the influence of lack of penis on the configuration of femininity as an *idée fixe,* I am of course defenseless." See also Sarah Kofman in "Ça cloche," p. 98, and, for the comparison of penis envy and the Medusa's head, *The Enigma of Woman,* pp. 82–83. For an account of the relation between the Medusa's head, women, and theory, see also Neil Hertz, "Medusa's Head: Male Hysteria Under Political Pressure," *The End of the Line,* pp. 161–92.

11. See Laplanche, *Problématiques II,* pp. 106–7, for the suggestion that Freud has here introduced, without pursuing, the implications of "an intersubjective point of view" for the problem of castration; may the boy be positioned here in relation to the desire of the mother?

12. Karen Horney, "The Dread of Woman," *Feminine Psychology,* p. 135.

13. Cf. Stephen Heath, "Difference," *Screen* (Autumn 1978), 19(3):53: "where a discourse appeals directly to an image, to an immediacy of seeing, as a point of its argument or demonstration, one can be sure that all difference is being elided, that the unity of some accepted vision is being reproduced." Heath's comment has an obvious bearing on my own use of visual images; my rationale is the exposure of what might be called the conditions of possibility for seeing these images as images at all— that is, their installation in the narratives which make them "legible." On the relations between castration and representation, see Neil Hertz, "Medusa's Head," pp. 165–67.

14. See Kofman, *Quatre romans analytiques,* p. 15: "opération violente qui a comme effet de 'déformer, de mutiler et de défigurer' l'original . . . celle-ci met fin au délire et à l'indécision du texte, suscitant la bonne entente d'un sens enfin univoque."

15. *Ibid.*, p. 84: "La 'puissance' de la mise en scène de Hebbel tient à ce qu'elle condense en une seule oeuvre les différents motifs exposés par Freud à partir de pièces détachées et fragmentaires."

16. *Ibid.*, pp. 97–98: "si la littérature peut, après traitement réducteur, sembler se plier à une lecture analytique, n'est-ce pas parce que les conceptions de Freud, par exemple, ici, celles sur la femme, rejoignent celles de la littérature qu'il exploite?

Adéquation entre la chose littéraire et la chose analytique qui, loin d'être indice de vérité, l'est seulement de l'emprise sur toutes deux d'une même tradition culturelle et idéologique, de l'identité des préjugés dont la force contraignante s'impose comme celle de la vérité."

17. *Friedrich Hebbel: Sämtliche Werke*, 14 vols., R. M. Werner, ed. (Berlin: B. Behr's Verlag, 1901), 11:14; cf. Georges Pernoud and Sabine Flaissier, eds., *The French Revolution*, Richard Graves, trans. (London: Secker and Warburg, 1961), p. 226.

18. *Friedrich Hebbel: Briefe*, 8 vols., R. M. Werner, ed. (Berlin: B. Behr's Verlag, 1904–07), 2:103. For a compilation of Hebbel's comments on his play, see Ulrich Henry Gerlach, *Hebbel as a Critic of His Own Works* (Göppingen: A. Kümmerle, 1972), pp. 8–82, and, for a recent critical reading of *Judith*, see also Mary Garland, *Hebbel's Prose Tragedies* (Cambridge: Cambridge University Press, 1973), pp. 23–135.

19. *Friedrich Hebbel: Tagebücher*, 4 vols., R. M. Werner, ed. (Berlin: B. Behr's Verlag, 1903), 1:404, entry 1802: "In der Judith zeichne ich die *That* eines *Weibes*, also den ärgsten Contrast, dies Wollen und Nicht-Können, dies Thun, was doch kein Handeln ist."

20. *Friedrich Hebbel: Briefe*, 2:28, 85: "wäre es Nichts, so wäre ich selbst Nichts"; "die Judith lähmt mich in meinem Innern."

21. *Three Plays by Hebbel*, Marion W. Sonnenfeld, trans. (Lewisburg: Bucknell University Press, 1974), p. 71. Subsequent page references in the text are to this volume.

22. *Friedrich Hebbel: Tagebücher*, 1:376, entry 1677: "Von meiner Poesie hängt mein Ich ab; ist jene ein Irrthum, so bin ich selbst einer!"

23. *Three Plays by Hebbel*, pp. 52, 54, 72. On the incorporation imagery in *Judith*, see Kofman, *Quatre romans analytiques*, p. 96.

24. Cf. the language of Shakespeare's *Rape of Lucrece*; after the rape, it is Tarquin who experiences the "crest-wounding, private scar" of castration, "the wound that nothing healeth,/The scar that will despite of cure remain" (11.828, 731–32). See Ian Donaldson, *The Rapes of Lucretia* (Oxford: Clarendon Press, 1982), pp. 40–56 for a discussion of Shakespeare's poem, and particularly the imagery of wounds. As Donaldson points out, the subject of *Judith and Holofernes* is often pictorially paired with that of *The Rape of Lucretia*.

25. See Mitchell and Rose, *Feminine Sexuality*, p. 7: "The selection of the phallus as the mark around which subjectivity and sexuality are constructed reveals, precisely, that they are constructed, in a division which is both arbitrary and alienating."

26. See Hebbel's foreword to *Judith;* see also *Sämtliche Werke*, 1:410, *Briefe*, 7:303, and J. Sadger, *Friedrich Hebbel: Ein Psychoanalytischer Versuch* (Nendeln/Liechtenstein: Kraus, 1970), p. 321, for accounts of the impact on him of this painting. I have been unable to trace the reattributed picture; Richard Spear, *Domenichino*, 2 vols. (New Haven: Yale University Press, 1982), 1:273 (Plate 329) lists only one painting on this subject, in Rome rather than Munich.

27. *Friedrich Hebbel: Briefe*, 3:67: "Ich verweilte lange vor dem Bilde. Könnte ich Französisch und Horace Vernet Deutsch, so würde ich ihn aussuchen, er hat in seinem Bilde dieselben Motive ausgedrückt, die ich in der Tragödie in Bewegung setzte."

28. Philippe Comte, "Judith et Holopherne ou la naissance d'une tragédie," *La Revue du Louvre et des Musées de France* (1977), 27(3):139: "Paradoxalement, ce que nous avions pris pour la mise en image d'un discours, a functionné ici comme image première, image signifiante, appelant une lecture, des lectures, dont aucune ne l'épuise et qui toutes nous enseignent."

29. *Französische Maler* (1831) in Hans Kaufman, ed., *Heinrich Heine: Sämtliche Werke*, 14 vols. (München: Kindler, 1964), 8:14–15: "Das vorzüglichste seiner

ausgestellten Gemälde war eine Judith, die im Begriff steht, den Holofernes zu töten. Sie hat sich eben vom Lager desselben erhoben, ein blühend schlankes Mädchen. Ein violettes Gewand, um die Hüften hastig geschürzt, geht bis zu ihren Füssen hinab; oberhalb des Leibes trägt sie ein blassgelbes Unterkleid, dessen Ärmel von der rechten Schulter herunterfällt und den sie mit der linken Hand, etwas metzgerhaft und doch zugleich bezaubernd zierlich, wieder in die Höhe streift; denn mit der rechten Hand hat sie eben das krumme Schwert gezogen gegen den schlafenden Holofernes. Da steht sie, eine reizende Gestalt, an der eben überschrittenen Grenze der Jungfräulichkeit, ganz gottrein und doch weltbesleckt, wie eine entweihte Hostie. Ihr Kopf ist wunderbar anmutig und unheimlich liebenswürdig; schwarze Locken, wie kurze Schlangen, die nicht herabslattern, sondern sich bäumen, furchtbar graziös. Das Gesicht ist etwas beschattet, und süsse Wildheit, düstere Holdseligkeit und sentimentaler Grimm rieselt durch die edlen Züge der tödlichen Schönen. Besonders in ihrem Auge funkelt süsse Grausamkeit und die Lüsternheit der Rache; denn sie hat auch den eignen beleidigten Leib zu rächen an dem hässlichen Heiden. In der Tat, dieser ist nicht sonderlich liebreizend, aber im Grunde scheint er doch ein bon enfant zu sein. Er schläft so gutmütig in der Nachwonne seiner Beseligung; er schnarcht vielleicht, oder, wie Luise sagt, er schläft laut; seine Lippen bewegen sich noch, als wenn sie küssten; er lag noch eben im Schosse des Glücks, oder vielleicht lag auch das Glück in seinem Schosse; und trunken von Glück und gewiss auch von Wein, ohne Zwischenspiel von Qual und Krankheit, sendet ihn der Tod durch seinen schönsten Engel in die weisse Nacht der ewigen Vernichtung. Welch ein beneidenswertes Ende! Wenn ich einst sterben soll, ihr Götter, lasst mich sterben wie Holofernes!" See also the brief discussion by S.S. Prawer, *Heine's Jewish Comedy* (Oxford: Clarendon Press, 1983), pp. 229–31.

    30. Cf. Alfred Moir, *The Italian Followers of Caravaggio*, 2 vols. (Cambridge, Mass.: Harvard University Press, 1967), 1:4: "Holofernes supine, physically powerful but helpless, shrieking and writhing in the surprise, anger, pain, and fear of his last instant of consciousness; opposing him, Judith, upright, young, and beautiful, physically weak—flinching her whole body and frowning in distaste—but determined; the blood-thirsty old hag urges her on." See also Alfred Moir, *Caravaggio* (New York: H.N. Abrams, 1982), p. 90: "It might serve as an emblem for 'women's lib': the *macho* oppressor destroyed by a virtuous resolute woman, whom he had intended to victimize in sexual exploitation." For a "psychoanalytic" reading of Caravaggio in the light of Freud's "Medusa's Head" and his own painting of the subject with himself as the severed head, see Laurie Schneider, "Donatello and Caravaggio: The Iconography of Decapitation," *American Imago* (Spring 1976), 33(1):83–91.

    31. Cf. Kofman, *Quatre romans analytiques*, pp. 87–88.

    32. *Friedrich Hebbel: Tagebücher*, 2:2: "Meine Judith wird durch ihre That paralysirt; sie erstarrt vor der Möglichkeit, einen Sohn des Holofernes zu gebären." For Freud, the irony here is that a child, and especially a son, would represent the only resolution to Judith's penis envy. For the effect of "petrification," see also Moir, *Caravaggio*, p. 90.

    33. See Janson, *The Sculpture of Donatello*, 2 vols. (Princeton: Princeton University Press, 1957), 1:199.

    34. See Schneider, "Donatello and Caravaggio," pp. 76–83.

    35. See Janson, *The Sculpture of Donatello*, 1:200–4; Edgar Wind, "Donatello's Judith: A Symbol of 'Sanctimonia,'" *Journal of the Warburg Institute* (1937), 1:62–63; and Michael Greenhalgh, *Donatello and His Sources* (New York: Holmes and Meier, 1982), pp. 181–92.

    36. See Greenhalgh, *Donatello and His Sources*, p. 192.

37. See Janson, *The Sculpture of Donatello*, 1:199.

38. See *ibid.*, p. 201, and, for the "star-shaped 'plan'" of Donatello's design, its exact center marked by the axis of Judith's body, with the rectangular cushion superimposed on the triangular base and Holofernes' thighs forming a superimposed triangle, see *ibid.*, p. 204.

39. See the account given by Germaine Greer in *The Obstacle Race: The Fortunes of Women Painters and Their Work* (New York: Farrar Strauss Giroux, 1979), pp. 191–93. A more detailed account is to be found in Ward Bissell, "Artemisia Gentileschi—a New Documented Chronology," *Art Bulletin* (June 1968), 50(2):153–75; see also Rozsika Parker and Griselda Pollock, *Old Mistresses: Woman, Art and Ideology* (New York: Pantheon, 1981), 20–26.

40. Cf. also "Some Psychical Consequences of the Anatomical Distinction Between the Sexes," *SE* 19:253: "Thus a girl may refuse to accept the fact of being castrated, may harden herself in the conviction that she *does* possess a penis, and may subsequently be compelled to behave as though she were a man."

41. Moir, *The Italian Followers of Caravaggio*, 1:136.

42. Greer, *The Obstacle Race*, pp. 189–90.

43. Cf. Hans J. Kleinschmidt, in his "Reply" to Laurie Schneider's paper on "Donatello and Caravaggio: The Iconography of Decapitation," *American Imago* 33(1):95: "The scene is filled with dramatic action and is pervaded, furthermore, by erotic tension, since the powerful, heavy arms of Holofernes resemble thighs, and his head, partly covered by hair and foreshortened, could well be mistaken for his genital area at first glance. The impression is unavoidable that the iconographic ambiguity— this, so to say, incomplete displacement of the action from below to above—is intentional: this is a scene depicting castration." One can think of many other "narratives"; the two women, for instance, might be midwives assisting at a particularly bloody and violent birth.

44. Ernst Pfeiffer, ed., *Sigmund Freud and Lou Andreas-Salomé: Letters*, William and Elaine Robson-Scott, trans. (New York: Harcourt Brace Jovanovich, 1972), p. 89.

45. *Ibid.*, p. 90.

46. *Ibid.*, pp. 89–90. Cf. *The Psychopathology of Everyday Life*, *SE* 6:168.

47. See Rudolph Binion, *Frau Lou: Nietzsche's Wayward Disciple* (Princeton: Princeton University Press, 1968), p. 371.

48. *The Freud Journal of Lou Andreas-Salomé*, Stanley A. Leavy, trans. (New York: Basic Books, 1964), pp. 88–89.

49. See "On Narcissism: An Introduction" (1914), *SE* 14:88–89: "The charm of a child lies to a great extent in his narcissism, his self-contentment and inaccessibility, just as does the charm of certain animals which seem not to concern themselves about us, such as cats and the large beasts of prey." See also Sarah Kofman, "Narcissistic Woman," *The Enigma of Woman*, pp. 50–65.

50. Pfeiffer, *Sigmund Freud and Lou Andreas-Salomé: Letters*, p. 67.

51. *Ibid.*, p. 81.

52. See, for instance, Binion, *Frau Lou*, pp. 240–41, 349, 354, 397.

53. *The Freud Journal of Lou Andreas-Salomé*, p. 111. Cf. Mitchell and Rose, *Feminine Sexuality*, p. 41: "Sexual difference is then assigned according to whether individual subjects do or do not possess the phallus, which means not that anatomical difference *is* sexual difference . . . but that anatomical difference comes to *figure* sexual difference. . . . The phallus thus indicates the reduction of difference to an instance of visible perception, a *seeming* value."

3. *DORA* AND THE PREGNANT MADONNA

1. Moustapha Safouan, "In Praise of Hysteria," in Stuart Schneiderman, ed., "*Returning to Freud: Clinical Psychoanalysis in the School of Lacan*, pp. 57–58 (New Haven: Yale University Press, 1980).

2. Gordon S. Haight, ed., *The George Eliot Letters*, 9 vols. (New Haven: Yale University Press, 1954–78), 2:471–72 and *n.*, and *George Eliot's Life as Related in Her Letters and Journals*, arranged and edited by her husband, J. W. Cross, 3 vols. (Edinburgh and London: W. Blackwood & Sons, 1885), 2:58. G. H. Lewes' journal records that he "looked at the Raphael Madonna di San Sisto, till [he] felt quite hysterical"; see Haight, ed., *The George Eliot Letters*, 2:472n.

3. Michel Foucault, *The History of Sexuality*, vol. 1, Robert Hurley, trans. (Harmondsworth: Penguin, 1981), p. 104.

4. First published in *Tel Quel* (Winter 1977), 74:30–49, Julia Kristeva's essay "Héréthique de l'amour" was republished as "*Stabat Mater*" in *Histoires d'amour* (Paris: Éditions Denoël, 1983).

5. See A. P. Oppé, *Raphael*, Charles Mitchell, ed. (London: Paul Elek, 1970), pp. 104–108, for an account of the Sistine Madonna which is itself sustained by the theology of Christian Incarnation; as Raphael's Madonna is to God (the innocent vehicle of divine desire), so Raphael's method is to his art. For the motif of the curtain and its significance, see in particular Johann Konrad Eberlein, "The Curtain in Raphael's Sistine *Madonna*," *Art Bulletin* (March 1983), 65(1):62–77.

6. Safouan, "In Praise of Hysteria," pp. 56–57, 58.

7. See Parveen Adams, "Mothering," *m/f* (1983), 8:40–52 for a critique of object-relation theories of mothering, especially the work of Winnicott and Chodorow, on which recent feminist writing about the mother have tended to draw.

8. See Adrienne Rich, *Of Woman Born: Motherhood as Experience and Institution* (New York: Norton, 1976) and Nancy Chodorow, *The Reproduction of Mothering: Psychoanalysis and the Sociology of Gender* (Berkeley: University of California Press, 1978).

9. Julia Kristeva, *Desire in Language: A Semiotic Approach to Literature and Art*, Leon S. Roudiez, ed. (New York: Columbia University Press, 1980), p. 237. Subsequent page references in the text are to *Desire in Language*.

10. D. W. Winnicott, *Playing and Reality* (New York: Basic Books, 1971), p. 107; cf. Kristeva, *Desire in Language*, p. 293n.

11. See Kristeva, *Desire in Language*, pp. 269–70n., and cf. her *Powers of Horror: An Essay on Abjection*, Leon S. Roudiez, trans. (New York: Columbia University Press, 1982), p. 14.

12. Cf. also Kristeva, *Desire in Language*, p. 235n., where Kristeva writes that the function of color "is related (in the domain of sight) to rhythm's function and, in general, to the musicality of the literary text, which, precisely in this way, introduces instinctual drive into language." In "Julia Kristeva in Conversation with Rosalind Coward," Kristeva alludes in passing to "this so-called crisis of representation [in modern art], which is a crisis . . . of representation. The breaking of the image, abstract art and so on"; see *Desire: ICA Documents* (London: Institute of Contemporary Arts, 1984), p. 23.

13. Leo Steinberg, *The Sexuality of Christ in Renaissance Art and in Modern Oblivion* (New York: Pantheon, 1983), pp. 41–42. See also p. 183, where Steinberg reproduces and comments on the retouched Anderson/Alinari reproduction of the Bergamo Madonna.

14. See Kristeva, *Desire in Language*, p. 260, and cf. Steinberg, *The Sexuality of Christ*, pp. 1–4, 110–16.

15. See *ibid.*, p. 109: "no less than 123 pictures are reproduced in the text of this essay and as many again in the back pictures, with many more cited in reference. . . . Readers in their sceptical phase will think half a hundred instances still too few. And once conviction has taken hold, more than six is too much. But the glut of the evidence is essential."

16. Kristeva, *Powers of Horror*, pp. 12–13. Cf. also the further account of the same process in Kristeva's "L'abjet d'amour," *Tel Quel* (Spring 1982), 91:17–32. For an excellent analysis of Kristeva's psychoanalytic argument and its implications, see Cynthia Chase's review of *Powers of Horror, Desire in Language,* and "L'abjet d'amour" in *Criticism* (1983), 26(2):193–201, and cf. also Neil Hertz, *The End of the Line*, pp. 231–33.

17. Cf. "Julia Kristeva in Conversation with Rosalind Coward," *Desire: ICA Documents*, p. 23: "maybe the good enough mother is the mother who has something else to love beside her child . . . what is necessary is to have three terms, if you prefer call them X and Y, why not?"

18. For an interesting reading of the role of art and science in Freud's *Leonardo*, see Sarah Kofman, *L'enfance de l'art: une interprétation de l'esthétique freudienne,* 2nd ed. (Paris: Editions Galilée, 1985), pp. 237–49.

19. See Kristeva, "Freud et l'amour: le malaise dans la cure," *Histoires d'amour*, p. 46; my translation. The entire passage runs:

"Si le narcissisme est une défense contre le vide de la séparation, alors toute la machine d'imageries, de représentations, d'identifications et de projections qui l'accompagnent dans la voie de la consolidation du Moi et du Sujet, est une conjuration de ce vide. La séparation est notre chance de devenir narcissiens ou narcissiques, des sujets de la représentation en tout cas. Le vide qu'elle ouvre est cependant aussi l'abîme à peine recouvert dans lequel risquent de s'engloutir nos identités, nos images, nos mots.

"Narcisse mythique se penchait en définitive héroïquement sur ce vide pour chercher dans l'élément aquatique maternel, une possibilité de représentation de soi ou d'un autre: de quelqu'un à aimer. Depuis Plotin au moins, la réflexion théorique a oublié qu'elle roulait sur le vide, pour s'élancer amoureusement vers la source solaire de la représentation, la lumière qui nous fait voir et à laquelle nous aspirons de nous égaler d'idéalisation en idéalisation, de perfectionnement en perfectionnement: *In lumine tuo videbimus lumen.*"

20. "Julie Kristeva in Conversation with Rosalind Coward," *Desire: ICA Documents*, p. 24.

21. *Ibid.*, p. 24.

22. See, however, for a more sophisticated political critique of Kristeva, Ann Rosalind Jones, "Julia Kristeva on Femininity: The Limits of a Semiotic Politics," *Feminist Review* (November 1984), 18:56–73; and cf. also Jane Gallop's questioning of Kristeva by way of Irigaray in *The Daughter's Seduction*, pp. 113–31.

23. Jacques Lacan, "Intervention on Transference," in Mitchell and Rose, *Feminine Sexuality,* p. 68.

24. Gallop, *The Daughter's Seduction*, pp. 156–57n.

25. Lacan, "Intervention on Transference," p. 70.

26. See Jacqueline Rose, "Dora—Fragment of an Analysis," *m/f* (1978), 2:12.

27. See Sharon Willis, "A Symptomatic Narrative," *Diacritics* (Spring 1983), 13(1):46–60, for a discussion of *Dora* in relation to the politics of visibility.

28. See Jerre Collins, et al., "Questioning the Unconscious: The Dora Archive," *ibid.*, pp. 40–41; cf. also the stage directions in Hélène Cixous's "Portrait of Dora," Anita Barrows, trans., *ibid.*, p. 11: "Suddenly, the evidence, unnoticed perhaps by everyone: the infant Jesus held by the Madonna is none other than a baby Dora."

29. See Lacan, "Intervention on Transference," pp. 30–31.

30. See "L'abjet d'amour," p. 46, and n. 19 above.

31. Jean Laplanche and J.-B. Pontalis, "Fantasy and the Origins of Sexuality," *International Journal of Psycho-Analysis* (1968), 49(1):16.

32. The figure is developed in Luce Irigaray's "When Our Lips Speak Together," *This Sex Which Is Not One*, pp. 205–18, as a metaphor for a female libidinal economy of language.

33. Laplanche and Pontalis, "Fantasy and the Origins of Sexuality," p. 17.

34. Lacan, "Intervention on Transference," pp. 67–68.

35. See Kristeva, *Powers of Horror*, pp. 2, 11.

36. See Mary Douglas, *Purity and Danger* (London: Routledge and Kegan Paul, 1966), p. 121; cf. Kristeva, *Powers of Horror*, p. 69.

37. Lacan, "Intervention on Transference," pp. 65–66.

38. See Gallop, *The Daughter's Seduction*, p. 140n.

39. *Ibid.*, p. 144. See also Sharon Willis, *Diacritics*, 13(1):58–60 for the duplicity of the bourgeois family structure as revealed in *Dora*.

40. See *The Psychopathology of Everyday Life* (1901), *SE* 6:240–41; cf. also Hannah S. Decker, "The Choice of a Name: 'Dora' and Freud's Relationship with Breuer," *Journal of the American Psychoanalytic Association* (1982), 30:113–36.

41. Gallop, *The Daughter's Seduction*, p. 147.

42. *Ibid.*, p. 145.

43. See Jim Swan, "*Mater* and Nannie: Freud's Two Mothers and the Discovery of the Oedipus Complex," *American Imago* (1974), 31:1–64, especially 10–20.

44. See *ibid.*, pp. 37–43 for Freud's interpretation of the dream which provokes these associations in the light of professional anxieties about payment for "bad treatment."

45. Kristeva, *Powers of Horror*, p. 64.

46. *Ibid.*, p. 71.

47. See Sarah Kofman, "The Sublation of Mothers," *The Enigma of Woman*, p. 76.

48. See Neil Hertz, "Dora's Secrets, Freud's Techniques," *Diacritics* (Spring 1983), 13(1):65–76 for a subtle account of Freud's epistemological anxieties; cf. also Toril Moi, "Representation of Patriarchy: Sexuality and Epistemology in Freud's Dora," *Feminist Review* (October 1981), 9:60–74.

49. See, for *couvade*, Sneja Gunew, "Feminist Criticism: Positions and Questions," *Southern Review* (March 1983), 16(1):151–60. Gunew's essay forms part of the collective "Forum: Feminism and Interpretation Theory," *ibid.*, 16(1):149–73.

IV. Anna (Wh)O.'s *Absences*: Readings in Hysteria

PREFACE

1. Juliet Mitchell, "Femininity, Narrative and Psychoanalysis," *Women: The Longest Revolution* (New York: Pantheon Books, 1984), pp. 289–90. Mitchell's linking of femininity, narrative, and hysteria is among the most suggestive recent discussions of the relation between feminism and psychoanalytic theory.

2. For an account of Bertha Pappenheim's later career, see Marion A. Kaplan, *The Jewish Feminist Movement in Germany* (Westport, Ct.: Greenwood Press, 1979), pp. 29–57; and see also Dora Edinger, *Bertha Pappenheim: Freud's Anna O.* (Highland Park, Ill.: Congregation Solel, 1968).

1. TAKING LIBERTIES WITH WORDS

1. William McGuire, ed., *The Freud/Jung Letters: The Correspondence Between Sigmund Freud and C. G. Jung*, Ralph Menheim and R. F. C. Hull, trans. (Princeton: Princeton University Press, 1974), p. 267.

2. See "History of the Psychoanalytic Movement" (1914), *SE* 14:13–15.

3. For a psychoanalytic account of Breuer's relation to Bertha Pappenheim, and of his countertransference, see George H. Pollock, "The Possible Significance of Childhood Object Loss in the Josef Breuer–Bertha Pappenheim (Anna O.)–Sigmund Freud Relationship," *Journal of the American Psychoanalytic Association* (1968), 16:711–39. Pollock points out that both Breuer's mother, who died when he was a young child, and his eldest daughter, were called Bertha.

4. See Dora Edinger, *Bertha Pappenheim: Freud's Anna O.* (Highland Park, Ill: Congregation Solel, 1968), pp. 78–79.

5. See Ernest Jones, *The Life and Work of Sigmund Freud*, 3 vols. (N.Y.: Basic Books, 1953–57), 1:225.

6. See Sander Gilman, "Jewish Jokes: Sigmund Freud and the Hidden Language of the Jews," *Psychoanalysis and Contemporary Thought* (1985) 7(4):591–614, for the link between Anna O.'s sexuality and her Jewishness, and particularly for the link between the language of prayer and Hebrew. Breuer wrote that "She is thoroughly unreligious. . . . Religion played a role in her life only as an object of silent struggles and silent opposition," despite her outward conformity to the religious rites of her orthodox Jewish family; see H. F. Ellenberger, "The Story of 'Anna O': A Critical Review with New Data," *Journal of the History of the Behavioural Sciences* (July 1972), 8(2):267–79.

7. See the persuasive account of Anna O.'s "unique use of languages" given by Dianne Hunter in "Hysteria, Psychoanalysis, and Feminism: The Case of Anna O.," *Feminist Studies* (Fall 1983), 9(3):465–88. Hunter's emphasis on language makes her essay the most illuminating feminist reading of the case of Anna O. so far.

8. The colleague was none other than Krafft-Ebing; the smoke which he blew in Anna O.'s face was from a piece of burning paper. See Ellenberger, "The Story of Anna O.," p. 276.

9. Cf. *The Adolescent Diaries of Karen Horney*, Marianne Horney Eckardt, ed. (New York: Basic Books, 1980), p. 246, for Horney's confession, in 1910, to the analytic fantasy that Karl Abraham would treat her "for nothing, nothing at all," i.e., for love: "I pictured to myself the situation as it would be when Dr. A. asked permission to write up my case scientifically and publish it—this would obligate him to study all the expressions of my neurosis with a special, almost 'affectionate' care."

10. See *SE* 1:133–43 for Freud's perface and notes to Charcot's *Leçons du Mardi de la Salpêtrière* (1887–88).

11. See Patrick J. Mahony, "Toward the Understanding of Translation in Psychoanalysis," *Journal of the American Psychoanalytic Association* (1980), 28(2):461–75.

12. Juliet Mitchell, "The Question of Femininity and the Theory of Psychoanalysis," *Women: The Longest Revolution*, p. 297.

13. See *The Diary of Alice James*, Leon Edel, ed. (Harmondsworth: Penguin, 1982), p. 150. Alice James is referring to William James' remark that "the nervous victim 'abandons' certain portions of his consciousness" (ibid., p. 148).

14. See Roy Schafer, "Narration in Psychoanalytic Dialogue," *Critical Inquiry* (Autumn 1980), 7(1):24–53, and, for narrative chronology and repetition, see also Paul Ricoeur, "Narrative Time," *ibid.*, 7(1):169–90.

15. See Freud's "History of the Psychoanalytic Movement" (1914), *SE* 14:12; Freud's phrase is in English in the original.

16. Ernst L. Freud, ed., *The Letters of Sigmund Freud*, Tania and James Stern, trans. (N.Y.: Basic Books, 1960), p. 413.

17. See Jones, *The Life and Work of Sigmund Freud*, 1:224–25. Following Freud, Jones mistakenly dates the birth of Breuer's daughter after the second honeymoon on which, he tells us, Breuer then embarked with his wife. In fact Breuer's youngest daughter, Dora, was born in March 1882 while his analysis of Anna O. was still going on.

18. See *ibid.*, 1:226.

19. "Freud told him of his own experience of a female patient suddenly flinging her arms round his neck . . . and . . . explained to him his reasons for regarding such untoward occurences as part of the transference phenomena characteristic of certain types of hysteria. This seemed to have had a calming effect on Breuer" (*ibid.*, 1:250).

20. *The Letters of Sigmund Freud*, pp. 412–13.

21. Cf. the 1924 footnote to "Katharina:" "I venture after the lapse of so many years to lift the veil of discretion and reveal the fact that Katharina . . . fell ill . . . as a result of sexual attempts on the part of her own father" (*SE* 2:134*n.*); with hindsight, Freud came to believe that "Distortions like [these] should be altogether avoided in reporting a case history."

2. AN UNNECCESSARY MAZE OF SIGN-READING

1. *The Living of Charlotte Perkins Gilman: An Autobiography* (New York: Harper & Row, 1975), p. 96.

2. See *The History of the Psychoanalytic Movement*, *SE* 14:13–15.

3. *The Living of Charlotte Perkins Gilman*, p. 121.

4. See Mary A. Hill, *Charlotte Perkins Gilman: The Making of a Radical Feminist 1860–1896* (Philadelphia: Temple University Press, 1980), pp. 27–43.

5. Juliet Mitchell, "The Question of Femininity," *Women: The Longest Revolution*, p. 299.

6. Charlotte Perkins Gilman, *The Yellow Wallpaper*, Elaine R. Hedges, ed. (Old Westbury, N.Y.: The Feminist Press, 1973), p. 10. Subsequent page references in the text are to this edition.

7. Annette Kolodny, "A Map for Rereading: Or, Gender and the Interpretation of Literary Texts," *New Literary History* (Spring 1980), 11(3):451–67; Jean E. Kennard, "Convention Coverage or How to Read Your Own Life," *New Literary History* (Autumn 1981), 13(1):69–88.

8. Kolodny, "A Map for Rereading," pp. 457–58.

9. *Ibid.*, pp. 457, 459; my italics.

10. Kennard, "Convention Coverage," p. 74.

11. Mary Wollstonecraft, *Mary, A Fiction and the Wrongs of Woman*, Gary Kelly, ed. (London and New York: Oxford University Press, 1976), p. 79.

12. See Jacqueline Rose, "Femininity and its Discontents," *Feminist Review* (June 1983), 14:17.

13. Kennard, "Convention Coverage," pp. 77–78.

14. See Neil Hertz's discussion of repetition and the uncanny in "Freud and the Sandman," *The End of the Line*, pp. 97–121.

15. See Hill, *Charlotte Perkins Gilman*, p. 186.

16. See Gilman, *The Yellow Wallpaper*, pp. 40, 37.

17. "The split-off mind is the devil with which the unsophisticated observation of early superstitious times believed that these patients were possessed" (*SE* 2:250).

18. *The Diary of Alice James*, Leon Edel, ed. (Harmondsworth: Penguin, 1982), p. 149.

19. See Hill, *Charlotte Perkins Gilman*, pp. 98–99; but see also pp. 144–45 for the course of feminist reading which Gilman undertook in 1887, the year of her breakdown.

20. "Once upon a time you 'spooned,' then you 'petted,' after that you 'necked' . . . but now you may 'smooch'" (1937); Harold Wentworth and Stuart Berg Flexner, *Dictionary of American Slang* (New York: Thomas Y. Crowell Co., 1975).

21. See Gallop, *The Daughter's Seduction*, pp. 27–28.

22. Michèle Montrelay, "Inquiry into Femininity," *m/f* (1978), 1:84; see also the discussion and critique of Montrelay by Parveen Adams, "Representation and Sexuality," *ibid.*, 1:65–82.

23. Gallop, *The Daughter's Seduction*, p. 27.

24. See Shoshana Felman, "Turning the Screw of Interpretation," *Yale French Studies* (1977), 55/56:125.

25. Montrelay, "Inquiry into Femininity," p. 96.

26. Felman, "Turning the Screw of Interpretation," p. 146.

3. HYSTERICS SUFFER MAINLY FROM REMINISCENCES

1. *The Diary of Alice James*, Leon Edel, ed. (Harmondsworth: Penguin, 1982), p. 41. Cf. James' reference to herself, in 1890, as "a mildewed toad-stool" (*ibid.*, p. 135). Subsequent page references in the text are to this edition.

2. Letter to William James, quoted *ibid.*, p. 15.

3. See Jean Strouse, *Alice James: A Biography* (New York: Bantam Books, 1982), p. 112.

4. *Ibid.*, p. 291.

5. See *ibid.*, p. 297.

6. Gordon S. Haight, ed., *The George Eliot Letters*, 9 vols. (New Haven: Yale University Press, 1954–78), 5:160–61.

7. George Eliot, "Margaret Fuller and Mary Wollstonecraft," *Essays of George Eliot*, Thomas Pinney, ed. (New York: Columbia University Press, 1963), p. 201.

8. *Ibid.*, p. 200; cf. Tennyson's *The Princess*, vii:253–54.

9. George Eliot, "Margaret Fuller and Mary Wollstonecraft," pp. 205, 202, 203.

10. George Eliot, "Silly Novels by Lady Novelists," *ibid.*, pp. 315–16.

11. *Ibid.*, p. 324.

12. Haight, ed., *The George Eliot Letters*, 3:67.

13. *Ibid.*, 5:380.

14. *Ibid.*, 6:75–76.

15. *Ibid.*, 6:116.

16. Gillian Beer, "Myth and the Single Consciousness: *Middlemarch* and *The Lifted Veil*, in Ian Adam, ed., *This Particular Web: Essays on Middlemarch*, pp. 96–97, 100 (Toronto and Buffalo: University of Toronto Press, 1975).

17. See Gilbert and Gubar, *The Madwoman in the Attic*, p. 448; George Eliot, "The Lifted Veil," *The Works of George Eliot*, Cabinet ed., 24 vols. (Edinburgh and London: W. Blackwood and Sons, 1878–85), 23:292. Subsequent page references in the text are to this edition.

18. Ruby Redinger, *George Eliot: The Emergent Self* (New York: Alfred Knopf, 1975), pp. 403–5.

19. Gilbert and Gubar, *The Madwoman in the Attic*, pp. 465–66.

20. For a brief account of Mary Shelley's story, see *ibid.*, p. 458.

21. See *SE* 12:295–96.

22. Peggy Kamuf, *Fictions of Feminine Desire* (Lincoln: University of Nebraska Press, 1982), pp. 47–48.

23. U. C. Knoepflmacher, *George Eliot's Early Novels: The Limits of Realism* (Berkeley and Los Angeles: University of California Press, 1968), p. 140. Gilbert and Gubar offer the reversed mirror image of Knoepflmacher's reading when they see Bertha's plot to kill Latimer as an understandable rebellion against the impoverishment of desire which he represents; see *The Madwoman in the Attic*, p. 464.

24. See "Is There a Woman in This Text?" (Section III.1, above).

25. See Gilbert and Gubar, *The Madwoman in the Attic*, p. 463.

26. See "Judith, Holofernes, and the Phallic Woman" (Section III.2, above).

27. See Haight, ed., *The George Eliot Letters*, 7:163 and *n*.

28. George Eliot, *Daniel Deronda*, Barbara Hardy, ed. (Harmondsworth: Penguin, 1967), pp. 691–92; subsequent page references in the text are to this edition. See Neil Hertz, *The End of the Line*, pp. 224–33 for an interesting discussion of the Princess as a scapegoated author-surrogate, who allows Eliot to turn problems of representation into moral problems, and then to cast them out.

V. Reading Correspondences

1. *Mary, A Fiction and The Wrongs of Woman*, Gary Kelly, ed. (London and New York: Oxford University Press, 1976), p. 124; subsequent page references in the text are to this edition.

2. "And the One Doesn't Stir Without the Other," Helene Vivienne Wenzel, tr., *Signs* (Autumn 1981), 7(1):60–61; subsequent page references in the text are to this volume and number of *Signs*.

3. "Interpreting the Self through Letters," *Centrum* (Fall 1981), n.s. 1(2):111.

4. For a brief reading of Irigaray's original sixteen-page text, *Et l'une ne bouge pas sans l'autre* (1979), in the light of Gallop's own "wish to fix Irigaray and Kristeva into daughter and mother roles," see *The Daughter's Seduction*, pp. 113–17.

5. *Ibid.*, pp. 57–58.

6. *Ibid.*, p. 68.

7. Ruthven, *Feminist Literary Studies: an Introduction* (Cambridge: Cambridge University Press, 1984), p. 45.

8. *Ibid.*, p. 46.

9. *Ibid.*, pp. 46–47.

10. *Ibid.*, p. 48.

11. See Johnson, "The Frame of Reference: Poe, Lacan, Derrida," *The Critical Difference*, p. 114.

12. "It is not how Lacan and Derrida meet each other but how they miss each other that opens up a space for interpretation;" *ibid.*, p. 119.

13. See *ibid.*, pp. 123–24.

Select Bibliography

Abel, Elizabeth, ed. *Writing and Sexual Difference.* Chicago: University of Chicago Press, 1982.

Breuer, Joseph and Sigmund Freud, *Studies on Hysteria* (1895), *SE* 2.

Culler, Jonathan. *On Deconstruction: Theory and Criticism After Structuralism.* Ithaca: Cornell University Press, 1982.

Freud, Sigmund. *The Standard Edition of the Complete Psychological Works of Sigmund Freud.* 24 vols. James Strachey, ed. London: Hogarth Press, 1953–1974. Cited *SE.*

The Interpretation of Dreams (1900), *SE* 4.

Fragment of an Analysis of a Case of Hysteria (1905), *SE* 7.

Delusions and Dreams in Jensen's Gradiva (1907), *SE* 9.

"The Taboo of Virginity" (1917), *SE* 11.

"The Uncanny" (1919), *SE* 17.

"Female Sexuality" (1931), *SE* 21.

"On Femininity" *New Introductory Lectures on Psycho-Analysis* (1932), *SE* 22.

Gallop, Jane. *The Daughter's Seduction: Feminism and Psychoanalysis.* Ithaca: Cornell University Press, 1982.

Gilbert, Sandra and Susan Gubar. *The Madwoman in the Attic: The Woman Writer and the Nineteenth-Century Literary Imagination.* New Haven and London: Yale University Press, 1979.

Hertz, Neil. *The End of the Line.* New York: Columbia University Press, 1985.

Irigaray, Luce. *Speculum of the Other Woman,* Gillian C. Gill, trans. Ithaca: Cornell University Press, 1985.

—— *This Sex Which Is Not One,* Catherine Porter, trans. Ithaca: Cornell University Press, 1985.

Jacobus, Mary, ed. *Women Writing and Writing about Women.* London: Croom Helm, 1979.

Johnson, Barbara. *The Critical Difference: Essays in the Contemporary Rhetoric of Reading.* Baltimore: Johns Hopkins University Press, 1981.

Kofman, Sarah. *Quatre romans analytiques.* Paris: Éditions Galilée, 1973.

—— *The Enigma of Woman: Woman in Freud's Writings,* Catherine Porter, trans. Ithaca: Cornell University Press, 1985.

Kristeva, Julia. *Desire in Language: A Semiotic Approach to Literature and Art.* Leon S. Roudiez, ed. New York: Columbia University Press, 1980.

—— *Powers of Horror: An Essay on Abjection*. Leon S. Roudiez, trans. New York: Columbia University Press, 1982.

Lacan, Jacques. *Écrits: A Selection*. Alan Sheridan, trans. London: Tavistock, 1977.

Marks, Elaine and Isabelle de Courtivron eds. *New French Feminisms*. Amherst: University of Massachusetts Press, 1980.

Mitchell, Juliet. *Women: The Longest Revolution*. New York: Pantheon Books, 1984.

Mitchell, Juliet and Jacqueline Rose, eds. *Feminine Sexuality: Jacques Lacan and the école freudienne*. London and New York: Norton, 1983.

Index